anglo-saxon poetry:
essays in appreciation

John C. McGalliard

anglo-saxon poetry:
essays in appreciation

For John C. McGalliard

edited by

LEWIS E. NICHOLSON
DOLORES WARWICK FRESE

UNIVERSITY OF NOTRE DAME PRESS

Notre Dame   London

Library of Congress Cataloging in Publication Data
Main entry under title:

Anglo-Saxon poetry.

    "Essays . . . in honor of John C. McGalliard."
    CONTENTS: Gerber, J. C. Foreword.—Secular heroic
poetry: Beowulf: Eliason, N. E. Healfdene's
daughter. Gardner, J. Guilt and the world's complexity.
Donahue, C. Potlatch and charity. Burlin, R. B.
Gnomic indirection in Beowulf. Nicholson, L. E.
Hunlafing and the point of the sword. [etc.]
    1. Anglo-Saxon poetry—History and criticism—
Addresses, essays, lectures. 2. McGalliard,
John Calvin. I. Nicholson, Lewis E. II. Frese,
Dolores Warwick. III. McGalliard, John Calvin.
PR201.A5   829'.1   74–27893
ISBN 0–268–00575–3
ISBN 0–268–00576–1 pbk.

Manufactured in the United States of America

Contents

v

THE RUNIC TRADITION: Cynewulf's Signed Poems

WISDOM LITERATURE: Maxim, Riddle, and Gnome

Preface

THIS VOLUME OF ORIGINAL ESSAYS ON ANGLO-SAXON POETRY HAS BEEN created and collected in honor of John C. McGalliard on the occasion of his retirement from the University of Iowa after a distinguished career as a scholar-teacher of medieval literatures. To accommodate essays from all those former students and present colleagues now engaged in medieval teaching and research who would have wished to so signal their affection and esteem for him would have necessitated an encyclopaedic project. For John McGalliard's humane range, even as a medieval specialist, is so various that admirers might easily compile similar volumes of essays on medieval Scandinavian literatures, Middle English studies, linguistics, Dante, Chaucer—all specific concerns of his teaching, research and publication—as well as the Anglo-Saxon language and literature of which he has been, for many years, so generous and profound a master and disciple.

Our decision to limit the essays in this *Festschrift* volume to specific topics concerned with Anglo-Saxon poetry was shaped by our sense of a very real need for such a volume of studies: to create a collection of essays responsive to the whole of that poetry seemed to us a valuable contribution worthy of its honoree. We felt that the ongoing usefulness of such a book, whose attractive critical unity would spring from the self-limited nature of the Anglo-Saxon poetic corpus, would constitute an added honorific dimension. Accordingly, we have collected here a set of new essays that respond to all of the major and most of the minor poems in the Anglo-Saxon canon.

The lively willingness of the contributors to accept specific titular assignments in order that the project might take this unique shape is a tribute to the man who inspired it. Indeed, the generous response of the community of Anglo-Saxonists both here and abroad, to the notion of such a collection of essays in his honor, is a symptom of the extraordinary professional and personal regard with which John McGalliard is held. We believe that novice and devotee alike will find here a range and depth that is structured, after a fashion, on the large architecture of his acquisitive mind and generous spirit. That there are practising poets, novelists and translators among the men and women contributing to this scholarly volume seems to us an emblem of the genuine humanism and erudition that has been both beacon and boon to several generations of those privileged to call John McGalliard by the names of teacher, colleague, friend.

L.E.N.
D.W.F.

Foreword

WHEN I FIRST CAME TO IOWA IN THE SUMMER OF 1944 JOHN MCGAL-
liard was not on campus, but he quickly became a presence for me, if
only a mythical one. Whenever a question about a course came up, I
was told how John McGalliard would probably handle it; when an
aspect of the curriculum was questioned, someone would say that we
shouldn't change it while John McGalliard was away; and more than
once I was encouraged to think that I would like Iowa even better when
John McGalliard got back. I was led to expect a teacher who could
make learning unusually personal and exciting, a scholar with an extraordinary breadth of information, a humanist who believed in and
fought for liberal education, and a warm, direct, and thoroughly honest
person. When John finally appeared I was not disappointed in any of
these expectations. The years since have only strengthened my liking and
respect. I welcome this opportunity, therefore, to mention some of his
remarkable accomplishments.

John Calvin McGalliard's formal training was ideal for an aspiring
medievalist. With a major in English and considerable training in Latin
and Greek, he was graduated as an A.B. from the University of North
Carolina in 1924, and went on to an M.A. the following year. He then
served three years as a full-time instructor at Northwestern University,
taking further graduate work there as well as at the University of
Chicago where he spent two summers. Having completed almost all of
the course work necessary for a Ph.D. in English he went to Harvard in
1928 to study other languages and literatures: medieval French, Old
Irish and Welsh, Old Icelandic, Provençal and medieval Latin. George
Lyman Kittredge directed the dissertation that led to a Ph.D. from
Harvard in 1930. Harvard then sent him off to the University of Paris
on a post-doctoral Sheldon Fellowship, where he took seminars and
advanced courses in medieval Latin, Irish and Welsh, and general

linguistics. Study in this last area, linguistics, he had begun at North-western under Hans Kurath, continued at Harvard under Whatmough, and explored still further in Paris under Meillet and Vendryes. While in Paris, too, he lived with a French family and acquired notable fluency in French. In 1931, a few weeks before his twenty-fifth birthday and perhaps by that time the best trained young medievalist in the country, he came to the University of Iowa where for forty-three years he has been teaching medieval literature and linguistics. This work at Iowa has been interrupted only by visiting professorships at Colorado (twice), North Carolina (twice), Wisconsin (twice), Duke (three times), Virginia, and Notre Dame.

By those who have known him well, John McGalliard will be best remembered as a witty and challenging teacher. His regular courses have been in the areas of Old and Middle English, especially *Beowulf* and Chaucer, and in linguistics. An equally distinctive part of his work has been the two-semester course on "European Literature from St. Augustine to Dante," which he has offered for at least thirty years. Regularly, too, he has insisted on giving a section of the sophomore Literature Core course in order to keep in touch with beginning students. And as if this weren't enough, almost every year he has voluntarily increased his teaching load so as to meet requests for Old Norse or Old Irish or comparative grammar. His grateful "alumni" include not only graduate students in medieval literature and linguistics but poets and novelists from the Writers Workshop and literally thousands of BA's who still single out his undergraduate courses as the ones that first made them realize the excitement of humane learning.

As his colleagues at Iowa are quick to point out, John McGalliard was teaching linguistics at Iowa before Leonard Bloomfield's *Language* came out in 1933. The first course he offered in the field was not only a pioneer venture at Iowa but one of the earliest such courses in the country. In 1962 he was one of those who helped to create the Linguistics program at Iowa, a program that achieved departmental status eight years later. For the last twelve years, at the insistence of his colleagues he has held a joint appointment in English and Linguistics. Though he has kept up with the new developments in language study and compe-tently directs advanced work in the area, his major contribution in linguistics has been in making countless students in other fields aware of the relevance of language scholarship to their own disciplines.

Despite his interest in advanced work, John McGalliard has never lost his concern for basic undergraduate education. With Norman Foerster in the early thirties he helped reshape the required literature program in the Liberal Arts College at Iowa so that freshmen and sophomores could be introduced to the literature of the past in the light of the present, and the literature of the present in the light of the past. He not only taught in the course but prepared syllabi for it. One Colorado "vacation," for example, he spent writing an account of ancient Greek literature for Iowa sophomores. On another occasion he undertook to do the same for Chaucer. And still another outgrowth of the program was *A College Bible,* co-edited with Joseph Baker. Through the years, though the general education program of the University has changed substantially, the required course in literature, at least in its basic philosophy, has changed little—and largely because of John McGalliard's formidable defense of it, not only in departmental meetings but in College faculty meetings as well. It remains a tribute to his tenacity and his deep convictions about what literature is and how it should be taught.

John McGalliard's publications exhibit the same breadth of interest and depth of insight as his teaching. Articles on *Beowulf, The Pearl,* and Chaucer's *Merchant's Tale* and *Shipman's Tale* exhibit the precision and judgment of the well-trained scholar, as does his translation of the Old Icelandic saga of *Hrafnkel Priest of Frey.* Such an essay as "Science in Poetry" reveals his concern that literature be viewed not narrowly but in the context of learning generally. Many, perhaps most, of his publications demonstrate his conviction that teaching and scholarship are inextricably bound together; he has often said that for him there is no line between teaching and research. For class use he has co-authored *A College Bible* (1938), mentioned above, and contributed the chapter on "Language" in *Literary Scholarship* (1941), the chapter on "Beowulf and Bede" in *Life and Thought in the Early Middle Ages* (1967), and the section on medieval literature in the Norton Anthology, *Masterpieces of Literature* (1956, 1965). In addition, he has written many reviews and served on the editorial boards of *Philological Quarterly, The Chaucer Review,* and *Language and Style.* Among others, Harvard, Yale, Oxford, Chicago, and Northwestern University presses have sought his advice on manuscripts. So has the editor of *PMLA.* His writing has been all of a piece, for even the shortest review exhibits the same clarity of statement and soundness of judgment as the longest article. One hesitates to revert to the old cliché that style is the man. Yet in John McGalliard's writings one constantly senses the force and integrity of the spirit behind the words.

Even this brief summary cannot close without a comment about John McGalliard as an influence upon the profession. He has been an active member of the Modern Language Association, the Midwest Modern Language Association, the Mediaeval Academy of America, the Linguistic Society of America, the Archaeological Institute of America, the National Council of Teachers of English, and the Iowa Council of Teachers of English. In the MLA he has served as secretary and chairman of the Old English and Chaucer Groups and of the section on "From the Beginning to 1650." In the MMLA he has been secretary and chairman of the English section "From the Beginning to 1600." In activities more directly related to teaching he was an official observer in 1962 of the C.E.E.B. summer institutes for the U.S. Office of Education; as a member of a panel he has helped to evaluate a variety of departments of English in the country; and at Iowa he has served on the Graduate Council, the Faculty Council, the AAUP executive committee, and the steering committee for the Literature Core program. Also at Iowa he has been president of the Humanities Society and of the local chapters of Phi Beta Kappa and the Archaeological Society.

John McGalliard is one of the few who have been able to excel in all aspects of academic life—scholarship, teaching, and service to his own university and to the profession at large. For years he has been a distinguished presence on our scene, and because of him our profession has a vigor and an integrity it would not otherwise possess.

John C. Gerber
The University of Iowa

Acknowledgments

The editors wish to acknowledge their particular appreciation to the Graduate College and the English Department's Sloan Fund at the University of Iowa for their generous gifts contributed to assist the publication of this volume.

The editors and the University of Notre Dame Press wish to acknowledge the generosity of the Board of Trinity College, Dublin, in granting permission for the reproduction of f. 124^v of the Book of Durrow on the cover of this volume.

Abbreviations

AN&Q—*American Notes & Queries*

ASPR—*Anglo–Saxon Poetic Records*

BT—*Bosworth–Toller*

BTS—*Bosworth–Toller Supplement*

CCSL—*Corpus christianorum series latina*

CL—*Comparative Literature*

CSEL—*Corpus Scriptorum Ecclesiasticorum Latinorum*

EEMSF—*Early English Manuscripts in Facsimile*

EETS—*Early English Text Society*

ELH—*Journal of English Literary History*

ES—*English Studies*

HBS—*The Henry Bradshaw Society Publications*

JEGP—*Journal of English and Germanic Philology*

M&H—*Medievalia et Humanistica*

MÆ—*Medium Ævum*

MGH—*Monumenta Germaniae Historica*

MLN—*Modern Language Notes*

MLR—*Modern Language Review*

MP—*Modern Philology*

MS—*Mediaeval Studies*

N&Q—*Notes and Queries*

NDEJ—*Notre Dame English Journal*

Neophil—*Neophilologus*

NM—*Neuphilologische Mitteilungen*

NMS—*Nottingham Medieval Studies*

PL—*Patrologia Latina*

PLL—*Papers on English Language and Literature*

PLS—*Patrologiae Latinae Supplementum*

PMLA—*Publications of the Modern Language Association of America*

PQ—*Philological Quarterly*

RES—*Review of English Studies*

SP—*Studies in Philology*

TAPA—*Transactions and Proceedings of the American Philological Association*

UTQ—*University of Toronto Quarterly*

ZfdPh—*Zeitschrift für deutsche Philologie*

Secular Heroic Poetry

BEOWULF

Healfdene's Daughter

NORMAN E. ELIASON

THE NAME OF HEALFDENE'S DAUGHTER AND THE IDENTITY OF HER HUS-
band pose problems which *Beowulf* scholars have long sought to solve,
seeking the solution by emending the line which presumably contained
this information. Since the line is obviously defective—something or
other having been omitted there through scribal error—emendation is
clearly in order. But unlike most *Beowulf* emendations, which merely
correct palpable errors of little or no substantive significance, this one
undertakes to provide important factual information. Unless it can be
authenticated somehow, this information remains dubious and the emendation accordingly questionable.

Lines 59–63, telling about the four children of King Healfdene, the
three sons who are named and the fourth, presumably the daughter married to a Swedish king, read thus in Klaeber's edition:[1]

> Ðæm feower bearn   forðgerimed
> in worold wocun,   weoroda ræswa[n]
> Heorogar ond Hroðgar   ond Halga til,
> hyrde ic þæt [. . . . .   wæs On] elan cwen,
> Heaðo-Scilfingas   healsgebedda.

[1] *Beowulf and the Fight at Finnsburg*, 3rd ed., (Boston, 1950).

[To him, the leader of the hosts, four children all told were born into the world, Heorogar and Hroðgar and good Halga. I have heard that . . . was Onela's queen, the dear bedfellow of the Battle-Scylfing.]

Line 62 appears in the MS as *hyrde ic þ elan cwen,* and most scholars now emend it as Klaeber does,[2] supplying *Onela* as the name of the Swedish king to whom Healfdene's daughter was married but cautiously and regretfully refraining from supplying hers. Malone,[3] however, supplies both names, emending the line to read:

Hyrde ic þæt Yrse   wæs Onelan cwen. . . .

Both emendations, the partial one adopted by Klaeber and the complete one advocated by Malone,[4] are based upon two assumptions: (1) that, like Healfdene's three sons, the daughter must also have been mentioned by name, and (2) that the name of the Swede (*Heaðo-Scilfing*) whose queen and consort (*cwen, healsgebedda*) she became was mentioned as well. The second assumption seems to be confirmed by the fact that the MS form *elan* contains not only the correct grammatical ending *-an*[5] but also a name-ending *-ela*, readily expandable to *Onela*, the only name of a Swedish king mentioned in *Beowulf* which ends thus. *Onela* is therefore now confidently entered in line 62, and with equal confidence Healfdene's daughter is assigned him as his wife. Our only doubt at this point arises from the fact that there is no further mention of Onela's wife in the poem and that nowhere else is his wife said to be Healfdene's daughter.

But if, apart from this small doubt, the second assumption works out

---

[2] Other emendations are cited in the excellent surveys of Johannes Hoops, *Kommentar zum Beowulf* (Heidelberg, 1932), pp. 17–18, and Elliott van Kirk Dobbie, *Beowulf and Judith* (New York, 1953), p. 118. All construe þ as the abbreviation of *þæt*, silently expanded thus by Klaeber, and also construe *Heaðo-Scilfingas* as genitive singular, the ending *-as* being a not exceptional variant of the more common *-es*.

[3] Kemp Malone, "The Daughter of Healfdene," originally published in 1929 but reprinted in his *Studies in Heroic Legend and in Current Speech* (Copenhagen, 1959), pp. 124–41. I have relied heavily on this article, for Malone clarifies much which is obscure in the Scandinavian accounts about Healfdene's daughter. Most of the accounts which he cites are briefly referred to by Klaeber (pp. 256–66) and less briefly by R. W. Chambers, *Beowulf: An Introduction to the Study of the Poem*, 3rd ed. (Cambridge, England, 1959), pp. 129–244, and by G. N. Garmonsway and Jacqueline Simpson, eds. *Beowulf and its Analogues* (London, 1968), pp. 124–221, who provide translations.

[4] Concerning which Dobbie, p. 118, remarks: "The lady's name is now believed to have been Yrse . . . but as yet no editor has ventured to put her name into the text."

[5] Genitive singular, agreeing with Heaðo-Scilfingas (see footnote 2).

4

very well, the first does not work out at all. With *Onela* established in the second half of line 62, the name of Healfdene's daughter, preceding it in the first half of the line,[6] must begin with a vowel in order to alliterate properly there. Among the names given serious consideration, *Signy, Elan,* and *Yrse,* the first must therefore be ruled out.

In favor of *Signy,* however, is the indubitable fact that this is the name which Healfdene's[7] daughter bears in Scandinavian tradition. But there her husband is not Onela, the Swedish king; he is Sævill, a Danish earl. If on the strength of the Scandinavian evidence, *Signy* is inserted in line 62, *Onela* must be abandoned in favor of *Sævill.* Satisfactory as the alliteration then becomes, problems arise about the man's identity and the form of his name, which to fit with the MS form *elan* must be rendered as *Sæwelan* or some other equally unlikely English name. These problems are best disposed of by disposing of *Signy* on the very plausible grounds that the name is a mistake, erroneously applied to Healfdene's daughter because she bore the same stigma as the legendary Signy, infamous for her incestuous union with her brother Sigemund.[8]

Unlike *Signy,* both *Elan* and *Yrse* meet the metrical requirements of the line with *Onela* established there. The objection to both is the lack of evidence indicating that either of these two women was Healfdene's daughter and Onela's wife. For Yrse, whose name is unknown in English tradition, such evidence must be sought in Scandinavian tradition, where her name is well known. The accounts about her there, however, are confused and confusing, and not until Malone succeeded in untangling them could a good case be made out for her. They reveal clearly that Yrse was the wife of Eadgils, Onela's nephew, and also, though less certainly, that she may have been the wife of Halga, Healfdene's son. This uncertainty, Malone sought to show, is clarified by the reference to her

---

[6] Modern scholars quite rightly assume that there is only one lacuna and that it occurs within the line. Though possibly wrong, the assumption is necessary in order to prevent fanciful speculations of the kind earlier scholars indulged in—for example, Holthausen's emendation (cited by Dobbie, p. 118) *Hyrde ic [eorlas cweðan], þæt [heo wæs On]elan cwen,* justified by the further assumption that the scribe also omitted a preceding line containing the name of Onela's wife.

[7] Throughout the discussion I shall use the English name-forms, not bothering to cite their Scandinavian equivalents.

[8] Malone, pp. 132–34, believes—quite rightly I think—that the remarkably similar incestuous union of Healfdene's daughter with her brother Halga is without historical foundation, the notion having arisen in later Scandinavian tradition through misapprehension about the identity and familial relationship of the two people involved. However erroneous the notion, there is no compelling reason to believe that incest did not figure in the story much earlier—early enough to have been known to the *Beowulf* poet and possibly therefore the reason for his cryptic reference to Healfdene's daughter. When he refers to the Signy-Sigemund story (lines 875–97), he delicately avoids mentioning the incest.

5

in line 62, where he believed the *Beowulf* poet erred, taking Yrse to be Healfdene's daughter whereas she was actually his daughter-in-law (Halga's wife). That she was not actually Healfdene's daughter, as Malone maintained—correctly I believe—is indicated by the fact that her name does not alliterate with that of her father, as the names of the three sons, Heorogar, Hroðgar, and Halga, all do.[9] But reasonable as the poet's mistake may be in confusing Healfdene's daughter-in-law with his daughter, it is not reasonable to believe, as Malone did, that the poet mistook Yrse as the name of the daughter. For if he did so, it would mean that he was unaware of the naming-tradition requiring that the name of Healdene's daughter should begin with an *h*—the very point Malone kept insisting upon and used as the keystone of his argument.[10]

The argument in favor of *Yrse* amounts simply to this: line 62, emended to read *Hyrde ic þæt Yrse wæs Onelan cwen,* is metrically satisfactory, the two names supplied there alliterating as they should. Instead of Healfdene's daughter, however, Yrse was his daughter-in-law, married first to his son Halga (a fact which the *Beowulf* poet was unaware of), second to the Swedish king Onela (a fact established only by line 62 as emended), and third to Onela's nephew Eadgils (a fact which the poet ignored). This argument is unconvincing, I believe, not only because of the flaw in it mentioned in the preceding paragraph but also because the evidence linking Yrse to Healfdene as daughter or daughter-in-law and to Onela as wife is too tenuous to be credible. If *Yrse* is accordingly rejected, we are left with *Elan,* the only other name given serious consideration in the past.

For *Elan* the claim seems even weaker since there is no evidence whatever, in either English or Scandinavian tradition, that Healfdene's daughter or Onela's wife was named thus. But the claim is stronger than

---

[9] Malone, p. 137, points out that all twelve of the historical members of the Scylding dynasty, ten men and two women, have names beginning with *h*. The only apparent exception is Hroðgar's daughter, for whom the poet used the nickname *Freawaru* rather than her real name *Hrut*.

[10] Malone, p. 137, summarizes his argument thus: "So far as verse 62 is concerned, we may cast our conclusions into the form of a syllogism:

1. The name of the princess of verse 62 must begin with a vowel.
2. The name of any daughter of Healfdene must begin with an *h*.
3. Therefore, the princess named in verse 62 cannot be a daughter of Healfdene.

"But, though the princess cannot be Healfdene's daughter, she can readily be his daughter-in-law. A daughter-in-law's name would naturally be chosen in accordance with the system of name-giving traditional in her own family, not the family she later married into. Hence the name of Healfdene's daughter-in-law might perfectly well begin with a vowel. . . . *Nor would it be surprising to find the English poet mistaking Yrsa for a true daughter of Healfdene*" [italics mine].

its early proponents seem to have realized, for unlike *Onelan,* present in MS only in part (i.e.—*elan*), *Elan* is there in full, and acceptance of it requires a minimal emendation to produce the metrically satisfactory line, *Hyrde ic þæt Elan [wæs On]elan cwen.*[11] Moreover, of all the emendations which have been proposed, this is the only one that is paleographically plausible, in that the MS gap is then not an unaccountable scribal error but one which is reasonable and of frequent occurrence, a simple eye-skip—in this instance from *elan* (the name of the woman) to *-elan* (the last part of the name of her husband). The possibility of explaining the scribal error thus and of emending the line accordingly seems to have been previously overlooked, as Dobbie's comment, p. 118, indicates:

> The early edd. accepted the MS. *elan* as a Germanic feminine name; the usual reading of l. 62 was *hyrde ic þæt Elan cwen [Ongenþeowes wæs],* an arrangement which is still found in Sedgefield (l. ed.). But as early as 1841 Grundtvig . . . had identified the letters *elan* as part of the gen. sing. form of the name *Onela.* . . . The gap in the text, then, is before *elan.* . . .

Thus the establishment of *[On]elan* in the line, which ought to have strengthened the claim for *Elan* there, led to complete dismissal of it.

The main objection raised against *Elan* was that it is an unlikely Germanic name. This valid objection can be met, however, by construing it as a nickname, formed from *el* "foreign, strange" and *an* "one." Such a nickname "Foreign one" corresponds remarkably well with the nickname *Wealhþeow* "Foreign captive" applied to Healfdene's daughter-in-law, wife of the Danish king Hroðgar. For her "Foreign captive" seems utterly inappropriate,[12] but for Healfdene's daughter, wife of a man in another realm, the Swedish king Onela, "Foreign one" is quite appropriate: As a nickname, *Elan* of course—alliterating as the line requires with *Onela*—need not alliterate with *Healfdene,* the name of her father.

Despite the plausible case that can thus be made out for *Elan,* it must be rejected nonetheless both because there is no other evidence that Healfdene's daughter bore such a name or that she was married to Onela, and because the assumptions upon which the emendation is based are dubious—dubious in and of themselves, unnecessary for emending the line, and, as we have seen, failing to work out satisfactorily.

Both assumptions, that Healfdene's daughter must have been men-

---

[11] In the first half-line (Sievers' type A3) the short syllable of the second lift is not exceptional (see John C. Pope, *The Rhythm of Beowulf* [New Haven, 1966], pp. 273–74). In the MS, names are usually not capitalized.

[12] As Malone points out, pp. 139–40.

7

tioned there by name and that her Swedish husband was mentioned thus there too, are inspired by wish rather than logic. The fact that no such alliance is referred to elsewhere in *Beowulf* or in any other account should have led scholars to question the assumptions. Instead, out of their desire to determine precisely what the alliance was and who was involved, they have clung tenaciously to them. Plausible as both assumptions are or seem to be, they need to be more carefully considered than they have been.

The second assumption, that the husband's name must have been mentioned in line 62, seems reasonable enough until we recall that the *Beowulf* poet sometimes fails to mention a name where he might be expected to and often designates someone by a descriptive epithet rather than by his name. The hero of the poem, whose exploits begin with line 194, is not called *Beowulf* until line 343, being referred to earlier as *Hygelaces þegn, se goda, se yldesta,* and various other descriptive epithets. The name of the Danish warrior *Hondsció,* seized and devoured by the monster Grendel (740–45), is not mentioned until line 2076. The Danish king Hroðgar, though referred to by name a number of times, is also referred to by a variety of descriptive epithets and so too are the Swedish kings Onela and his father Ongenþeow. The use of epithet rather than name, abundantly exemplified in *Beowulf,* is a well-known characteristic of all Old English poetry, where—regardless of the confusion or annoyance it now often causes—it must be accepted as a consciously employed stylistic trait. If then *-elan* in line 62 refers to the Swedish husband, we are not compelled to assume that this must be the ending of his name, for it could be the ending of any noun or adjective suitable here as a descriptive epithet—such as *gamelan* "the old one" or *æþelan* "the noble one."

The second assumption is obviously two-fold, including both the assumption that it is Healfdene's daughter who is referred to there and also the assumption that, whoever the woman may be, she is mentioned by name. The latter may be disposed of readily, for, like the man, she might have been designated by a descriptive epithet (*seo yldesta* or *gingesta*),[13] or simply by a noun (*seo ides* "the lady") or even a pronoun (*oþer* "the other one").[14]

The other part of the second assumption cannot be disposed of so

[13] In Scandinavian tradition Healfdene's daughter (Signy) is said to be the oldest of his children. *Beowulf* scholars take her to be the youngest, inferring this from the fact that her three brothers, mentioned before her, are listed in order from eldest to youngest.

[14] *Oþer,* regularly referring to one of two, would be appropriate here as referring to the daughter vs. the three sons.

quickly. It needs careful examination because both of the assumptions, the first as well as the second, insofar as they are not inspired merely by wishful thinking, stem from the conviction that the woman referred to in line 62 must be Healfdene's daughter. The passage in which it occurs (59–63, cited above p. 3) seems at first glance to imply this very clearly, for four children of Healfdene are mentioned there and only three are accounted for, the three sons listed as *Heorogar ond Hroðgar ond Halga til.* Quite naturally this leads to the expectation that the daughter, who though possibly not mentioned by name, will at least be referred to. Enhancing the expectation and seemingly confirming it beyond doubt is the fact that immediately following (62) there is a reference to a woman.

Several words in the passage are worth notice: *forðgerimed* (59), *til* (61), and *hyrde ic* (62). For the nonce-form *forðgerimed,* any of the meanings usually ascribed to it, "counted up," "all told," or "in succession" will do well enough provided it is correctly applied to yield the proper sense there (e.g. "To Healfdene four children all told were born") and not loosely construed as implying that all four children are to be accounted for in much the same way as the three sons are. Following the names of the three sons is the adjective *til* "good," modifying *Halga,* the last of the three, and definitely marking the end of the list. This function of *til* as an end-marker has long been recognized,[15] but its possible significance has been ignored. If it marks the end of the list of names, the expectation that the name of the daughter is to follow seems rather unlikely. Further doubt about the expectation arises from the way the next line begins. *Hyrde ic þæt* may be a mere formula, as it is here regularly taken to be, but instead of a pointless remark, serving no purpose whatever except to get the sentence underway in an aimless manner, the phrase seems more likely to be quite pointed in meaning, function, or both. Whatever the poet went on to say, *hyrde ic* would thus seem either to mean that he was doubtful about it or reluctant to mention it, or to indicate that he was now shifting away from Healfdene's children to someone else.

Still more doubt about the expectation that the poet was to go on and mention Healfdene's daughter, by name or not, arises from two other considerations—his usual avoidance of women's names and his apparent unconcern about daughters. Throughout the poem he leaves most of the women unnamed, naming only Hildeburh, a minor figure in the poem,

15 "In accordance with an ancient idiom . . . well known from Homer . . . the last of three coordinate nouns, in particular proper names, is marked by the addition of an epithet or some other qualifying element; thus 11. 2434 . . . " (Klaeber, note on line 61).

9

and Hygd, who as wife of Hygelac, king of the Geats, is a prominent figure there.[16] For the other women, whether their role is prominent or not, the poet uses only nicknames—*Wealhþeow* for Hroðgar's queen and *Freawaru* for his daughter—or leaves them nameless: the Geatish woman mourning at Beowulf's funeral; Ongenþeow's wife, whose capture and recapture in the war with the Geats would seem to be an exciting enough episode to call for some more specific designation of her than merely *iomeowlan* "old woman" (2931); Hygelac's only daughter, given in marriage as a reward to the slayer of Ongenþeow (2997–98); the mother of the monster Grendel, who fought Beowulf more fiercely than her son did; and the mother of Beowulf, whose father Ecgþeow is mentioned by name sixteen times.

The poet's failure to mention the hero's mother by name is especially noteworthy since it is parallel to the way he treats Healfdene's daughter. Like her, Beowulf's mother is a princess, the only daughter of Hreþel, king of the Geats, and also she has three brothers who are named in a list: *Herebeald ond Hæðcyn oððe Hygelac min* (2434). This list of Hreþel's sons is remarkably like the list of Healfdene's sons (61), for the arrangement—from oldest to youngest son—is the same and both lists conclude with an end-marker, *min* functioning thus here just as *til* does in the other.[17] The context in which line 2434 occurs also raises the expectation that the daughter of Hreþel will be mentioned too, for in the preceding lines (2428–33), where Beowulf is reminiscing about his childhood when Hreþel took him into his household, loving him no less than he did any of his own children, it seems apparent that Beowulf has in mind all of Hreþel's children, not just the three sons. Yet despite the fact that Hreþel's daughter is Beowulf's mother—a fact brought out early in the poem (372–75)—she is not mentioned here at all. The *Beowulf* poet evidently felt that sons merit special notice but daughters do not—even so illustrious a one as Hreþel's, the mother of the hero of the poem.

If we therefore reject the questionable assumptions that in line 62 Healfdene's daughter must be mentioned—whether by name or not—and that the man mentioned there is her husband Onela, to what con-

---

[16] Her prominence becomes greater if, as some scholars prefer to think, she later married Beowulf and is the Geatish woman mourning at his funeral (3150–55) or if, as I believe, before her marriage to Hygelac she was married to Offa (see "The 'Thryth-Offa Digression' in *Beowulf*" in *Franciplegius: Medieval and Linguistic Studies in Honor of Francis Peabody Magoun, Jr.* [New York, 1965], pp. 124–38). Those who interpret the digression (1931–62) otherwise are forced to conclude that Offa's wife was left nameless or bore the strange name *Modþryðo*.

[17] As Klaeber recognizes (see footnote 15) but so obscurely that the point may easily escape notice. Hoops, *Kommentar*, pp. 17 and 259, brings it out clearly.

10

clusion are we led? Certainly not to the conclusion that emendation of the line is impossible, for if two names are not required there, other terms are readily available, opening up many interesting possibilities. I have already suggested what they are, pointing out that descriptive epithets or other suitable terms might have been used to designate the man or the woman or both. Accordingly, *-elan* may then be expanded to [*gam*]*elan* or [*æþ*]*elan* and preceding it any word may be supplied which is metrically satisfactory and applicable to the situation. If we assume that the situation involves the marriage of Healfdene's daughter to a Swede, he would remain unidentified because these descriptive epithets could refer to any of several men[18]—*æþela* to either Onela or his brother Ohthere and *gamela* to their father Ongenþeow. Ongenþeow is repeatedly referred to as old in the stirring account of his death and his wife's rescue later in the poem (2922–98). The mention of her here (62) would accordingly not be pointless, as it is if the woman is Onela's wife, who, as I have said before, is never referred to again.

Those who, like Klaeber, insist upon identifying the man as Onela would have no trouble with the rest of the emendation if they were content to leave Healfdene's daughter nameless. Various terms, such as the ones I mentioned earlier, *ides, yldesta,* or *oþer,* all clearly referring to her, would fit with *æþelan* as well as with *Onelan.* But of course with *gamelan* other terms would be required—*gingestan,* for example.[19]

If, however, we assume that the situation does not necessarily involve Healfdene's daughter, or a Swedish king, or their marriage, other ways of emending the line are possible. Thus *gamelan,* instead of referring to Ongenþeow, could refer to Healfdene, described as *gamol* only four lines earlier (58). If so, the line might be emended to read *Hyrde ic þæt geo wæs þæs gamelan cwen,* which, with the following phrase *Heaðo-Scilfingas healsgebedda,* would mean, "I have heard that formerly the old man's (Healfdene's) queen was the consort of a Swede." Though stylistically somewhat awkward, the reading is defensible, I think, and gains some plausibility from the fact that in Scandinavian tradition Healfdene's wife was a foreigner. Scandinavian tradition, however, was concerned more about Healfdene's mother than his wife, for it was thus that his name "Half-Dane" was explained. His Danish father carried off the daughter of a Swedish king, making her his concubine and the mother of his illegitimate son Healfdene. If this sordid tale is what the *Beowulf* poet had heard and reluctantly mentioned, the line could then be

---

18 Though not necessarily a king—as *cwen* (62) might seem to imply but actually does not since the word may mean merely 'lady'—I shall limit the choice to the Scylfing dynasty.
19 See footnote 13.

emended accordingly to . . . *seo ealdmodor wæs æþelan* . . . , meaning "the grandmother (Healfdene's mother) was the queen or consort of a Swedish nobleman." If, on the other hand, it was the incestuous stigma attached to Healfdene's daughter[20] that the poet had heard about and felt compelled to mention, the line might be emended to read, *Hyrde ic þæt seo gyngesta* (Healfdene's daughter) *wæs ær þæs gamelan cwen,* which with the following phrase[21] would mean that after her incestuous union with her father she became the consort of a Swede.

Taking *gamelan* or *æþelan* as referring to Healfdene—regardless of whether the woman is his daughter, wife, or mother—provides a fitting conclusion for the passage, which marks the end of the introductory section of the poem. In it the Scylding dynasty is traced from its mythical founder down to Hroðgar, a central figure in the action which follows. In this action, his sister and two brothers play no part whatever, Heorogar being barely mentioned later (467, 2158) and Halga and his sister not at all. Mention of them in lines 59–63 is incidental. Mention of Healfdene, the father, is essential there. And with him the introductory section comes to its proper end.

My concern throughout has not been to show how line 62 should be emended but rather to show how it should not be. There are many possible ways of emending it, all of them more or less satisfactory but none really satisfactory at all because it is impossible to demonstrate that any of them is correct. This is certainly true of the way hitherto assumed to be correct, whereby the name *Onela* is confidently entered there and identified as the husband of Healfdene's daughter. Both are merely guesses—not even very good ones, it seems to me.

Guesses, even good ones, do not constitute facts. Yet the alliance of Onela with Healfdene's daughter is now accepted as a fact, duly entered in the genealogies of both the Swedish and the Danish royal lines.[22] Tucked away thus in a genealogical table, this "fact" is too inconspicuous to attract much attention and seems too inconsequential to arouse any concern. But for scholars attempting to piece out the main events of Scandinavian history during this period on the basis of the few solid facts available, this Danish-Swedish alliance is of considerable importance.

If history scholars are ill served by this pseudo-fact, so also are

---

[20] See footnote 8.

[21] *Heaðo-Scilfingas healsgebedda* is then in apposition with *seo gyngesta.* Construing it more naturally as in apposition with *gamelan cwen* would require emending *Scylfing* to *Scylding,* which, though certainly plausible, must be ruled out for the reason given in footnote 6.

[22] As in Klaeber, pp. xxxi and xxxviii.

Beowulf scholars, who unwarily are led to believe that it is a fact recorded in the poem and are accordingly tempted to attribute far-reaching significance to it. Thus Klaeber, for example, regards the alliance as a clue to the strange favoritism shown by Onela toward the Wægmundings, the family to which Beowulf belongs, and also says that Onela's role in "the dynastic struggle within the royal Swedish line is perhaps to be explained . . . by the existence of a foreign or pro-Danish party led by Onela (the son-in-law of Healfdene). . . ."[23] In both instances Klaeber is wrong but this need not concern us here, for I mention them only as examples of how risky it is to regard the marriage of Onela and Healfdene's daughter as an established fact.

There is, as I have said, no really satisfactory way of emending line 62, and the safest course therefore is to leave it unamended. For those who are not content to leave it thus, the least unsatisfactory way is to emend it to something like *Hyrde ic þæt seo ides wæs þæs æþelan cwen,* leaving Healfdene's daughter nameless and her husband unidentified. In proposing this I am motivated not by any desire to deprive her of her name and her husband but by the hope that it may both put an end to the long and fruitless quest to determine her name and also prevent any further mischief caused by incautious emendations of the line.

---

[23] P. xliii, immediately followed by his conjecture about Onela's connection with the Wægmundings.

2

Guilt and the World's Complexity: The Murder of Ongentheow and the Slaying of the Dragon

JOHN GARDNER

THE STORY OF THE SWEDISH KING ONGENTHEOW, MURDERED BY GEATS, and the story of Beowulf's dragon have odd similarities: both the king and the dragon are "old and terrible" and "crafty"; both retreat to caves which they mistakenly put their trust in, and die there defending their treasure hoards, the dragon defending his hoard of gold, Ongentheow defending a different kind of treasure (*hord forstandan, bearn ond bryde,* 2955b–56a)—his children and wife; both the king and the dragon are wounded in the forehead, strike back ferociously, and are later finished off; and both are killed not by one man alone but by two kinsmen working together. In a poem as carefully constructed as *Beowulf,* a parallel so close can hardly be accidental. But what does it mean?

Beowulf bristles from end to end with curious echoes and parallels, repeated or pointedly juxtaposed details of language, imagery, or thought which bind the poem together and establish its assumptions and values—if we can figure the equations. The parallels show up in many forms and serve a variety of purposes, from textural interest to allegorical patterning. We hear repeatedly, for instance, of the sleep that follows the feast, the sorrow or joy which comes in the morning (Ongentheow claims he will hang his Geatish attackers in the morning), the great difference between words and works, the troubles brought on by drunkenness or by gold, and God's payment of his friends (the repetitions of *frofor*) and grim repayment of his enemies (e.g., of Cain, *he him ðæs lean forgeald,* 114b). We also hear key words repeated and occasionally echoed by related words, *bearm,* for instance, and its near-relation, *fæþm,* words used throughout in many senses, from the bosom of the family or the bosom of the death-ship to God's embrace or Grendel's hug.

Whether or not the poem was composed orally, the theory of oral-formulaic composition comes nowhere near accounting for this patterning.[1] It is true that brilliant, difficult poets who lean heavily on repetition and structural parallel have sometimes composed orally—if not Homer, then certainly John Milton and James Joyce—but the central tenet of those who preach the oral-formulaic dogma, that formulas swing in to give the poet time to think, though it may work for rambling Yugoslavian oral poems, will not work in the case of *Beowulf* (as it will not work for the *Iliad* or the *Odyssey*). The Beowulf-poet obviously thought out his poem with care, at his leisure and in private, writing or saying his lines over and over until everything was right. When he makes use of mechanical formulas like *Beowulf maþelode, bearn Ecgþeowes,* he does so in sophisticated imitation of the archaic native style, not because he needs the formulas but because he likes them, that is, because the old-fashioned formulas give textural interest and enhance his treatment of the poem's main subject, "the good old days." (For similar application of old devices to a new, strictly aesthetic purpose, consider the use of stained-glass windows in department stores and Unitarian churches.) One evidence that the poem's more rigid formulas are mainly ornamental is the fact that most of the poem's repetitions, instead of freeing the poet to think ahead, involve him in more or less tortuous allegorical equation making.

Take one equation that seems at first glance not unduly complex and hence the kind of thing a poet might come up with on his feet, slightly drunk, in the presence of an audience. The *Beowulf*-poet sets up, in the Grendel's mere episode, a contrast between Hrunting, the sword Unferth gives Beowulf, a fine sword which never before failed, and Beowulf's chainmail, which holds good—a contrast pointedly recalling that between Unferth, Hrothgar's bravest warrior until the advent of Grendel, and Beowulf, whose courage remains firm. Read simple-mindedly, the parallel merely underscores the difference between Beowulf's glory and

---

[1] For the standard articles on oral formulaic theory and for criticism of the theory's weaknesses, see the essays collected in *Essential Articles for the Study of Old English Poetry,* eds. Jess B. Bessinger, Jr. and Stanley J. Kahrl (Hamden, Connecticut, 1968), pp. 319–403.

a lesser man's. Since Unferth lacks the courage to swim down to almost certain death, he gives up his splendid reputation: (*þær he dome forleas, / ellenmærðum,* 1470b–71a); and in the same way the sword, when it fails to bite, gives up its glory (*his dom alæg,* 1528b). But the equation involves more. Unferth is a *þyle*—a troublemaking priest of Woden[2]—and a man of violence, a slayer of kinsmen, while Beowulf is treated throughout the poem as, though pagan, Christlike (*manna mildust*), a hero who never got drunk and slew kinsmen (2179b–80a). Thus the weapon contrast (sword *vs.* chainmail)—as well as the scene's emphasis on courage—subtly reinforces a contrast that runs throughout the poem, between what might be called the old heroic ethic and the new, the Old Testament ethic and the New, or, to put it still another way, the ethic of fearless, thieving Hama, who won glory among men by stealing the Brosing necklace, and the ethic of Beowulf, whose gentleness except in defense of right wins him not just the eternal praise (*ece rædas*) of men but also that of God (cf. lines 1741b–60a and 1197–1201). Except in self-sacrificing defense of right, the sword has, in the Christian scheme, laid down its glory; the thing to be trusted is "the whole armor of God."

Such complex equations are far more the rule than the exception in this poem. Think of the ingenious double equation of (1) Heorot and the world, introduced by, among other things, verbal parallels in the passage describing the creation of the hall and the passage on God's creation of the world, and (2) Heorot and the tri-partite human soul: at Heorot watchmen fall asleep, drunk on beer, allowing devil-like Grendel to have his way, while within the human soul, according to Hrothgar, *se weard swefeð* [the watchman (intellect) falls asleep] and a murderer all too near (Satan, or the passions) comes and kills.[3] Or think of the beautifully ambiguous raven symbolism, whose traditional significance as a bird of war and death flowers magnificently in the nightfall passage near the end of section XXV:

> Reste hine þa rumheort;   reced hliuade
> geap on goldfah;   gæst inne swæf,
> oþ þæt hrefn blaca   heofones wynne

[2] See Joseph L. Baird, "Unferth the 'þyle,'" *MÆ,* 39 (1970), 1–12.

[3] For more detail on Heorot symbolism and the importance of the idea of the tri-partite soul in *Beowulf,* see John Gardner, "Fulgentius's *Expositio Vergiliana Continentia* and the Plan of *Beowulf:* Another Approach to the Poem's Style and Structure," *PLL,* 6 (1970), 238–40 (hereafter "Fulgentius and *Beowulf*"). I should note here that my eccentric translation of 170b–72a (p. 240) is wrong, but the point I make is still valid, for reasons I explain in *The Construction of Christian Poetry in Old English,* to be published by the Southern Illinois University Press in 1975.

bliðheort bodode. Ða com beorht scacan
[scima ofer sceadwa]; scaþan onetton,
wæron æþelingas eft to leodum
fuse to farenne; wolde feor þanon
cuma collenferhð ceoles neosan.

(1799–1806)[4]

[Then the great-hearted one rested; the hall stood high, vaulted and gold-adorned; the guest slept within until the black raven, blithe-hearted, announced heaven's joy. Then the bright light came passing over the shadows. The warriors hastened, the nobles were eager to set out again for their people. Bold of spirit, the visitor would seek his ship far thence.]

Beowulf bristles, I have said, with parallels and echoes; and no passage illustrates that quality better than this one. The passage is joyful on the literal level: a bird announces sunrise and Beowulf's companions are eager to depart, return home, on their ship, to their people. But the bird is the black raven, image of death, and morning is "heaven's joy," in other words, the happiness of the future life. The sailors' eagerness to be gone recalls the splendid passage on their earlier eagerness to come to Hrothgar's aid, *weras on wilsið* [warriors on a well-wished voyage] when their ship flew *fugle gelicost* [most like a bird] urgently driven by winds and waves, with the blessing of both men and the omens—a passage allegorically suggesting the divine aid God sends all men as he sent the physical hero Beowulf to Hrothgar. (See lines 194–223a and, also, 1888–1916.) The poet's echoes hint that what seems good to pagans, a return to the homeland, is to Christians a false hope, though not a hope to be despised: friends die, kingdoms fall; the homeland to be eagerly sought is heaven. Not that death's terror is forgotten for a moment. Light comes in syntactical constructions formerly associated with Grendel: *Com on wanre niht* [Came gliding in the black night, 702b], *Ða com of more* [Then came from the moor, 710a], and *Com þa to recede* [Came then to the hall, 720a]—descriptions of Grendel's approach to Heorot—are echoed in the phrase on the approaching sun: *Ða com beorht* [Then the bright light came, 1802b]; and the verbal key to the syntactical envelope pattern on Grendel's first approach to Heorot, *Gewat ða neosian* [He (Grendel) went then to survey, 115a] and *wica neosan* [to seek his dwelling, 125b], has its echo in *ceoles neosan* [to seek the ship, 1806b].

[4] Quotations are from the 3rd edition of F. Klaeber, *Beowulf and the Fight at Finnsburg* (New York, 1950). Here and throughout this essay, translations are taken from E. T. Donaldson, *Beowulf* (New York, 1960).

Juxtapositional and echoing devices are the poet's chief aesthetic method in *Beowulf*. They are the means by which he interweaves history and legend, as Bonjour pointed out in his most famous essay,[5] and the means by which he defines the moral principles of the new heroic ethic, as when he gives Hrothgar's scop the three contrasting stories of corrupt Heremod, who was bloodthirsty and selfish, imperfect Sigemund, who was courageous but secretive (not even telling Fitela what business he had in hand), and the ideal hero Beowulf, courageous and open-hearted, a man who (now that he is mature) acts for the welfare of others, with their knowledge and approval. Indeed, as I have argued elsewhere in detail,[6] symbolic juxtaposition gives the poet his three major episodes, Beowulf's successive encounters with Grendel, Grendel's dam, and the dragon. The profluence of *Beowulf* is not causal, each event generating the next by the laws of *energeia,* as in a good Aristotelian plot, but schematic, as in a typical medieval plot: Beowulf fights first a creature of *perverse rationality* (a criminal, a "hell-counsellor," a hater of order), then a creature of *perverse irascibility* (an avenger who seeks to glorify wrong, that is, win vengeance for a criminal), and finally a creature of *perverse concupiscence* (a dragon whose nature is to seek out gold and sit on it). This is of course not to deny that the plot is borrowed from pagan legendry[7] but only to say that the borrowed plot has been rationalized in a new way, hence philosophically transformed.

In this forest of echoes and parallels, what are we to do with those verbal and imagistic echoes which invite us to compare old Ongentheow and the dragon? Certainly the answer is not that Ongentheow, like the dragon, is evil. He is explicitly called "the good" (2949a), and in his war with Hygelac he is the victim, not the aggressor. When he dies, his gold has already been stolen; the only "treasure" he defends is his family; and though Ongentheow is *eald ond egesfull* [old and (to his enemies) terrifying, 2929a] he is not, like Heremod, bloodthirsty. In other words, if evil in the poem is defined by the monsters—evil-minded Grendel, Grendel's wrongfully vengeful dam, and the mindlessly concupiscent dragon—Ongentheow is innocent. Beowulf acknowledges this, in effect, when he shelters the old Swede's legitimate heir.

Perhaps we should try a different tack. What has Ongentheow to do with the death of Beowulf?

Beowulf, when the dragon attacks his people, has the painful thought

---

[5] Adrien Bonjour, *The Digressions in Beowulf* (Oxford, 1950).

[6] John Gardner, "Fulgentius and *Beowulf*," pp. 243–60.

[7] See Nora K. Chadwick, "The Monsters and Beowulf," in *The Anglo-Saxons: Studies in some Aspects of their History and Culture, presented to Bruce Dickens,* ed. Peter Clemoes (London, 1959), pp. 171–203.

that some sin of his own may have brought on the tribe's catastrophe, in other words that the dragon is a punishment sent by God (2327b–31a). That is, of course, a natural, psychologically realistic touch, and one need do no more with it; but some recent critics have made it the basis of a theory that Beowulf is indeed a guilty man: the dragon has done no real harm, according to Professor John Leyerle (merely burned the meadhall and other houses, leaving "nothing alive" [2314b]!), yet Beowulf becomes furious, as is not his wont, and foolishly strikes out single-handedly, an act excusable, even praiseworthy, in a hero, but for a king, on whose life the whole tribe depends, a sign of overweening pride.[8] Leyerle supports this annoying theory with a glance at Hrothgar's warning to Beowulf in section XXV, where Hrothgar speaks of how Heremod became bloodthirsty (an effect of perverse irascibility) and stingy (an effect of perverse concupiscence), then tells how a king's long years of good fortune can lead to miserliness.[9]

In Leyerle's defense it must be said that the dragon episode does certainly deal with concupiscence and irascibility, the passional forces which overthrow reason. That is the point—beyond plot necessity—of the focus on Hygd and Hygelac. Once cruel and proud, Hygd has been tamed by her former husband Offa and is now, as her name suggests, a model of reasonableness. (*Modþryðo* has lately been proved a misreading: when young, Hygd was *mod-þryð*.)[10] Her lord, as Professor Kaske has shown, is her foil, *hyge-lac,* that is, *mind-lack.*[11] His raid on Ongentheow, a piece of raw thievery which ultimately brings his own kingdom to ruin,[12] shows the appropriateness of his name. But it is not exactly clear that Beowulf shares, to any significant degree, his dear lord's faults. In the poem's first two episodes, Beowulf stands in absolute contrast with the monsters he opposes. Whereas Grendel is a figure of perverse rationality, Beowulf is the very emblem of right thought—in his speech to the coastguard, Wulfgar, Hrothgar, Unferth, Wealhtheow, and finally his own men, his "wide-mindedness" and discernment, his full and articulate knowledge of the code, are the poet's main emphasis. (A central point in

8 John Leyerle, "Beowulf the Hero and the King," *MÆ,* 34 (1965), 89–102.

9 The parenthetical identifications of the soul's two lower faculties are of course mine, not Leyerle's.

10 Norman E. Eliason, "The 'Thryth-Offa Digression' in *Beowulf,*" in *Franciplegius: Medieval and Linguistic Studies in Honor of Francis Peabody Magoun, Jr.,* eds. Jess B. Bessinger, Jr. and Robert P. Creed (New York, 1965), pp. 124–38. Eliason (p. 126) translates *mod-þryð* "guilty of haughtiness."

11 R. E. Kaske, " 'Hygelac' and 'Hygd,' " in *Studies on Old English Literature in Honor of Arthur G. Brodeur* (Eugene, Oregon, 1963), pp. 200–06.

12 Historically, the raid was apparently a military move aimed at weakening the Franks. See G. Storms, "The Significance of Hygelac's Raid," *NMS,* 14 (1970), 3–26. But this is not the way the raid is used in the poem.

that code, as I have elsewhere shown, is that the hero must act for others and with their full approval.)[13] And whereas Grendel's dam seeks to avenge evil, Beowulf is the absolute model of the legitimate avenger. Is he in fact tainted by concupiscence in the dragon episode? And if so, does concupiscence lead him, as it did Heremod, to perverse irascibility?

Not really. When his hall burns, Beowulf swells with rage: *breost innan weoll / þeostrum geþoncum, swa him geþywe ne wæs* [his breast welled within with dark thoughts, as was not usual with him, 2331b-32]; and in this Beowulf is similar to the dragon, who, when he finds his gold stolen, *gebolge(n) wæs* [was swollen with rage, 2220b]. But the real point here is contrast, not comparison. The dragon is furious at the loss of gold which is useless to him (2277b). Beowulf, whom the poet has insistently presented as (at least until now) a good, wise king (2207-10a), is furious at the loss of his meadhall, not a private but a public possession, a place where, as in Hrothgar's meadhall (71-73), a good king deals out to old and young alike all that God has given him. The poet's remark that Beowulf's anger is not usual with him means not so much that he has changed for the worse as that in ordinary situations he was not at all a man of wrath—indeed, he was a warrior-hero of incredibly gentle ways. In other words, the interjection *swa him geþywe ne wæs* is the poet's attempt to prevent any misunderstanding by the listener: though Beowulf was exceedingly angry this once, anger was by no means his usual mood. And since Beowulf seeks the dragon's gold not for himself but for his people (2794-2801a), the charge of perverse concupiscence is even weaker than the charge of perverse irascibility.

His attacking the dragon all alone is, admittedly, a tactical error and a slight failure by the code (as Wiglaf indicates), but we need not make too much of this. Leyerle may be right philosophically in arguing that what is fitting for a hero is foolishness in a king; but that judgment comes from outside the poem, where error is defined in terms of reason's guardianship, rule of the passions. There is nothing—or almost nothing— wrong with Beowulf's tri-partite soul. He makes only the minor mistake of refusing counsel, precisely the mistake he made, as he in effect admits to Unferth, when he swam with Breca. And in that case, despite his error, all turned out well. He was at that time a trifle foolish, being a mere boy, *cnihtwesende / . . . þa git / on geogoðfeore* [like boys / . . . then still in first youth, 535b-37a], refusing to take advice (510b-12a), but he nevertheless achieved results beneficial to man (565-69a). Error or no error, he was protected by fate: *Wyrd oft nereð / unfægne eorl, þonne his ellen deah!* [Fate often saves an undoomed man, when his

[13] John Gardner, "Fulgentius and *Beowulf*," p. 251.

courage is good, 572b–73]. Making the same fairly trifling mistake, now that he is old, he dies—as Wiglaf says: fated. Perhaps it is foolish to ask why. Fate is fate. Nevertheless, since fate is also providence, as the poet may have known through Boethius, one does ask.[14]

Though he committed no great sin, it is not quite true that Beowulf, like Ongentheow, died "absurd." Ongentheow dies as the indirect victim of Hygelac (Mindlack), who is in command of the raid, and as direct victim of two men named Eofor (Boar, a creature famous for irascibility) and Wulf (Wolf, a creature famous for its ugly eating habits, ravenous concupiscence), two sons of a man called Wonred (Darkcounsel). Ongentheow, in other words, is the sad victim of the Heremod principle among men, fallen reason, the supremacy of the passions. By the divine law of the poem, he will be avenged. Beowulf dies, I should like to suggest, because when Ongentheow was murdered, he was there, fighting in the foremost. He tells us why he fought: Hygelac gave him treasures; it was therefore Beowulf's duty to fight for his beloved lord, to "repay" him (2490–93a). Thus

> Sinc eaðe mæg,
> gold on grund(e)   gumcynnes gehwone
> oferhigian,   hyde se ðe wylle!

> (2764b–66)

[Easily may treasure, gold in the ground, betray each one of the race of men, hide it who will!]

Involved, however distantly, in the Ongentheow raid—and despite his attempt to make amends by granting asylum to Ongentheow's heir—Beowulf is tainted. The poet hints that Beowulf may be tainted, too, by some more general force unexplainable by the warrior's ethic. Grendel once slew thirty men; Beowulf has the strength of thirty men in his fist, and after the fight with the Hetware, he rows back to Geatland[15] bearing thirty suits of armor. If the numerical echo has any significance, it would seem to be that Beowulf is in some way a little like Grendel, mixed up with Cain. Symbolically at least, he is perhaps tainted by his killing of

---

[14] On *Beowulf* and Boethius see Bertha Phillpots, "Wyrd and Providence in Anglo-Saxon Thought," *ES*, 13 (1913), 20, and B. J. Timmer, "Wyrd in Anglo-Saxon Prose and Poetry," in *Essential Articles for the Study of Old English Poetry*, pp. 124–58.

[15] See Karl P. Wentersdorf, "Beowulf's Withdrawal from Frisia: A Reconsideration," *SP*, 68 (1971), 395–415. Wentersdorf speaks of Fred Robinson's earlier demonstration that Beowulf rowed instead of swimming (as critics used to think), in an article for *SP* in January, 1965. I have not read Robinson's article.

Daeghrefn as well, that fight of which he so proudly boasts; for the name of Beowulf's mighty opponent recalls that day-raven who sings of *heofones wynne,* [heaven's joy].

The name Daeghrefn is of course a mystery. Kaske speculates that Daeghrefn may have been Hygelac's murderer, a Frisian giant.[16] If so, by the poem's morality Beowulf may be at least partly wrong in killing him, avenging Hygelac, Ongentheow's (indirect) murderer. But perhaps the name is purely symbolic. It is curiously close to Swedish *dag-gryning* [dawn], Danish *daggryning* [dawn], German *tagesgrauen,* or, by another line, Irish *dei-grine* [sunbeam, Finn MacCool's standard], or *dio-ghrein* in the Magnus ballads on Finn (Fingal), derived from the Irish *grian* [sun], from **greina.*[17] Daeghrefn is of course not close to Old English *dægrima* [dawn], but it might derive as a folk etymology from some such word as *daggryning,* which to Anglo-Saxon ears made no sense. This is pure speculation, but it is interesting to note that the name Ongentheow (beginning + servant or priestly servant; cf. Wealh-theow) seems to fit with a reading of Daeghrefn as dawn or somehow related to dawn. And if dawn is viewed as a Christian resurrection symbol—as it seems to be intended in lines 1799–1806—Beowulf's killing of Daeghrefn would seem to put him (as his pagan birth does) on the wrong side.

I suggest, in other words, that though Beowulf is not guilty of sinful irascibility or concupiscence, he is nevertheless mysteriously guilty. His errors, in the warrior world he inhabits, are as inescapable as, say, original sin. And that, I think, may be the poet's point. Beowulf had nothing to do, directly, with the murder of Ongentheow; if he bears any guilt at all, it is strictly guilt by association. But the parallel between the old Swedish king and the flame-spewing dragon suggests that in some way it is Ongentheow's ghost that kills him.

[16] R. E. Kaske, "The Eotenas in *Beowulf*," in *Old English Poetry: Fifteen Essays,* ed., Robert P. Creed (Providence, 1967), p. 302.

[17] E. L. Epstein, who put me onto these related words, reminds me that in *Finnegans Wake* Joyce writes, "Dayagreening gains in schlimninging" (607.24).

3

Potlatch and Charity:
Notes on the Heroic in *Beowulf*

CHARLES DONAHUE

PERHAPS THE *Beowulf* POET'S GREATEST IMAGINATIVE ACHIEVEMENT was to body forth such an image of an heroic and good but non-Christian Germania as enabled him—and doubtless some of his audience —to reconcile admiration for ancient heroic ancestors with a new Christian faith. The poet, influenced by pre-Augustinian theological views of human history, portrayed his non-Christian Germania as an essentially good society, whose members followed the natural law engraved in their hearts and looked with gratitude towards God, Whose existence they had discovered by considering His works. There were heathens in this society. Heathens are men who seek the aid of evil spirits and who do not know the true God. Such was Grendel, and doubtless Grendel's dam. Such were also the Danes who sacrificed at heathen shrines. The heathens, however, are the antagonists in the poem. They are opposed to God and given over to evil practices, such as murder and refusal to pay wergild (154–56). The protagonists, however, true representatives of Germania in days of yore, Hrothgar and most of the Danes, Beowulf, Hygelac, and, so far as our knowledge goes, all of the Geats, were theists who knew God and followed the law of nature, the *ealde riht* (2330). There are no good pagans in the poem. (The poet, I suspect, would have found the phrase *god hæpen* an unintelligible paradox.)

Potlatch and Charity: Notes on the Heroic in *Beowulf*

The poet is obviously concerned to make his religious conviction a part of his work. The references to God are very numerous throughout the poem. The first is the poet's declaration that God granted a son to Scyld to comfort the Danes who had long been without a lord (12–16a). The last is Wiglaf's command to the Geats to carry Beowulf's body to the place he would long abide *in Wealdendes wære* [in the peace of God the Ruler, 3107–09]. The poet makes God part of the action of the poem and is concerned to make it clear to his audience that the Judaeo-Christian God is present by His power and providence in the non-Jewish and non-Christian world in which his theistic protagonists and heathen antagonists move.[1]

Despite the poet's strong theistic conviction, however, I believe it is a critical error to approach his poem as primarily a doctrinal work, one designed to inculcate Christian beliefs or recommend Christian conduct either directly or cryptically, by truths hidden under the veil of allegory. The poet was clearly well-schooled in Germanic heroic poetry. That poetry knew nothing of allegory. It celebrated heroic deeds and encouraged emulation of them. It served to keep up morale in meadhalls. *Beowulf* is an extremely elaborate and sophisticated example of its genre, affected by biblical narrative and, perhaps, by the *Aeneid,* but the poet, as he assures us at the outset of his poem, proposes to celebrate the glory of Germanic heroes in days long past, "how those princes showed forth their prowess." The poet holds to his purpose from the beginning to the end of his work. I propose to trace some of this development with particular attention to the way in which the poet has used it as a means of unifying his composition.

As the poet sees it, the heroic is a characteristic of warrior societies consisting each of a warlord (*dryhten*) and a body of retainers (*gedryht*). Heroic munificence is incumbent on the *dryhten*. He is keeper of the treasure. The arms and the rings he distributes ceremoniously at feasts are of practical use to his warriors and they convey status (*weorþ*). The warrior is bound in honor to make a counter-gift of his military services and all that they bring. He is bound to lay down his life in defense of his *dryhten* or to die in an effort to avenge him if the defense fails. Heroic loyalty is the counterpart of heroic munificence.

---

[1] Two papers have been devoted to the poet's view of his pre-Christian ancestors and the possible theological origins of that view: "Beowulf, Ireland, and the Natural Good," *Traditio,* 7 (1951), 263–77, and "Beowulf and Christian Tradition: A Reconsideration from a Celtic Stance," *Traditio,* 21 (1965), 55–116. Both of these were primarily concerned with theological assumptions implied by the poem; any literary explication was introduced to that end. The purpose of the second paper was expressly declared (p. 59) to be an attempt to persuade historians of religious thought to take the good pre-Christian monotheists in *Beowulf* more seriously. The present paper is an attempt at a literary explication of one theme of the poem.

The poet was doubtless familiar with this system of gift and counter-gift, munificence and loyalty, in the traditional poems which he certainly knew. He could probably still observe it motivating action in aristocratic circles in his own day, for the system is not a poetic convention but a social fact. The main outlines of it can be found in Tacitus and similar values were apparently still valid in the tenth-century English society for which *Maldon* was composed. The system was not confined to the Germanic nations. Other northern Europeans, notably the Thracians and the Celts, organized their societies by similar systems of gift and counter-gift. The French anthropologist M. Mauss is apparently the first to have called attention to the similarity between such customs and the competitive exchange of gifts at feasts among the American Indians of the northern Pacific coast for which American anthropologists use the term potlatch.[2] The term can become, I believe, a useful speculative instrument for the investigation of *Beowulf*. It serves to remind us that the poet's handling of the munificence of lords and the loyalty of retainers reflects very ancient customs and very ancient ways of feeling. If we think in terms of modern or even classical notions of private property and exchange of goods and services, we can go astray in our response.

The justly admired prologue with which the poem begins (1–52) reaches its climax in a potlatch and, prior to the climax, is much concerned with questions of giving and counter-giving, of munificence and loyalty. Scyld Scefing arrived alone, a child (46), and without treasure (7) at the shores of the Danes who were suffering great need (14) because they were without a lord to give them treasure. He became their leader and won booty (5b) and tribute (11). His son, the Danish Beowulf, was already famous in Denmark and the neighboring lands before his father's death (18–19). The poet assumes that such fame can come to a young prince only as a result of his munificence, and he makes his first gnomic statement: "Thus a young man ought to do good with ready gifts of treasure while he is still under his father's protection" (20–21). If he does so he will have willing companions in his age if war comes. "It is the rule in every tribe that a man thrives by praiseworthy deeds" (*lofdædum*, 24 b).[3] For a prince or a king, the poet believes, *lofdæde* are deeds of munificence.

The poet's account of the death of Scyld, the ship burial, and its accompanying potlatch follows. The dead king's *comitatus* laid their dear and munificent lord in the ship and put in the hold with him many

---

[2] See Marcel Mauss, "Sur un texte de Posidonius. Le suicide contre-prestation suprême," *Revue Celtique*, 42 (1925), 324–29; H. Hubert, "Le système des prestations totales dans les littératures celtiques," *Revue Celtique*, 42 (1925), 330–35.

[3] The last word in the poem may contain a reminiscence of this passage. See text at note 16.

treasures from afar (29–37). A multitude of treasures, presumably from the hoard, was being sacrificed, sent out to sea with the dead *dryhten*. The warriors, as the poet says, are expressing their sorrow (49b–50a). At the same time, the notion of counter-gift is apparently present. Scyld's warriors have not been called upon to die for their lord. Consequently, they respond to his munificence by loading the ship with treasure from the national hoard. That is the counter-gift.

Potlatch and its associated loyalties is a carefully developed theme in the Danish section of the poem. The main action of the poem begins with the construction of Heorot. Hrothgar had made a formal promise that the hall would be a center of gift-giving. He kept his word: *he beot ne aleh, beagas dælde* [he did not leave unfulfilled his promise, gave out rings, 80]. When Grendel began his attacks and finally became at night the thane in charge of the hall (142), God denied him access to the gift-seat and the treasure (169–70), for these, intimately associated with munificence and loyalty, symbolized the values at the core of the warrior community. These Grendel, a heathen, might not share.[4]

The banquet following Beowulf's victory over Grendel (991–1238), a scene conducted with great care by the poet, is a potlatch. As a counter-gift for Beowulf's purging of Heorot (cf. 1176b), Hrothgar gave him four noble treasures, a battle standard, a helmet, a byrnie, and a sword (1020–30), together with twice four horses, all with decorated bridles, one bearing Hrothgar's jeweled war-saddle (1035–40a). In addition, Hrothgar gave a treasure to each of the thirteen companions of Beowulf and ordered that wergild be paid for Hondscioh (cf. 2076) whom Grendel had devoured (1050–55a). The poet pauses to note that the counter-gifts were adequate: "Thus the glorious lord paid manfully for the battle with such horses and treasures as no man wishing to speak truth rightfully will find fault with" (1046–49). In short, Hrothgar's munificence was such as to assure his *dom*.

There is a second great potlatch in Denmark following Beowulf's victory over Grendel's mother. It takes place in two scenes. In these scenes the poet begins to develop the theme of munificence and loyalty by portraying its reflection in the sensibility of his characters, particularly Hrothgar. The first scene (1644–1790) takes place in the evening when Beowulf and the Geats return with the rune-inscribed hilt of the old giant sword (cf. 1557) and the head of Grendel. The hilt was a gift

---

[4] The poet, of course, sees nothing pagan in Hrothgar's sacral gift-seat. The true God by his power prevented the holy seat of the pre-Christian theist Hrothgar from being contaminated by the murderous pagan Grendel. On the gift-seat, cf. W. A. Chaney, *The Cult of Kingship in Anglo-Saxon England* (Berkeley, 1970), pp. 135–37.

to Hrothgar (1677–86) and the head of Grendel was a proof that a second great service had been performed (cf. 1778–81). Hrothgar's immediate reply is his pre-Christian theistic homily in which he expounds the ethos of the *ealde riht* particularly as it applies to a young man who will some day be king.[5] His affection for Beowulf is the motive for this homily. He is trying to give his adopted son advice which will assure him a long and glorious career as a ruler and, after death comes as it must to all men, that *dom* which Beowulf has already declared to be the best thing for a warrior whose life is ended (1388–89). Consequently, he reminds him of that other strong man Heremod, who had been both cruel and niggardly to his *comitatus;* "he remained without hall-joys to the end" (1720b). He failed, in short, in the king's function of serving as the center and chief mover of a circle of warrior companions. Beowulf will succeed if he learns the lesson of that failure.

Long continued success, however, can bring with it an arrogant selfishness (*oferhygd,* 1740).[6] Hrothgar develops the case of a hypothetical prince of great power (1728–34). *Oferhygd* grows and flourishes in him until he thinks his hoard too small. He becomes greedy and no longer gives decorated rings (1748–50a). Finally, he dies. Another, apparently of no near kin, succeeds him. Without sorrow, the successor distributes to his followers the hoard of the dead prince. He has no respect for him (1753–57). These lines gain in clarity and force if one reads them in the context provided by the burial of Scyld in the prologue. Scyld was an antitype of the hypothetical prince. Like the prince he had received from God wealth and power, but he had practiced generosity and taught it to his son. When he died, he left behind dear companions who esteemed him. Moved by their esteem, they loaded the ship with treasures, their last counter-gift, tangible evidence the Scyld possessed that *dom* which is the best thing for a warrior whose life has ended. Hrothgar looked forward to a similar end for Beowulf. Therefore, he advised him to think of death and avoid *oferhygd* (1758–68). Thus he will ward off the disaster which befell the greedy prince, a death after which none of his treasures was used to give testimony to his *dom.*

Next morning, the potlatch is concluded in a second scene (1813–82a). Beowulf bids farewell to Hrothgar in a very correct speech ex-

---

[5] This "homily" is discussed with particular reference to the poet's adaptation of a Christian homiletic vocabulary to Hrothgar's pre-Christian heroic ethics in *Traditio* 21, 81–83, and, with reference to Margaret Goldsmith's Christian interpretation, in *Anglo-Saxon England,* 2 (Cambridge, 1973), pp. 294–95.

[6] By *oferhygd,* Hrothgar did not mean pride in a Christian sense, a conviction that one can act well without divine aid. Both Heremod and the hypothetical prince ignored their need for other human beings. As a result, the one was driven out of his kingdom and lost his life. The other died with none to mourn or remember him.

pressing his awareness of the obligations he has assumed in accepting Hrothgar's gifts and hospitality. He is ready to return again to aid Hrothgar if it is necessary and in a pointed reference to Wealhtheow's request (cf. 1226–27), he assures Hrothgar that Hrethric will find friends at the Geatish court if he chooses to go there (1818–39). Hrothgar replies by praising that wisdom which Beowulf unites to his great strength (1841–45). He predicts that Beowulf will one day be chosen king by the Geats (1845b–53a). Beowulf's journey has put an end to the hostilities which existed between the Geats and the Danes (1855–58). Now there will be peace between them and exchange of gifts. Potlatch will become a means of strengthening an alliance between peoples, but Hrothgar views such a ceremonious exchange not primarily as an instrument of policy but as an expression of affection. The gifts as the splendid and well-known lines 1860b–63a tell us are to be not only *lac* [gifts], but *luftacen* [tokens of love]. The potlatch concludes with Hrothgar's gift of twelve treasures to Beowulf. The old king's tears, embrace, and kiss prove that the treasures are *luftacen* (1866–80a).

The next long scene (1963–2199), the first in the land of the Geats, is another important potlatch. At the end of the banquet and the story-telling (2144), Beowulf began the formal exchange of gifts. He mentioned Hrothgar's munificence and declared that he would now put the treasures he had received at Hygelac's feet as gifts. His hope of favor in the future now rested with Hygelac (2139–50a). He then commanded that the war-standard, the byrnie, the helmet, and the sword, the four treasures of lines 1020–29, be fetched into the hall (2152–54). The treasures were followed by four of the eight horses (2163–66, cf. 1035). Beowulf gave the horses and treasures to Hygelac. He then gave to Hygd, together with three slender horses, the great neck-ring he had received from Wealhtheow (2172–75a, cf. 1195). Beowulf presumably gave away all the more important gifts, thereby making himself dependent on the answering generosity of Hygelac.[7]

Hygelac's counter-gift was magnificent. First, he ordered the great sword of Hrethel to be fetched. It was the best treasure the Geats had (2190–94), and, probably, when Hygelac put it into Beowulf's arms,

---

[7] The eighth horse is not mentioned nor the twelve treasures (1867) given as a reward for the conquest of Grendel's dam. Are we to assume that Beowulf gave the horse and the twelve treasures to his thirteen surviving companions? Each of them had already received a treasure from Hrothgar for the Grendel fight (1050–55). Perhaps Beowulf kept Hrothgar's royal saddle (1037–40) for himself and gave the wergild for the slain Hondscioh (1053b–55, 2076) to Hondscioh's family. Our version of the poem may have been shortened. The poet tends to be meticulous about such details.

he recognized him as heir presumptive to the Geatish throne. He gave him seven thousand hides of land together with a house and high seat worthy of a king. Hygelac's act of munificence concludes the first part of the poem, the poet's portrayal of the hero in his youth.

The second part of the poem is more compact than the longer first part and perhaps equal to it in poetic weight. The poet portrays the death of King Beowulf and reveals that the old king had undergone a considerable moral and religious development since he "trod the grassy earth" (1881) in Denmark. In connection with that development the poet succeeds in ringing some surprising changes on the potlatch theme.

The poet moves to the main themes of the last part by mentioning the death of Hygelac. He presents Beowulf, now an old king, after fifty years of rule. He had ruled well and was a king wise in years, an old and successful guardian of his inheritance until a certain dragon took to ruling in the dark nights (2200–20). Beowulf's *dom* is now endangered by the dragon as Hrothgar's had been by Grendel, but the malevolent force of Grendel, the fellowships with evil spirits which made him heathen, is not shared by the dragon. The hoard he guarded, however, is heathen (2216) and, therefore, represents the antagonistic forces in the last section. The atmosphere is dark, there are no celebrations, no feasts, and the heathen hoard becomes the symbolic center of the pot-latch theme.

Having searched for a slave who stole a decorated cup from the hoard, the dragon attacked and burned the royal burg of the Geats. Whether performed by man or beast that was a deed calling for vengeance. When Beowulf, who held his own well (2737), heard the news, his immediate reaction was to suspect that he had somehow angered the Lord by acting contrary to the *ealde riht* (2330), the moral law, written by God in the hearts of pre-Christians of good will. This notion was, however, a mere scruple. Beowulf had not offended God. He took only a moment to dismiss his scruple and to give orders for the hunt that was to avenge the beast's insult. He ordered an iron shield to be made to protect himself against the dragon's fire. He then decided to go alone against the dragon. He scorned to attack the dragon with a host (2345–46). Having perceived that his conscience was clear, he did not fear the combat nor set great store by the worm's prowess (2347–48).

A long section of narration by the poet follows (2349b–95). These lines give the poet's justification for Beowulf's decision to fight the dragon without assistance. He had been successful in many previous engagements, against the Grendel kin and against the Franks and Frisians when Hygelac was slain. He refused the throne offered by

Hygd. He acted as protector of Heardred until the boy was old enough to rule. The poet doubtless viewed Beowulf's scrupulous respect for the right of the successor in the male line as a great display of virtue on Beowulf's part. When the male line ended with Heardred, Beowulf succeeded as nearest male kin to Hrethel in the female line. As king he aided Eadgils in his war against Onela, thus fulfilling his obligation to avenge his dead lord Heardred. Beowulf was thus assured of continued military success by his previous victories and of divine favor by his virtues. *Swa he niða gewhane genesen hæfde, / sliðra geslyhta, . . . oð ðone anne dæg, / þe he wið þam wyrme gewegen sceolde* [In that way he had survived fierce combats, . . . until that one day when he was to fight against the worm, 2397–400]. Clearly it is not the poet's opinion that his hero was guilty of arrogance or foolish over-confidence in refusing aid against the dragon. He seems to regard the act as evidence as a fine excess of heroism, all the more commendable because as an old king, Beowulf could have left the dragon to others. No one had suggested that Hrothgar ought to fight against Grendel.

The next few lines bring the hero, bent on revenge (*torne gebolgen* [swollen with wrath]) together with his eleven companions, with the slave as guide, to the dragon's lair, near the sea and full of treasure. A monstrous guard held those treasures: *Næs þæt yðe ceap / to gegangenne gumena ænigum* [That was no easy bargain for any man to get, 2415b–16]. This is the first hint by the poet that the purpose of the hunt was not only to wreak vengeance on the dragon but to get possession of the hoard. We are told, too, that the hero's mood had changed. He was no longer swollen with wrath and in fine martial spirits. He was *fæge*, tired and ready for death. He sat down and began his final words (2426–509) to his hearth companions.[8]

After concluding a discourse of great eloquence, Beowulf began his formal promises. The first is that he, an old leader of the people, will seek battle if the dragon comes out of his lair against him (2511–15). The second, that he would not retreat a single pace. He asked his comrades to wait. They need not regard it as their duty to fight monsters (2524–35). He added a promise about the hoard: *Ic mid elne sceall / gold gegangan, oððe guð nimeð . . . frean eowerne* [I shall get the gold with valor, or warfare will carry off your lord, 2535–37]. Beowulf stood, and with the full approval of the poet—*ne bið swylc earges sið* [not such is the going forth of a coward, 2541]—strode off to the barrow to summon the dragon.

---

[8] This long talk is of great importance and handled in *Traditio* 21, 100–03. Beowulf remembered that his maternal grandfather, Hrethel, had risen above the demands of the heroic code to a higher morality.

The poet handles his hero's fight with a fabulous beast in the same grim realistic manner that he employed for the two earlier fights with fabulous anthropoid monsters. All the fights illustrate the prowess of the hero, but the fight with the dragon is complicated by the episode of the ten cowardly thanes, so that the ethical interest of the episode is greatly enhanced. Beowulf met the dragon's first attack with his sword. It failed to "bite" (2575–80). Contrary to his *beot* (cf. 2524–25), Beowulf was compelled to yield ground. But the dragon pursued him, belching fire. The lord of the people was in serious straits (2593–95). As a group, his selected thanes betrayed him, "turned to the woods to save their lives" (2598–99). One alone suffered great sorrow at this betrayal. "For a right-thinking man," the poet observes, "nothing can alter kinship" (2600–01). He then introduces Beowulf's successor, Wiglaf, Weohstan's son. Wiglaf is a man of the Scylfings, a Swede not a Geat, and his family, the Wægmundings, are related to Beowulf's father, Ecgtheow (2813–14). The hunt of the dragon is Wiglaf's first military engagement (2625–27), and the poet gives him a fine formal speech in which he treats of the obligation of good warriors in the present situation. He and his comrades had been generously supplied with mead and gear for war. The generous lord had honored them by choosing them for this perilous expedition. The lord's life was now endangered by the dragon's fire. The fact that Beowulf wanted to finish the hunt alone can no longer be regarded as an excuse. The clear duty of all is to serve their lord or die with him in the fire (2631–60).

Wiglaf strode through the smoke to find Beowulf. He encouraged him with words that I suspect the poet meant to be tactful (2663–68). The dragon then made his second attack, and Beowulf's sword broke. In the third attack the dragon seized Beowulf's neck and inflicted a mortal wound. Wiglaf then showed his valor. He burned his hand when he struck the dragon somewhat lower down. His sword sank in, and the dragon's fire began to abate. Beowulf still had his wits about him; he drew his dagger and slashed the dragon in his middle, the soft underbelly. The poet expresses his approval of the deed. "The noble kinsmen, acting together, had felled their enemy. . . . Thus should a thane behave when his lord is in need. By his own deed, the lord had achieved his final hour of victory" (2706–10).

The poet then moves on to his notable handling of the final words of Beowulf. Wiglaf revived the dying hero and "he spoke formally (*maþelode*), deathly pale and struggling against his wound" (2724–25). He declared that he had ruled his people fifty years and kept them free from attack. Although he held well what was his own, he had not resorted to stealthy combat (*searoniðas*) nor had he sworn false oaths.

Sick with mortal wounds, all this comforted him, particularly the fact that God would have no need to call him to account after his death for the murder of kinsmen (2732–43). His conscience was clear. His reference to God implied a deep humility towards Him, and he was not conscious of anything that Hrothgar might have called *oferhygd*.

His thought was still on the treasure. He asked Wiglaf to hasten into the barrow and fetch some of the precious objects so that he might die more easily after seeing them. Wiglaf obeyed and came back from the barrow loaded with treasures. He had to revive Beowulf with water a second time. The hero recovered to see the gold and began his last speech, which is, in my opinion, the key to the principal ethical movement of the poem. "For the treasure I see here before me, I raise words of thanks to the Master of all, the King of Glory, the eternal Lord, since, before my death, I have been able to win it for my people. Now I have sold my old life, laying it down for a hoard of treasures. Those treasures will hereafter take care of the people's need.[9] I may be here no longer" (2794–801). The sight of the treasure leads Beowulf to break out into thanks to God. He reveals the reason for his interest in treasures. He has laid down his life for them, and now they will take care of the people's needs.

From the poet's point of view, and doubtless from the point of view of schooled Christians among his audience, Beowulf's decision to lay down his life for his people was an indication that he had moved upward to a higher moral sphere. He had examined his conscience and found it clear. He had done nothing contrary to the *ealde riht*. God would have no grounds for reproaching him in the afterlife. But in his decision to sacrifice his life for the people, he was moving according to impulses which owed nothing to the *ealde riht*. The *ealde riht* included, to be sure, the warrior code and that did demand that the warrior, who owed everything to his lord, must, if necessary, sacrifice everything, including his life, to protect his lord or to avenge him. But the king, the law-giver, had no recognized obligations to sacrifice himself. Here the lord was

---

[9] Traditionally *fremmaþ* (2800) and also *hataþ* (2802) have been taken as imperative plurals. Beowulf is talking to Wiglaf and there is no one else present to justify a plural imperative. There is no case in *Beowulf* where a second person plural is used in speaking to a single unaccompanied person. (In line 1985, Hygelac is addressing Beowulf and his companions, who are present.) *Fremmaþ* as a plural present gives a very satisfactory meaning. It is plural because after the phrase *maþma hord* (2799), the subject of *fremmaþ* is *maþmas* "understood." The poet was thinking of treasures to be separately expended, perhaps for champions. In lines 2493–96, Beowulf says that while he was Hygelac's champion, Hygelac did not need to buy champions from other nations.

putting himself in the place of the servant. To do that is to move beyond the moral realm of potlatch into the realm of charity.[10]

The poet, however, is not implying that his hero, a perfect man according to the *ealde riht,* is also a perfect Christian. In the lines we have been considering, he touched a moral sphere more elevated than the *ealde riht* when he expressed his joy and his gratitude to God that he had won, by the sacrifice of his life, a hoard that would meet the needs of the people. He was thinking also, however, of that fame *(dom)* which, in his youth, he called "the best thing that a dead warrior has" (1387–89). Immediately after mentioning the treasure, he continued the discourse, talking of the great barrow, which battle famous men could cause to be built for his ashes on the Whales' Headland. Sailors would call it Beowulf's barrow (2802–08). These are innocent sentiments, but not the thoughts of a Christian saint in his last few moments. The poet knew that and so, I suspect, did a considerable number of his audience.

Concerning Beowulf's last words, his short but important utterance after he gave his weapons and ornaments to Wiglaf (2813–16), and the poet's deliberately ambiguous farewell to his hero's soul (2817–20), I have nothing to add to my remarks in *Traditio* 21, 109–110. More important for our present theme, potlatch and the hoard, are the poet's remarks that begin a new fit. First he tells his audience that it was very difficult for Wiglaf, a warrior lacking the wisdom derived from experience *(guman unfrodum,* 2821) to see his dearest lord at his life's end faring so wretchedly. The poet then adds a consolation. The slayer, the dragon, also lay dead. Beowulf was the victor. The poet composes a vaunt over the defeated dragon. Both conquered beast and victorious hero had arrived at the end of this transitory life (2836–45).

Meanwhile, the poet tells us, the ten thanes who had deserted their lord returned and looked at Wiglaf, who sat weary at his lord's shoulder, trying to call him to life with water. Wiglaf was loyal but *unfrod,* and the poet, who is presumably *frod,* has an opportunity to state a theological opinion of the first importance. "He [Wiglaf] had not the power, though he was filled with longing, to hold life in his lord nor to change a whit of what the Ruler had decreed. The judgment of God was in those times to control the deeds of every man, as it still does today" (2855–59).

The Beowulf poet does not use the kenning *wyrda Wealdend,* but it

---

[10] Beowulf's decision to sacrifice himself is first made clear in lines 2794–2801. It must have been made sometime after his loss of martial spirits at coming to the barrow. See text at note 8.

is clear, from the passage under consideration and a number of other passages in the poem, that he regarded God as Ruler of events (or destinies). The decisive event, *wyrd,* was at the same time a judgment (*dom*) of God. The kenning reflects a commonplace of Judaeo-Christian theism which, being closely related to the knotty problem of evil, has resulted in elaborate theological developments. Our poet is not an elaborate theologian, but he insists on the main point, namely that these deaths, that of the beast and that of the hero, were the results of the doom of God. God had withdrawn his gift of martial prowess and left Beowulf weak at the time of the dragon fight. The poet, however, gives no indication that God was punishing Beowulf in bringing death to him. On the contrary, Beowulf was an old man, and God gave him an opportunity to die in action, and as victor in that action, at peace with his conscience, examined according to the *ealde riht,* comforted by the certainty that his fame would be kept alive among his people, cheered by the sight of the treasures which would help meet their needs. His wonderful strength, the gift that God had withdrawn, was replaced by the higher and far greater gift of charity that enabled him to sacrifice his life for his people. It is this grace of charity that makes it possible for the poet to suggest (2817–20) that he died capable of beatitude.

The hero has died his sacrificial death. There remains for the final episode the problem of the counter-gift on the part of his people. The first necessity is to purge that people of the ten thanes who had betrayed their trust. The poet gives to Wiglaf a speech both eloquent and contemptuous in which he sends the ten into exile. When princes hear of their inglorious deed, they will find that they must wander without right to a homeland anywhere. "Death is better for any earl than a life of reproach" (2864–91). Presumably at this point the traitors left the scene.

Wiglaf ordered a mounted messenger to bring word back to the Geatish fort. The messenger was obviously an important person, old and acquainted with battles long ago, *frod.* The poet gives him a speech of one hundred and twenty-five lines. He began with a succinct account of what had happened and of how Wiglaf is now keeping watch over Beowulf and the dragon (2900–10). He then mentioned Hygelac's expedition against the Franks and Frisians, hinted at military threats from the south (2910–21), and followed it with a fairly lengthy account of the Swedish wars, centering attention on the death of another old king, the Swede Ongentheow. He concluded with a tribute to Hygelac's munificence in rewarding the champions Eofer and Wulf, who won for their lord the title *Ongenþeowes bana* (cf. 1968) (2922–98).

The death of Ongentheow remained unavenged. The messenger, obviously a stern old warrior like Saxo's Starcatherus, warned that the Geats must be ready to defend themselves when the Swedes learned that the lord who held the rule and hoard of the Geats against enemies was dead (2999–3004). For the present, he urged the *comitatus* to hasten off, look upon their lord and then "bring him who gave us rings to the pyre" (3009–10). The following lines (3010b–14) are astonishing: "No mere portion of a single man shall be destroyed with the brave king, but there is a hoard of treasures, . . . bought in grim battle, and now, finally, there are the rings purchased with the king's own life. All these the flame shall devour." In Scyld's funeral, Scyld's royal standard (and doubtless his own war gear) were put into the ship. A grateful *comitatus* added a generous portion of the Scylding hoard; they sent it to sea as an expression of their grief (*murnende mod,* 50). For Beowulf, the *comitatus* is asked to sacrifice much more. They are to destroy the hoard won by the Geatish soldiers under Beowulf's leadership and, finally, the dragon's hoard, for which Beowulf, acting above and beyond the call of duty, had laid down his life. The *comitatus* could honorably reply with nothing less than a total sacrifice of the treasure, in partial return for the supreme sacrifice of Beowulf.

The messenger, as an *eald æscwiga,* does not think of the possibility of buying champions with treasure.[11] The treasure, if kept, would be used for frivolous purposes. Noble warriors might wear some of the precious objects as mementos of the dead lord, or beautiful maids might decorate their necks with the rings (3015–17). Everybody should be ready to suffer the worst, poverty and exile, "now that the war-lord has laid laughter aside, song and the harp-filled noise of the hall" (3020–21). The sacrifice of the treasure will be followed by a period of martial austerity where many will be called upon to sacrifice their lives as counter-gifts for Beowulf's sacrifice of his. The impressive speech of the messenger closes with the poet's admirable use of the commonplace of the raven, wolf, and eagle on the field of battle (3021–27).

No one opposed the messenger's proposal. The *comitatus* moved out to the headland, where they found "him who had given them rings" (3034). There, too, they found the dragon, fifty feet long (3042). Beside him were the treasures that Wiglaf had brought out of the barrow (3047–48, cf. 2783 and 2788–89). Here, for the benefit of those who need to know, the poet gives us his version of the story of the dangerous curse that had been put upon the hoard: "That inheritance, the gold of men of long ago, was of a singular power (*eacencræftig*); it had been bound about by an enchantment (*galdor*) so that no hu-

---

[11] Cf. end of note 9.

man being was permitted to touch the hiding place of the rings with safety, unless God Himself, true King of Victories—He is man's safeguard (*gehyld*)—gave to some such man as seemed fit, the power of opening the hoard without harm" (3051–57). These are the *verba poetæ* and we must take him at his word. He believed in the power of evil spirits and hence in the power of heathenism, which was the cult of evil spirits. From evil spirits came the power of the Grendel race in the earlier parts of the poem. At the end of the poem the enchanted hoard became the symbol of the antagonistic force and its power. It was the heathen *galdor* that made the hoard heathen. It had real power to harm. Of course, the reference to God, Who could prevent when He would the action of that power, was not a part of the *galdor*. The ancient and heathen lords (3070) who had buried the enchanted hoard centuries ago, like those Danes who sacrificed at pagan shrines to get protection from Grendel, "did not know the Lord God" (180). It is the poet who, in lines 3053–57 is expressing his conviction that God had greater power than the *galdor*. His point is that God did intervene in the case of Beowulf, and, as a final gift or grace in this world, permitted him to see the hoard which he had bought for his people by his death. The much controverted lines 3074–75, reading without emendation, *næs he goldhwæte / gearwor hæfde / Agendes est / ær gesceawod* can be translated "Never before had he [i.e. Beowulf] looked more readily upon the gold-abounding munificence, the grace of God."[12] The lines, then, point to the previous scene (2785–93) where Wiglaf brought treasures from the hoard and the sorely wounded old man looked upon the gold—*gold sceawode* (2793)—and broke into his great speech of thanksgiving and concern (2794–2808).

My conviction that the poet is not presenting his hero as the victim of a heathen *galdor* is strengthened by three lines immediately preceding 3074. It is generally agreed that the lines contain an account of the sanction attached to disturbing the enchanted hoard. The lines state that one who removed the hoard from its hiding place would be *synnum scildig, / hergum geheaðerod, hellbendum fæst / wommum gewitnad*. Most commentators since Klaeber have interpreted those lines as meaning that the sanction was death followed by punishment in a Christian *infernus*. So taken, the lines are an instance of what older commentators

---

[12] The translation follows Kock in taking *goldhwæte* as the acc. sing. of a noun. *gold-hwatu*, cited in J. Hoops, *Kommentar zum Beowulf* (Heidelberg, 1932), p. 318, and Chambers (cited in C. L. Wrenn, *Beowulf* [Boston, 1953] p. 227) in taking *est* to mean "grace" in a theological sense. I hope to consider this passage in a separate article where justice can be done to the context, to other opinions, and to linguistic detail.

regarded as the poet's habitual blunder of attributing Christian thoughts to pagan characters. There is, however, nothing in the four lines that is distinctly and exclusively Christian. *Heargas* can certainly mean pagan altars and the groves associated with them. *Synn* is an ancient Germanic word for any kind of act involving guilt. *Hell* was the pagan word for the land of the dead. In this case the poet was either choosing his words carefully or quoting from an older poem which contained the original version of the pagan curse. The lines can be translated "guilty of violating a taboo, confined for sacred groves [pagan ones, of course], fast in bonds of death, dreadfully tormented." The situation envisaged is clear.[13] A man bound up for pagan shrines was very likely a prisoner of war, destined to be hanged in a sacred grove, as a sacrificial victim. The poet knew of this pagan custom and had it in mind. He alluded to it in the passage he put into the messenger's speech (2935–40). Old Ongentheow had driven the forces of the slain Haethcyn into a refuge in the wood. He besieged them with his whole army, threatening them all during the night.

> cwæð, he on mergenne   meces ecgum
> getan wolde,   sum[e] on galgtreowu[m]
> [fuglum] to gamene.

(2939–41a).

[He said he would settle the matter in the morning with swords' edges, some (he would hang) on gallows trees as sport (for the birds).]

The text is corrupt but the meaning is sufficiently clear. Ongentheow intended to dispatch most of his enemies by the sword. Some, however, were destined for the more dreadful fate of being hanged, probably as victims in sacred groves.[14] Such was the fate that hung over the head of Beowulf when he ordered the despoiling of the hoard, but God had

[13] The practice of ritualistic human sacrifice among the Germanic peoples is well established both for the continent and for Scandinavia. For the continent, see Jan de Vries, *Altgermanische Religionsgeschichte* I (Berlin, 1935), pp. 180–81, on Tacitus' report of sacrifices in groves by the Semnones; p. 252, hanging on trees, as the usual way of sacrificing victims in the Roman period; for Scandinavia, II (Berlin, 1937), p. 119, sacrificial hangings at Uppsala.

[14] As a Scylfing king, Ongentheow probably had his seat at Uppsala where human sacrifices were offered in a sacred grove. See note 13. The poet may have learned about pagan practice in Sweden from heroic poems of Geatish origin. Alistair Campbell in "The Use in *Beowulf* of Earlier Heroic Verse," *England Before the Conquest* (Cambridge, 1971), p. 286, suggests his use of "an heroic lay summarized and probably in part reproduced in lines 2922–98, which dealt with the death of Ongentheow."

37

annulled the heathen force of the *galdor* and granted Beowulf a glorious death. For an audience who understood lines 3071–73, the poet was simply stating the obvious when he declared in lines 3074–75 that the treasure was still another grace that the hero received from God. God had enabled him to win it and still to die a glorious death, in no way similar to the horrible death called for by the pagan curse.[15]

After the poet's assurance that God's grace was with Beowulf until the end, we find Wiglaf at the center of the stage. He proposed that the rest of the dragon's hoard be removed and Beowulf carried "to the place where he shall long abide in the peace of God" (*on ðæs Waldendes wære geþolian,* 3095–3109). The last phrase connects Beowulf's funeral with that of Scyld: he departed after death, *on Frean wære* [in God's peace].

Wiglaf and seven men removed the hoard. There was no fear of the dragon now, and the carcass was shoved over the cliff into the water. Loaded on a wagon, the hoard accompanied the dead hero (3120–35). The people built a great funeral pyre and hung it with helmets, shields, and byrnies. These treasures were presumably from the national hoard mentioned by the mounted messenger in line 3011. If his instructions were fulfilled, the whole hoard was placed on the pyre, which was very large, *bælfyra mæst* (3143). With lamentations, the warriors laid their king on the pyre. A Geatish woman, possibly Beowulf's wife, sang a dirge wherein she expressed her fear of battles to come and consequent slavery (3137–55).

For ten days the people worked in building the great barrow Beowulf had desired. The ashes of the pyre were contained within it, whatever the fire had left of the nation's hoard and the bones of the king (3156–62). Obeying the commands of the messenger, the people then made the final sacrifice. The hoard won from the dragon had apparently been reserved. Now they put into the barrow the rings and jewels, all such precious objects as men of ill will had taken from a hoard long ago. "They left the treasure of earls for the earth to hold, gold in the sand, useless to men as it was in the days gone by" (3163–68). The advice of the stern messenger had been followed. Whatever utilitarian advantages

---

[15] Among the characters mentioned in the poem, the only ones who could have and probably did suffer from the effects of the curse are the relatives of the sole survivor, who buried the hoard for a second time with a lament that "death in war, grime bale to life," had taken away all his kin. Some of them may have been captured alive and hanged in groves. The poor slave was saved, presumably by the divine compassion. Beowulf (and, presumably his agent Wiglaf and Wiglaf's seven helpers) were also saved by divine grace. The living Geats, however, face warfare with the Swedes but they are good pre-Christian theists and perhaps *Waldend* will protect them.

the hoard might have had for meeting the needs of the people had been sacrificed. The people preferred to put the hoard in the barrow with the *manes* of Beowulf. There it remained, a counter-gift for the life he sacrificed to get it for them, a symbol of their stern adherence to the rules of a warrior society and of their grateful affection for their dead king. Warned by the messenger's speech and by the dirge of the Geatish woman, the Geats, men and women, awaited the worst, "firmly disposed towards foe and towards friend, blameless in each case, in the old manner" (1864–65).

The poet gives his last words to twelve mounted thanes who rode about the barrow reciting a song to express their sorrow and make fitting mention of the king (3169–71). "They took notice of his qualities as a noble warrior (*eorlscipe*) and appraised worthily his works of prowess. Thus it is fitting that a friendly lord be praised, loved heartily, when he is taken out of his body" (3173–77). These words summarize the general content of the usual dirge for a brave king and warrior, which Beowulf certainly was. The following lines dwell on the particular virtues of Beowulf: "This is how his hearth companions, men of the Geats, mourned their lord's fall: they said that he was of all the kings of the world, the mildest of men and the most civil, most gentle to his people, and most eager for praise" (*lofgeornost,* 3178–82). The four superlative adjectives here express the poet's view of his hero as reflected in the grateful breasts of his hearth companions. The first three all point to qualities of civilized behavior. To be much eager for praise is not civilized. The term used here needs a context. That contrast is supplied early in the poem in the poet's first gnomic statement where he implies that in the case of a ruler *lofdæde* are primarily deeds of munificence.[16] Surely the twelve sons of princes had such deserved praise for munificence in mind when they concluded their elegy with the word *lofgeornost.* Beowulf, in the eyes of these men of the *ealde riht,* was not guilty of that insolent aloofness (*oferhygd*) of which Hrothgar had warned him in his pre-Christian homily. He had a decent regard for the esteem of his companions and assured himself of that esteem by *lofdæde,* acts of munificence. At the end, he bought the dragon's treasure for them with his life. For that gesture the Geats would remember him as long as the nation survived.

The poet has stated his heroic theme with clarity and persistence. During the first part, it alternates constantly with the scenes of fighting. When the poem was sung in a royal meadhall, the less sensitive members of the *comitatus,* whose principal interest was probably in the fights,

16 Cf. at note 3.

perhaps benefited by absorbing some appreciation of the meticulous manners of Hrothgar's court. Some of the more sensitive of the audience, the kind of thane who if he survived to old age retired to a monastery, might have discerned that the poet helped him to resolve the tension between his loyalty to his pre-Christian ancestors, whose deeds heroic poetry celebrated, and his Christian faith. The poet was suggesting to such men that their ancestors might not, all of them, have been pagans. Some perhaps knew the true God and did His will, insofar as they knew it through the natural law. God was present to them through His power and providence. In the universal battle against the powers of evil, fallen spirits and those who worshiped them, the good pre-Christian ancestors were, like their admiring descendants, on the side of *Wealdend*. The sensitive thane could take comfort.

The poet, some of the thanes, perhaps, and the monastic audiences who heard the poem saw a deeper level of significance in the career of the hero. In his last deed Beowulf, through God's grace, had moved from the *ealde riht* to the higher moral sphere of the deutero-Isaiah and the voluntary self-sacrifice of Christ, the sphere of charity. This important development, however, was a part of what we may call the esoteric Beowulf, those elements in the poem intended primarily for monastic audiences. Like Shakespearean plays, *Beowulf* contains interlocking elements addressed to different strata of the audience.

The present paper has been concerned primarily with the exoteric *Beowulf,* the indispensable core of the poem, the poem directed mainly to the audience in the royal meadhall. The esoteric *Beowulf* was the principal concern of the paper in *Traditio* 21. The exoteric *Beowulf* shows a real sensitivity to the spiritual and intellectual needs of the more intelligent members of the warrior class. The esoteric *Beowulf* could have been of real assistance to monks who were giving spiritual counsel to the *eorlas*. Tolkien was weighing his words when he wrote that *Beowulf* was "one of the chief contributions to the controversy" about the eternal destiny of the unbaptized. Well schooled in heroic poetry, our poet combines his knowledge of the heroic ethos wisely with a knowledge of Christianity such as he might have acquired from the monks in an English monastery of Celtic origin. He showed forth in his poem the esthetic value of right conduct in the heroic mode and, at the same time, provided a guide to those perplexed about the relation of heroic ancestors to Christian teaching. His concern was not with abstract moral precepts from the fathers but with the concrete spiritual problems of the Englishmen he knew. That is why his heroic elegy is one of the greatest meditative poems in the English language.

4

Gnomic Indirection
in *Beowulf*

ROBERT B. BURLIN

EXCEPT FOR THE BRIEF DISCUSSION BY BLANCHE WILLIAMS IN HER BOOK
on the *Gnomic Poetry in Anglo-Saxon*[1] and a rather bland survey by
Kemp Malone,[2] the gnomic passages in *Beowulf* have attracted relatively little comment and less enthusiasm. No longer confident of our
ability to distinguish the Christian and "heathen" elements, critics seem
content to relegate these moments of aphoristic didacticism to the category of "Germanic Antiquities," formal, if not always conceptual, sur-
vivals of an older poetic mode, reformulated unimaginatively where
congenial to a monkish Christianity. They may confirm the literary anthropologist's notion of a deep-rooted connection between story-telling
and wise counsel, but they run counter to the modern critical preference
for the inexplicit, for the discovery of "meaning" in the organic whole
rather than the sententious assertions of the narrative voice. In *Beowulf*
particularly, the flatfootedness of the gnomic formula with its emphatic
sceal or *biþ* seems uncharacteristic of the poet at his most inventive, not

[1] Williams (New York, 1914).
[2] Malone, "Words of Wisdom in *Beowulf*," in *Humaniora*, eds. Wayland D.
Hand and Gustave O. Arlt (Locust Valley, New York, 1960), pp. 180–94. A
significant advance in appreciation of this apsect of Old English poetry is implied
by T. A. Shippey's use of the term "wisdom" in his discussion of the "elegies" and
related poems, *Old English Verse* (London, 1972).

in the same artistic league with the obliquity of the "digressions," the subtleties of diction and the rhetorical suavity, on which recent criticism has justifiably heaped such admiration. Yet even in his moments of gnomic blandness this poet is not always as merely "conventional" or as straightforward as he seems. In some instances he demonstrates that this bardic posture may be manipulated with the resourcefulness and freedom he accords other inherited features of the Old English poetic vocabulary.

The apparent function of the gnomic set-pieces in a poem such as *Beowulf* is twofold. At times the "words of wisdom" provide a useful rhetorical service. Kemp Malone observed that they offer a ready-made introduction or conclusion to a speech or section of the narrative; "roundings of periods" was Blanche Williams's earlier phrase.[3] Conceptually, however, their function is primarily normative and communal. Stepping momentarily out of his narrative, the poet takes the occasion to pronounce some accepted verity, usually concerning the forces which govern the great world—nature, wyrd, divine Providence—or the way man should respond to such forces—principally by respecting the values of the heroic society or observing divine decree. In resorting to the gnomic mode, then, the speaker may give both shape and scope to his utterance, lifting it for the moment out of the flow of narrative (or the press of events, if it is a character speaking), relating the actuality of his fiction to familiar universals in the appreciation of which his audience can easily concur. In so doing the poet may seem to interrupt the action, to shift his stance from story-teller to sage, but in fact—and this is particularly true of *Beowulf*—he intensifies his communion with the audience, flattering them into contemplation of the narrative by providing secure resting-points which comfortably evoke the ideal norms of their society and their world.

An obvious case in point occurs in the midst of the Scyld "Prologue," rounding off the first long verse paragraph:

> Swa sceal (geong g)uma   gode gewyrcean,
> fromum feohgiftum   on fæder (bea)rme,
> þæt hine on ylde   eft gewunigen
> wilgesiþas,   þonne wig cume,
> leode gelæsten;   lofdædum sceal
> in mægþa gehwære   man geþeon.

(20–25)[4]

---

3 Williams, p. 33.

4 The text is that of Fr. Klaeber, *Beowulf and the Fight at Finnsburg,* 3rd ed. (Boston, 1950).

[So should a young man do good deeds with splendid gifts while in his father's protection, that in his old age, should war come, his chosen companions will still stand by him, the people follow him; by praiseworthy deeds, in every nation man shall prosper.]

The lines seem to give prominence to young Beowulf (or Beow) the Dane, prompting early critics like Earle and Brandl to invoke Renaissance epic theory, raising the poem as a whole to a monitory level— "The Institution of a Prince" or "fürstenspiegel."[5] But the second gnome (24b–25) reaches beyond the immediate concern for royal lineage and performance to embrace the nation as a whole (*mægþ*). The "praiseworthy deeds" by which men thrive are not merely those of the aggressive king and his open-handed son, but those of the comitatus (*wilgesiþas*) and even the less distinguished multitude, the *leode,* whose support is necessary in times of national emergency. The passage which follows this gnomic pointing returns us to Scyld and the impressive obsequies which anticipate the end of the poem. But here again the emphasis falls on the community as a whole, for it is they who must observe these proprieties, as the Geats will with greater ceremony for Beowulf:

> . . .swa hit gede(fe) bið
> þæt mon his winedryhten   wordum herge,
> ferhðum freoge,   þonne he forð scile
> of lichaman   (læded) weorðan.

> (3174b–77)

[. . . as it is fitting that a man honor his liege lord with words and love him in his heart, when he must be taken forth from his body.]

This final gnomic passage of the poem supports its structural coherence, just as the first conjoins the two parts of the Prologue. Thematically, both direct our attention to that societal interdependence which determines the heroic ethos. The gnomic exhortations which draw the poet's audience more deeply into the significance of his narrative thus become the bardic correlative for one of his major themes, the ties that hold together the human society he celebrates, bonds of such splendid yet inherently fragile nobility.

Beowulf is not merely the story of the rise and fall of one exceptional being; it takes its elegiac cast from the paradox that lies at the heart

---

[5] J. Earle, *The Deeds of Beowulf* (Oxford, 1892), p. lxxv and A. Brandl, *Geschichte der Altenglischen Literatur* in Paul's *Grundriss,* 1908, I, p. 1001, cited by Williams, p. 32.

of the heroic life, a paradox which has been much debated in recent criticism, but is best expressed in the gnomic despair of Beowulf's successor:

> Oft sceall eorl monig   anes willan
> wræc adreo*gan,*   swa us geworden is.

(3077–78)

[Often shall many an earl endure sorrow through the will of one man, as has now come to pass for us.]

The major exploits of the poem have been Beowulf's alone, but we have seen his retainers dwindle from the sword-flourishing attackers of Grendel, to the faithful patient watchers at the mere, to the cowardly hangers-back from whom Wiglaf detaches himself. Less schematically, but with a grimmer aura of historicity, the sub-plots or "digressions" dramatize the entanglements of human activity which require heroic conduct of all men if their society is to prosper: *Lofdædum sceal / in mægþa gehwære man geþeon.* The commonplace gnomic utterance with which the poet rounds off his first period touches upon some of the deepest concerns of the poem and its immediate audience, enticing even the lowliest of its hearers to reflect upon his place in the heroic action. *The Battle of Maldon* reminds us of the continued potency and inclusiveness of such ideals. Yet the *Beowulf* poet's next words, the conclusion of the Prologue, suggest that the characteristic service which falls to such an "audience" may be no more than to supply a fitting commemoration for their heroic king.

A faintly ironic resonance does not, of course, attend all the poet's gnomes. Those expressed by the actors themselves tend to confirm heroic values or refer human activity to such mysteries as death, wyrd, or God, which may delimit its scope. Most of the poet's own generalizations, too, seem in a straightforward way to suit the immediate context. When for example he again exults in the achievement of longlasting fame in battle (1534b–36), the gnomic interruption merely provides a dramatically effective pause for narrative breath, as Beowulf, struggling with Grendel's mother, turns from reliance on the ineffectual Hrunting to the trial of his mighty grip. Even the notoriously difficult Christian "excursus" on Danish idolatry (183b–88) has obvious pertinence to the occasion, whatever other problems it may raise. For the most part, then, one is forced to agree with Kemp Malone's conclusion that the *Beowulf* poet's use of inherited "words of wisdom" demonstrates the richness of his art "in the aptness of what he has to say and the rightness of his way of saying it."[6]

[6] Malone, p. 194.

In some instances, however, Malone's notion of "aptness" appears unnecessarily facile, underestimating perhaps the deviousness of the poet's art. In particular, two passages related to the fight with Grendel require a reassessment of the precise locus of the presumed aptness. The first (1002b–08a), which Malone considers "beautifully integrated into Grendel's flight,"[7] must be recalled in full context. Section XV begins with the preparation of Heorot for the banquet to celebrate Grendel's defeat, then under the pretext of explaining the need for decorative wall-coverings drifts into a gratuitous allusion to Grendel's departure and the gnomic statement:

> Wæs þæt beorhte bold   tobrocen swiðe
> eal inneweard   irenbendum fæst,
> heorras tohlidene;   hrof ana genæs
> ealles ansund,   þe se aglæca
> fyrendædum fag   on fleam gewand,
> aldres orwena.   No þæt yðe byð
> to befleonne   —fremme se þe wille—,
> ac gesecan sceal   sawlberendra
> nyde genydde,   niþða bearna,
> grundbuendra   gearwe stowe,
> þær his lichoma   legerbedde fæst
> swefeþ æfter symle.
>   Þa wæs sæl ond mæl
> þæt to healle gang   Healfdenes sunu;
> wolde self cyning   symbel þicgan.

(997–1010)

[The bright dwelling was greatly shattered, though all was fast within with ironbands; its hinges split; the roof alone survived all unharmed, when the monster, guilty of criminal deeds, turned to flight, despairing of life. That is not easy to flee—let him try as he will—, but he must seek out the ready place, compelled by necessity, for all soul-bearers, all earth-dwellers, children of men, where his body, fast in the grave, will sleep after the feast.

Then the time was fitting that the son of Healfdene should go to the hall; the king himself wishes to partake of the feast.]

Note that there are two curious grammatical features in the sequence: þe seems to introduce a temporal clause,[8] and the antecedent of þæt (1002) is somewhat ambiguous. The clause depicting Grendel's flight

---

[7] Malone, p. 184.

[8] A unique instance in the poetry, but prose examples are cited by Arthur Adams, *The Syntax of the Temporal Clause in Old English Prose* (New York, 1907), pp. 26 ff.

45

does not really explain the condition of the hall; instead, it emphasizes his spiritual condition (*fyrendædum fag, aldres orwena*). "Death" is the easily assumed referent for *þæt*, but the generalization is not what one would expect at this juncture. The gnome more or less confirms the fatality of Grendel's wound, but his final resting-place (*legerbed*) is as yet a mystery and the inconclusiveness of the struggle is a source of some discomfort to Beowulf, who had hoped to make Heorot the monster's *wælbed* [bed of death] (cf. 963 ff.). From one point of view, then, the passage seems to anticipate the next major episode and the hero's satisfaction in the ritual decapitation.

The disquieting element in this sequence of statements lies in the fact that though Grendel, guilty (or stained?) with criminal deeds, despairs of his life, the impossibility of escaping death is extended to all men (*niþða bearna*), earth-dwellers and soul-bearers, who are equally compelled by necessity (*nyde genydde*), presumably "under the sentence of death" (cf. 2454, *deaðes nyd*). Of course, Grendel's creaturely status has been kept ambiguous throughout the poem: he must in some indeterminate theological sense bear a soul if he is to be consigned to hell, and he had been granted warrior rank, though with grim irony, while he had occupied Heorot by night. Yet the element of sympathy which creeps into the gnomic passage as the generalization expands is hardly consonant with the prevailing attitude toward Grendel throughout the poem, and the final phase, *swefeþ æfter symle* [sleep after the feast], points up the distance we have moved from the ostensible occasion for the gnomic utterance. Grendel's prescribed after-life can hardly be thought of as a sleep, and his earthly existence could be considered a feast only by forcing the tone into a gruesome irony, which the context at this point cannot tolerate.

In short, these "apt" words of wisdom have finally little to do with Grendel at all, but they do have a powerful impact on the scene into which they have intruded, a scene of joyous feasting. The word *symbel* [feast], which recurs almost immediately (1010), ties the poet's apparent drift into helpless philosophizing back to the main action, reinforcing a rhythmic pattern of narrative which pulses insistently through this first part of the poem. During the dragon fight, the complexities of the subordinate narratives entangle the central action with a patterned intricacy which suggests the universality of its tragic outcome. The tone of the Grendel fights is, on the contrary, youthfully and unambiguously victorious. The hero's conquests can be followed only by general rejoicing, sumptuous rewards, and the mandatory banquets. Such occasions are the prevailing symbol in Old English poetry for human happiness, the health and comfort of human society, and even the best available analogue for eternal bliss. But the feasts of the meadhall receive their intensity from an awareness of what lurks outside, be it monster or man. It is never far from the *Beowulf* poet's mind at least that the great celebrations of human communality share in the precariousness of the "feast of life." By his apparently meandering bardic utterance, he prepares us for the events of this night *æfter symle,* the advent of Grendel's mother. But at a deeper level, the gnomic inconsequence reintroduces the alternation of human security and fear, comfort and agony, the inexorable rhythm on which the poet has chosen to organize his narrative.

This fundamental thematic pattern is most easily recognized in the intercalated performances of the royal scop, significant social events which rank with the king's munificence as focal ceremonies in the festive banquet. The *Beowulf* poet, by his consistency of purpose, insinuates a functional kinship between his own self-conscious gnomic pronouncements and those more easily apprehended fictive moments of poetic speaking within the narrative. The first interpolated song (90b–98) effectively interrupts the entrance of Grendel into the poem, providing both the earthly *dream* [joy] which so offends the monster, and the absolute metaphysical dimension by which he is to be measured —the song of Creation within the hall and the race of Cain without. The *swutol sang scopes* [clear song of the minstrel] (90a) draws into the pristine Heorot the innocent freshness of the newly quickened earth, while the monstrosity (*untydras*) of fallen man is relegated to darkness and the wasteland of moors and mist. The possibility of internal disruption has been hinted at, of course, in the allusion to the firing of Heorot (82b ff.), but the full measure of such a threat is not realized until the next song, the extempore celebration of Beowulf's feat, which in its inverted symmetry pairs the heroic rise of Sigemund with the degeneration of Heremod into physical and moral exile. The full force of the tragic potential which informs all heroic society is, however, reserved for the scop's performance at the great banquet whose preparations were overshadowed by the gnomic passage on the inescapability of death.

The feast begins with the conferral of sumptuous treasures on Beowulf and his men, but before the song of Finn and Hengest occurs, the poet rounds off with another gnomic period. The point of departure is the wergild for Handscio, but the poet moves away from the immediate occasion with a deviousness strikingly similar to that exhibited by the previous passage:

> ... ond þone ænne heht
> golde forgyldan,   þone ðe Grendel ær
> mane acwealde,—   swa he hyra ma wolde,

47

nefne him witig God   wyrd forstode
ond ðæs mannes mod.   Metod eallum weold
gumena cynnes,   swa he nu git deð.
Forþan bið andgit   æghwær selest,
ferhðes foreþanc.   Fela sceal gebidan
leofes ond laþes   se þe longe her
on ðyssum windagum   worolde bruceð!
   Þær wæs sang ond sweg   samod ætgædere
fore Healfdenes   hildewisan . . .

(1053b–64)

[. . . and he promised to recompense with gold the one whom Grendel had previously killed sinfully—as he would have done to more, had not wise God averted that fate, and the bravery of the man. The Lord governed all the race of men, as He still does. Therefore discernment is at all times best, and prudence of spirit. Much good and evil must he endure, who has long experience here of this world in these days of strife.

There was song and music mingled together before the battle-leader of Healfdene . . .].

Grendel is reintroduced, not in a temporal clause, but in a conditional aside (1055b) which emphasizes in retrospective potential the magnitude of his viciousness. This in turn leads into a formulaic collocation of *Metod, wyrd,* and the man whose courage meets with the favor of these mysterious forces. The expression recurs frequently enough in *Beowulf* alone to brand it as a commonplace, and we are not at this point invited to explore its implications. God rules all, of course, but the remainder of the passage turns upon the value of the word *mod,* a wide-reaching term for the non-physical components of the human animal, but here defined particularly in terms of the relatedness of mental activity to bravery of spirit. The qualities of discernment and prudence (*andgit, foreþanc*), however essential to the heroic posture as dramatized in the poem as a whole, were not, however, noticeably prominent in the struggle with Grendel. (It seems unlikely that the poet means to return to the awkward question of Beowulf's solitary wakefulness.) The gnomic formulation requires a larger generalization. In context, these virtuous attributes seem to imply a more embracing spiritual resolution, some such stoic fortitude as will enable any one to endure the world's strife-filled days, the *fela leofes and laþes* [many things of good and evil] which are man's lot.

Once again, though the pat gnomic utterances are too comprehensive for the particulars on which they syntactically depend, their very presence at this point contributes to the thematic rhythm of the poem, baldly asserted in the final sentence of the passage. The applicability of the poet's wisdom is subtly reinforced by what follows. *Fela leofes* bursts immediately upon the scene with the sound of the scop's performance, *sang ond sweg,* but *fela laþes* is inherent in the story of Hildeburh and Hengest, in spite of the grim triumph of its conclusion. The alternation of joy and sorrow has quickened in pace, and though Beowulf has another unqualified victory still before him, the tone of the poem has begun to shift away from the comforts of the hall.

The textual difficulties attending the opening of the Finn episode present an ambiguity which, though unlikely to have been the poet's, appropriately characterizes the situation. *Healgamen* (1065a) may be the scop's entertainment in Hroðgar's hall or, with savage irony, the bloody sport in Finn's. In any case, there is an aesthetic irony in the scene, which might be considered quintessentially Beowulfian. The *scop's* contribution to the joyful celebration of Beowulf's victory injects a disconcertingly somber anticipation of the elegiac tone which will dominate the latter part of the poem. The smaller formal unit functions paradoxically within the larger; its tonal and thematic implications cannot be contained by the apparent occasion. This much has been generally acknowledged to be the ultimate purpose of the fictive poetic interpolations into the narrative. A similar obliquity may, I believe, be conceded the poet's own gnomic statements analyzed here. They seem self-sufficient and straightforward; they give the illusion of locally satisfying "aptness" and immediate, if slight, semantic value, while rhetorically they round off the period with a comfortable metrical security. Yet, when examined closely, they slip their syntactic bonds and, like their more impressive formal counterparts, manage a significant resonance within the larger structure. Even in his moments of apparent gnomic superficiality, it is difficult to be sure one has caught the *Beowulf* poet nodding.

5

Hunlafing and the Point of the Sword

LEWIS E. NICHOLSON

THE SECOND ELEMENT OF THE NAME "UNFERTH" HAS LONG BEEN IN-
terpreted by *Beowulf* scholars as a metathesized form of *frith* [peace],
but a recent provocative study by Fred C. Robinson asks us to consider
anew "what the name would mean if taken at face value without assuming distortion."[1] Because names in Anglo-Saxon poetry frequently offer
valuable hints as to the character's meaning and function in a poem[2]—
i.e., "Wulf," "Eofor" [wild boar]—Robinson's focused discussion on the
meaning of Unferth's name is especially valuable, as is his replacement
of the conventional modern distortion, "Unfrith," (which translates as
"non-peace" or "discord") with the form "Un-ferth," as it consistently
appears in the manuscript. Any attempt to restore a manuscript reading
is attractive, and more especially so as in Robinson's essay, where such
a suggestion is supported by a full discussion of the entire medieval tradition of name-meanings. A further value in considering Robinson's
proposals to restore the manuscript reading is that his argument invites

[1] Fred C. Robinson, "Personal Names in Medieval Narrative and the Name
of Unferth in *Beowulf*," in *Essays in Honor of Richebourg Gaillard McWilliams*,
ed. Howard Creed (Birmingham, Ala., 1970), p. 46.
[2] Robinson, "Some Uses of Name-Meanings in Old English," *NM*, 69 (1968),
161–71.

us to bring under careful scrutiny not only the *-ferth* part of the name, but the emended first part as well.

The arguments for changing *Hun* to *Un* are, of course, all familiar ones; they range from the view that the initial *h* is inorganic and a scribal habit borrowed from the Celts, to the idea that the alliterative rules of the poem "show conclusively that the *h* is to be disregarded in reading the name."[3] Since Rieger first made his emendation in 1871, editors of *Beowulf* have consistently deleted the *h* in Hunferth's name, until this century-old practice of reading the name as *Unferth*, rather than *Hunferth*, has become a firmly established literary tradition, one which only the *collen-ferð*—the bold in spirit—would dare to question.

The name Hunferth occurs four times in *Beowulf*, in lines 499, 530, 1165, and 1488, and, with the single exception of line 530, the name alliterates with vowels. Ordinarily, such imperfect alliteration would suggest a corrupted text, an unhistoric insertion of the *h* by the scribes; but, as D. G. Scragg observes in his useful study of the initial *h* in Old English,[4] many Anglo-Saxon poems contain lines in which an *h* before a vowel alliterates with a vowel. Most readers are perhaps only vaguely aware of this alliterative pattern, since editors of Anglo-Saxon texts long ago decided that these irregular lines were corrupt, and therefore emended-out such "unhistoric insertions." There are, however, a sufficient number of instances of *h* coupled with vowel alliteration in the Anglo-Saxon poetic corpus to allow us at least to question and examine anew the validity of many of these editorial emendations. It is true that in *Beowulf* itself one finds only a handful of such lines containing an omitted *h*, a so-called "unhistoric insertion."[5] Furthermore, Hunferth is the only proper name in *Beowulf* where an initial *h* followed by a vowel is allowed to alliterate with a vowel.[6] But such alliterative practice is certainly not without significant parallels. In other Anglo-Saxon poems such as *Daniel, Andreas, Judith, Juliana,* and *Fates of the Apostles,* such proper names from Latin sources as "Hebreos," "Herodes," "Heliseus," "Holofernus," and "Habrahame" are all allowed to alliterate regularly with vowels.[7]

Bloomfield and others have pointed out the possibility that the *Beo-*

---

[3] Robinson, "Personal Names," p. 48.

[4] "Initial *H* in Old English," *Anglia,* 88 (1970), 165–96.

[5] In line 332 of *Beowulf* if the manuscript *hæleþum* is retained, the *h* of *hæleþum* must alliterate with a vowel. In lines 2929 and 2972, if the manuscript *hondslyht* is retained, the *h* of *hondslyht* must again in both instances alliterate with a vowel. If the *h* is restored to *handlean* in lines 1541 and 2094, *handlean* alliterates with an *h*.

[6] Lines 499, 1165, 1488.

[7] Scragg, p. 187.

wulf scribe seems to have altered the original form because the name Unferth was not understood, and because Hunferth was a more familiar form.[8] On this last point, rather than "not fully understanding," as Bloomfield and others suggest, I would like to venture the outside possibility that the poet himself might not have understood the meaning of the form "*Un*ferth," or if he did understand it as "mar-peace" or "discord" or "unintelligence" (as Robinson argues), he might have found such an editorial change alliteratively acceptable but at the same time perceived it as being so poetically reductive and so mechanically wooden in its imaginative consequences as to seriously compromise certain of the poem's demonstrably subtle poetic relationships which register on our consciousness only if the form "Hunferth" is retained.

Having postulated this outside possibility, and temporarily invoking a quasi-Coleridgean "willing suspension of all historical emendation," it is interesting to examine certain poetic potencies that immediately energize the narrative with the reconstitution of the name "Hunferth." It should be noted at the outset that a restoration of the manuscript form, Hunferth, is not merely a gratuitous exercise in editorial wishful thinking. In *Widsith,* line 33, one finds the name "Hun Hætwerum," and although Malone, in his edition of *Widsith,* is able to offer no certain historical informations about Hun Hætwerum,[9] a cursory reading of the text of that poem does reveal that this name occurs in a context curiously and persuasively rich in proper names that are common to the *Beowulf*— Breoca Brondingum, Fin Folcwalding, Ongenþeow, Sceafa, Offa, Hroþwulf, Hroðgar—altogether there are about two dozen place-names and proper names in *Widsith* that also turn up in *Beowulf.* Furthermore, these Hetware, a Frankish people on the Rhine whom we can assume to be the tribe of the unidentified "Hun," referred to in line 33 of *Widsith,* appear again on two occasions in *Beowulf* (2363, 2916), where they are the peoples attacked by Hygelac when he went journeying with his sea-army to Frisian lands. The proper name "Hun" however does not occur in *Beowulf* as such; rather it appears as one part of two compound names, *Hunferth* and *Hunlafing,* both of them rich with unexplained connective suggestion.

Many years ago, two nineteenth-century German scholars, Bugge and Trautmann, actually suggested that lines 1143 and 1144 of the *Beowulf* (*þonne him Hunlafing hildeleoman / billa selest on bearm dyde*) should be read as follows: "Hun placed Lafing [a sword] on his lap . . . ," but

---

[8] Morton W. Bloomfield, "Beowulf and Christian Allegory: An Interpretation of Unferth," in *An Anthology of Beowulf Criticism,* ed. Lewis E. Nicholson (Notre Dame, 1963), p. 156.

[9] Kemp Malone, ed., *Widsith, Anglistica,* 13 (Copenhagen, 1962), pp. 81, 176.

Klaeber and others found that reading less acceptable than "son of Hunlaf," basing their interpretation on the analogical similarity of the name Hunlaf to Guthlaf and Oslaf, both mentioned in the *Finnsburg Fragment* and *Beowulf*. Malone's idea was that "Hunlafing" was a sword owned by Hunlaf and given by the dying Hnæf to Hengest on the occasion of the fight at Finnsburg.[10] Klaeber reacted to Malone's suggestion with a faintly wistful reservation, hedging his rhetoric of admiration somewhat by calling the speculation "so brilliant that one might wish it could be forthwith assented to."[11] Klaeber's critical reservation apparently carried more weight than his qualified admiration: so far as I know, the idea was too speculative, and met with few takers.

Nevertheless, the repetition of "Hun" in "Hunlafing" and "Hunferth" is still a tantalizing possibility and continues to cause readers of the poem to look for a significant connection between the two names, even though we know that the nameless son of Hunlaf is certainly not Hunferth, since the latter is specifically called "the son of Ecglaf" (499, 590, 980, 1465, 1808). To speculate more profitably, could the strange form "Hunlafing," be he man or sword, perhaps represent a shortened or contracted form of "Hunferth Ecglafing" [Hunferth, the son of Ecglaf], where the names of both father and son are reduced to "Hunlafing," a shortened form which, incidentally, would seem to enhance the special importance already attached to Hunferth's sword by this further wordplay on his father's name?

> Swa he ne forwyrned   worold rædenne,
> þonne him Hunlafing   hildeleoman,
> billa selest   on bearm dyde;
> þæs wæron mid Eotenum   ecge cuðe.
>
> (1142–45)

[Thus, he (Hengest) did not refuse the worldly terms or conditions (namely, war), when Hunferth, the son of Ecglaf, placed on his lap the battle-light, the best of swords; its edges were to that extent well-known among the giants.]

Directly following the singing of the Finnsburg episode, we recall, the narrrator-poet remarks of the present moment that "there was still peace among the Danes, each true to the other. Moreover, there sat *Hunferth þyle*, at the feet of the Scylding chieftains; each of them trusted in his *ferþe* [spirit], that he had much courage, though he was not merciful to

---

[10] Kemp Malone, "The Finn Episode in Beowulf," *JEGP*, 25 (1926), 159, 167.
[11] Fr. Klaeber, ed., *Beowulf and The Fight at Finnsburg*, 3rd ed. (Boston, 1950), pp. 175–76.

his kinsmen at the play of swords," (1164–68). It is impossible not to hear again in these lines the *Beowulf* poet's characteristic word-play on a person's name, with the repetition of the form *ferth* (a word which, incidentally, appears elsewhere in *Beowulf* in the compounds *collen-ferð* [bold in spirit, 2785] and *sarig-ferð* [sad at heart, 2863]). Moreover, the reference to Hunferth's lack of mercy toward his kinsmen is peculiarly consonant with the etymological intelligence that escapes when we unlock the two parts of his compounded name: taken together, the compound translates as "hun heart," or "hun spirit," and when we consider the rude wit and invective with which the poet characterizes Hunferth in an otherwise polite court, we are probably safe in concluding that the name "Hun" for the eighth century audience must have had exceedingly unpleasant associations.

The barbarous, savage, and destructive nature of the Huns was, of course, already an old and well-established tradition by the time the *Beowulf* poet wrote. Jordanes, writing in about 550, spoke of the Huns as "half-Gothic in origin, derived from a group of Gothic witches who, expelled from the tribe of King Filimer, wandered about in Scythia where they mated with vile spirits and begat the savage and hideous Huns."[12] For both Jerome and Isidore, the Huns were a wild and savage peoples from behind the Caucasus, "in the farthest reaches of Maeotis, between the icy Tanais and the territory of the giant Massagetae," held back by the gates of Alexander from striking terror throughout the civilized world.[13] And the name "Hunferth" itself appears, in fact, in the *Parker Chronicle* under the years 744 and 754 (Laud MS 754). But if the *Beowulf* poet had the Hun Hætwerum of *Widsith* in mind when he created Hrothgar's *þyle,* the *-ferth* part of his name might well have been added to emphasize adroitly that his "Hunnish-ness," far from being a mere tribal or genealogical identification, is in fact a part of his essential nature, his mind, soul, and spirit. The poet's deliberate intention to construct such values into his compounding of names is not a gratuitous suggestion, nor even a new one, as Robinson and others have ably demonstrated.[14] The name of the hero himself, it could be plausibly argued, might have been constructed from the shorter form "Beaw" which appears on regnal lists in the Anglo-Saxon Chronicle, and elsewhere in the poem the poet clearly engages in onomastic exercises with such names as "Hygd" [thought], "Hygelac" [instability of mind], "Wonred" [unreason],[15] not to mention the name of Hrothgar's great hall, Heorot, a name with double or possibly triple significance.

[12] Cited by Jane Acomb Leake in *The Geats of Beowulf* (Madison, 1967), p. 30.
[13] Leake, pp. 40–41.
[14] Robinson, "Personal Names," p. 44.
[15] Robinson, "Personal Names," p. 45.

Assuming for the nonce that Hunferth in *Beowulf* is indeed the same man as "Hun Hætwerum" in the *Widsith,* and recalling the information given by the *Beowulf* poet that the Hetware are Frisians (2915–16), then we may entertain the possibility that Hunferth is not a Dane at all, but a Frisian who occupies a position of honor as Hrothgar's chief spokesman or *þyle.* Such a possibility gives rise to an immediate political and poetic question: how is it that a Frisian, a foreigner, could rise to such a position of honor in a Danish court, sit at the feet of the king in the very heart of the court, and speak the mind of the king and his people? The poem itself supplies a possible answer. Hunferth Ecglafing ("Hunlafing") was a Frisian in Finn's court, and for whatever personal or political reason, he betrayed his own people and placed the best of swords, the battle-light, in the bosom or lap of Hengest, a Dane—an act which results in a wholesale slaughter of Frisians and the death of Hunferth's brothers. That Beowulf knew about the events at Finnsburg long before he hears the Danish scop recite the events in the mead-hall is made clear by his specific subsequent reference to Hunferth's traitorous act, the slaying of his brothers and near kinsmen, an act for which, Beowulf says, Hunferth must now suffer damnation in hell (588). It is ironic, of course, that Beowulf will himself, at a much later date, journey with Hygelac to Frisia and become involved in another battle which results in the death of "brothers" (2490–2506, and elsewhere).

Critics have often raised the question of how Hunferth could live in the Danish court and occupy a seat of honor if he has killed his brothers, but the problem is more apparent than real, for a cogent rationale can be supplied. The Danes, who generally looked upon the Frisian enemy as *eotenas* [giants, monsters],[16] might well have tended to respect and honor—almost in the later sense of special honor accorded a religious convert who had forsworn his pagan past to embrace a new Christian allegiance—such a man of acknowledged stature who had forsworn an unenlightened and heathenish people as the Frisians were considered to be. A man such as Hunferth, under such circumstances, could plausibly come then to Denmark along with the liberated queen, Hildeburh, and be given a seat of honor in the Danish court as a reward. If we can thus account for Hunferth's honored presence in Hrothgar's court, even though he has been instrumental in the death of his brothers, we are in a position to appreciate even more securely the compelling and intricate ironies that are subsequently implied by certain of the poet's indirect references to Hunferth.

The subtlety of these ironies has been sensitively explored by Bro-

---

[16] R. E. Kaske, "The Eotenas in Beowulf," in *Old English Poetry, Fifteen Essays,* ed. Robert P. Creed (Providence, 1967), pp. 288–89.

deur: treacherous to his own kin in Frisia, Hunferth is to become once more a traitor to the Danish King and his court. In lines 1017b-19, "Heorot was filled within with friends. Not yet had the Scylding people used treachery." Brodeur understands this to mean "that Hrothulf was not *yet* conspiring against Hrothgar and Hrethric."[17] After the Finnsburg episode, the narrator comes back to the subject of treachery within the Danish court: "There sat the two nobles, uncle and nephew (Hrothgar and Hrethric); then still was their peace together, each true to the other. Likewise, there sat Hunferth the *þyle* at the feet of the Scylding chieftain. Each of them trusted in his spirit, that he had much courage, though he was not merciful to his kinsmen at the play of swords" (1163ff.). Of this key moment in the text Brodeur remarks, "No one doubts that these two passages forecast allusively the impending revolt of Hrothulf against his uncle and cousin, his murder of them, and his usurpation of the throne. The immediate adjunction of the statement about Unferth, *in this context,* can be nothing else than a clear intimation that he is to have a hand in fomenting the revolt, and perhaps its bloody consequence."[18]

If Hunlafing then, is in fact Hunferth, as I am now suggesting may be the case, then Hunferth's gift of a sword to Beowulf on the occasion of his joining battle with Grendel's mother takes on more meaning for the reader than a mere "sportsmanlike act," as Brodeur designates it. Indeed, the courtly forms of such "sportsmanship" are here freighted with a rich ironic resonance when we perceive that the sword which he gives Beowulf may be the same sword that was used at Finnsburg to kill brothers. And now, as Beowulf prepares to descend into hell to fight the monster, the sword that he carries may well be the instrument of that fratricide which Beowulf says will cause Hunferth to suffer damnation in hell. Beowulf tells Hrothgar that he (Beowulf) will gain *dom* [glory] with Hrunting, or "death will take me off," (1490). He, of course, does not gain glory with Hrunting. A few lines later he finds that the "battle light" is of no use—a battle-light that had often cut through the helmet, the war-garment of the doomed. "That was the *first time* for the precious treasure that its *dom* failed" (1527–28).

If the carefully suggested fratricidal credentials of this sword have been properly apprehended by the reader or listener of the poem—an audience accustomed to communal listening might well have had a distinct advantage in being tonally and emotionally induced toward ironies that an audience of solitary readers tends to perceive through structures that are more rational and intellectual—then these words of the poet

---

[17] Arthur Gilchrist Brodeur, *The Art of Beowulf* (Berkeley, 1969), p. 156.
[18] Brodeur, p. 156.

fairly drip with irony. And in fact, there are poetic reasons to suspect that the sword which now fails Beowulf is indeed the sword involved in that shameful battle at Finnsburg, where brother killed brother. *Beadoleoma* [battle-light] in line 1523 is also the kenning used earlier (*hildeleoma*) to describe the sword which Hunlafing places in the bosom of Hengest (1143), the sword which touches off the final bloody civil war between the Danes and the Frisians. This reference to the sword as "battle-light" occurs in *Beowulf* only in these two instances, and this restricted usage may well be another indication of the poet's controlled suggestion that we see the two swords as one and the same.

Beowulf is angry when Hrunting fails him, and he casts aside the "sword with the curved serpentine markings" (1531). The description of the military artifact here suggests the texture of the poetry itself, with an elaborate interweaving of themes and events themselves constructing a serpentine interweave, a *wundorsmiþa geweorc* [work of cunning craftsmen, 1681]. For Hunferth's fratricidal weapon—this gift of an *eotenisc* fratricidal donor which Beowulf now casts aside—is replaced by an ur-fratricidal weapon made by giants, and on the hilt of which there is runically inscribed the origin of the ancient strife when Cain killed Abel. This is a giant sword, larger than any other man could carry to battle-play, made by giants and monsters, which the poet (ironically?) characterizes as "a gift of God." What follows from this tellingly monstrous sword replacing the worthless, merely human smaller weapon, Hrunting (a runt?)?

Once perceived in its proper ironic context, a host of intricate consequences follow on the poetic employment of the weapon which is now, indeed, a two-edged sword. When Beowulf later becomes a gift-giver, a treasure dispenser, returning from the underworld, it is a death's head and a bladeless hilt which he presents to the Ar-Scyldings [the Honor Scyldings], the Ecgwela [sons of sword-wealth]. Hrothgar's attack on Heremod (1719) because he gave no rings and his own nothing-short-of-lavish gifts to Beowulf are ironically shadowed by Beowulf's counter-gift of "sword wealth" which consists of the fratricidally inscribed hilt of the now non-existent blade. Beowulf, we recall, had found Hrunting to be without value, and he was angry when the edges of that sword failed him at a critical moment; nonetheless, the hero, who "did not swear many false oaths," returns the sword with a concealment of his true feelings, forging a formal statement that is gracious and polite and patently false on the face of it: "He said he considered the *guðwine* [war-friend, sword] good, mighty in war, not at all with words did he find fault with the edge of the sword" (1810). Later, after Beowulf returns to Geatland, this faint caul of falsification again hoods the narrative as he tells Hygelac about his fight with Grendel's mother, but glosses over certain details that might seem shameful. Neither does he tell about Hunferth's sword and its failure, nor about the specifics of *where* he obtained the great sword, nor who made it. Almost as in dreams, Beowulf's version evades, with a kind of self-deception, certain points of information that have been previously situated as decisive. His psyche acts as a censor to evade definite informations which might make him appear shameful, not honorable (2138).

Beowulf's last act before he departs for home is the giving of a sword to the boatguard. Ever afterwards, because of this gift, the poet says, the boatguard was honored on the meadbench for that treasure, that ancient heirloom. This statement appears innocent enough looked at in isolation; but when studied with the larger design of *Beowulf* in mind, the reader may well sense an intended irony in this honored sword-gift, coming as it does after the recounting of the gift of the fratricidal sword at Finnsburg, and after the gift of that same sword to Beowulf by Hunferth, and after the granting of the giant sword with the fratricidal inscription to Beowulf as he engages in battle with Grendel's mother, and echoing Beowulf's prior gift of the bladeless hilt to Hrothgar.

The precise ways in which the sword and the gift of the sword figure in the larger design of *Beowulf* are beyond the scope of this essay, but if we were to approach the problem from the point of view of interlace structure, we would no doubt find here the same elaborate patterns of intricate weaving that John Leyerle finds elsewhere in the poem. Leyerle, in studying the structure of *Beowulf* as an analogue of the interlace designs in Anglo-Saxon art, considers not only verbal or stylistic interlace but narrative and thematic threads as well. He finds in the four Hygelac episodes, for example, which occur in the poem without regard for chronological order, an example of a narrative thread, where each episode has "positional significance." Leyerle observes, "Unravel the threads and the whole fabric falls apart." All swimming episodes, to consider another instance, if taken together, become for Leyerle an elaborate thematic thread; fights with or without weapons, or the recurrence of marriages to establish bonds of tribal kinship form an equally important part of the poetic design, or interlace structure.[19]

Following Leyerle's method, then, if we were now to take a single strand, namely, the sword and gift of the sword, and trace this strand through the entire "knot-work design" of the poem, we would want to see some connection between the gift of the sword which touches off the

---

[19] John Leyerle, "The Interlace Structure of *Beowulf*," *UTQ*, 37 (1967–68), 1–17, esp. 7–8.

final, fatal battle at Finnsburg, and the precious sword (2050) which belonged to the father of the young, unnamed Heathobard, a sword now worn by the enemy, a Dane. To parallel the role played by the sword in the Finnsburg episode, it is this sword, worn now by an exulting Dane, which touches off anew the battle between the Heathobards and the Danes. If Leyerle is right, as he surely is, to see the sword as part of an overall design, we are invited by such insight to seek new meanings and to dis-cover additional resonances in the reappearance of the sword theme when Beowulf returns to Geatland and Hygelac offers him gifts: "There was not among the Geats a better precious treasure in the form of a sword, that he laid on the lap (*bearm*) of Beowulf, and gave him seven thousand hides of land, a hall and princely throne," (2210). Such a scene clearly echoes that earlier description when Hunlafing (Hunferth Ecglafing?) placed the "battle-light" in the lap of Hengest. And in that earlier episode, just as here, the poet rigorously arranges for death and disaster to follow hard upon the presentation of such a gift.

With the rise of Beowulf's worldly fortune and the gift of the sword, the story suddenly breaks, and we hear with a swiftness that is only superficially discontinuous how Hygelac lay dead, and Heardred lay dead. The narrator passes quickly over Beowulf's fifty year reign, and now he tells us how, on dark nights, the dragon comes to attack "the old guardian of the land" (2210). Whether we wish to attach significance to the above parallelism or see it simply as coincidence, Leyerle's observations concerning the nature of the interlace structure are surely apt: "design reveals the meaning of coincidence, the recurrence of human behaviour, and the circularity of time, partly through coincidence, recurrence, and circularity of the medium itself. . . . The significance of the connections is left for the audience to work out for itself. Understatement is thus inherent in interlace structure. . . ."[20]

Understatement, and its hearth-companion, literary irony, are retainers constantly employed by the *Beowulf* poet. The final scene of Beowulf's fight against the dragon may acquire an additional resonance if we see the events in that last great battle as a part of such an interlace structure with deliberately wrought ironic intricacies whose pattern the poet has been at some pains to rehearse for us. In an important article on Weohstan's sword, R. E. Kaske focuses his attention on the "critical moment of the dragon fight in *Beowulf*, as Wiglaf is on the point of coming to Beowulf's aid," and notes that "the action is strangely interrupted by a reminiscence on the history of the sword he carries."[21] The inter-

[20] Leyerle, p. 8.
[21] R. E. Kaske, "Weohstan's Sword," *MLN*, 75 (1960), 465.

ruption may seem "not so strange" if we have retained a foregrounded sense of the fratricidal ironies that have been so allusively and ongoingly adduced by the poet, and indeed, Kaske finds attractive Adrien Bonjour's explanation of the significance of the sword as a reminder of tribal enmities with ominous overtones of a future renewal of the latent feuds between the Geats and Swedes. Kaske studies the history-of-the-sword passage in terms of its immediate context, and concludes that the sword serves as an amplification and illustration of "the important Germanic ideal of good retainership."[22] He sees, further, "a parallel between the good retainership of Weohstan and that of his son Wiglaf; and in the contrast between Weohstan and the other retainers, who in an unambiguous situation, involving no ethical peculiarities, abandon their lord in time of need. The contrast is sharpened by the prominent mention of Weohstan's well-earned war-gear as against Wiglaf's references to the equipment fruitlessly bestowed on Beowulf's retainers, both here (2636–38) and in his later reproach (2864–72)." This example of the Germanic ideal of retainership is further set off and stressed by what appears to Kaske to be "some violation of the ties of kinship, whether by Onela or Eanmund or both" (467).[23] Kaske's stress in this article on the Germanic ideal is certainly valid and sensible, but the dragon fight and sword description acquire additional complex reverberations and resonances if viewed as a part of the total design of the poem, and more especially for our purposes here, if viewed as part of the poignantly ironic design I perceive in the structuring of the Hunlafing episode.

The history of Wiglaf's sword, after all, parallels in a strange and interesting way the history of Beowulf's sword, Hrunting, which he had acquired from Hunferth. Both swords have been involved in a Cain-like feud. Onela, we recall, gave Weohstan that sword to slay his brother's son, and Weohstan "had kept that sword for many years until his son could perform heroic deeds just as his old father" (2622). So too the "heroic deeds" Beowulf would earlier perform with Hrunting, deeds— if my interpretation is correct—similar to those performed at Finnsburg by Hunlafing and the other Danes. Now, in the dragon fight, Beowulf's sword, Nægling, with an apparent contagion of insufficiency, bursts apart, even as Hrunting had failed earlier. There seems to be a hint of more-than-merely-physical qualification upon the employment of these swords, and even though the precise history of Nægling is unknown, other than the fact that it had been previously tried in battle, the same

---

[22] Kaske, "Weohstan's Sword," p. 466.
[23] Kaske, "Weohstan's Sword," p. 467.

Cain-like associations are invited by a description of the sword as a "weapon hardened by wounds" (2687).

Just as Beowulf was previously rescued at the critical moment by an *ealdsweord eotenisc* [ancient giant-made sword, 1558], so here in this final episode it is again an *ealdsweord etonisc* (2616), carried by Wiglaf, that dispatches the monster at the critical moment. By attending to the larger design of the poem, we may discover some of the deeper meanings of this strange coincidence. In light of the poet's own clearly inscribed Christian ideal, it is a final coincidence that makes both cumulatively poignant and devastatingly ironic Beowulf's dying wish and last testament: "Now I should wish to give battle-garments to my son, if it was so granted to me that there would be afterwards any heir belonging to my body" (2729).[24]

[24] I am grateful to my colleague, Dolores Frese, for reading my manuscript and for suggesting important revisions.

Religious Heroic Poetry
THE LIVES OF HOLY MEN AND WOMEN

6

Guthlac A and *Guthlac B:*
Some Discriminations

DANIEL G. CALDER

COMPILERS OF MEDIEVAL ANTHOLOGIES WORKED ON PRINCIPLES BEST
described as idiosyncratic. Some seem to have arranged their materials
with no eye to order at all; others rested content with vague notions of
a format that could, and often did, encompass an extraordinary variety
of "literary" pieces. The cataloguer who received Leofric's donations to
Exeter Cathedral notes two items that characterize The Exeter Book for
him—it is in English and in poetry. As for its contents, they are about
"various things" (*.i. mycel englisc boc be gehwilcum þingum on
leoðwisan geworht*).[1] This codex, the most important of all the Anglo-
Saxon poetic records, does indeed comprise "various things," and why
the original collector fixed the poems in their present sequence will
remain a vexed question until the unlikely discovery of a "key" to its
order. The volume begins with two large divisions that both the medieval
scribe and modern scholars have separated into five poems: the three
parts of *Christ* and *Guthlac A* and *B*. Although the total scheme may

---

[1] George Philip Krapp and Elliott van Kirk Dobbie, eds., *The Exeter Book* (New
York, 1936), p. ix. All quotations are taken from this edition. For comments on
the contents of other important collections, see Kenneth Sisam, "The Compilation
of the Beowulf Manuscript," in *Studies in the History of Old English Literature*
(Oxford, 1953), pp. 65–96; Krapp, ed., *The Junius Manuscript* (New York, 1931),
pp. xi–xii; and D. G. Scragg, "The Compilation of the Vercelli Book," *Anglo-
Saxon England*, 2 (1973), 189–207.

elude us, perhaps we may assume that the *Christ* poems come first because they are about Christ, and that the two *Guthlac* poems follow
because they are about an English saint.

Guthlac A and *Guthlac B* have no doubt always existed as distinct
compositions, yet their placement in the Exeter manuscript suggests that
someone intended them to approximate a single account of the saint's
life and death. The first tells of Guthlac's temptations in the fens near
Cambridge, ending with a brief report of his death and ascension; the
second relates that death in great detail. But the arbitrary ties between
the poems scarcely hold them together at all. Not surprisingly, then,
critics have ignored the medieval editor's rough attempt at a biographical
unity and concentrated instead on the two parts.

Having set aside that medieval perspective which can see *Guthlac A*
and *B* as one "composite" poem, modern criticism should at least define
the two "sections" more precisely. This it has not done. Beyond noting
the obvious shift in subject matter, most analyses give only impressions
of the variations in style and treatment.[2] In the end, *Guthlac A* usually
receives blame for being abstract, repetitive, and didactic, while *Guthlac
B* customarily garners praise for its clarity, humanity, and poetic power.[3]
Guthlac A may not be as good a poem as *B,* though they differ so
markedly that such a distinction is hard to make. We can, nevertheless,
exploit the fortunate accident of our having two poems on the same
saint and put the necessary discriminations on a firmer base. By exploring the formal features of these narratives—the prologues and
their ritual actions—we discover that the two works embody entirely
different symbolic modes. Both modes approach or resemble allegory:
Guthlac A derives its symbolism not only from traditional Christian
interpretations of the desert saint, but also from the psychomachia;
Guthlac B does not depend on any other literary genre, but draws
directly on the symbolism of Christian typology.

I THE PROLOGUES

Each Old English poem on Guthlac has a prologue, quite unlike the
preface to the Latin saint's life.[4] Textual problems, however, attend the

[2] Cf. T. A. Shippey, *Old English Verse* (London, 1972), p. 128.

[3] See Rosemary Woolf, "Saints' Lives," in *Continuations and Beginnings: Studies
in Old English Literature,* ed. Eric Gerald Stanley (London, 1966), p. 57; Benjamin P. Kurtz, "From St. Antony to St. Guthlac: A Study in Biography," *University of California Publications in Modern Philology,* 12 (1925–26), 144–46;
Theodor Wolpers, *Die Englische Heiligenlegende des Mittelalters* (Tübingen,
1964), pp. 112, 115; and Stanley B. Greenfield, *A Critical History of Old English
Literature* (New York, 1965), p. 123.

[4] Professor Jones has written amusingly of the "wanderings of that conventional
preface"; not trusting inspiration, Latin hagiographers borrowed wholesale from

prologue to *Guthlac A:* do the first 29 lines, which depict an angel's welcome of a blessed soul into heaven, belong to *Guthlac A* or to the end of *Christ III?* Strictly on grounds of subject, the lines could fit *Christ III.* In his metrical investigations Professor Pope finds additional support for this position.[5] But Fr. Shook's seminal article on the theology of both prologue and poem seems to have dispelled most doubts. He writes:

> The poet . . . succeeded in binding the two parts together by the following devices, meaningful to him in his character of theologian: the journey of the departed soul to paradise under the guidance of its heavenly psychopomps; the symbolic figure of the eternal city, the heavenly Jerusalem, as the final end of the Christian life; the sharp contrast between the temporal joys of earth and the eternal joys of heaven; and a mysterious even apocalyptic atmosphere common to both parts of the poem and springing from an acquaintance with apocryphal materials.[6]

One small pattern would seem to reinforce Fr. Shook's theological argument. Just prior to the angel's official greeting to the newly-arrived soul, the poet intrudes an unexpected, parenthetical half-line: *Hafað yldran had* [(the angel) will have the higher *rank,* 4a (emphasis added)]. Angels do in fact have "the higher rank," but unless the poet means to elaborate on that idea for some purpose, then the line by itself stands awkwardly apart from its context. The word *had* appears four more times within the opening 94 lines, that is, within the 92-line general introduction and the first two lines of the narrative proper. This fairly striking example of "clustered repetition"[7] prompts two observations: first, the word *had* does not occur in *Christ III* at all, and we may add this fact to the cumulative evidence that the scribe was correct in assigning the first 29 lines to *Guthlac A;* second, the use of the word helps clarify the prologue's structure and establishes some concerns that occupy the poet throughout.

Even those who accept Fr. Shook's theological justification for attaching these lines to *Guthlac A* express an uneasiness with the prologue's rhetorical and logical structure. Professor Lipp can find no

---

the major early lives—Evagrius' translation of the *Life of Saint Anthony,* Sulpicius' *Life of Saint Martin,* and Bede's *Life of Saint Cuthbert.* See Charles W. Jones, *Saints' Lives and Chronicles in Early England* (Ithaca, N.Y., 1947), p. 54.

[5] John Collins Pope, *The Rhythm of Beowulf* (New York, 1966), p. 101.

[6] Laurence K. Shook, "The Prologue of the Old-English *Guthlac A,*" *MS,* 23 (1961), 304.

[7] See James L. Rosier, "Death and Transfiguration: *Guthlac B,*" in *Philological Essays: Studies in Old and Middle English Language and Literature in Honour of Herbert Dean Meritt,* ed. Rosier (The Hague, 1970), p. 91; and Rosier, "The Literal-Figurative Identity of *The Wanderer,*" *PMLA,* 79 (1964), 366–69.

specific "thematic relevance" that would connect the lines to the rest of the poem, and she decides that "the five subdivisions . . . constitute five separate passages."[8] The passages may be separate, but they follow a necessary and clear progression. We begin with a generalized picture of the joy accompanying a righteous soul's entrance into heaven;[9] we are reminded—suddenly and intrusively—that there is an order of creation in which God, "the highest King of all kings" (16b–17a), sits at the pinnacle and "rules the city" (17b). Angels rank below God, though above the righteous souls "who perform His commands here on earth" (14a–15b). Creation, however, is varied; it exemplifies plenitude, and so the prologue moves on—and down—to the second division:

> Monge sindon   geond middangeard
> *hadas* under heofonum,   þa þe in haligra
> rim arisað.

> (30a–32a; italics added)

[There are many *ranks/men* throughout the world under heaven who belong to the number of the holy.]

From the generalized picture of the individual redeemed soul, the prologue descends to the many on earth who may potentially enjoy that same bliss, and "we" can "by right belong to any one [of these ranks], if we fulfill the holy commands" (32b–34b). Again the same emphases: God's order described in hierarchical terms and the necessity for obedience.

The initial words of the first three sections are in themselves guides to the structure: *Monge, Sume, Sume;* and the next two verse paragraphs treat variant possibilities in the earthly sphere. Pointing out that "some want to have the fame of a [good] *man / rank* in words and not do the deeds" (60a–61b; italics added), the poet then proceeds to his second category which both counters the first and edges closer to his eventual topic: "some dwell in deserts; they seek and live in homes in dark places of their own accord" (81a–83a). Most important, "these men are proven warriors who serve the King" (91). Finally the poet approaches Guthlac himself, underscoring his own sense of the rhetorical climax by using a familiar formula:

> Magun we *nu* nemnan   þæt us neah gewearð
> þurh haligne   *had* gecyþed,

[8] Frances Randall Lipp, "*Guthlac A:* an Interpretation," *MS,* 33 (1971), 57; see also Woolf, p. 56.

[9] I cannot agree with Fr. Shook's claim that this soul belongs specifically to Guthlac and that "one has to wait until the end of the poem—which thus becomes a long flashback on Guthlac's life and trials—for the final carrying of the soul to heaven by the psychopomps" (p. 300).

<pre>
hu Guðlac his   in godes willan
   mod gerehte,   man eall forseah.
</pre>

(93a–96b; emphasis added)

[May we *now* tell what recently was revealed to us by a holy *man*, how Guthlac governed his mind according to God's will, renounced all evil.]

Here *had* must take its other meaning, "man" or "being," though the poet often plays with the double meaning. And the poet's assertion that he received his information about Guthlac *þurh haligne had* legitimizes the spiritual account, as well as completing his pattern. The poem moves in five bold steps down the ladder from a cosmic perspective to Guthlac's temptations. Obvious rhetorical devices highlight these steps and each contains a rehearsal of the dominant themes: the hierarchical order of the world, the necessity for obedience, and the positive force of God's love that makes salvation possible for holy men of all ranks.[10]

In the prologue to *Guthlac B* the poet takes another cosmic view— not "down" through space from heaven to earth, but "back" in time to the creation of Eden and man. The opening of *A* provides a glimpse of heaven itself as the land the sinless reach; the opening lines of *B* move from a sketch of the earthly paradise to death's entrance into the world as a consequence of Adam's sin. Implied associations rather than logical progressions govern the movement in *B,* and after a short section on "Death's" rule, the poet gets directly to the presentation of his saint. He arrives at this destination by asserting that although "Death ruled over earth-dwellers" (871b–72a), many holy men do exist, one of whom is Guthlac, "blessed among the English" (880). Since Guthlac's death will be the poem's matter, any general discussion of death could bring the poet to his subject. Nonetheless, he suppresses this natural transition momentarily, and makes a swift tour back through the trials Saint Guthlac suffered *on þam westenne* [in the desert, 899a], recounting at the same time Guthlac's miraculous works and deeds of charity. This epitome marks an important departure from the rhetorical structure outlined for *A:* rather than being another in a progressive series, the recapitulation of Guthlac's life delays the movement, though not without purpose. For in its perfection Guthlac's devotion to the eremitical life atones for Adam's sin, just as in retreating to the desert he eventually recaptures the paradise Adam lost. Without this suspension, many of the symbolic links between the poem and prologue would be lost.

---

[10] Since the positive force of God's love and the poem's unusual "mildness and encouraging tone" (p. 58) are the main subjects of Lipp's essay, I have not felt it necessary to dwell on this point.

One can also trace a complex metaphorical pattern in the prologue to *B* which operates in the narrative on several levels. Images of a paradise with all its beauty gone pervade the prologue and extend throughout the poem;[11] and a partly-personified Death stalks through the action in several forms: as the separation of soul from body; as a bitter drink mankind sips from the cup Eve gave Adam; and as a thief in the night who unlocks life's treasure and steals it away.[12] This pattern counterpoints, in its own context, the simple motifs that comprise the Christian "message" in the *A* prologue.

The different schemes of the two prologues have pronounced effects on their succeeding narrative structures. One turns to Guthlac-A's temptations ready for the battle because of the repeated assurance that God does reward those who love and obey Him with a seat in heaven; one turns to Guthlac-B's death with an awareness of all Christian history, but fortified by the expectation that Guthlac's holy life will permit him to vanquish Death and regain paradise. Although each saint re-enacts the drama of salvation, the poems start at quite different points.

II RITUAL ACTION

In both *Guthlac A* and *B* the narrative action can be called ritual, even though the poets use that ritual in distinct ways for diverse ends. Ritual action necessarily implies a degree of repetition and T. A. Shippey lists this as a significant fault in *A:*

> There is little narrative interest or change in the saint's circumstances. . . .
> Three times toward the start we are referred back to the devil's discomfiture *siþþan he for wlence . . . beorgas bræce* [once (Guthlac) broke the mounds in the wilderness, out of daring], *siþþan biorg gestah eadig oretta* [once the noble warrior ascended the mound], *þa he ana gesæt dygle stowe* [when he alone settled the secret place]. In these repetitive structures the poet seems to be projecting effort and triumph when none is clearly visible.[13]

And one of the poem's ablest defenders, Professor Lipp, still finds occasion to remark that "The poet merely expresses a few basic Christian

[11] See Daniel G. Calder, "Theme and Strategy in *Guthlac B,*" *PLL*, 8 (1972), 227–34.

[12] See Rosier, "Death and Transfiguration," *passim.*

[13] Shippey, p. 130. The translations in brackets are his; the passages he quotes should be identified as lines 208a–09a, 175b–76a, 158b–59a. See also Wolpers, p. 114; and Laurence K. Shook, "The Burial Mound in *Guthlac A,*" *MP*, 58 (1960), 2.

ideas, using repetition and changing context for emphasis and variety."[14] Regardless of their final pronouncements, all agree that the action of *Guthlac A* becomes a maze of repetitions.

At one point in the midst of what appears to some as a poem gone berserk, the poet says, *Ða wæs eft swa ær* [Then it was again as it had been before, 390a]. This seemingly empty formula indicates that for the poet a continual return to the same events was not a senseless effort. Rather than trying to avoid the stigma of repetition, he calls our attention to it both by his own words and by his depiction of Guthlac always facing the same encounters with the same effects. The return itself has meaning, because the repetition becomes a ritual.[15] But such iterative movement interrupts the narrative progress: if we always return to exactly the same place, then we have obviously not gone forward. For the time being, everything continues to be "as it had been before," and the insistent note struck by the constant returns does indeed, as Shippey claims, project "effort and triumph when none is clearly visible." However, none *should* be clearly visible, for Guthlac has not yet been supremely triumphant; and the ritual action creates a symbolic sense of his extreme effort with a corresponding recognition of his great victory.

Shippey's reading stems from a general, though not universal, misunderstanding of Guthlac's "effort." Since he assumes that "both *Guthlac*-poems almost entirely erase one of the best points of the 'Antonian' tradition, its sense of psychology," then he must logically conclude that the demons' attacks in *A* are external and not projections of human responses from the saint's mind.[16] The debate concerning the demons' origins and type finally comes down to questions about mimetic and abstract art. In his *Life of Saint Anthony* Athanasius does give the saint attributes of a recognizable person; so we can accept more easily the attacks of beasts and demons as projections of a real mind under considerable stress as it attempts to cope with the rigors of asceticism. On the other hand, the poet of *Guthlac A* portrays his saint in a relentlessly abstract manner;[17] he strips away all vestiges of a mimetic ap-

---

[14] Lipp, p. 59.

[15] On repetition and ritual, especially in their relation to allegory, see Angus Fletcher, *Allegory: The Theory of a Symbolic Mode* (Ithaca, N.Y., 1964), pp. 147–219.

[16] Shippey, pp. 129–30.

[17] This abstract portrayal corresponds to historical developments in art. Citing Adolf Katzenellenbogen as his source, Morton W. Bloomfield writes that there is a "cyclic movement in the psychomachias of [the Middle Ages] which might be described as naturalistic-abstract-naturalistic. The naturalistic treatments emerge in the fifth century with Prudentius himself, are submerged in the ninth to twelfth centuries by the more abstract style, and in the Gothic period gradually regain ascendancy, finally bursting out with full force in the Renaissance" (*The Seven*

proach to character. Predictable consequences follow from each method: Athanasius' realism allows us to see a connection between Saint Anthony's mind and the demons who attack him; the *A*-poet's abstract art demands that he state these same equivalences bluntly. And so he does. No situation, action, or reaction in *A* may seem to have profound psychological roots, but without exception the poet *says* they do:

> Swa him yrsade,   se for ealle spræc
> feonda mengu.   No þy forhtra wæs
> Guðlaces gæst,   ac him God sealde
> ellen wiþ þam egsan   þæt þæs ealdfeondes
> scyldigra scolu   scome þrowedon.

> (200a–04b)

[So the one who spoke for the whole host of fiends angered him. Guthlac's soul was not afraid of that, for God had given him strength against fear, so that the guilty gang of the old enemy suffered shame.]

We must accept his statements, even if they are at odds with our preconceptions about psychological narratives. In *Guthlac A* the devils do not have a separate and external reality; the number of times the poet uses Old English words for Guthlac's heart, mind, soul, and spirit cancels even the possibility of a discrete existence for the demons.

Without doubt the poet faces a difficult problem: he must use the repetitive device to create an abstract ritual which symbolizes Guthlac's spiritual and psychological "effort," "strife," "battle," "war." Because that concern remains ever-present through most of the poem, the means that express and symbolize it must recur. Guthlac cannot take care of the "devils" in one fell swoop; as spiritual doubts, fears, and terrors, the devils present him with a constant battle that cannot be won until his trials prove him worthy and he vanquishes his own demons. But the "present" battle also moves through a sequence that resembles a chronology recounting Guthlac's life as a recluse in the fens. This overlay of conflicting patterns—one direct (the straight narrative progession) and the other repetitive (the ritual symbolizing of his spiritual struggle) —has led to many of the objections about the poem. A sharper perception of that ritual scheme and its functions may help solve the

---

Deadly Sins [East Lansing, Mich., 1952], p. 81). Several critics have recently called attention to this abstract quality in the Old English poem: see Lipp, *passim;* and Alvin A. Lee, *The Guest-Hall of Eden: Four Essays on the Design of Old English Poetry* (New Haven and London, 1972), p. 103.

puzzle. Fortunately, the poem provides a single center for his double narrative pattern. Some time ago Fr. Shook pointed out that "the poem has no significant passage which does not somehow hinge upon this 'return the barrow or die' motif."[18] The barrow Guthlac "builds"[19] locates the poem's center and clarifies both the need and purpose of the ritual action: through his perseverance—his repeated words and deeds—Guthlac finally wins his barrow. He has fashioned it as the center of his psychological world, and, consequently, it becomes the center of his and all spiritual worlds. To paraphrase Professor Eliade, Guthlac has transformed profane space into a transcendent space,[20] an achievement realized only through the poem's sanctifying ritual action.

In *Guthlac A* the poet has to find a means to represent and symbolize Guthlac's creation of his own spiritual perfection; Guthlac may be assured of God's help and protection at every interval, but the struggle must be endured. Thus the poet designs a double narrative pattern whose temporal confusions and ambiguities are resolved by a spatial symbol of the "center"—the *beorg*. In *Guthlac B* the spiritual struggle with the demons has long since passed, and we assume Guthlac's sanctity from the outset, waiting only for the moment of transfiguration to occur. Once more, we discern an emphasis on space in one poem, and an emphasis on time in the other.

While the spiritual struggle may be over for Guthlac-B, another struggle has taken its place: the saint's encounter with Death. Extended considerably beyond the material in Felix's chapter,[21] the account of Guthlac-B's death also turns repetition into ritual. But these ritual devices are concealed by the clear narrative line and we do not notice that the poet (or the characters) return again and again to the same subject. In a series of meetings with his disciple, Beccel, Guthlac keeps the discussion centered on his approaching death. Beccel's understandable grief is one of the details that makes *Guthlac B* more "human" for

---

[18] Shook, "Burial Mound," p. 2.

[19] Cf. Lee, p. 105.

[20] Mircea Eliade, *Cosmos and History: The Myth of the Eternal Return,* trans. Willard R. Trask (New York, 1959), p. 21.

[21] The source for *Guthlac B* is "Chapter L" of Felix of Crowland's *Vita Sancti Guthlaci;* see Bertram Colgrave, ed., *Felix's Life of Saint Guthlac* (Cambridge, 1956), pp. 150–61. All quotations are taken from this edition, including the translations. The arguments about the relationship of *Guthlac A* to Felix are long, heated, and complex; one may read Gordon Hall Gerould, "The Old English Poems on St. Guthlac and their Latin Source," *MLN,* 32 (1917), 77–89, as an example of those who believe *A* does derive from Felix; and Claes Schaar, *Critical Studies in the Cynewulf Group* (Lund, 1949), pp. 39–41, as an example of those who believe the poet relied mainly on oral traditions. I tend to agree with Lipp (p. 51n.), who tends to agree with Schaar.

many critics.[22] This response has, in turn, made it more difficult to grasp the abstract pattern behind the "realistic" surface. Here a comparison with the source illustrates what the Old English poet has done. Felix writes: *Fili mi, tristitiam ne admittas; non enim mihi labor est ad Dominum meum, cui servivi, in requiem venire aeternam* [My son, do not give way to sadness, for it is no hardship for me to enter on eternal rest with my Lord whom I have served, pp. 154–55]. These words, comforting as they may be, provide the sole instance in Felix where Guthlac offers consolation to his servant. By contrast, in the Old English poem, Guthlac has four long speeches in which he comforts Beccel and prophesies his coming death. These speeches are set in and among four additional lengthy descriptions of the advancing disease and four expressions of grief on Beccel's part. Even the one departure from this plan—Guthlac's report of his angelic visitations—comes back at the end to the familiar refrain. What the poet writes near the beginning pertains until the saint's death:

> He on elne swa þeah
> ungebylged bad   beorhtra gehata
> bliþe in burgum
>
> (940b–42a)

[Nevertheless he waited bravely, unafraid, for the bright promises, glad in his stronghold.]

Guthlac B concerns "fulfillment," a term with several layers of meaning, but in this case the fulfillment is the heavenly reward Guthlac will receive. Guthlac's prophecy of his death-day gives him control over the time that moves toward this apotheosis; it also enables him to endure the "struggle" of his fatal disease with an equanimity denied to ordinary men, who are represented by Beccel. So the poet's triple subjects for his ritual action—the disease, Guthlac's calm assurance of reward and the servant's grief—serve related ends: the disease which mankind inherits from Adam offers a cause for the action and its severity only sets Guthlac's serenity into higher relief. The same is true of Beccel's repeated expressions of grief and desolation. As for Guthlac, he remains absorbed in the idea of his own death and imminent reward. Each successive return to these same matters lessens the narrative's mimetic force and heightens the abstract pattern of the ritual. However, in *Guthlac B* the "returns" are not confusing; the ritual action supports a simple narrative. This clarity in the temporal order permits a climactic reso-

[22] Cf. Lee, p. 109; and Woolf, p. 57.

lution in and beyond time itself: Guthlac's death and transfiguration; the temporal confusions in *Guthlac A* require a climactic resolution, not beyond time, but rather separate from it: Guthlac's winning of the barrow. We can now discriminate between two entirely different uses of ritual action: that of *Guthlac A* consecrates a space; that of *Guthlac B* fulfills and redeems time.

III SYMBOLIC MODES

Following Fr. Shook's lead, most critics describe the actions of *Guthlac A* and *B* as "symbolic."[23] But it should be obvious by now that the variances between the poems ought to result in quite different symbolic modes; the term "symbolic" cannot serve as a single cover for all the disparities of subject, structure, and theme. In refining the distinctions, several possibilities present themselves. One could use established exegetical commentary and work out a full allegory; Professor Bolton reads the Guthlac legend in this way:

> The concept of spiritual warfare . . . had its basis in Scripture. The central document in the formulation of the Scriptural tradition was Augustine of Hippo's *De Agone Christiano,* and the key idea in it is expressed in the first sentence: *Corona uictoriae non promittitur nisi certantibus* [The crown of victory is not promised except to those who fight]. . . . The Temptation in the Desert was a model for man's spiritual life. Bede calls the desert *locum certaminis* [a place of struggle], and points out that Christ's voluntary exile *admonet nos ut accepta in baptismo remissione peccatorum, et gratia Spiritus sancti contra antiqui hostis insidias accingamur . . .* [admonishes us to accept the remission of sins in baptism and to gird ourselves with the grace of the Holy Spirit against the traps of the ancient enemy]. . . . Christ is both the example and the eternal leader in the fight. Augustine quotes Paul, I Corinthians 11:1, *Imitatores mei estote, sicut et ego Christi* [Imitate me, just as I did Christ]. . . . To the reader this meant that eremitical saints like Guthlac could in a sense be regarded as figures of all mankind, and that their lives were the figurative lives of all who accepted Christ as their leader and model.[24]

Within the framework of Christian exegesis, Bolton's interpretation makes perfect sense. Yet it is also reductive, and its archetypal figures and images—Christ, devil, desert, saint—let us read allegorical meaning

---

[23] See Shook, "Burial Mound," p. 10; Lee, p. 107ff.; and Lipp, *passim.*
[24] W. F. Bolton, "The Background and Meaning of *Guthlac*," *JEGP,* 61 (1962), 597–99. The translations of the Latin quotations are mine.

into the life of any holy recluse. On this level, Christian allegoresis parallels the theological notion of a communion of saints.[25] While Bolton's view is in harmony with the theological uses of allegory, it impedes our understanding of the kinds of allegory present in *Guthlac A* and *B*. Theological and literary allegory need not be mutually exclusive (especially in saints' lives), although they need not be the same either. As Christian literary documents, saints' lives can be read from both vantage points.

Many of the comparisons between *Guthlac A* and *B* already presented adapt themselves readily to an important general statement recently fashioned by Raymon Farrrar. Reviewing the range of Anglo-Saxon saints' lives, he writes:

> Their conventionality suggests a certain degree of repetitive abstraction rather than concretion, however graphically their actions may be described; and this abstractness poses the question of what it is they represent if they cannot primarily (or finally or most importantly) be said to "represent" themselves. The implication is . . . that elements of something akin to allegory are present and of greater value in comprehending saints' lives than are questions of historicism or lack thereof.[26]

Guthlac-A's war with his demons could certainly pass over into allegory at any stage in the ritual; its action moves in the directions of a psychomachia—that *bellum intestinum* [internal struggle] which C. S. Lewis calls "the root of all allegory."[27] The requisite scaffolding for literary allegory is certainly present—the battle form itself, the presence of a good and bad angel as participants in that battle, a cosmic perspective that insists upon more than a literal reading, and a ritual action that func-

[25] The anonymous Monk of Whitby writes in his *Life of Gregory the Great:* "So let no one be disturbed even if these miracles were performed by any other of the saints, since the holy Apostle, through the mystery of the limbs of a single body, which he compares to the living experience of the saints, concludes that we are all 'members one of another.'" See Bertram Colgrave, ed., *The Earliest Life of Gregory the Great* (Lawrence, Kansas, 1968), p. 131; and Jones, pp. 57–64.

[26] Raymon S. Farrar, "Structure and Function in Representative Old English Saints' Lives," *Neophil,* 57 (1973), 86.

[27] C. S. Lewis, *The Allegory of Love* (New York, 1958), p. 68. See also Fletcher, who remarks: "The tendency is for allegories to resolve themselves into either of two basic forms, and they do not merely arise out of the bare rudiments of these two forms; they keep returning to insist on them. The two may be labeled *battle* and *progress*" (p. 151). Michael D. Cherniss has written that the strife between the good and bad angels "for Guthlac's allegiance is clearly a *psychomachia* which takes place in Guthlac's mind immediately prior to his final decision to serve God rather than the World (114–140)." See *Ingeld and Christ: Heroic Concepts and Values in Old English Christian Poetry* (The Hague, 1972), p. 229.

tions in a like manner. But these elements do not come together in an obvious allegory. By juxtaposing *Guthlac A* (a kind of psychomachia) with Prudentius' original *Psychomachia,* the reasons become apparent. However abstract the patterned action in *Guthlac A* may be, it does not involve the clear-cut and absolute personification of inner forces. A good and bad angel are projections of a divided spirit; yet they are not Good and Evil *per se.* Neither can we classify the demonic apparitions under any other heading than the various aspects of Guthlac's troubled soul. The schematic narrative does not produce a schematic allegory, for the shift in battleground from the "soul of man" in Prudentius to the *beorg* in *Guthlac A* has real importance. In the barrow the poem has so powerful a focus for its action and so strong a symbol for its center that the need for explicit allegory disappears. This barrow is all that Fr. Shook and Paul Reichardt have claimed and more: [28] it is the object Guthlac desires after his conversion to the eremitical life and so it represents his highest hopes for spiritual achievement. On it, as well as through it, he projects his fears and doubts, and in his decisive winning of it we recognize the outer sign of an inner victory. As a *ham* [home] for his body, the barrow also symbolizes the perfect soul he, like all wise men, builds (800b–02a). Taking another perspective, we see that as a perfected soul the home is also the eternal home, the New Jerusalem, to which "a" soul is welcomed at the opening and to which Guthlac is brought at the end. Circular in its structure, ritual in its action, the poem begins and ends in heaven, incorporating into its fabric an earthly setting which symbolizes all that God demands of a Christian desiring perfection and all that the Christian will receive as a reward if he succeeds. The blossoming of the barrow at the end of *Guthlac A* (732b–51b), the reign of peace that follows the saint's violent battles, presages Guthlac's heavenly bliss and reveals an interesting relation between saint and barrow: the poet tells us that Guthlac was happy and enjoyed his dwelling (772, 744b–45b), but it is the landscape which undergoes the transformation. The *beorg* has consistently symbolized both the means and end of Guthlac's spiritual perfection and thus when he reaches it, the symbol and not the man reflects that triumph.

Guthlac A misses the mark of "pure allegory" (if such a thing exists) [29] for two reasons: first, the battleground is not the saint's soul, but a symbolic object in a landscape outside that soul, an object that ties together all the threads of action and theme. Allegory demands the sepa-

---

[28] See Shook, "Burial Mound," p. 10; and Paul F. Reichardt, *"Guthlac A* and the Landscape of Spiritual Perfection," *Neophil,* 58 (1974), 331–38.
[29] See Fletcher, p. 312.

ration of the individual threads in order to tie them to one or to a series of themes. Second, the oft-noted and sometimes scorned "didactic" or "homiletic" quality of *A* works against the presence of a literary allegory. Angus Fletcher puts it clearly: "allegory," he says, "recedes into the background . . . when commentary takes over on the figurative level."[30] The recurring moralizations—encouraging, affirmative and loving—replace the last elements that could have turned *Guthlac A* from a saint's life "akin to allegory" into a specific allegory more closely resembling Prudentius' *Psychomachia,* the most significant of the Old English generic ancestors.[31]

The symbolic mode of *Guthlac B* derives from those aspects of Christian thought that give a meaning to time: the typological interpretation of history. Here too the mode is "akin to allegory,"[32] although of a completely different kind from the shadowy psychomachia that stands behind *Guthlac A.* Furthermore, as Professor Manning rightly warns us, "Typology . . . is not properly a literary technique, nor can it be reduced to one. But it is a mode of spiritual perception and can affect literary technique and can resemble literary modes."[33] Yet from the prologue on, there is no doubt that the poet of *Guthlac B* explores the figural connections between the English saint and the major characters in Christian history: Adam, Christ, and Satan. Guthlac-B continues the line of men who have both lost and redeemed time. What Adam took away from mankind and Christ restored, Guthlac-B likewise restores through his saintly life. As Christ in traditional typology is the second Adam, so Guthlac-B (and, theologically, all the saints) is both a second Adam and a model of Christ.[34] He is the exemplar, "the Christian in sacramental imitation configured to Christ."[35] The historical fact reported by Felix that Guthlac died during the Easter Octave offers the poet more material to extend his typological parallels. The poet begins his account of the saint's own death with a description of that event in universal history when Christ stripped power from the devil by harrowing hell (1098b–

---

[30] Fletcher, p. 321.

[31] It is interesting to note that the two *Guthlac* poems "contain the first literary appearance in English of the Christian battle theme." See Bloomfield, p. 108.

[32] R. P. C. Hanson notes how at all times and in all places typology has a habit of "slipping gradually into allegory" (*Allegory and Event: A Study of the Sources and Significance of Origen's Interpretation of Scripture* [Richmond, Va., 1959], p. 22).

[33] Stephen Manning, "Scriptural Exegesis and the Literary Critic," in *Typology and Early American Literature,* ed. Sacvan Bercovitch (Amherst, Mass., 1972), p. 58.

[34] See Jean Danielou, S. J., *From Shadows to Reality: Studies in the Biblical Typology of the Fathers,* trans. Dom Wulstan Hibberd (London, 1960), pp. 30–47.

[35] Hanson, p. 69.

1104b);[36] he also "turns Guthlac's death into a symbolic recreation of Christ's Passion and Resurrection."[37] Felix in his rendering includes none of these typological equivalents; and the highly symbolic concept of the saint's death in *Guthlac B* we can credit to the poet himself, though he drew, quite naturally, on the main items of Christian typology to accomplish his aim.

A last look at the death scenes in both poems elucidates these distinctions. At the moment of his death Guthlac-B has fulfilled his mission within time and slips out of his human form to become a saintly artifact:

> Ahof þa his honda,   husle gereorded,
> eaðmod þy æþelan gyfle,   swylce he his eagan ontynde,
> halge heafdes gimmas,   biseah þa to heofona rice,
> glædmod to geofona leanum,   ond þa his gæst onsende
> weorcum wlitigne   in wuldres dream.

> (1300a–04b)

[Then he raised his hands after he had eaten the Eucharist; he was humble with the noble food. So he opened his eyes, the holy jewels of his head, and looked, glad in heart, towards the kingdom of heaven, towards the rewards of grace. Then he sent forth his soul, made beautiful by his deeds, into the joy of heaven.]

The house and landscape in which he dwells do emit a lambent glow and a sweet odor; however, in sharp contrast to the analogous scene in *Guthlac A*, the emphasis is on the saint's transformation as well as the radiance of the setting. Guthlac-B is transfigured because the poem is about his fulfillment; the barrow in *Guthlac* is transformed because it is the symbol of the saint's perfection. While all the clamor appropriate to a saint's ascension into heaven accompanies Guthlac-B's journey, we do not see him "there," as we see Guthlac-A firmly established on his *setl on swegle* / [seat in heaven, 785a]. The symbolism of space in *A* requires that we see heaven itself; the symbolism of time in *B* demands only that we know of the saint's reward. To a certain degree each poem has a structure that simulates one of the basic forms Fletcher identifies at the heart of allegory: *Guthlac A*, the *battle*; *Guthlac B*, the *progress*. And the models themselves suggest the terms we have used: battles happen in space; a progress moves through time. However, the two Old English poems are both deflected allegories; some aspect of each keeps it from being a clear example of its pattern. The displaced *battle* in *A*

---

[36] See Calder, p. 238.
[37] Calder, p. 239.

occurs on a barrow that is at once real and densely symbolic; it gathers rather than disperses the poem's themes. The true *progress* in Guthlac-B's life is already over when the poem begins and the ritual action, by suspending time, converts it to eternity. These fundamental differences define the crucial ways in which both poems may be "akin to allegory" and at the same time quite removed from it.

Any theological system that asserts a "communion of saints" whose earthly deeds conform to a perfect divine pattern must inevitably produce a conventional and abstract biographical literature. If all the saints are in essence the same, then so should be their "Lives"; but the facts belie this simple equation. Theologically the lives may be identical, but as literature they are not. Differing from their Latin models more than has been granted, the Old English saints' lives do not show a strict adherence to set conventions even among themselves. *Guthlac A* and *Guthlac B* share a common theology and Guthlac-A and Guthlac-B achieve the same reward. Still, as literary works they are distinct, and they serve as paradigms for a large corpus of Anglo-Saxon Christian poetry.

7

Andreas and Beowulf:
Placing the Hero

DAVID HAMILTON

Andreas AND *Beowulf* HAVE LONG BEEN COMPARED WITH RESULTS RUN-
ning the full gamut of possibilities. *Beowulf* has been taken as the model
for *Andreas*,[1] and *Andreas* as all but incidentally independent of the
epic.[2] More recently, critics have taken less radical positions by saying
that though the *Andreas* poet was clearly familiar with *Beowulf,* he went
beyond the epic in his direct cultivation of religious interests and
themes.[3] Peters, who has urged the separation of the two poems most

[1] Arthur Fritzsche, "Das Angelsächsische Gedicht Andreas und Cynewulf,"
Anglia, 2 (1879), 441–96; George Philip Krapp, ed., *Andreas and the Fates of
the Apostles* (Boston, 1906), pp. li–lviii; Thomas Arnold, *Notes on Beowulf*
(London, 1898); Fr. Klaeber, ed., *Beowulf,* 3rd ed. (Boston, 1950); Satyendra
Kumar Das, *Cynewulf and the Cynewulf Canon* (Calcutta, 1942); Claes Schaar,
Critical Studies in the Cynewulf Group (Lund, 1949). Schaar's position is cau-
tious: *Andreas* is more nearly related to *Beowulf* than to the poems of Cynewulf,
pp. 275–87.

[2] R. M. Lumiansky, "The Contexts of the Old English 'Ealuscerwen' and
'Meoduscerwen,'" *JEGP,* 48 (1949), 116–26; L. J. Peters, "The Relationship of
the Old English *Andreas* to *Beowulf,*" *PMLA,* 66 (1951), 844–63.

[3] Thus with various emphases, Robert E. Diamond, "Theme as Ornament in
Anglo-Saxon Poetry," *PMLA,* 76 (1961), 461–68; Arthur G. Brodeur, "A Study
of Diction and Style in Three Anglo-Saxon Narrative Poems," in *Nordica et
Anglica: Studies in Honor of Stefan Einarsson,* ed. Allan H. Orrick (The Hague,

strongly, stated that proof of *Beowulf's* influence would require, among other things, our showing that the later poet altered his source to fit the epic.[4] That source, as Peters points out, is a lost Latin translation of the Greek *Acts of Andrew and Matthew,* a story that contains almost all the features of plot and incident that we find in the OE poem. Another possibility is that as the poet of *Andreas* brought this story to the poetic idiom of OE, to a language that expressed an unavoidable relationship to *Beowulf,* he cultivated ways of marking departures from the epic, or from the old heroic tradition that *Beowulf* best conveys for us. In this essay I shall expand on this possibility, and expand also, I hope, on a way of reading *Andreas* that I have previously described.[5]

One admits, first of all, that certain details found in both *Beowulf* and *Andreas* seem strained if not inappropriate in the later poem. The coinage of *meoduscerwen* [deprival of mead, 1526b] is a possible example of such strained usage though the case for admiring it is strong.[6] The northern connotations that cling to phrases like *heah ond horngeap* [high and horn-gabled, 668a] and *windige weallas* [windy cliffs, 843a] detract more noticeably from their usefulness to *Andreas*. Equally uncertain is the use of *landes ne locenra beaga* [of land nor of locks of rings] as a description of payment Andrew lacks:

> Næbbe ic fæted gold   ne feohgestreon,
> welan ne wiste,   ne wira gespann,
> landes ne locenra beaga,   þæt ic þe mæge lust ahwettan,
> willan in worulde,   swa ðu worde becwist.

> (301–04)

[I have no plated gold nor rich possessions, neither food nor goods nor twists of wire, of land nor of locked rings, that I may stir your desire for wants in the world as your words suggest.]

The genitive seems wrong in a context that is accusative otherwise. Schaar, whose discussion of parallels between these two poems is the

---

1968), pp. 97–114; and Thomas D. Hill, "Two Notes on Patristic Allusion in *Andreas,*" *Anglia,* 84 (1966), 156–62; "Figural Narrative in *Andreas,*" *NM,* 70 (1969), 261–73; and "The Tropological Context of Heat and Cold Imagery in Anglo-Saxon Poetry," *NM,* 69 (1968), 522–32. See also Kenneth R. Brooks in the introduction to his edition of *Andreas and the Fates of the Apostles* (Oxford, 1961) and Hans Schabram, "Andreas and Beowulf," *Nachrichten der Giessener Hochschulgesellschaft,* 34 (1965), 201–18.

4 Peters, p. 851.

5 "The diet and digestion of allegory in *Andreas,*" *Anglo-Saxon England,* 1 (1972), 147–58.

6 Lumiansky and Brodeur cited in notes 2 and 3 above provide the fullest discussions.

most thorough, finds it clumsy and suggests that it may be taken from *Beowulf* 2994ff., in which passage the genitive carries a fully partitive sense:[7]

> [he] sealde hiora gehwæðrum   hund þusenda
> landes ond locenra beaga.[8]

[(he) gave each of them a hundred thousandsworth of land and locked rings.]

An objective genitive is a common OE form, however, and need not have seemed strained to the original audience even when so singularly placed.[9] It may have derived from the genitive *wira* in the preceding half-line. Still, these passages suggest a poet who by his verbal echoes of *Beowulf*, shows that he tries to write in the heroic style, but sometimes muddles it.

A more obvious parallel is the proem which echoes *Beowulf, Juliana,* and several other poems as well. The introduction there of the apostles as retainers and warriors is both curious and inapposite, but it is harder to dismiss these lines as ineptly borrowed.[10] The word order in *Andreas* suggests a different conception of purpose. Whereas the *Beowulf* poet allows his proem to sift through widening historical and genealogical allusions, *Andreas* is aggressively straightforward; it pushes ahead and precisely narrows a heroic context until it focuses on Matthew whose imprisonment compels the main action. A verb appears in the first half-line and carries the alliteration: *Hwæt! We gefrunan on fyrndagum.* *Beowulf* tosses up a number of concrete images instead—Spear-Danes, kings, nobles, and Scyld Scefing—and underplays the verbs that regulate their interaction. *Beowulf* delays its verbs until the second staves of lines two and three and deemphasizes them by placing the alliteration on more substantive elements. The movement of *Beowulf* supports, if it did not elicit, Klaeber's observation that OE poetry tends to dwell on "the result of an action . . . on a state or situation when a straightforward

---

[7] Schaar, p. 278.

[8] All citations from *Beowulf* are from Klaeber's 3rd edition, but I have deleted his diacritical marks. Those from *Andreas* follow Krapp's edition of *The Vercelli Book, ASPR,* II (New York, 1932).

[9] I am indebted to the unpublished dissertation of Dennis E. Baron, "Case Grammar and Diachronic English Syntax," (Michigan, 1971), for a full discussion of this form.

[10] E. G. Stanley finds the proem of *Andreas* inept; see "Beowulf" in *Continuations and Beginnings,* ed. Stanley (London, 1966), pp. 112–13; Stanley Greenfield defends it, *A Critical History of Old English Literature* (New York, 1965), pp. 105–06; Schaar cites the passages without critical comment.

account of action would seem to be called for."[11] But *Andreas* behaves differently; it sets out to analyze a process and define a direct sequence of action. Its attention falls on the full process of predication, and its verbs are more prominent therefore.

The *Beowulf* poet has only to mention glory before shifting to its various manifestations. He seems confident of his audience's ability to attach Scyld Scefing to the heroic context that he suggests only briefly. Then, leaving the connections to us, he skims the high points of Danish history and interposes occasional authorial commentary. The *Andreas* poet's progress is more labored. He expands to ten and one-half lines the generalized heroic background that the *Beowulf* poet sketches in three. He prepares for his announcement that Matthew accepted the duty God assigned him by saying first that all the apostles assumed burdens. God showed them their duty, and they performed heroically. Matthew was one of those heroes, and God appointed him to go to that island *þær ænig þa git / ellþeodigra eðles ne mihte / blædes brucan* [where as yet no stranger could enjoy the pleasures of home, 15b–17a].

The *Andreas* poet seems self-consciously determined to define and pin down all that he mentions. Throughout the poem he amplifies the idea of the joylessness of Mermedonia, as in the proem he generalizes about the apostles' labors before specifying Matthew's burden. If *Beowulf's* style answers to the familiarity of his audience with his material, it may follow that the *Andreas* poet, writing after the appeal of heroic themes had faded and after Christ's direct influence, as the model Christian hero, on the world of poetic action, could not depend upon the same kind of traditional associations. He depends more upon himself therefore to develop his own subject completely and to enforce the progress of his poem. The presumed dependence and inferiority of *Andreas* might first be seen as a difference of intention and need; and the self-conscious control of the proem suggests that the *Andreas* poet works hard at putting the materials of *Beowulf* to new uses.

Other passages in which *Andreas* makes use of heroic motifs bear out this point, and more often than not the passages in *Andreas* are compelling in their own terms. The half line *eodon him þa togenes,* for example, occurs in both poems. The clause is colorless and might pass as a routine narrative statement. But the exact repetition indicates that its utility was consciously sought, and it suggests finite limits within which the poetic language operates.[12] It bears witness, that is, to an unavoid-

---

[11] Klaeber, p. lxvi.

[12] In his essay, "Towards a Generative View of the Oral Formula," Michael Nagler interestingly cites Chomsky as having said that every sentence he utters is original; repetition therefore may legitimately appear purposeful; *TAPA,* 98 (1967), 291 n. 40.

able relationship to *Beowulf* that would be limiting unless creative use were made of it.

> Eodon him þa togeanes,   Gode þancodon,
> ðryðlic þegna heap,   þeodnes gefegon,
> þæs þe hi hyne gesundne   geseon moston.

(Beow. 1626–28)

[Then they stepped toward him, gave thanks to God, the splendid troop of thanes rejoiced in their prince, that they themselves might see him sound.]

> Eodon him þa togenes,   garum gehyrsted,
> lungre under linde,   (nalas late wæron),
> eorre æscberend,   to þam orlege.

(Andr. 45–47)

[Then they stepped toward him armed with spears, quickly under their shields; not at all slow were the angry ash-bearers to the battle-play.]

In both passages the repeated half-line occupies an a-verse, alliterates on *g* and coordinates with a band of warriors separated from the protagonist. In *Beowulf* the opposition is friendly; Geatish retainers rush to welcome the hero as he emerges from Grendel's mere. In *Andreas,* it is angry; the Mermedonians attack their captive Matthew. Peters has already pointed out that words and phrases in *Andreas* that appear also in *Beowulf* are apt to occur in different contexts.[13] The contrast here of help to opposition bears out his point. But what is most important about these passages is that there is a system of compatibility between them that extends beyond the repeated half-line. In spite of the contrasting actions, the repeated half-line associates with a troop of armed men who are noticeably eager to meet or greet a hero.

In either passage the half-line that is exactly repeated may be said to interact with certain details of its context. Quirk speaks of this kind of relationship as collocation,[14] and though he describes principally the interaction of stressed words in phrases like *lungre under linde* in the passage from *Andreas* above, these relationships broaden, so that not only the phrasing alone, but the events and ideas at play seem to exhibit patterns of expectancy for each other. The formulaic and traditional properties of *Beowulf* enforce this kind of ordering and suggest that the

---

[13] Peters, pp. 849ff.
[14] "Poetic Language and Old English Metre," in *Early English and Norse Studies,* eds., Arthur Brown and Peter Foote (London, 1963), pp. 150–71.

poetic language of OE was a closed field, or gave the sense of being a closed field, wherein the probabilities of repetition were increased and were meaningful. In *Andreas,* moreover, as in this instance, collocations often invert the expectations that one infers from the evidence of *Beowulf.* One suspects then that the *Andreas* poet tries to create a different pattern of expectation and that he achieves this aim by deliberately thwarting traditional collocations. For *Andreas* these repetitions become more meaningful insofar as they reverse traditional patterns, and the strength of those patterns is perhaps underscored by the fact that Peters and Schaar both ignore the passage from *Andreas* quoted above and compare the lines from *Beowulf* to these lines instead:[15]

> Aras þa togenes, gode þancade
> þæs ðe hie onsunde æfre moston
> geseon under sunnan.

(*Andr.* 1011–13a)

[Then he arose to meet him, and thanked God that they might ever see each other in safety under the sun.]

These lines are far more congruent with the passage in *Beowulf.* Andrew and his companions greet Matthew whom they have just freed from prison. But this parallel is offered after, as we shall see, a number of divergences have been stressed.

There are several other instances of the kind of reversal that we have seen. Some are straightforward enough. When Andrew, for example, frees Matthew from prison, the phrasing resembles Grendel's entrance into Heorot:

> Duru sona onarn
> þurh handhrine haliges gastes,
> ond þær in eode, elnes gemyndig,
> hæle hildedeor.

(*Andr.* 999b–1002a)

[The door opened quickly at the hand's touch of the holy visitor, and the battlebold warrior, mindful of valor, strode inside.]

The *Andreas* poet reverses what we may think of as the received point of view. The language that expresses Grendel's attack conveys deliverance in this instance. Schaar suggests that it is one of the *Andreas* poet's

---

[15] Peters, p. 861; Schaar, p. 283.

better borrowings: the force of Grendel's hand, he says, is transmuted to Andrew making the sign of the cross.[16]

In a more complex example of apparent borrowing, *Andreas* accumulates references to several scattered passages in *Beowulf*.

> Ða wæs first agan   frumrædenne
> þinggemearces   butan þrim nihtum,
> swa hit wælwulfas   awriten hæfdon
> þæt hie banhringas   abrecan þohton,
> lungre tolysan   lic ond sawle,
> ond þonne todælan   duguðe ond geogoðe,
> werum to wiste   ond to wilþege,
> fæges flæschoman.   Feorh ne bemurndan,
> grædige guðrincas,   hu þæs gastes sið
> æfter swyltcwale   geseted wurde.

(Andr. 147–56)

[Then the period alotted was past, the marked interval, except for three nights as the slaughter-wolves had written down; after that they thought to break open the bone-rings, eagerly separate body and soul, and then apportion to old warriors and young, as food for men and as desired feasting, the flesh of the fated man. The greedy battle-warriors mourned not for his life, how the soul's journey would be destined after the agony of death.]

In corresponding passages in *Beowulf,* the hero attacks Grendel's dam:

>   [he] yrringa sloh,
> þæt hire wið halse   heard grapode,
> banhringas bræc;   bil eal ðurhwod
> fægne flæschoman.

(Beow. 1565b–58a)

[He struck savagely so that (the sword) grasped her neck fiercely, broke the bone-rings. The blade went through the fated flesh completely.]

Shortly afterwards, Beowulf's retainers help disarm him:

> Ða wæs of þæm hroran   helm ond byrne
> lungre alysed.

(Beow. 1629–30a)

[Then from the brave man helmet and corselet were eagerly loosened.]

---

16 Schaar, p. 283.

Much earlier, the *Beowulf* poet had also described Heorot as a place where Hrothgar

> . . . on innan   eall gedælan
> geongum ond ealdum,   swylc him God sealde
> butan folcscare   ond feorum gumena.[17]

(Beow. 71–73)

[inside divided everything to young men and old, all that God gave him, except the people's lands and the lives of men.]

The *duguðe ond geogoðe* occur, of course, as the paired recipients of favor throughout *Beowulf* (160, 621, and 1674).

The use of these passages in *Andreas* is in several ways remarkable. First, the poet combines phrasings scattered through *Beowulf,* and thereby suggests his awareness of their traditional nature rather than their specific use in a particular poem. On the other hand, he employs them differently with respect to *Beowulf,* and the difference inverts again the expectations that *Beowulf* establishes. It is the flesh of Grendel's dam that is fated and her bone-rings that break; whereas in *Andreas,* the Mermedonians threaten Matthew. In *Beowulf,* further, the other parallel phrases occur neutrally and casually; they indicate a friendly disarming of the hero and a beneficent sharing of Heorot's treasure. In *Andreas,* on the contrary, the Mermedonians move to divest Matthew of his body and soul, not his helmet and corselet, and they wish to share his flesh among themselves who are cannibals. The *Andreas* poet wrenches greater literal intensity from these phrases, and the effect is for casual description to become grotesquely significant.

A more extended pattern of collocations begins with these lines in which Andrew repeats Christ's command to the apostles:[18]

> Faraö nu geond ealle   eorðan sceatas
> emne swa wide   swa wæter bebugeð,
> oððe stedewangas   stræte gelicgaþ.
> Bodiaö æfter burgum   beorhtne geleafan
> ofer foldan fæðm.   Ic eow freoöo healde.
> Ne ðurfan ge on þa fore   frætwe lædan,
> gold ne seolfor.   Ic eow goda gehwæs
> on eowerne agenne dom   est ahwette.

(Andr. 332–39)

---

[17] Schaar notes these lines as parallel to the passage from *Andreas* last given, and that *Andreas* makes a "grotesque caricature" of them, p. 276.

[18] Schaar notes these passages also, but without comment, p. 279.

[Journey now through all quarters of the earth, even so widely as waters reach flowing, or as fields lie along the roadways. Proclaim the shining faith among villages over the earth's expanse; I shall safeguard you. Nor need you carry jewels on that journey, gold nor silver; but I shall give plenty of all things to you as you desire.]

Wealhtheow praises Beowulf in similar language:

> Hafast þu gefered,   þæt ðe feor ond neah
> ealne wideferhþ   weras ehtigað,
> efne swa side   swa sæ bebugeð,
> windgeard, weallas.   Wes þenden þu lifige,
> æþeling, eadig!   Ic þe an tela
> sincgestreona.
>
> (*Beow.* 1221–26a)

[You have fared so that far and near men will esteem your valor forever, even as widely as the seas surround the cliffs, the wind-houses. Be blessed, O hero, while you live. I grant rich treasure to you.]

The most parallel lines in these passages contrast sharply. Wealhtheow comments on Beowulf's spreading fame. Andrew defines his mission which is to spread the fame of Christ. These lines collocate in both instances with a more extended description of the earth, of the habitations of men, and with the idea of treasure. And again the usages contrast. Wealhtheow hopes that Beowulf will receive rich treasure; Andrew repeats Christ's assurance that the apostles will not require worldly wealth. Wealhtheow speaks unambiguously. Her praise of Beowulf leads to a simple request that he look after her son. The import of Andrew's lines is made clear less quickly. Andrew is unaware that he speaks to Christ. We read his words ironically, and the irony invites a delayed response. The irony extends the impact of the speech, for the injunction against treasure that Andrew expresses serves finally as sufficient treasure in itself. Andrew's echo of the treasure Beowulf might expect, converted here to a denial of any such need, does more than justify Christ's acceptance of him aboard ship. It reflects also on another passage that obviously echoes *Beowulf,* that associates Andrew with great treasure, and that vexes readers who have not learned to take the treasure metaphorically, as a quality of spirit, rather than literally as a hoard:[19]

> Gesæt him þa se halga   holmwearde neah,
> æðele be æðelum;   æfre ic ne hyrde

---

[19] Brodeur in "A Study," p. 98, feels that the *Andreas* poet had *Beowulf* well "in mind" at this point; Brooks goes further and finds the parallel a bit absurd, p. xxiv.

þon cymlicor   ceol gehladenne
heahgestreonum.   Hæleð in sæton,
þeodnas þrymfulle,   þegnas wlitige.

(Andr. 359–63)

[Then the saint sat down near the helmsman, nobleman by nobleman. Never have I heard of a more splendid ship laden with fine treasure. The heroes sat in it, the peerless princes, the bright thanes.]

The metaphorical burden of the treasure-laden ship in the passage just quoted is one of the more striking reversals of traditional expectations that *Andreas* affords, and it attaches to a pattern of dramatic irony that is important to the thematic development of *Andreas*.[20] Another reversal that depends less on our ironic view of the incident and that also draws together a number of related moments in both poems may be approached from the passage in which the Mermedonians prepare to eat a young boy. Andrew, who is invisible for the moment, observes the preparations:

Ða þæt Andrea   earmlic þuhte,
þeodbealo þearlic   to geðolianne,
þæt he swa unscyldig   ealdre sceolde
lungre linnan.

(Andr. 1135–38a)

[Then Andrew thought that pitiable, a cruel public punishment to endure, that one so guiltless should suddenly yield his life.]

The thoughts imputed to Andrew reflect Beowulf's hypothetical talk about being killed by Grendel's mother: *Geþenc nu,* he says to Hrothgar, *gif ic æt þearfe þinre scolde / aldre linnan* [Think now . . . if I, at your need, should yield my life, 1474–78a]. In each case the premonitions centering on the verb *linnan* collocate with the verbs *ðencan* [to think] and *ðyncan* [impersonal, to seem to] which are themselves closely related. Each passage also leads to a miraculous event. God answers Andrew's concern by commanding that the *wæpen wera wexe gelicost / on þam orlege eall formeltan* [The men's weapons were made like wax; they all melted in the strife, 1145–46]. And in the fight that follows Beowulf's speech another sword dwindles until *hit eal gemealt ise gelicost* [it all melted like ice, 1608].

[20] See n. 5 above.

90

Andreas continues then by relating the reaction of the Mermedonians:

> Þa wæs wop hæfen   in wera burgum,
> hlud heriges cyrm.   Hreopon friccan,
> mændon meteleaste,   meðe stodon,
> hungre gehæfte.

(Andr. 1155–58a)

[Then a cry arose in the city of men, a loud clamor of the host. Heralds shouted, lamented the famine; they stood listless, snared by hunger.]

These lines recall a passage that comes early in *Beowulf* on the morning when Grendel's *guðcræft* [war-strength] is first known clearly at Heorot:

> Þa wæs æfter wiste   wop up ahafen,
> micel morgensweg.   Mære þeoden,
> æþeling ærgod,   unbliðe sæt.

(Beow. 128–30)

[Then after feasting a cry rose up, a great shout in the morning. The famous chief, the long-honored prince, unhappily sat.]

The parallel is complex. It begins in both passages with *wop* and continues with a variation on that word in each of the next a-verses: a loud or great cry of the host in *Andreas,* a loud or great cry in the morning in *Beowulf.* It extends then to a more general expression of sorrow in the next few half-lines of each poem. In *Andreas,* as we might expect by now, the sorrow has a more grotesque character; its terms are "meatlessness" and "hunger." In *Beowulf* the alternation of joy with sorrow is a central motif; the collocation of *wop* with *wiste* extends the pattern of *swefan æfter symble* upon which the epic depends. In *Andreas, wop* collocates also with the idea of *wiste;* the meatless Mermedonians starve. But the collocation is reversed and applied to the cannibals rather than to the Danes. This whole theme, gradually and explicitly developed in *Andreas,* seems to play off Grendel's cannibalism, and it connects at least tangentially with the figure of the melting sword that occurs in both narratives. From the evidence gathered here, it is impossible to determine the extent to which the connection of so many passages is consciously designed. It seems clear though that their assemblage is not gratuitous and that in some sense these motifs attract each other.

Many of the parallels observed so far may stem from traditional poetic diction and need not indicate close knowledge of *Beowulf* specifically.

Beowulf, however, is where we find them. It seems most probable, further, that the literal description of a treasure-laden ship in *Beowulf* would precede its metaphorical use in *Andreas,* and, similarly, that the routine unbinding of *helm* and *byrne* from Beowulf should be the precedent for the attempt upon Matthew's body and soul. The more strained sense of some of the other passages in *Andreas* supports these assumptions.

We can observe also that these passages cause no problematic reverberations in *Beowulf.* One reads them literally and appreciates certain internal symmetries—the burial at the beginning and end of that poem for example—and rhythms such as are implied by the phrase *swefan æfter symble* [to sleep after feasting]. Insofar as these expressions require substantiation from outside the poem, we appeal to the record of contemporary customs such as we understand them and to literary tradition. We read the ship burial as a literary handling of factual report and understand it as something that enters the poem naturally from the life that surrounds and antedates *Beowulf* precisely because it is the job of *Beowulf* to depict that life. It may be a heightened report, but we find it true to life in the main.

Andreas affords fewer footholds of this kind. Its audience must be led to consider a different kind of treasure and to understand treasure metaphorically. The terms of this change arise from within the poem; by and large they exclude or diminish reference to the natural world. This difference is most clearly illustrated by the role of patristic learning in *Andreas.*

In his longest speech to Christ, Andrew describes the venom that rises in the breast of an antagonistic priest:

> Man wridode
> geond beorna breost, brandhata nið
> weoll on gewitte, weorm blædum fag,
> attor ælfæle.
>
> *(Andr.* 767b–70a)

[Sin flourished in the breast of the man, boiling hatred surged in the mind, a worm stained with success, with dire venom.]

Wiglaf observes similarly that

> symle wæs þy sæmra, þonne ic sweorde drep
> ferhðgeniðlan, fyr unswiðor
> weoll of gewitte.
>
> *(Beow.* 2880–82a)

92

[He grew ever weaker when I struck the deadly enemy with the sword; fire less fierce surged from his head.]

The word *weorm* in the first passage recalls also the dragon in *Beowulf,* and Schaar extends the parallel to this passage:

> he þæt sona onfand,
> þæt him on breostum   bealoniðe weoll
> attor on innan.

(Beow. 2713b–15a)

[Then he found immediately that the baleful venom surged in his breast, the poison within him.]

    Hill attributes these passages to the patristic image of the *draco militæ* that surges in the minds of the wicked.[21] In *Andreas* this image defines the perverse rage of the Jewish elders when they confront Christ, and it may indicate similarly the internal struggle that animates Beowulf's last combat.[22] This allegorical reading is possible in either poem, but *Andreas* requires it. Schaar, who assumes that a literal reading is to be preferred, finds that the descriptive image is "more suitable" for the dragon's bite than for describing the attitude of Christ's enemies.[23] Schaar's point is apt. We can visualize the flames that rush from the dragon and fester in Beowulf's breast. The change of preposition (*weoll on gewitte* in *Andr., weoll of gewitte* in *Beow.*) stresses the literal sense of *Beowulf.* The dragon as conveyed in *Beowulf* is a sufficient image and requires no explication in patristic or other terms. In *Andreas,* on the contrary, the metaphorical rendering of the *draco militæ* makes sense of a passage that we could not well imagine otherwise. This patristic usage, moreover, corresponds to the poet's imaginative alteration of other traditional terms that he uses. The imagery of *Beowulf* always embodies a sensible, literal factor that corresponds to the natural world either as we know it from direct experience, or as we imagine it in a specific historical context or in the heightened world of adventure stories. That fidelity to literal fact remains intact in *Beowulf,* even as we read it allegorically. *Andreas,* on the other hand, consistently violates the literal narrative for its metaphorical sense.

    This distinction indicates a separation of genres and also of styles. The

---

21 "Two Notes," pp. 156ff.
22 Hill cites Kaske's *"Sapientia et Fortitudo* as the Controlling Theme of *Beowulf," SP,* 55 (1958), 445–55.
23 Schaar, p. 282.

evidence gathered so far supports the usual view that *Beowulf* represents a prevailing style that was prior to *Andreas*. Its style expresses an easy relationship with the world around it: it assumes the audience's familiarity with that world but requires no esoteric knowledge in order to be understood. It is apparently prior to *Andreas* because when usages overlap, the passages in *Andreas* read as specialized interpretations of events that *Beowulf* conveys more naturally. We add only that *Andreas* takes particular pains to mark itself off from that prevailing style.

For one last example of the *Andreas* poet's control over his poem, let us return to a sequence of events in the early action of *Andreas* that illustrates most of the characteristics that we have described: *Andreas's* extended analysis of a situation, its reversal of expectations, its development of metaphorical and ironic understanding that verges, when literally taken, on the grotesque. This sequence is of further interest because the beach scene from which it begins is one of the best attested traditional passages in OE literature, and the poet's handling of this kind of scene, one that has been entitled "the hero on the beach,"[24] places the ensuing action in a traditional context by recalling poems such as *Beowulf* for us. It is striking, therefore, that, as in other instances, the poet should rearrange this scene decisively.

Andrew's arrival on the beach in the company of his thanes, at the beginning of a journey, and with a bright light flashing (241ff.) designates the traditional context from which he hails the sailors and initiates a dialogue that leads eventually to his voyage. As Andrew calls to the pilot, his words parallel the challenges the coastguard and Wulfgar put to Beowulf. This entire sequence of testing is comparable to the pattern of testing that precedes Beowulf's arrival at Heorot. *Andreas,* however, devotes almost twice as many lines to this sequence in a poem that is roughly half as long. *Andreas's* extension of the sequence is another indication of its greater tendency to protract and exhaust the development of a given theme.

As Andrew approaches the seamen, he calls to them:

> Hwanon comon ge   ceolum liðan,
> macræftige menn,   on mereþissan,
> ane ægflotan?   Hwanon eagorstream
> ofer yða gewealc   eowic brohte?

(Andr. 256–59)

---

[24] See David K. Crowne, "The Hero on the Beach: an Example of Composition by Theme in Anglo-Saxon Poetry," *NM*, 61 (1960), 362–72; Donald K. Fry, "The Hero on the Beach in 'Finnsburh'," *NM*, 67 (1966), 27–31; and "The Heroine on the Beach in 'Judith'," *NM*, 68 (1967), 168–84.

[Whence have you come, journeying by ship, you skillful men in the vessel, sailors alone? Whence has the ocean-stream over the waves' surge brought you?]

This challenge differs from its form in *Beowulf*. Andrew issues the challenge as the protagonist rather than answering to it. He addresses Christ, to be sure, and thus speaks from the inferior position, but the fact that the protagonist can be placed in such a position and held there for several hundred lines—until after he arrives in Mermedonia—is a significant development of the experience of heroes like Beowulf.

Schaar finds the passage in error for a different reason. He finds Andrew's question incomprehensible and wonders why Andrew does not ask *Hwider willað ge of waroðe liðan?* [Whither will you journey from this shore?] or as the OE prose version puts it, *Broðor, hwider wille ge faran mid þis medmiclum scipe?* [Brother, whither will you go with your medium-sized boat?].[25] We should remember, however, that God has just assured Andrew (205ff.) that it is within His power to find passage for Andrew to distant Mermedonia, and that Andrew should go to the beach on the next day. Andrew can assume that the ship will be going his way, and by asking the question in the way he does, he allows the Pilot to stress, on the basis of his experience, the dangers that lie ahead. Here again, *Andreas*'s single-minded focus on a particular aspect of the situation is typical of its narrative style.[26]

In some ways, this testing of the hero carries increased complexity in *Andreas*. Andrew's inferior position opens into an ironic design that is foreign to *Beowulf*. Irony is a narrative technique that *Beowulf* does not explore, not in this fashion at least, because it does not suit the needs of that poem, and because the epic does not stem from a Christian point of view that holds worldly matters at bay. But the demands of irony influence *Andreas* greatly. In *Andreas,* the hero grows in awareness as his testing progresses, and he becomes by stages a wiser and holier man. Christ changes too. At first he appears as a heavenly voice, God the Father, who commands Andrew's departure. Throughout the greater part of the poem, he is a pilot whom Andrew perceives as a young and unusually wise man. At the end of the voyage, he appears as a child (910ff.), in which form Andrew recognizes him at last. All these factors, the irony, the dual character development, and the process of recognition modulating with the development of both characters, are original

25 Schaar, p. 277. I have quoted the prose version from *Bright's Anglo-Saxon Reader*, revised by James R. Hulbert (New York, 1963), p. 116.
26 See likewise the unpublished dissertation of Milton Riemer, "The OE Andreas: A Study of the Poet's Response to his Source" (Texas, 1965), p. 179.

to *Andreas*. Assuming then that *Beowulf* adheres more closely to a traditional narrative form, *Andreas* departs from that tradition. *Andreas* takes significant liberties with an old story; the poet, however, matches his adventuresomeness on some fronts with restraint in other matters.

The speech last quoted, for example, is both shorter than comparable speeches in *Beowulf* and more selective about the interests it expresses. In four lines, Andrew mentions the sea, ships, or sailors five times. He phrases essentially the same question twice, and he refers only to the skill of the sailors, not to their valor or might. Insofar as this speech characterizes Andrew, it limits his interest to a single aspect of the situation he confronts. He speaks only as a prelude to travel. The isolation of this single interest is an aspect of the narrowing focus and forced progress that, from the opening of the proem, typify *Andreas*'s style.

This extended dialogue contains five exchanges before Andrew gains passage and the first stage of his testing ends. Being unbroken by narrative action and adhering closely to the narrow issue of getting to Mermedonia, it is more continuous than comparable portions of *Beowulf*. Irony is one device that enforces the continuity. Throughout this dialogue and throughout the voyage also, the hero addresses the pilot as if the latter were simply a fine sailor. The audience knows from the first and receives continuous reminders that the pilot is Christ in disguise. Each time the pilot speaks, the poet reminds us that we are listening to *ælmihti God* [almighty God, 260b], the *engla scippend* [guardian of angels, 278b], the *engla þeoden* [prince of angels, 290b,] the *beorna brego* [protector of men, 305a], and the *ece dryhten* [eternal lord, 343b]. Consequently the audience, the poet, and the pilot share a superior level of awareness, and Andrew's success depends upon his attaining our point of view. When Andrew discovers the truth, the dramatic irony collapses and Christ disappears.

In *Beowulf*, the poet carefully identifies his speakers also, but as *weard Scildinga* [guardian of the Scyldings, 229b] when it is the shore-guard, or *helm Scyldinga* [leader of the Scyldings, 371b] in the case of Hrothgar. The first time Wulfgar speaks, we know him only as an important warrior (331–32), then a few lines later the narrator adds that among the Wendels *wæs his modsefa manegum gecyðed, / wig ond wisdom* [his character was known to many men, his valor and wisdom, 349–50a]. Similarly, the poem introduces Unferth as *Ecglafes bearn* [Ecglaf's son, 499b], and Wealhtheow as *cwen Hroðgares* [Hrothgar's queen, 613a] and *ides Helminga,* [lady of the Helmings, 620b]. The *Andreas* poet partially follows traditional form in that he supplies speakers with epithets, but by making his identifications theological rather than genealogical he alters the received tradition. Each time the *Beowulf* poet identifies a speaker in geographical, historical, or genealogical terms, he ties another loose end onto the narrative and invites the kind of digression we associate with Swift, Stern, Burton, or Montaigne. Whenever he fulfills that opportunity, even briefly, as with the few cryptic remarks directed at Unferth's past, he turns from the main action into a narrative pattern that is associative and discontinuous. At these points the fictional impulse of *Beowulf* tends to be encyclopedic, and, as Tolkein did not quite put it, the poet invites us to attend to the periphery of his poem. *Beowulf* spreads out on a horizontal plain; the poet knows every point on the plain and digresses freely.[27] His inclination is to be all-inclusive and thus the poem acquires a kind of disintegrating, centrifugal force. The *Andreas* poet, on the contrary, reinforces our attention to the main action by repeating so frequently the central dramatic fact: Andrew converses with Christ. Perhaps it scarcely requires adding that the ease by which we grant Unferth a father when contrasted to our difficulty in imagining the conversation aboard Christ's ship correlates with the epic's casual attraction of related matter on the one hand and the reiteration and development of a few central issues on the other. Since we are at ease with knowing that men have fathers, we find the movement from Unferth to his father unforced. But since men rarely converse with Christ, that event must be imposed upon us, and it helps to have all potential distractions, even genealogical tags, stripped away.

At every opportunity, the *Andreas* poet intensifies the selectivity of his narrative and, as with the tags identifying Christ, emphasizes the few ideas he handles. The speeches in these first five exchanges are short with a single exception—when Andrew in the last of them accuses Christ of pride, the situation is pushed to its grotesque extreme—and each speech deals directly and exclusively with the main issue. The sequence begins with Andrew's hailing the sailors and asking whence they have come. Their reply is equally restrictive. We have come from afar, from Mermedonia, the pilot says, on a high-prowed ship over the sea to the land. Andrew replies,

> Wolde ic þe biddan,   þeh ic þe beaga lyt,
> sincweorðunga,   syllan meahte,
> þæt ðu us gebrohte   brante ceole,
> hea hornscipe,   ofer hwæles eðel
> on þære mægðe.   Bið ðe meorð wið god,
> þæt ðu us on lade   liðe weorðe.

> *(Andr. 271–76)*

[27] I am in debt to Joan Blomfield's essay, "The Style and Structure of *Beowulf*," *RES,* 14 (1938), pp. 396–403, for my descriptive terms at this point.

[I would ask you, though I have few rings, few worthy treasures that I might give you, that you convey us in the lofty ship, the high-prowed vessel, over the whales' home to that people. Your reward will be with God if you are kind to us on the voyage.]

By suggesting that the pilot's reward will be with God, Andrew intensifies the irony and his admission that he has no treasure introduces the issue upon which the next few passages center.

But with this passage we return to the metaphorical identification of the hero's nature with his treasure, to patterns of irony and metaphorical imagery touched on already in this essay and better developed in another.[28] The lines quoted earlier, however, offer a rich image of the situation we discuss. For when Andrew, *se halga,* takes his place beside the *holmwearde, æðele be æðelum,* he takes his place not beside Christ only but beside Beowulf too who was a worthy sea-leader in his time: Andrew takes his place beside both heroes yet acquires his own distinctive characteristics, and when so much has been assembled for us, we may well say with the narrator of *Andreas*—

                              æfre ic ne hyrde
        þon cymlicor   ceol gehladenne
        heahgestreonum.

---

28 See n. 5 above.

8

Arithmetical Design of the Old English *Andreas*

ROBERT D. STEVICK

IN THIS ESSAY I PROPOSE A SCHEMA FOR THE COMPOSITIONAL DESIGN of *Andreas* to represent an arithmetically computed plan for the length of the principal sections (or fitts) as well as the length of the complete poem. If this schema should be accepted as representing the poet's plan for the larger quantitative features of the verse narrative, then *Andreas* will be a second lengthy poem in Old English recognized to have an arithmetically based structure. The other one is *Beowulf.* To propose this schema is to answer (tentatively) one set of questions about *Andreas,* those concerning the rationale of the manuscript's sectional divisions and the line-count of the text from which the Vercelli Book copy ultimately derives. It also adds (tentatively) a very important datum to Anglo-Saxon literary history, namely, the further use—after *Beowulf*—of an arithmetical structuring principle for extended verse narrative in Old English. *Andreas,* then, may have a place in a putative tradition in Anglo-Saxon literary art, as well as a place in a larger tradition of compositional design that embraces such other works as the *Heliand* and *Pearl.*

This schema, on the other hand, raises a number and variety of questions whose answers are not implicit in it and to which answers may be difficult to find. Some of the questions will be briefly examined in the last section of this essay in the hope that they may encourage continued study of the poem and the numerical design for the *dispositio* of the text.

To mention *Andreas* and *Beowulf* together and to associate them with a particular mode of poetic structuring will immediately raise for many readers anticipation that "influence" of one poem upon the writer of the other may be a topic to which this study will tend: debate over the relation of the two poems has a very long history.[1] The topic of relationship will be noticed briefly but with no assertion that *Beowulf* influenced the composition of *Andreas*. That *Andreas* may be, after *Beowulf*, another early English poem exhibiting a numerically controlled structural principle is no more than a statement about a pair of discoveries—that both poems utilize a particular kind of structure and that that structure was discovered first in *Beowulf*.

Without the example of tectonic analysis provided by Thomas E. Hart[2] for the major surviving Old English poetic composition, *Beowulf*, analysis of this kind would never have been likely to be undertaken for a long poem of secondary concern. For not only is *Andreas*—like about every other Old English poem—of lesser literary interest than *Beowulf*, but the extant text of *Andreas* is incomplete, with both small lacunae and one folio missing. The model set by Hart will be especially important to the present analysis in two ways. First, he has established securely the fact of controlled quantitative extension of poetic text as a structuring device known and utilized (with amazing skill) in Anglo-Saxon England;[3] hence he has provided heuristics for a new kind of structural analysis for *Andreas*. Second, he has explicated the logical foundations and artistic implications of tectonic design. These have to do

---

[1] Leonard J. Peters, in "The Relationship of the Old English *Andreas* to *Beowulf*," *PMLA*, 66 (1951), 844–63, after reviewing earlier claims of "influence," argues that some verbal parallels "can scarcely be called meaningful influence"; but he concedes that "one cannot establish that the Old English hagiographer was in no sense indebted to the secular epic" (p. 863). In *Andreas and The Fates of the Apostles* (Oxford, 1961), Kenneth R. Brooks reverses the concession and opinion of Peters, saying that "such a close resemblance" of certain passages in the two poems makes "the theory of conscious imitation . . . hard to deny, especially when an expression that is appropriate in *Beowulf* appears in an incongruous context in *Andreas*" (p. xxiv).

[2] The initial study was presented in "*Beowulf*: A Study of the Tectonic Structures and Patterns," Ph.D. dissertation, University of Wisconsin (Madison), 1966; cf. *DA*, 28 (1967), 631-A. See further "A Tectonic Consideration of the *Eotenas* in *Beowulf*," *Thoth*, 10 (1969), 4–17; "*Ellen*: Some Tectonic Relationships in *Beowulf* and their Formal Resemblances to Anglo-Saxon Art," *PLL*, 6 (1970), 263–90; and especially "Tectonic Design, Formulaic Craft, and Literary Execution; the Episodes of Finn and Ingeld in 'Beowulf,'" *Amsterdamer Beiträge zur älteren Germanistik*, 2 (1972), 1–61.

[3] The assessment of Hart's analysis, by W. F. Bolton, in his revised third edition of C. L. Wrenn, *Beowulf, with the Finnsburg Fragment* (New York, 1973), is a just one.

with numerical individuality of the line as a basis for establishing numerical proportions between loci of recurring elements (chiefly words, formulas, and themes), so that parallels, oppositions, and ultimately unity can be created from them by a poet; and if we understand his devices and standards, we can trace and verify them in a non-subjective way. The extensiveness and functions of such design features in *Beowulf* point to the likelihood of their recurring in poetry of Anglo-Saxon England.

I

The only known copy of the poem now called *Andreas* makes up a portion of the Vercelli Book, and that copy is imperfect. To develop the latent design of the poem we must therefore rely on the authority of the single manuscript where it has all the signs of being good copy, and reconstruct at least the quantitative features of the text where physical aspects of the manuscript or discontinuity in the meter or the sense show that some portions of the text have been lost. In practical terms, we need take only one step beyond the conclusions regarding the text established by (or incorporated in) the most recent editions. The most thorough and reliable edition is in Kenneth R. Brooks's *Andreas and The Fates of the Apostles*;[4] while in most ways it supersedes the edition in George Philip Krapp's *The Vercelli Book*,[5] Krapp's edition provides a much fuller description of the manuscript. Needless to say, no step beyond these editions should be attempted without reference to the facsimile edition, in *Il Codice Vercellese*, by M. Foerster.[6]

Both Brooks and Krapp (as well as Foerster) count 1722 verse-lines. Their count includes lines metrically incomplete, as at 1036 *swylce feowertig . . .*, 1040 *anes wana þa fiftig . . .*, 1434 *Me is miht ofer eall . . .*, where preceding and following verse-lines are intact; the count also includes, of course, lines requiring emendation to supply the key alliterating word, as at 1562 and 1571. They differ in two instances. Brooks divides the sequence of words at 1090 to indicate two defective verse-lines, which (to maintain conventional line-count) he numbers 1090a and 1090b. The sequence of words standing between 1089 and 1091 lacks alliteration, which Krapp makes good by supplying one word (*deade*). There is no indication in the manuscript that any word(s) may be missing, and there is no break in sense. The other difference is at 1667–68, where Krapp divides the words to indicate two defective lines but Brooks supplies *me* as an alliterating word for the second half-line, thus collapsing the conventionally numbered pair of lines into one, des-

4 See note 1, above.
5 Volume II of *ASPR*, New York, 1932.
6 Rome, 1913.

ignated as 1667–68. Both editors indicate that, from comparison with parallel prose versions of the narrative, it is clear that little has been omitted. The manuscript copy is continuous.

The count of verse-lines, by convention, does not include full lines supplied by editors to fill in obvious lacunae. At three places in the text omission of one or more verse-lines has been determined, and for two of them conjectural lines have been constructed. One is following line 828; both editors agree that little has been lost, printing a line of asterisks or dots not included in the numbering of lines. Another is following line 1663, where more than one verse-line seem to have been dropped out, represented in both editions by a line of asterisks or dots. (Reconstruction of the missing lines is given by Brooks in both instances in his "Commentary," in the first instance by Krapp in his "Notes.") At neither place in the manuscript is the copy discontinuous or illegible. The third gap in the text occurs between the incomplete verses numbered 1024 and 1025: loss of text here results from one folio having been excised. Physical evidence of the manuscript indicates the loss, and the length of narrative that is missing—calculated from lengths of corresponding passages in other versions of the Acts of Matthew and Andrew in the City of the Cannibals—corresponds to the approximate number of lines to be expected on recto and verso of the missing leaf.[7]

The beginning and ending of *Andreas* seem to be fully established. Following after a series of prose homilies, the text begins stylistically, metrically, and grammatically as the commencing of a separate, metrical work. The text follows closely a well-attested narrative throughout. And it concludes where the narrative ends, again with stylistic, metrical, and grammatical signs of being complete.[8]

In short, the Vercelli manuscript preserves a completed poem in a copy that is for the most part "good" and whose omissions can be detected with a high degree of confidence. Prose versions of the same narrative in Greek, Latin, and Old English enable comparisons that make possible a close calculation of the quantity of verse omitted in the extant copy. In reconstructing the quantitative measure of the lost text, we have to reckon, then, with two short lacunae, a missing folio, and two points at which defective alliteration may or may not reflect loss of two (or more) half-lines.

It is in order to mention at this point a recurring set of graphic features

---

[7] In Milton Henry Riemer, *The Old English Andreas: A Study of the Poet's Response to His Source,* Ph. D. Dissertation, University of Texas, 1965, the narrative material of the prose versions is summarized on p. 46 and an additional summary is given on p. 245, with a note that parallel text in *Recensio Casanatensis* constitutes thirty printed lines.

[8] See Brooks, pp. xix–xx.

of the manuscript, readily apparent in the facsimile, quite obscured in Brooks's edition, though generally noted by Krapp. Prominent capitalization occurs fifteen times. In all but one instance the first letter of a line exceeds in height the measure of two lines of normal writing and the other letters of the initial word (or syllable of *Ge-wat* 1058 or words *We ðe* 1352) are smaller capitals. The exception is at the beginning of line 1253, where a large capital *S* has been erased and a small capital *a* remains; emendation restores *Þa* as the initial word. In all fifteen instances there is a blank line separating the line with initial capitalization from the preceding line of text, unless capitalization occurs at the head of the page (as at lines 1 and 950). In addition, punctuation more elaborate than a single point follows the end of the line of writing preceding capitalization. The recurrent combination of "initial capitals, terminal pointing, and intercapitular space"[9] marks segmentation of the copy representing "sectional divisions" in the text, or "fitt divisions" of the poem. The sections, or fitts, are not numbered in *Andreas,* although they are (incompletely) numbered in *Elene* in the same manuscript, just as they are in *Beowulf.*

II

The sectional divisions are recorded by Krapp in Table II of the Introduction to *The Vercelli Book* in terms of the line numbers in his edition of the poem. They are given here with addition of the number of lines in each section (in parentheses) and an asterisk marking sections with unquestioned lacunae:

I.	1–121	(121)
II.	122–229	(108)
III.	230–351	(122)
IV.	352–468	(117)
V.	469–600	(132)
VI.	601–695	(95)
VII.	696–821	(126)
VIII.	822–949*	(128)
IX.	950–1057*	(108)
X.	1058–1154	(97)
XI.	1155–1252	(98)
XII.	1253–1351	(99)
XIII.	1352–1477	(126)
XIV.	1478–1606	(129)
XV.	1607–1722*	(116)

[9] Rudolph Willard, review of Brook's *Andreas and The Fates of the Apostles,* *MP,* 62 (1964), 46.

Fitts I–VII (lines 1–821) and fitts X–XIV (1058–1606) are the two series of fitts in which the text appears to be complete, and it is therefore in these sets of sections that numerical patterning should be examined first. Among the line-sums of two or more successive fitts the first of any complexity to appear is that of fitts I–III, comprising 351 lines, divisible by 3, 9, 13, . . . 117. With the succeeding fitt, comprising 117 lines, the line-sum of fitts I–IV is 468; this is divisible by 2, 3, 4, 6, 9, 12, 13, . . . 117, 234. The constant multipliers, or moduli, common to these sets are 3, 9, 13, . . . 117. Both the first and the last of these can be disregarded as uninteresting, since 3 is too small to operate significantly in a poem of this length and 117 is too large for the poem, besides being a unique line-sum for a fitt and being operative only in the first four fitts of the poem. The one modulus found elsewhere is 13. It is a factor of 221 (= 13 × 17), the number of verse-lines in fitts VI–VII, and also of 195 (= 13 × 15), the sum of lines in fitts X–XI. It does not operate in other single fitts or fitt groups.

Fitts I–V comprise 600 lines, the moduli of which are many:

$$
\begin{array}{ll}
2 \times 300 = 600 & 6 \times 100 = 600 \\
3 \times 200 = 600 & 10 \times \ 60 = 600 \\
4 \times 150 = 600 & 12 \times \ 50 = 600 \\
5 \times 120 = 600 & 15 \times \ 40 = 600 \text{ etc.}
\end{array}
$$

Again, some of these can be discarded as uninteresting because of their extreme size—large or small—and their non-recurrence elsewhere. It is 12 and 15 that recur in other parts of "good" text. The line-sum of fitts X–XI is 195 (= 15 × 13), as noted above; the line-sum of fitts XII–XIII is 225 (= 15 × 15). Combined, then, fitts X–XIII, with 420 verse-lines, will have the same modulus (15 × 28). The same four fitts also have the same modulus 12: 420 = 12 × 35. In an additional pair of fitts, XIII–XIV, the sum 255 contains again the modulus 15: 255 = 15 × 17.

The principal moduli of "good" text, then, are 12, 13, 15, and they are displayed in Figure 1.

In moving now to those parts of the text in which independent editorial considerations indicate loss of one or more verse-lines, simple arithmetical analysis must be supplemented by controlled conjecture: the task, so to speak, is one of counting verse-lines that are lost, at the same time analyzing line-sums of fitts and fitt-groups for recurrence of moduli found to be present in the complete sectional divisions of the poem. Inevitably there will be some circularity of argument, but at each turn the independent textual evidence will provide rather tight controls for the reconstruction and the inferences about tectonic structure.

I	II	III	IV	V	VI	VII	VIII	IX	X	XI	XII	XIII	XIV	XV
121	108	122	117	132	95	126	128*	108*	97	98	99	126	129	116*
121	229	351	468	600	695	821	949	1057	1154	1252	1351	1477	1606	1722

3(13 x 9) = 351

13 x 9 = 117

4(13 x 9) = 468
13 x 36 = 468
etc.

15 x 40 = 600
4 x 150 = 600
5 x 120 = 600
etc.

13 x 17 = 221

13 x 15 = 195

15 x 17 = 255

15 x 13 = 195

15 x 15 = 225

15 x 28 = 420
4(15 x 7) = 420
15 x 35 = 420
etc.

Figure 1

105

After line 828, as noted earlier, at least one full verse-line has been dropped. Krapp's note on the passage observes that "nothing of importance has been lost," gauging apparently by narrative continuity; Brooks's commentary on the passage is that "the loss of a single verse may perhaps be assumed" at this point. Now, if one additional verse-line is counted to fill the lacuna, fitt VIII would have 129 lines. The pair of fitts VII–VIII then would have a line-sum of 255 ($= 15 \times 17$), exactly matching the pair XIII–XIV. It brings the total for fitts I–VIII to 950 lines. Counting 129 lines in fitt VIII does not, though, reveal any other moduli of 12, 13, or 15 in the first eight sections of the poem. Also it misses only by 1 generating a second fitt group with a total of 600 verse-lines: fitts IV–VIII now have a total of 599 verse-lines. On the other hand, if two verse-lines are missing after 828, the original text would have a second large segment of 600 verse-lines ($= 5 \times 120$, 15×40, etc.), but not a second segment of 255 ($= 15 \times 17$). Neither alternative of positing one line or two is precluded by the context or by comparison of *Andreas* with other versions of the story; probability of more missing lines drops sharply for three or more. Other considerations, to be taken up later, will have to help settle whether one line or two should be counted here.

In the final fitt (XV, by the surviving sectional divisions), the loss between lines 1663 and 1664 seems to be slightly larger. The clause ending line 1663 introduces a speech (. . . *ond þæt word gecwæð weoruda dryhten*) [and he (God), Lord of hosts, spoke the speech (that follows)], and a sentence of the speech terminates with the first half-line of 1664. Brooks's commentary includes quotation of parallel prose versions and concludes that "a lacuna of some three or four verse-lines is probable here." For reconstructing the original line-sum for the final fitt there is also the problem of whether 1667–68 constitute two verse-lines or one. No clear solution to the problem appears to be possible by conventional editorial criteria. All editors other than Brooks have assumed loss of two half-lines here. His emendation, reading *murnende mod, fore [me] sneowan,* remedies the lack of alliteration and counts one verse-line, adequate to match the content of the Latin text (*Recensio Casanatensis*) most nearly corresponding to *Andreas* but not the immediate source. The emendation is reasonable but does not preclude loss of two half-lines rather than a single word—does not, in fact, make the larger loss any less probable. The full range of the original count of verses for the final fitt, thus, is 118–121, according to textual considerations independent of arithmetical design, with highest probability for 119–120.

To the 116 verse-lines (by conventional count) the addition of 3 yields

119, a sum that neither the fitt alone nor in combination with line-sums of preceding fitts has one of the moduli found elsewhere. On the other hand, the addition of 4 to the line-count yields 120, a structurally viable number in two immediately apparent ways. It has the modulus 15 ($120 = 15 \times 8$), as well as 12 ($120 = 12 \times 10$), and it brings the sum of lines in the final three fitts, XIII–XV, to 375, which also has a modulus of 15 ($375 = 15 \times 25$).

It will be useful at this point to abstract the modular units based on the numbers 12 and 15 and represent them schematically. Those incorporating reconstructions are marked with an asterisk. See Figure 2.

Before attempting to deal with the very large lacuna caused by excision of a folio, it may also be useful to consider arithmetical relations suggested by the modular units both found and provisionally reconstructed thus far. If the final fitt did have originally a total of 120 lines, that number not only has a modulus of 15. It is also related to 15 by a type of calculation mentioned commonly in medieval treatment of numbers—as, say, in Byrhtferth's treatment of the symbolism of numbers[10] or Augustine's rationalizing the number (153) of fishes caught and drawn to land by the disciples:[11] the sum of digits from 1 through 15 ($1 + 2 + 3 \ldots + 15$) is 120. This calculation may be represented $\Sigma 15 = 120$. Further, both 15 and $\Sigma 15$ (or 120) are moduli of the fitt groups consisting of 600 verse-lines—I–V of "good" text, IV–VIII as possible reconstruction; in either instance it is a group of five fitts, so that 5×120 may be an intentional relation between number of fitts and a major—perhaps dominating—modulus, 15. It may also be that it is $\Sigma 15$ that generates or at least controls the modulus 12, as a decimal of 120.

These considerations provide internal, "closed system" heuristics for further attempt to reconstruct quantitative features of the lost text and the possible arithmetical plan of the poem. Suppose, for the moment, that the excised page did not record a section division of the text, hence 15 is not only a modulus for some fitt groups and perhaps for the final fitt, but also the number of fitts in which the poem was constructed. A third of the poem's sections, fitts I–V, with its moduli of 15 and $\Sigma 15$ could possibly constitute a third of the poem's lines, the total projected by this hypothesis being, then, 1800. This line sum for the original poem would extend and complement dramatically the arithmetical structural details already described: $15 \times 120 = 1800$, or expressed in another way, $15 \times \Sigma 15 = 1800$.

[10] *Byrhtferth's Manual*, ed. S. J. Crawford (*EETS*, o. s. 177, London, 1929).
[11] See, for example, Gunnar Qvarnström, *Poetry and Numbers: On the Structural Use of Symbolic Numbers* (Lund, 1966), p. 19.

I	II	III	IV	V	VI	VII	VIII	IX	X	XI	XII	XIII	XIV	XV
121	108	122	117	132	95	126 (129*)	130*	108*	97	98	99	126	129	120*
121	229	351	468	600	695	821 (950*)	951*							

$15 \times 40 = 600$
$4 \times 150 = 600$
$5 \times 120 = 600$
etc.

$(15 \times 17 = 255^*)$

$15 \times 40 = 600^*$
$5 \times 120 = 600^*$
$4 \times 150 = 600^*$
etc.

$15 \times 13 = 195$ $15 \times 15 = 225$

$4(15 \times 7) = 420$
$5(12 \times 7) = 420$
etc.

$15 \times 17 = 255$ $15 \times 8 = 120^*$

$15 \times 25 = 375^*$

Figure 2

108

This conjecture, on total line-count for the poem, is the largest one to be set forth here, and it must now be tested with great care. It also involves, of course, quantitative reconstruction of text lost by excision of a folio that contained lines between those now counted as 1024 and 1025.

To the 1722 verse-lines that can be counted in surviving text need to be added 78, if the total length had once been 1800. Thus far one or two verses after line 828 and three or four verses after line 1663 can be counted with some confidence, reducing the needed addition by four, five, or six; that is, to complete the design of total line-count of 1800, we have still to account for 72–74 lines. The missing folio may be assumed to have been ruled for twenty-four lines of writing, since ff. 33a–47b are all ruled thus, and the gap occurs between f. 42 and f. 43. It may also be assumed to have contained approximately the same number of verse-lines as the average of folios preceding and following, since the writing elsewhere is generally uniform in size. The number of verse-lines on the three preceding and the three following folios are these: 75, 75, 74½, . . .74+, 68, 73+, the measurement including pieces of verse-lines. The range of probability for the number of verse-lines on the lost leaf, then, is about 73, plus or minus 2.

No closer calculation of the number of lines at this place can be made with assurance. Folios 40 and 41, containing 75 verse-lines, leave blank one and one and a half lines, respectively, for sectional divisions; f. 44 leaves blank less than a full line for a sectional division and works around a small blemish in the parchment, yet contains only 68 verse-lines; ff. 42 and 45 do not have sectional divisions and contain 74½ and 73+ lines, respectively; f. 43 has a sectional division, two half-lines missing (at line 1036 and line 1040), and contains 74+ verse-lines.

Neither will the number of verse-lines that would fit on the missing folio provide unambiguous evidence for there having been an additional sectional division within this large lacuna.[12]

Now, if the lost leaf contained the equivalent of 73 verse-lines, the total count for the poem should be increased by 72, since just less than half of line 1024 concludes the preceding folio and just over half of line 1025 begins the succeeding folio. (It may be noted, too, that the fragment of line 1024 appears to begin a hypermetric line, and as Brooks

---

[12] Mention should be made here of a claim by Riemer (see note 7) that the missing folio contained a fitt division (pp. 8, 143). No clear evidence is adduced to support the claim, and the "basic balance and symmetry" of fitts grouped by narrative movements, as 1 – 3 – 3 – 3 (or 4) –3 – 2 (see p. 145) lacks both precision and non-thematic correlates for a fitt boundary having occurred on the lost leaf.

observes,[13] it is possible that a passage in which hypermetric lines occur with some frequency may begin at line 1022, similar to the passage at line 795 ff.) Addition of 72 lost verse-lines for the missing folio, 2 verse-lines after line 828, and 4 verse-lines after line 1663, for a total of 78, would yield the 1800 verse-lines for the complete poem, as projected on a different basis above.

Not only that, the additional count of 72, combined with the 108 verse-lines extant, would yield a total of 180 verse-lines for fitt IX, a number having several ramifications for the arithmetical design thus far found or projected. For one thing, the line-sum 180 has the modulus 15 as well as the modulus 12 ($15 \times 12 = 180$). For another, this line-sum replicates, as a decimal, the line-sum of 1800 that can have been the length of the original text. For yet another, fitts IX–XIII would then have a total of 600 lines—a second, or perhaps a third, fitt-group of this length which, again, comprises five fitts.

Still further ramifications appear in secondary effects. If fitt IX did originally contain 180 lines, the three fitts IX–XI would have had a line-sum of 375 ($= 15 \times 25$), repeating the pattern of the three fitts XIII–XV containing 375 verse-lines if the lacuna in the final fitts is restored as proposed earlier. Also, the ten fitts IV–XIII would have had exactly 1200 verse-lines if the alternative of reconstructing two verse-lines rather than one after line 828 is taken as more probable. (If not, the 1199 lines of this fitt-group could be brought to 1200 by positing 73 additional lines for the missing folio, a reconstruction just as plausible if the folio size is considered in isolation from other aspects of the text.) Reconstruction of two verse-lines after line 828 and 72 verse-lines for the lost folio produces a brace of successive fitt-groups, IV–VIII and IX–XIII, each consisting of 600 verse-lines. Furthermore, there would then be a pair of fitt-groups comprising 1200 verse-lines: the one just proposed (IV–XIII), as well as the one in VI–XV complementing the fitt-group of 600 verse-lines that begins the poem. An additional correspondence is that of 1200 as a line-sum of these fitt-groups to its decimal 120, the latter being a modulus of 600 (and 1200), the $\Sigma 15$ which is also a modulus of the complete poem, and the unique line-sum of the concluding fitt of the poem.

Finally, all these pieces falling into place in an arithmetical design provide indirect but converging evidence for the original text having just the fifteen fitts that the sectional divisions of the extant folios show.

By collecting the extant and proposed structural units in diagrammatic form, a schema for the reconstructed compositional design of *Andreas* can be shown as in Figure 3.

[13] Brooks, p. 90 (commenting on line 795 ff.).

121	108	122	117	132	95	126	128*	108*	97	98	99	126	129	116*
121	229	351	468	600	695	821	949	1057	1154	1252	1351	1477	1606	1722
I	II	III	IV	V	VI	VII	VIII	IX	X	XI	XII	XIII	XIV	XV

| 121 | 108 | 122 | 117 | 132 | 95 | 126 | 130[a] | 180[b] | 97 | 98 | 99 | 126 | 129 | 120[c] |
| 121 | 229 | 351 | 468 | 600 | 695 | 821 | 951 | 1131 | 1228 | 1326 | 1425 | 1551 | 1680 | 1800 |

$3(13 \times 9) = 351$

$4(13 \times 9) = 468$

$13 \times 9 = 117$

$13 \times 17 = 221$

$15 \times 12 = 180$

$15 \times 13 = 195$

$13 \times 15 = 195$

$15 \times 15 = 225$

$15 \times 8 = 120$

$\Sigma 15 = 120$

$15 \times 17 = 255$

$15 \times 25 = 375$

$15 \times 25 = 375$

$4(15 \times 7) = 420$

$\Sigma 15 \times 5 = 600$

$\Sigma 15 \times 5 = 600$

$\Sigma 15 \times 5 = 600$

$2(\Sigma 15 \times 5) = 1200$

$2(\Sigma 15 \times 5) = 1200$

$\Sigma 15 \times 15 = 1800$

$15 \times \Sigma 15 = 1800$

ANDREAS
15 Sections [I-XV]
$\Sigma 15 = 120$

[a] Lacuna of 2 verse-lines
[b] Lacuna of 72 verse-lines
[c] Lacuna of 4 verse-lines

Figure 3

111

III

Immediately one tends, from the modern point of view, to ask what the various key numbers "mean." There may be answers, assigning non-arithmetic, "qualitative" meanings to 13, 15, 60, 120, etc., in *Andreas*. Trial and error matching of items from the vast inventory of medieval number symbolism may be the only way to find them. A cycle of Indictions comprises 15 years, Paul is said to be the thirteenth in the list of holy men, the great year in which celestial bodies return to the same place they were at the beginning takes 600 years, and so on. None of these "meanings" has apparent consonance, though, with narrative or thematic elements of the poem. St. Andrew's Day cannot be calculated from the modular numbers of the poem through any generally used medieval system of reckoning time. Unless some correlations between numbers and non-numerical meanings can be made for the design and the "content" of *Andreas,* the interpretation of the numerical scheme cannot proceed.[14]

A question can also be directed at the internal structure of the poem. Within *Andreas* there might be—if *Beowulf* were its model—a disposition of lexical elements according to the schematic design. There is, for example, a recurrence—and *in identical order*—of several words and word-roots in the concluding four and five lines, respectively, of fitts I and II, shown here by italicization:

> *Ge*[*wat*] *him þa se halga*   helm ælwihta,
> engla scyppend,   to þam *up*lican
> *eð*elrice;   he is onriht cyning,
> staðol*fæst* styrend,   in stowa gehwam.

(118–21)

> [Then the Holy One departed, Protector of all creatures,
> Creator of angels, to the celestial
> domain; He is rightful king,
> steadfast ruler, in every place.]

> *Gewat him þa se halga*   healdend on wealdend,
> *up*engla fruma,   *eð*el secan,
> middangeardes weard,   þone mæran ham,
> þær soð*fæstra*   sawla moton
> æfter lices hryre   lifes brucan.

(225–29)

[14] On the problem of "interpretation," a step above both initial "description" and subsequent "correlation," see Qvarnström, p. 15. Qvarnström has assembled a generous sampling of instances of "numerical symbolism or allegory in literature."

[Then the Holy One departed, Guardian and Ruler,
Prince of heavenly-angels, to seek his native land,
Protector of the world, (to seek) the glorious habitation,
where, of the righteous, the souls are granted
after body's fall to enjoy life.]

Again, the last six lines of fitts VIII and X begin similarly:

> þu hine secan scealt,
> leafne *alysan* of laðra *hete*.

(943b–44)

[Thou shalt seek him out,
set free the beloved one from persecution of the hateful.]

> Swa wearð *alysed* of leod*hete*,
> geong of gyrne.

(1149–50a)

[Thus he was released from persecution,
the young man (was released) from affliction.]

Forms of *wuldor* recur in the second lines from the end of fitts VIII and IX (lines 948 and 1056); other forms of *wuldor* recur in the fifth line of fitts IV and XV (lines 356 and 1611).

There may be a good many more of these correspondences and they may be worth searching for. But it should be pointed out that *wuldor,* for example, as a separate word and as initial root in six separate compounds, appears a great many times and more often than not a numerical pattern of its disposition is not apparent: the correspondences need to be exact, and to be convincing they need to involve most (if not all) occurrences of the lexical form. *Þrym(m)* is another instance; while it occurs in the third line of the poem and in the third line from the end of the poem, most other of its occurrences do not have readily apparent schematic placement. The patent error in copying *heofon* for *geofon* (lines 393, 1508, 1585) does not recur in a readily discernible pattern. And so on.

To approach the question from a different position, tectonically patterned disposition of lexical elements, while it is a characteristic of *Beowulf,* may not be a characteristic of *Andreas.* There are some reasons, in fact, to guess that the two poems will inevitably differ in this respect. The progress of *Andreas* is thoroughgoing chronological narra-

113

tive, quite unlike that of *Beowulf*. A single narrative line neither invites nor accommodates verbal parallels (such as appellatives) that can fit—and at the same time manifest—patterns. *Andreas* does not have internally repeating action-types comparable to the hero's three fights with monsters in the other poem, hence lacks another means of developing lexical repetitions on which patterns depend for their existence.

Neither does the arithmetical design appear to have been exploited for positioning of recurrences of thematic elements. God's regular exit after speaking—the *he astag on heofonas* of the prose translation—occurs at the conclusion of fitts I and II, for example, but after ending a speech in the first part of fitt IX, within no discernible pattern of fitt numbers or line numbers; the departure can be used to end a scene, as in the case of the opening two fitts, but it remains a stage direction without establishing a theme. There are abundant miracles in the story—the sea-crossing, the series with the images in the temple in fitt VII, Andrew's restoration to health, the flood, to name only the main ones—so many, in fact, that they seem to be less thematic elements than the stuff of the legend. In this respect, and in their following the order of the source text(s), their disposition in the poetic text may not be within the control of the poet for developing a tectonic design. Further, the two long divisions of the narrative—the calling of Andrew and the sea journey, and the passion of Andrew among the Mermedonians—do not have intrinsic thematic parallels lending themselves to repetitions of which tectonically patterned recurrences can be created. Just as a Gothic tale lacks leisure and possibility of thematic embellishments to fit linked, long stanzas like those in *Pearl*, or just as a fabliau or tale of intrigue could hardly fill out the formal potential of a sonnet sequence, so *Andreas* seems to leave unused some structural resources of tectonic form.

All this is not to say that the fitt divisions represent arbitrary, mechanical segmenting of the verse narrative. Riemer's study of the contents of the fitts[15] shows that "the *Andreas* poet is very conscious of his fitt boundaries, making of each fitt a structural unit roughly equivalent to a chapter in a novel, or more germanely a capitulum in a lectionary";[16] "there is within the boundaries of each of the fitts of the poem a sequence and structure as to the grouping of the materials";[17] and the poet "for the most part used traditional formulaic motifs and themes to mark

---

[15] Especially Chapter XI, "The Fitt Divisions of Old English Poetry" (pp. 103–10), and a fitt-by-fitt summary in Chapter XII, "The Fitts of the *Andreas*" (pp. 111–45).

[16] Riemer, p. 108.

[17] Riemer, p. 110.

the beginning and end of his fitts."[18] Yet the accommodation of "structural and dramatic" elements to fitt boundaries in no way establishes that the placements of these elements "determine fitt length," as Riemer claims.[19]

We may suppose, rather, that the direction of determination was exactly the opposite—the "matter" being adjusted to the schema laid out in advance for the compositional design of the poem. Whether that schema holds symbolic (or even quasi-allegorical) meaning is a question I have posed at the beginning of this section without having an answer to propose. Whether the poet exploited an arithmetically devised plan for locating—and thus marking—correspondences in wording and theme is a problem to which I have given preliminary consideration and a tentative answer essentially negative. Modular design of the quantitative extension of the text is the aspect of *Andreas* I have attempted to establish. If that design, like the one in *Beowulf*, is recognized as a primary part of the author's plan for his poem, our understanding and assessment of the literary qualities of *Andreas* will have a new foundation.

[18] Riemer, p. 110.
[19] Riemer, p. 106.

9

The Speech of Stephen
and the Tone of *Elene*

JAMES DOUBLEDAY

Elene IS, AT FIRST GLANCE, ONE OF THE LEAST ATTRACTIVE OF THE Old English poems to a modern audience. Elene herself, with her threats, her torture, and her arrogant self-righteousness, seems to be one of the most unpleasant saints in the calendar. The modern reader may well consider the work important primarily as a document in the long and painful history of anti-semitism. Moreover, the work is a translation of an earlier Latin work, *De inventione crucis dominicae* (Latin at least in the version Cynewulf knew), and the poet makes no major changes in the events of the story.[1]

Thus, scholars had until recently shown little or no interest in *Elene* as a work of literary art.[2] But recently a number of scholars have been

---

[1] This tractate *De inventione* was in existence by at least the early sixth century and was widely read: see Butler's *Lives of the Saints*, rev. & supp. by Herbert Thurston S.J. and Donald Attwater, II (New York, 1956), 221–22. There are a number of texts of *De inventione*, all slightly different, none exactly the text Cynewulf used: see P. O. E. Gradon, ed., *Cynewulf's Elene* (New York, 1966), pp. 15–20, and J. J. Campbell, "Cynewulf's Multiple Revelations," *M&H*, n.s., 3 (1972), p. 258 and n. 1 p. 276.

[2] Gradon's edition (the standard one, used in this paper throughout) has no discussion of the literary qualities of the poem in the introduction and no section on literary criticism in the bibliography. C. L. Wrenn, in *A Study of Old English Literature* (New York, 1967), devotes only two pages (pp. 124–25) to *Elene*, and of these only part of one sentence is given to the body of the poem.

examining the poem anew.[3] There is remarkable agreement among these scholars on how the poem ought to be seen. Viewed in their light, the poem is a more remarkable feat intellectually and artistically than it was previously considered. Their consensus, put briefly, seems to be the following: the subject of *Elene* is not primarily the discovery of the Cross, but the conversion of Judas, his "Invention of the Cross" in a spiritual sense. The pattern of the poem is the pattern of conversion. Judas and Elene are not simply characters in a narrative, but typological figures: Judas represents the whole unconverted Jewish nation, and Elene the Church Militant. Looming behind the poem, then, is the great medieval contrast between Church and Synagogue,[4] and the medieval Christian sense that the New Law is the fulfillment of the Old.

In this framework, a number of things about the poem that were formerly puzzling make sense. In particular, the statement that Stephen the protomartyr was Judas' brother is typologically significant. The statement is a deliberate anachronism; both Cynewulf and his audience knew perfectly well that any brother of Stephen would have died long before the reign of Constantine. And any such use of anachronism leads the reader to question why. There seem to be two principal implications for the instructed audience in this pairing of Judas and Stephen. First, Stephen (like Saul / Paul, who is mentioned along with Stephen in 489a–516) is the type of the Jewish convert, as Judas is the type of the unconverted Jew. Second, the speech of Stephen to the Sanhedrin is a model for the Church's approach to the unconverted.

Let us recall the account of Stephen's martyrdom as it is given in Acts 6 and 7. Stephen, one of the first seven deacons of the Church, *plenus gratia et fortitudine* [full of grace and fortitude],[5] did great won-

---

[3] The best of these articles (from which I have derived many of the ideas in this paper) I list in order of publication: Robert Stepsis and Richard Rand, "Contrast and Conversion in Cynewulf's *Elene*," *NM*, 70 (1969), 273–82; J. Gardiner, "Cynewulf's *Elene:* Sources and Structure," *Neophil*, 54 (1970), 65–76; Thomas D. Hill, "Sapiential Structure and Figural Narrative in the Old English 'Elene,'" *Traditio*, 27 (1971), 159–77; Daniel G. Calder, "Strife, Revelation, and Conversion: The Thematic Structure of *Elene*," *ES*, 53 (1972), 201–10; Campbell, cited above, n. 1; and Catherine A. Regan, "Evangelicalism as the Informing Principle of Cynewulf's 'Elene,'" *Traditio*, 29 (1973), 27–52.

[4] The standard discussion of this theme is Hiram Pflaum, "Der allegorische Streit zwischen Synagogue und Kirche in der europäischen Dichtung der Mittelalters," *Archivum Romanicum*, 18 (1934), 243–340. See also Margaret Schlauch, "The Allegory of Church and Synagogue," *Speculum*, 14 (1939), 448–64, and Wolfgang S. Seiferth, *Synagogue and Church in the Middle Ages: Two Symbols in Art and Literature*, trans. Lee Chadeayne and Paul Gottwald (New York, 1970).

[5] The text of the Bible used in this paper is the Vulgate, the version Cynewulf would have known best; the translation is that of Rheims, the closest to a literal version of the Vulgate NT.

ders among the people. But certain Jews, who had disputed with Stephen but had not been able to conquer *sapientiæ et Spiritui qui loquebatur* [the wisdom and the spirit that spoke], brought him before the council, claiming that he had spoken blasphemy *adversus locum sanctum et legem* [against the holy place and the law]. Stephen then defended himself and his Church before the council. His speech is in form a brief history of the Jews from the appearance of the Lord to Abraham up to the building of the temple. He deals almost equally with the mighty acts of God, particularly the promises of deliverance that He gave to Abraham and Moses, and the sins of the people who rejected Him and turned to idol-worship. The last section of the speech, or at least the last words that Stephen was allowed to say, are a direct attack on the council-members. This part of the speech runs as follows:

> Dura cervice et incircumcisis cordibus et auribus vos semper Spiritui sancto resistis; sicut patres vestri, ita et vos. Quem prophetarum non sunt persecuti patres vestri? Et occiderunt eos, qui prænuntiabant de adventu Iusti, cuius vos nunc proditores et homicidæ fuistis, qui accepistis legem in dispositione angelorum et non custodistis. (Acts 7:51–53)

> [You stiff-necked and uncircumcised in heart and ears, you always resist the Holy Ghost; as your fathers *did,* so *do* you also. Which of the prophets have not your fathers persecuted? And they have slain them who foretold of the coming of the Just One; of whom you have been now the betrayers and murderers; who have received the law by the disposition of Angels, and have not kept it.]

This speech angers the council: *stridebant dentibus in eum* [they gnashed with their teeth at him]. And when immediately afterwards he proclaims his vision of Christ standing at the right hand of God, they make a dead set at him, run him out of the city, and stone him. The last act of his martyrdom is to pray for his persecutors, *Domine, ne statuas illis hoc peccatum* [Lord, lay not this sin to their charge].

The early Church, naturally enough, thought of Stephen's life and death as a model. Isidore indeed explains the name as meaning *norma, quod prior fuerit in martyrio ad imitationem fidelium* [pattern, because he was first in martyrdom for the imitation of the faithful], and Bede repeats the comment.[6] Moreover, the Church took Stephen's speech to the Sanhedrin as a model of how one spoke to the proud. Gregory points out that Stephen's *verba altitudinis* [high words] are not to be taken as exhibiting his own pride, but rather his *zelo veritatis* [zeal for truth],

---

[6] Isidore, *Etymologiarum*, ed. W. M. Lindsay, VII, xi (Oxford, 1911), translation mine; Bede, *Super Acta Apostolorum expositio, PL,* 92, 956.

asking, reasonably enough, *quomodo ergo Stephanus proferre increpationem per elationem potuit, qui pro eisdem quos increpaverat, ad deteriora crescentibus, seque lapidantibus, flexis genibus oravit, dicens:* Domine, ne statuas illis hoc peccatum. [Accordingly, how could Stephen utter reproach in pride, who with bended knee prayed for those whom he reproached, when they went on to worse and stoned him, saying, *Lord, lay not this sin to their charge.*][7] Augustine likewise emphasizes that Stephen rebukes from charity, not from pride: *quasi sæviebat enim Stephanus; sæviebat ore, corde diligebat; et non est victa charitas ipsa in eo* [for Stephen seemed in a manner to rage against them; he raged in word, but loved in heart, nor was his charity overcome].[8] Gregory even considers that this particular attitude towards wrongdoers, severe rebuke from a loving heart, is characteristic of the Church *because* it was that of Stephen:

> Hæc per quosdam santa Ecclesia in fine factura est, hæc per quosdam in suis jam exordiis fecit. Primum quippe martyr Stephanus Judæis persequentibus prodesse prædicando conatus est, quos tamen post verba prædicationis, dum videret ad jaciendos lapides convolasse, fixis genibus orabat, dicens: *Domine Jesu, ne statuas illic hoc peccatum.*

> [Such things is Holy Church to do by certain persons in the end, these things has she already done by certain (persons) in her beginnings. For the first martyr Stephen endeavoured by preaching to benefit the Jews that persecuted him, which persons when he saw, notwithstanding, after the words of preaching to have flocked together to throwing stones, he prayed with his knees set fast, saying, *Lord Jesus, lay not this sin to their charge.*][9]

If, then, this is the Church's view of Stephen's speech, it is significant that Elene's speech to the assembled Jews is so like his in theme, except that the theme is thrice repeated (287–319, 333–76, 386–95 and 406b–10): first to six thousand, next to one thousand, and last to five hundred Jews. In each division of her speech, Elene contrasts the gifts of God to the Jews in times past with their folly in resisting both the law (*æ*) and the word of the prophets (*wigena word*). As other critics have commented,[10] after Judas' speech to the other wise men among the Jews and

[7] Gregory the Great, *Moralia,* VII, 54, *PL,* 75, 797; translation from *Morals on the Book of Job* (Library of the Fathers: Oxford, 1844–47), I, 407.

[8] Augustine, *Enarratio in Psalmum CXXXII,* 8, *PL,* 37, 1734; translation from *St. Augustine on the Psalms,* VI (Library of the Fathers; Oxford, London, 1857), 117. See also *Enarratio in Psalmum LXX,* 14, *PL,* 36, 884.

[9] *Moralia,* XX, 79, *PL,* 76, 186; translation from *Library of the Fathers,* II, 512.

[10] See esp. Campbell, "Cynewulf's Multiple Revelations," p. 265, on the difference in Elene's tone before and after Judas has given his account of the knowledge passed down from his fathers.

when they still refuse to admit any knowledge of the Cross (in what is now an undoubted lie), Elene directly threatens the Jews. But earlier her tone is that of Stephen: a tone of anger and reproach that the chosen people, who have had the benefit of the law and the prophets and moreover the special grace of the coming of Jesus Christ, have blindly and rebelliously resisted and slain both the prophets and Christ Himself.

As generally in *Elene*, Cynewulf's text in Elene's speech is close to, but not simply a translation of, *De inventione*. Cynewulf constantly varies his original. He also adds, and one addition here in the second part of the speech is thematically important. In *De inventione*, Elene simply quotes two passages from Isaiah (Is. 7:4 and 1:1–2) prophesying the birth of Christ and lamenting that Israel would not recognize Him, and then demands again that her hearers choose men wise in the law to answer her. In the poem, Elene directly contrasts the *dom* [power] that the Lord had given the people of Israel with their rejection of the right way and following after error *ofer riht Godes* [against the law of God, 364–72a].

Immediately after Elene's speech comes the first mention of Judas. Judas is, as has been remarked, a typological figure, representing the whole unconverted Jewish nation. The pattern of the poem, in which the field has been progressively narrowed—from three thousand to one thousand to five hundred and finally to this one chosen spokesman—forces the audience to see this figure as a representative one. But Judas is not simply the type of the unconverted Jew. He is, above all the others, the one who *should* have been a convert, for he knows more than the other wise men. Moreover, the difference is not only one of knowledge, but of faith. His speech to the others is given, not simply in the objective tone of intellectual knowledge, but in the emotive tone of religious assent. It sounds like a creed. The truth about Christ's crucifixion and resurrection and the beginning of the Christian Church is for him a family tradition. It has been handed down from father to son for three generations, and he obviously believes in it.

That family itself is a further reason that Judas should have been a Christian already, if there is anything to the notion of heredity (and certainly to an Old English audience there is a great deal to it). Judas is not only the brother of Stephen, he is the son of Simon and the grandson of Zacheus. As with his brotherhood to Stephen, these details are historically impossible and typologically meaningful. Zacheus (see Luke 19:1–10) was the chief tax-gatherer who climbed a tree to see Jesus, and Jesus invited Himself to Zacheus' house. The people around murmured that Jesus was making Himself the guest of a sinner, but Zacheus promised Jesus to give half his goods to the poor and make four-fold restitution to those he had wronged, and Jesus answered, *Quia hodie salus domui huic facta est, eo quod et ipse filius sit Abrahæ* [This day is salvation come to this house; because he also is a son of Abraham]. Simon is more difficult to identify, for there is only one Zacheus in the New Testament but several Simons: Simon the Cananean, one of the twelve apostles (Matt. 10:4, Mark 3:18); Simon the brother of Jesus (Matt. 13:15, Mark 6:3); Simon the leper, at whose house Jesus was anointed with ointment (Matt. 26:6, Mark 14:3); Simon of Cyrene, who carried Christ's cross (Matt. 27:32, Mark 15:21, Luke 23:26); Simon the father of Judas Iscariot (John 6:72, 13:2, 26); Simon Magus (Acts 8); and Simon the tanner, with whom Peter stayed at Joppa (Acts 9:43, 10:6). Peter also is called Simon in many places in the New Testament. There is no way to decide, from either *De inventione* or *Elene,* which of these Simons is the father of Judas. Apparently it does not matter, since with any of them the audience would recognize a Jew in close contact with our Lord and / or His disciples. In other words, Judas is not only a son of Abraham, but the son of a house to which salvation has come.

Why is Judas not himself a Christian already? Why does he resist the truth? This question of the spiritual obduracy of the Jews has plagued the Church from the beginning; the figure of Judas simply puts the question in its most extreme form. Judas knows the truth, not only from the prophets as do the other Jews, but from personal and direct contact with believers. Yet he does not believe. His ostensible reason—that if Christianity conquers, Israel will no longer "rule the world," *ofer middangeard ma ricsian* (434)—hardly seems adequate, for Israel is not "ruling the world" at the time in the poem. The harshness of Elene with Judas later, which makes the modern reader so uneasy, is in direct proportion to the frustration the Church feels with the Jews for obstinately remaining outside the faith they ought to accept so eagerly.

But this harshness (to give it an over-weak name), this persecution and torture of Judas gives the modern reader an uneasiness that seems justified. Even if Elene's actions can be understood psychologically, they cannot be accepted. Moreover, Elene's tone earlier is unacceptable in the same way, when coming from Elene. It changes the force and meaning of the rebuke when it comes from a queen in power rather than from a martyr defying purely human authority. Rosemary Woolf makes the same point: "The heroic resolve of the martyr, who speaks from physical weakness, sounds false from Elene, surrounded by a strong well-armed company of soldiers. . . ."[11] Is there, perhaps, irony in this reversal of the usual roles in a saint's life?

11 "Saints' Lives," in *Continuations and Beginnings: Studies in Old English Literature,* ed. E. G. Stanley (London, 1966), 46–47; cited in Regan, "Evangelicalism," p. 34.

Perhaps. But it is not necessary to hypothesize irony; there is another, and to my mind more likely, hypothesis. That hypothesis is that Cynewulf is deliberately focusing on a central problem of Christianity: that there is no scriptural model for the Christian as citizen in power. The primitive Church, of course, existed for the most part as an illegal organization, at best a small, barely tolerated group of enthusiasts, seen by the huge secular state as fanatics and potential rebels. The New Testament is filled with models and advice for the Christian acting in that situation; but there are no models, there is no advice, for the Christian ruler of a state. And the lack continues, so great that it is not recognized. Gregory the Great was one of the great rulers of all time, but when he writes as teacher and counsellor (as distinct from his state letters) he sees the Christian as Job—afflicted, condemned by the prosperous and successful, with God alone as friend. This model is an excellent one in many ways, but it furnishes no help for one who is a prince in this world if not of it.

Elene thus has no scriptural model, and the lack shows. First she speaks in the tone of Stephen—a tone appropriate to the situation, but inappropriate to her position as queen. Then she falls back on her only other model, that of the Roman empire, and uses its means: threats, punishment, torture. And the reader becomes uneasy at this mode of action, as I think the poet intends.[12]

This uneasiness deepens in the rest of the poem. The miracles—the finding of the true cross and its nails—are the work of Judas's prayers, and the defeat of the devil results from the boldness of his faith. Elene is reduced to an approving chorus, and by the end of the poem she has to beg Judas's advice as to what to do with the nails. No doubt this pattern is typologically appropriate for Elene, since the work of the Church in conversion should be completed at the baptism of the convert. But Elene's passivity and subordinate position at the end of the

[12] There is some external evidence that medieval Christians, at least in the northern countries of Europe, did not think highly of conversion by force. In Bede (II, 13), the conversion of Northumbria is the result of a council called by the king; the decisive arguments in favor are given by a wise old pagan counsellor and a priest of the pagan gods; and the only violence employed is that of the priest against the idols of his former gods. The story of the conversion of Iceland, as given by Ari the Learned and substantially repeated by later writers, is even more firmly against forcible conversion. The priest Thangbrandr, sent over by King Olaf of Norway, failed to convert the land chiefly because of his violent deeds there, and indeed reported back to Olaf that the land was unchangeably hostile to Christ. The conversion was accomplished at the yearly *thing* (assembly), and again by the arguments of a pagan, the law-speaker, whose chief object seems to have been to keep the peace in Iceland. In the same year that Iceland was converted, King Olaf, the greatest practitioner of forcible conversion in the North, was betrayed to his death.

poem contrast rather oddly with her overwhelming dominance earlier. This pattern in itself seems to make a comment on Elene's limitations, on the problems with her method of achieving "her desire in the world" (*willan on worulde,* 1152a).

The "Jewish question" is not an important one for Anglo-Saxon England. But the question of the relationship of church to state, and especially the question of the proper action of a Christian ruler, is undoubtedly an important one. Cynewulf has chosen a narrative that raises this question at almost the earliest point in history it can be raised: immediately after the conversion of Constantine, when the Church (and Elene its representative) gained the power of the state (and Elene *its* representative, too). And the ambiguous position of Elene, saint and queen, with her different and probably irreconcilable models, is the position of the Christian in power ever since.

10

Judith: Hypermetricity
and Rhetoric

BURTON RAFFEL

I HOPE IT WILL NOT SEEM SENTENTIOUS IF I EXPLAIN THAT THE VALID-
ity of literary criticism depends, for me, on there being some substantial
connection between the critic's criticism and his own interior world. My
purpose in this essay, in accordance with that notion, is to account for
the sense of disquiet—sometimes reaching rather intense levels—which
I experienced while translating *Judith*.[1] I do not propose an elaborate
self-analysis; neither do I intend self-advertisement. Simply stated, my
primary relationship to *Judith* is as a translator into modern English, and
my basic perception about the poem is precisely that uncomfortable
awareness of there being something—not perhaps wrong, but certainly
not quite right. I have not been able to come to grips with that perception previously: the invitation to contribute to John McGalliard's *Festschrift* is thus an opportunity to remedy a gap in my own understanding.

Every critic who has commented on *Judith* has dealt with the hypermetrical lines. The most interesting observation, to my mind, is Stanley
B. Greenfield's connection between normal-length lines used "for rapid
narrative action" and hypermetrical lines reserved "for the most part for
reflective or psychological passages." Greenfield goes on to note that

---

[1] B. Raffel, *Poems From the Old English*, 2nd ed. (Lincoln, 1964), pp. 94–105.

"even in translation, the shift in stress can be observed at beginning and end, the movement into the short line at the end beautifully coinciding with the quickening of the narrative pace."[2] The translation he then cites is my own: without making any claim for the translation, or for my own authority in dealing with this particular passage, let me take the lines Greenfield has chosen, which are lines 54–68, as a useful point of departure.

In the lines immediately preceding, Holofernes has been described, swiftly and very effectively, lying wrapped in his *fleohnet fæger* [beautiful bed-curtain], from where *se bealofulla / mihte wlitan þurh . . . on æghwylcne þe ðær inne com* [the wicked (evil) one could look through . . . at anyone who came in there].[3] These lines, roughly 46–54a, are among the most frequently praised in the poem. C. L. Wrenn, whose remarks can stand here for the general tenor of critical discussion, says: "A canopy (*conopeum*) which was over the bed of Holofernes, mentioned in the Vulgate without comment (Chapter X, 19), is treated imaginatively by our poet. . . . The *Judith* poet entirely transforms the idea and expands it in a quite original way with a touch of Oriental knowledge."[4] I agree. It is a lovely passage. But it is *not* devoted to "rapid narrative action." True, in the lines just previous to these, the poet has had Holofernes' soldiers hurrying in Judith, ready for their master's bed. Nevertheless, lines 46–54a are precisely those "reflective or psychological passages" which, according to Greenfield, are "for the most part" expressed, in this poem, in hypermetrical language. Plainly, we do not know just why or when the *scop* would use hypermetrical lines, and Greenfield's perception of rhythmic shift is accurate. But just as plainly, the contrast between such normal lines as 46–54a and the hypermetrical lines, 54–68, which immediately follow, cannot be founded on a distinction between narrative and "reflective or psychological passages."

Further: lines 46–54a gave me no particular difficulty, in translation, nor any sense of dis-ease. But lines 54–68, the hypermetrical passage, *were* difficult and uncomfortable to deal with. Discussion of the passage must be limited, in view of our inability to understand the function of hypermetrical lines; still, detailed examination from even a limited perspective may be helpful, ultimately, in understanding both *Judith* and the *scop's* sense of the hypermetrical line.

Line 54, in which the poet begins this 15-line hypermetrical passage (I omit the problem of the truncated state of line 62; in any case, I have

---

[2] *A Critical History of Old English Literature* (New York, 1965), pp. 165–66.
[3] All citations to the Old English text are from *Beowulf and Judith, ASPR, IV*, ed., Elliott van Kirk Dobbie (New York, 1953).
[4] *A Study of Old English Literature* (New York, 1968), p. 178.

no useful solution therefor), concludes the sentence begun in line 46. Holofernes is able to call his soldiers *him . . . near,*

> rinca to rune gegangan. Hie ða on reste gebrohton
> snude ða snoteran idese; eodon ða stercedferhðe,
> haeleð heora hearran cyðan þæt wæs seo halige meowle
> gebroht on his burgetelde.

(54–57a)

[warriors came for secret consultation. Then they brought to his bed quickly the wise virgin; the brave ones went, the men, to announce to their lord that the holy maiden had been brought to his tent.]

This is not only metrically different from the normal passage just before it. It is also, it seems to me, rhetorically different—which is, I suspect, the basis for Greenfield's linkage of hypermetrical and "reflective or psychological passages."[5] Renwick and Orton speak of the *Judith* poet's "effective and contrasting use of passages in long and short lines."[6] It is undoubtedly contrastive—but is it in fact effective? Let me, for illustrative purposes, take the three and a half lines just quoted and make them more or less metrically normal, not by full-scale revision but simply by cutting (and also by a bit of minor tinkering):

> rinca to rune. On reste gebrohton
> ða snoteran idese; ða stercedferhðe
> eodon heora hearran cyðan seo halige
> gebroht wæs on his burgetelde.

[warriors for secret consultation. They brought to his bed the wise virgin; the brave ones went to announce to their lord that the holy one had been brought to his tent.]

After a rather different bit of re-casting an Old English original, Robert P. Creed, in a finely illuminating essay, confessed: "I don't like my poem nearly so much as I like the singer's. . . . But then this is where I've got by *trying* to be different from a great singer."[7] I must make a very different confession: I rather prefer my four lines to the *scop's* three and a half. I regret the omission of *snude* [quickly, at once]; on the other hand,

---

[5] By "rhetorical," here, I mean a fusion of stylistic and harder-to-define emotional effects, most of which should become clear as I proceed.
[6] W. L. Renwick and H. Orton, *The Beginnings of English Literature to Skelton, 1509,* 3rd ed. (London, 1966), p. 159.
[7] "The Making of an Anglo-Saxon Poem," *ELH,* 26 (1959), 454 and n. 10.

had I been free to truly rewrite, I could have gotten that idea in, I think. The point is that virtually all I have eliminated, in my recasting, is inessential—is, in short, pretty close to padding.[8] Is this what accounts for the difference in tone ("rhetorically different"), and also for my sense, while translating *Judith,* of dis-ease?

Three and a half lines is a slender sample on which to rest so large a conclusion. Let me turn, first to the rest of this hypermetric passage, and then to other hypermetrical passages in the poem.

> Þa wearð   se brema on mode
> bliðe, burga ealdor,   þohte ða beorhtan idese
> mid widle ond mid womme besmitan.   Ne wolde þæt wuldres dema
> geðafian, þrymmes hyrde,   ac he him þæs ðinges gestyrde,
> dryhten, dugeða waldend.

(57b–61a)

[Then was the famous one in heart
happy, commander of the cities, he thought the fair virgin
with impurity and with sin to defile. The Judge of glory would not
consent, the Keeper of glory, but He restrained him from that deed,
God, Lord of men.]

Do we really need *on mode* [in heart (mood, spirit)], in the first of these lines?[9] John S. Westlake, in *The Cambridge History of English Litera-*

---

[8] It is of course true, as Professors D. W. Frese and L. E. Nicholson pointed out to me, after reading an earlier draft of this essay, that the *Judith* poet makes regular use of phrases like *sea halige meowle,* "the holy maiden," in preference to the more usual Old English phrase, *seo halige,* "the holy one." An argument can therefore be made, and they did in fact make it, for *meowle,* "maiden," as an essential word rather than as padding. I think, however, that this is rather like lifting yourself by your own bootstraps. It is to argue backwards from the fact of a verbose poet's verbosity, and to use that verbosity to justify itself. The fundamental fact, here, is that the *Judith* poet *frequently* skates on the edge of padding, in *both* his normal and his hypermetrical lines.

This is also one of the ways in which the poem can be dated: the excessive—as I see it—verbiage helps point to a time of composition when the Old English poetic tradition was ripe, and even beginning to decay, rather than young and firmly flourishing. There are other signs of a late date, too, such as phonological evidence—discussed succinctly by Timmer in his edition of the poem, cited below in note 16; this weaving together of the various strands of evidence seems to me to make each individual strand stronger.

[9] Again, Professors Frese and Nicholson questioned my dismissal of *on mode* [in heart, (mind, spirit)], arguing that if the poet is here composing formulaically, then we must respect his formula as an essential part of his rhetoric. I am not sure I believe in a rigid application of the formulaic theory (or any other theory), but more importantly I am very clear about my belief in the primacy of literary (rather than technical) judgments about literature. The *Judith* poet is saying, literally, "Then was the famous one in heart (mind, spirit) joyful (happy)."

ture, refers to "an impression of intensity," "produced by the heaping of synonyms in moments of stress"[10]—but is that what happens in the next line, with the introduction of the synonymous *burga ealdor* [commander (lord) of the city (fortress)]? The heaping up of synonyms is surely one of the Old English poet's most formidable weapons; it is used to magnificent purpose in poems like *The Battle of Brunanburh.* One could almost argue, indeed, that in poems like *Brunanburh,* whose basic subject matter is war, the piled-up synonyms are themselves representative, evocative, of the actual events of war: *geslogon æt sæcce sweorda ecgum . . . bordweal clufan, heowan heaþolinde . . .* [they won by fighting, with the blades of swords . . . splitting the shield-wall, cutting through the battle-shields . . .]. Here, however, it seems to me very much inessential, neither adding to the portrait of Holofernes nor helping to build intensity. It does, admittedly, serve a delaying function; it impedes the flow of the verse. And that may be what the *scop* was after: in a poetry as rhythm-oriented as Old English poetry, it would hardly be surprising if Greenfield's insight about the differing tendencies of normal and hypermetrical lines turned out, in the end, really to get to the heart of things.

Let me put off further comment on rhythm here and move quickly through the rest of the lines quoted and then the balance of this initial passage. Surely *mid widle ond mid womme besmitan* [with impurity (filth) and with sin to defile] is conventional; it seems to me that there is nothing in *womme* [sin, stain, spot, disgrace, evil, crime, loss,

---

My *literary* reaction to "in heart" (*on mode*) is that it is—to insist on my own phrase—padding, and distinctly inessential. This judgment is one founded in perception—in taste, if you prefer. It is not founded on any technical approach, nor on any theory. One cannot read Old English or any other ancient literature without a certain amount of technical information: I am not plumping for some sort of "inspirationalist" approach to literary texts. What I am arguing is that "Then the famous one was happy" is *better writing* than "Then the famous one was happy in his heart." And, further, that it is better precisely because "in his heart" (*on mode*) is inessential and succeeds, really, only in filling the line out to the length the poet felt he wanted.

I must also add that one can take the business of giving the poet his head much too far. When a very great poet like T. S. Eliot, e.g., writes obscure, private lines in *The Waste Land,* say, I believe in pinning the tail on the donkey. Conversely, when Joyce Kilmer, in his execrable poem, "Trees," produces the most rigidly iambic of iambic lines, I believe in pointing out that no good poet ever writes such mechanical stuff. The poet, in short, is as entitled to his assumptions as is anyone else, but the critic is also entitled to claim that the poet's assumptions are *wrong.* Or inadequate. Or what-have-you. I say this, be it understood, despite the fact that I am myself a practicing, publishing poet and writer of fiction, and despite the fact that I do not by any means always agree with the critics of *my* work.

[10] A. W. Ward and A. R. Waller, eds., *The Cambridge History of English Literature* (Cambridge, 1933), I, 158.

hurt, injury, defilement, shame, misfortune] that is not conveyed by *widle* [impurity, filth, defilement]. From there to the end of the second snippet just quoted, it is possible to neatly rearrange things in normal four-stress lines, tinkering a bit with word order and eliminating yet another pleonastic expression, namely *dryhten* [God (Lord)]. As it stands, in line 61, *dryhten* works as an effective alliterative pair, with *dugeða* [of men], but is otherwise sheer padding—and in my suggested four-stress re-casting, *dryhten* seems to me to positively interfere with its synonymous but more potent siblings, *wuldres dema* [Judge (Ruler) of glory] and *dugeða waldend* [Lord of men]. That is, these latter two expressions both acknowledge God's power and presence and, at the same time, say something, and something not absolutely identical, about the nature of that power and that presence. But *dryhten* does neither of these things, only intoning the bare name of the Lord.[11]

Line 62, truncated as it is, must be skipped over. The remainder of the passage goes as follows:

> bealofull his beddes neosan, þær he sceolde his blæd forleosan
> ædre binnan anre nihte; hæfde ða his ende gebidenne
> on eorðan unswæslicne, swylcne he ær æfter worhte,
> þearlmod ðeoden gumena, þenden he on ðysse worulde
> wunode under wolcna hrofe. Gefeol ða wine swa druncen,
> se rica on his reste middan, swa he nyste ræda nanne
> on gewitlocan.

(63–69a)

[evil one his bed to seek, where he must his life abandon
at once in less than one night; he had then come to his end
on earth cruel, as he had previously striven after,
severe lord of warriors, while he in this world
dwelled under the roof of heaven. He fell then, with wine so drunken,
the powerful one in his bed, that his senses were totally deadened
in mind.]

This final segment does not seem to me to be padded. I would be hard put to it to omit anything. But I also find the tone, the rhetoric if you will,

---

[11] In some contexts such synonymous phrasing might help to emphasize the central conflict of the poem. But not, I think, here. The syntax of this passage uses *wuldres dema* [The Ruler (Judge) of Glory] at the start, making plain that He *ne wolde þæt . . . geðafian* [did not wish to (would not) consent to that] and then ties the moral together by adding that He, *Þrymmes hyrde* [Keeper (Guardian) of Glory], instead restrained Holofernes, ending with the reiteration, *dugeða waldend* [Lord of men]. In this syntactic overview, *dryhten* [Lord (God)] inserted just before *dugeða waldend* can be seen as conclusively pleonastic. It weakens the otherwise carefully constructed balancing of the rest of the passage.

of this final segment to be distinctly unlike that of the first two snippets I have quoted and discussed. It is taut, and even more interestingly, it moves more swiftly than those earlier lines. The rhythmical delays of the earlier portion, caused—as I would argue—by the (deliberate?) verbosity, have vanished. Indeed, though this entire sequence of lines 63–68 is hypermetrical, and lines 46–54a, just preceding it, are metrically normal, I feel a rhythmical similarity. It would be pleasant to be able to explain that similarity, rather than be forced to rely on an impressionistic judgment, but I cannot do it. I *feel* the similarity; I hear it, when I read the sequence aloud. And when I translated *Judith,* the "quickening of the narrative pace" which Greenfield noted, beginning with line 69, for me really began with line 63. Lines 63–68, that is, were for me a great deal easier to translate than the earlier portions of this whole hypermetrical passage (lines 54–68) had been: they moved, they swung, where the earlier portion of the passage hung, stuttered—almost bored, almost irritated me.[12]

A possible critical approach begins to suggest itself: namely, that in the hypermetrical passages of *Judith,* the *scop* uses two basic techniques, in one of which the rhetoric inflates and the rhythm delays, in the other of which the rhetoric goes taut and the rhythm drives ahead. This needs to be tested; even if accurate, it would not explain so much as describe. But, if accurate—indeed, even if only partly accurate—it may prove suggestive. And the subject of hypermetricity badly needs some new exploration.[13] Without plodding methodically through each and every hypermetrical passage in *Judith,* let me do some spot testing, particularly in the great battle scenes.

Judith's speech, in lines 83–94, is in both normal (lines 83–87) and hypermetric (lines 88–94) rhythm. It is followed, furthermore, by a single line which continues the hypermetric mode of the latter part of her speech, then by a line half in normal four-stress rhythm and half in expanded (i.e., hypermetric) rhythm, and then by three more lines of hypermetric rhythm, before returning (with the exception of line 132) to normal rhythm for over a hundred and seventy lines. Certainly, the

[12] Although this is not the place to detail my reactions to translating *Judith,* I hope it is clear from what has already been said, particularly in footnotes 8 and 9, above, and in the discussion of *Brunanburh* as contrasted with *Judith,* that there is a solid basis for those reactions.

[13] John C. Pope's classic study, *The Rhythm of Beowulf* (New Haven, 1942), p. 100, confesses more than once that "certain verses can be treated as normal or hypermetric according to the context"; as T. A. Shippey also notes, in *Old English Verse* (London, 1972), p. 102, "Knowledge of Old English metre is hard for critics to apply." A cautious and helpful recent article is Lewis E. Nicholson, "Oral Techniques in the Composition of Expanded Anglo-Saxon Verses," *PMLA,* 78 (1963), 287–92.

presence of both normal and hypermetric lines in the same brief speech (twelve lines in all), plus the rapid switching back and forth between normal and hypermetric lines in the six or seven lines that follow (not to mention the single-line leap into hypermetricity, at line 132), suggest at the least that extreme critical caution is needed. My sense of lines 83–87, which are in normal rhythm, is that they move unusually slowly. Contrast, e.g., the pacing, in these lines, with that employed in the rapid movement of lines 46–54a. Representative snippets of the two passages will do:

> Þær wæs eallgylden
> fleohnet fæger   ymbe þæs folctogan
> bed ahongen. . . .
>
> (46–48a)

> [There was all golden
> a beautiful curtain around the chieftain's
> bed hung. . . .]

> Ic ðe, frymða god   ond frofre gæst,
> bearn alwaldan,   biddan wylle
> miltse þinre   me þearfendre. . . .
>
> (83–85)

> [I to you, God of Creation and refuge of the spirit,
> Almighty Son, will ask
> Your mercy in my need. . . .]

And after five lines of such unusually slow but metrical normal verse (83–87), the *scop* moves to seven hypermetrical lines (six and a half— 88 to 94a—belonging to Judith's speech) of virtually the same full, heavy movement. It is very appropriate to the sentiments expressed, and to Judith's situation; the high rhetoric does not seem inflated, nor the synonyms redundant. Indeed, there is a deep and emotional resonance which made translation relatively straightforward. Further, the hypermetrical line and one half which follow the speech (94b–95) have the same feeling and the same movement, as I read them, as do the three additional hypermetrical lines (97–99) which follow after the sudden shift back to normal rhythm, in the on-verse of line 96. I can see no reason for this shift, incidentally. It seems to me to read in the same way as the lines preceding and following it—which suggests the possibility that there was *no* reason, as we usually understand the word, for the

131

shift. It happened; the poet felt like it; he did not feel that he needed a "reason," nor did his audience. I suspect that the same may well need to be said for the lapse into hypermetricity, in line 132: this six-stress line, again, seems to me to read much like the four-stress lines preceding it and following it. As Larry D. Benson neatly says, in puzzling out the green skin of the knight of that color, in *Sir Gawain and the Green Knight,* "The green skin is puzzling because that is what the poet intended it to be."[14] Are we to deny individuality to medieval poets because they happen to be medieval—or because we, in our attempts to recapture the artistic norms by which they worked, have evolved "rules" more rigid than their actual practice? As Peter Dronke has said, speaking to precisely this point, "A poetic tradition has no deterministic power over the poets of individual talent who take that tradition as their point of departure."[15]

The battle scenes may prove a more powerful testing ground. Note, first, that they are mostly *not* in hypermetrical mode. Lines 199–267a, in which most of the fighting is accomplished, are all in normal four-stress lines. The *scop* shifts to hypermetricity, suddenly, in lines 272–73, maintaining the six-stress line for only those two lines and not resuming it until lines 287–90, where he again maintains the six-stress line for just four lines. He uses it only once more, after almost fifty metrically normal lines, in the hymn-like passage at the very close of the poem, lines 337–48—of which more in a moment. Here are lines 272–73, suddenly hypermetrical:

> . . . mid toðon torn þoligende.   Þa wæs hyra tires æt ende,
> eades ond ellendæda.   Hogedon þa eorlas aweccan
> hyra winedryhten. . . .

(272–74a)

[with teeth (-gnashing) suffering enduring. Then was their glory at an end, prosperity and deeds of courage. The men had meant to awaken their lord. . . .]

Almost elegiac—the word is not strictly apposite—these lines have a kind of slow relish to them. The *scop* wants to linger over the wretchedness of the Assyrians. I feel no padding, here—and even a doubly appropriate slowing down of the poem's movement, for what follows

[14] *Art and Tradition in Sir Gawain and the Green Knight* (New Brunswick, 1965), p. 91.
[15] *Poetic Individuality in the Middle Ages: New Departures in Poetry 1000–1150* (Oxford, 1970), p. 11.

immediately on lines 272–73 is the desperate entry into Holofernes' tent and the discovery of his bloody, headless corpse. Lines 287–91, once more, occur in the middle of the Assyrian discoverer-of-the-corpse's speech to his comrades; their full, slow, sombre movement is distinctly appropriate:

". . . mid niðum neah geðrungen,   þe we sculon nyde losian,
somod æt sæcce forweorðan.   Her lið sweorde geheawen,
beheafdod healdend ure."   Hi ða hreowigmode
wurpon hyra wæpen of dune,   gewitan him werigferhðe,
on fleam sceacan.

(287–91a)

[". . . with affliction closely rushing on, that we must of necessity perish,
together in battle perish. Here lies, slain by (a) sword,
our lord, beheaded." They then sorrowful
threw away their weapons, (threw them) down, departing wearily,
into flight hastened.]

My comments on lines 272–73 are essentially true here as well. They are also applicable to lines 337–48, which again presented no special problems in translation.

The very tentative critical approach I have suggested—the use of two contrasting techniques in hypermetrical passages, one with inflated rhetoric and slowed rhythm, the other with taut phrasing and quickened rhythm—clearly must now be modified. The *Judith scop* is peculiarly fond of hypermetrical lines. As I read those lines, the *scop* more often than not—but not invariably—employs hypermetricity for moments of elevated rhetoric; he usually—but not invariably—further employs the hypermetric lines as a kind of rhythmic brake. He is more often than not—but not invariably—successful in this usage of hypermetricity; he seems more uniformly successful when, for reasons unknown, he uses hypermetrical lines which do not delay the poem's movement, which are not elevated in rhetorical content. This particular *scop* seems to draw as much on his literary predecessors as he does on his own creative powers; he frequently employs what B. J. Timmer has—I think accurately—called a "stereotyped and conventional" style.[16] It is not surprising that he has difficulty, at times, in sustaining the longer line.

It seems clear, too, and again not surprising, that my perception of

16 *Judith*, ed. B. J. Timmer (London, 1952), p. 13. In more modern terms, a reviewer might be tempted to say that the *Judith* poet, though in many ways gifted, is often rather too "literary."

something not quite right about *Judith* is related to certain turgid features in some of the hypermetric lines, but is in no way caused by the abundance of such lines in the poem. "We will see again and again," writes Bernard F. Huppé, "that the structure and language of the poem are at the service of a thematic design . . . [and] that the poet's art is subtle, profound, original. . . ."[17] Huppé criticizes Timmer's appraisal of the poem, and particularly Timmer's criticism of those who, like Sweet, have made very large claims for *Judith*'s literary worth. It should be clear that I find Timmer's sense of the poem more true to the text—and Greenfield's recent analysis of Huppé's *Judith* discussion, singularly calm and careful, makes it plain that Huppé is in many ways quite wrong.[18] There are perhaps too many uncertainties, some of them probably unresolvable, for us ever to know the full truth about *Judith*. If, however, as Greenfield nicely urges, "we must work from the poem itself outwards,"[19] then a brief excursus into some of *Judith*'s problems may be of help both in solidifying our estimate of that poem and, ultimately, even in understanding the significance and scope of hypermetricity and rhetoric in Old English prosodic practice.

[17] *The Web of Words* (Albany, 1970), p. 148.

[18] *The Interpretation of Old English Poems* (London, 1972), pp. 96–100. Apart from Huppé's outright errors which are carefully discussed and detailed here by Greenfield, it is not surprising, I think, to find that Greenfield's strictures, which I endorse both in detail and in principle, are rather similar to some of the things I have been saying in this essay. Huppé's argument, says Greenfield, shows "how reasonable expectations can be drowned in pumping external cultural knowledge into a text instead of allowing textual meaning to flow out." Or as Greenfield rephrases this position, at the end of his discussion of Huppé's manifold errors, "We must work from the poem itself outwards *and submit our cultural knowledge to the text's rein*" (emphasis added).

[19] Greenfield, p. 100.

11

Judith: A Fragmentary and Political Poem

DAVID CHAMBERLAIN

CONSIDERABLE DISAGREEMENT NOW EXISTS OVER THE ORIGINAL STRUC-
ture of the Old English *Judith* since several influential critics are contending that the poem is virtually complete in the 349 lines that have
survived. Formerly, this view was not advanced seriously because of
the seemingly obvious evidence against it: 1) the poem begins in the
middle of a sentence; 2) it omits the first eleven chapters of the Vulgate
Book of Judith; and 3) it includes section or "lection" numerals X,
XI, and XII at lines 15, 122, and 236 of the edited text, suggesting
that over eight sections are missing. The most recent editors, Dobbie
(1953) and Timmer (1961) briefly defend the older view of the fragmentary nature of the poem,[1] and recent critics such as Brodeur, Renoir,
and Campbell accept this fragmentary nature without discussion.[2] The
opposing critics are following the lead of Rosemary Woolf, who was

[1] Elliott van Kirk Dobbie, ed., *Beowulf and Judith, ASPR,* IV (New York, 1953),
pp. lix f.; B. J. Timmer, ed., *Judith,* 2nd ed. (London, 1961), p. 2. I will quote from
Timmer's edition.
[2] A. Brodeur, "A Study of Diction and Style in Three Anglo-Saxon Narrative
Poems," in *Nordica et Celtica: Studies in Honor of Stefán Einarsson,* ed. Allan H.
Orrick (The Hague, 1968), p. 105; A. Renoir, *"Judith* and the Limits of Poetry,"
ES, 43 (1962), 146; J. J. Campbell, "Schematic Technique in *Judith," ELH,* 38
(1971), 166.

the first to develop a set of rational arguments for the virtual completeness of the surviving poem.[3] Woolf drew slightly on the views of earlier
scholars, Foster (1892) and Cook (1904), who could believe, on
aesthetic grounds (if it were not for the section numbers) that "at most
a few lines" of *Judith* were missing.[4]

Woolf has influenced Stanley Greenfield, in his important *Critical
History of Old English Literature,* to conclude that *"Judith* should
properly be regarded as a religious lay, akin to the secular *Finn Fragment* or *Maldon,* and not as a fragment of a larger religious epic."[5] Her
arguments are also used by Bernard Huppé to defend a detailed interpretation of the poem as a "compact heroic ode" which draws from the
patristic tradition exemplified in chapters by Ambrose and Aldhelm
that treat Judith briefly as an heroic exemplum or allegory. Huppé concludes that the "Latin precedents ... seem to reinforce the likelihood
that the poem as we have it is almost complete."[6] Independently, it
would seem, and on grounds of the poem's style—its non-moral and
purely narrative interest—the German critic, C. Enzensberger, has
decided that "probably only a little, perhaps only the beginning of the
first sentence is missing."[7]

To all these critics, the question of length is not academic; the validity
of their interpretations depends to a large extent upon it. Huppé expresses this succinctly when he writes, "the reader must decide between
these two views; for a long epic paraphrase ... must be judged differently from a compact heroic ode centering on the slaying of Holofernes."[8] A careful study of the evidence needed to make such a
decision has led me to formulate some new suggestions about the
source, emphasis, and occasion of the poem, although these cannot
be explored fully in the present essay. Unfortunately, a study of what
Judith might have been requires a good deal of "speculation." Ordinarily
I prefer to anathematize such speculation, as Judith does the spoils of
Holofernes (in the Vulgate, though not in our poem), but I do not
see how it can be avoided on this subject.

The external manuscript evidence for a much longer poem consists
mainly of the sectional numbers X, XI, XII (at lines 15, 122, 236),

[3] R. E. Woolf, "The Lost Opening to the *Judith,*" *MLR,* 50 (1955), 168–72.

[4] A. S. Cook, ed., *Judith,* Belles Lettres Series (Boston, 1904), note to line one;
T. Gregory Foster, *Judith: Studies in Metre, Language and Style, Quellen und
Forschungen,* 71 (Strassburg, 1892), p. 92.

[5] Greenfield, *Critical History* (New York, 1965), p. 165.

[6] Huppé, "Judith," *The Web of Words* (Albany, 1970), pp. 136–37, 141, 147.

[7] Christian Enzensberger, "Das altenglische *Judith*—Gedicht als Stilgebilde,"
Anglia, 82 (1964), 443, n. 23 (translation mine).

[8] Huppé, p. 136.

although both Greenfield and Huppé accept Woolf's reasoning that these numbers provide no significant argument.[9] Only six Old English poems have such sectional numbers in the manuscripts, she reminds us. These are *Beowulf* and *Judith* in the Nowell Codex (the second part of Cotton Vitellius A XV), *Elene* in the Vercelli Book, and the four poems of the Junius MS, *Genesis, Exodus, Daniel,* and *Christ and Satan.*[10] Three of these six, however (*Genesis, Exodus,* and *Daniel*), are numbered *seriatim* from I to LV, rather than individually, so, it is argued, *half* of the available evidence implies that the sections of *Judith* also may have been numbered *seriatim* with other poems rather than numbered separately. Since the present fragment seems to these critics to be aesthetically complete—in part because its ending echoes very closely two crucial phrases from its beginning—the evidence weighs in favor of *seriatim* numbering also in the *Judith* manuscript. Thus Woolf infers we have only a "slight loss" at the beginning that relates "a few details concerning Judith's identity and her motive for visiting the camp of Holofernes."[11]

This argument needs scrutiny. In the first place, it would appear that the existing numbered poems strongly imply that at least *ninety* lines or so of *Judith* have been lost. All the other numbered poems begin with a *full* section, suggesting that *Judith* also began with a full section. The existing sections of *Judith* consist of 107, 118, and 113 lines, or an average of 112 lines. Despite considerable variation in the average length of sections from one numbered poem to another, the sections are surprisingly uniform in length *within* each poem, though, of course, there are exceptions.[12] Subtracting the opening 14 lines from the average of 112, then, we get a likely approximation of 98 lines that are missing from the opening of *Judith*. Such a number is considerably more than Greenfield, Enzensberger, and Huppé wish to allow. But one hundred lines of addition really would not pose an aesthetic challenge to the unity of form and theme that critics see in the present 349 lines. The *Judith* poet could certainly have added an excellent 100 lines that would not have jeopardized the present unity, but in fact, improved it. Nonetheless, a missing 100 lines would have one considerable effect on present thinking, signally qualifying the argument for completeness

[9] Woolf, p. 170; Greenfield, p. 164; Huppé, p. 136.

[10] For the most part, I have used the Introductions to the *Anglo-Saxon Poetic Records* for facts about the numbering.

[11] Woolf, p. 171.

[12] B. J. Timmer, "Sectional Divisions of Poems in Old English Manuscripts," *MLR*, 47 (1952), 319–22, averages them. Timmer suggests the sections may be "psychological units of composition," what a poet could compose at one time before resting. Woolf strongly disagrees.

based on the similar wording of the opening and closing of the poem. If the phrases that now appear at the start of the poem (*tweode gifena* and *trumne geleafan*) are to be considered as occurring about 100 lines from the beginning, they remain very important thematically, but they no longer provide the neat symmetry and sense of completeness that critics now see in them. From this point on in my discussion, therefore, I do not accept the similarity of opening and closing phrases as evidence for completeness. As Timmer says, they appear at the present beginning of the poem only by coincidence.[13] Other arguments implied by these phrases will be discussed later.

The actual nature of the numbered sections poses quite another problem; Timmer and Woolf have sketched the history of this question.[14] Woolf seems right to agree with Gollancz, that the numbers indicate "suitable pauses in the narrative, but often not structurally important points, . . . where the hearers might momentarily rest their attention," as in the "lections" of monastic study or *meditatio* (*lectio divina*). She may not be quite so right in arguing that the numbers do not represent an author's own structural divisions. Some sections or "lections," as in *Beowulf,* may represent an author's intentions, as Klaeber thinks,[15] while other sections may represent an editor's or lector's intentions, as in the *seriatim* numbering of the Junius MS, where Woolf observes that it is inconceivable that *Genesis, Exodus,* and *Daniel* are the work of one author.[16] What matters at present is not so much the conjecturable motive for the numbered sections as the objective facts regarding them, and this leads to another argument for the fragmentary nature of the *Judith* manuscript.

For the *seriatim* numbering of three poems in the Junius MS does not turn out, after scrutiny, to have much relevance to the numbering of *Judith,* since among the four great manuscripts of Old English poetry, Junius is a special case. It is the only exclusively poetic manuscript. It is unique in having illustrations, and in its provision of space for more of them. It shows markedly more systematic preparation and organization than the other manuscripts, even though that care has broken down somewhat with the fourth and last poem (*Christ and Satan*).[17] That the

---

13 *Judith,* p. 17, n. 1.

14 In the articles cited; Woolf cited from p. 169.

15 *Beowulf,* 3rd ed. (Boston, 1950), p. ci. He also quotes from the Latin *Prefatio* to the *Heliand,* which states that "whole work is marked by fitts ("vitteas") which we are able to call lections or readings ("lectiones vel sententias"), and from the *Erfurt Glossary:* "una lectio *fitt*" (p. c., n. 3).

16 Woolf, p. 170.

17 G. P. Krapp, ed., *The Junius Manuscript, ASPR,* I (New York, 1931), pp. xi–xii.

Junius MS differs then from the other manuscripts in having an obvious, intelligent plan appears evident. The first three poems, numbered *seriatim*, deal only with *major* aspects of the Old Testament, and in chronological order (*Genesis, Exodus, Daniel*). The fourth poem *Christ and Satan*, representing the New Testament, is numbered separately and ends with the statement *Finit Liber II. Amen.* As the editor Krapp points out, the missing end of *Daniel* may well have included a similar indication for *Liber I.*[18] In any case, the four poems are clearly intended to be two distinct coherent units, and this is sufficient to explain why the first three poems are numbered *seriatim.* They offer a unique case not found in other manuscripts and having little relevance to *Judith.* None of the other three great codices is organized according to such an obvious principle of chonology, genre, or theme, so far as scholars have determined. The Exeter Book shows limited organization in placing the longest, most significant poem first (*Christ*), and the four other major poems next, but it shows no clear principle in arranging these (*Guthlac, Azarias, Phoenix,* and *Juliana*). Even though the Nowell Codex may possibly have been organized deliberately, if not obviously, as a Book of Wonders, there is no evidence that justifies likening it to the special case of Junius. Even if Nowell were so unified as a Book of Wonders, it offers no evidence of internal arrangement into Books, as in Junius. There is room at the end of each item in Nowell—the *Wonders of the East*, the *Letter of Alexander to Aristotle*, and *Beowulf*, which is numbered separately—to indicate the end of a "Book," but we find no such indication.[19]

The external evidence suggests, then, that we are more reasonable to expect in *Judith* the separate numbering that appears in *Beowulf, Elene,* and *Christ and Satan,* than to expect the very special case of *seriatim* numbering found in the first three poems of Junius.

Other Old English poems that are not actually numbered in the manuscripts also help to strengthen this case for separate numbering in *Judith.* Such poems, although not numbered, do have one or more other signs of sectioning, usually a large capital, often a space, and often elaborate punctuation at the end (colon with a dash, mainly in the *Exeter Book*). It is such signs, not the numbers, that are the principal signs of sections. The existing *numbered* poems in fact imply that these clear sections in the unnumbered poems would not have been numbered *seriatim* unless some clear principle of arrangement dictated it. In the Exeter Book, for example, the three different, but coherently grouped, parts of *Christ*

18 *The Junius Manuscript*, p. xii.
19 *The Nowell Codex,* ed. Kemp Malone, *EEMSF,* XII (Copenhagen, 1963).

(Advent, Ascension, Judgment), we could reasonably expect to be numbered *seriatim,* in the same way that the less disparate episodes of *Christ and Satan* (Fall of Angels, Harrowing of Hell, Christ's Temptation) are numbered *seriatim* in the Junius MS. But there is no equivalent reason to expect the miscellaneous sequence of *Guthlac* (A and B), *Azarias, Phoenix* and *Juliana* to be numbered *seriatim.* They are not a coherent series that is likely to have constituted a "Book" such as *Genesis, Exodus,* and *Daniel,* that would have provided a coherent series of "lections" in a monastic refectory or noble hall.

If the sections, then, were intended to mark reasonable pauses, or "lections," in some kind of coherent program of reading, as seems most likely, then there would seem to be no clear reason to number *seriatim* the two versions of *Guthlac* and the problematic *Azarias* with the complete and coherent *Phoenix* and *Juliana.* In the Vercelli Book, we recall, the only numbered poem is *Elene,* which is preceded and followed by a prose homily. *Andreas,* also preceded by a prose homily, has fifteen sections, each marked by capitals, so if it were numbered it would undoubtedly run from I to XV. It is possible that the one section of *Fates of the Apostles* which follows *Andreas* could have been numbered *seriatim* with it, somewhat as the Epilogue of *Elene* is numbered with that narrative (even though the word *finit* appears at the end of section XIV just before the Epilogue), but the greater differences, evident between *Andreas* and *Fates,* and the fact that *Elene's* numbering follows the numbering in the Latin sources of that poem reduce the likelihood that *Andreas* and *Fates* were conceived by the compiler as continuous reading, in the way the Epilogue is definitely conceived as continuous with *Elene.*[20]

The evidence of numbering, then, is at least three to one in favor of an original *Judith* of twelve sections. *If* the long poems in the Exeter Book were numbered, they would furnish only one instance (*Christ*) of *seriatim,* but four likely instances of separate numbering (*Guthlac, Azarias, Phoenix,* and *Juliana*). In the other manuscripts, there are three examples of separate numbering (*Beowulf, Elene, Christ and Satan*), and only one very special case, the Junius, of *seriatim* numbering. This hypothesized loss of eight-plus lections in *Judith* is not difficult to explain. The present fragment begins at the top of one folio (202a). As Dobbie computes, about 24 folios of *Judith* are lost. The scribe could have been copying from a complete version of *Judith,* but sometime after he finished, three quarters of the poem was lost. The same scribe

---

[20] On the similarity of *Elene's* sections to those of Latin sources, see P.O.E. Gradon, ed., *Cynewulf's* Elene (London, 1958), p. 19.

also copied *Beowulf* from line 1940 to the end, but the last leaf of *Beowulf* is battered and looks as if it once were the outside leaf of the manuscript book.[21] So appearances suggest that *Judith,* the product of the same scriptorium, was separate from *Beowulf* for a long period of time, thus allowing ample opportunity for twenty-four folios to have been lost. They may well have been separated and misplaced in the process of reading from them in a refectory or a hall.[22]

A final minor external argument can be based on the general nature of surviving Old English poetry. If *Judith* were virtually complete at present, it would be an anomaly in length and genre. Most obviously, *Judith* is a narrative religious poem and should be compared with others of this kind. Other Biblical narratives are much longer, and apart from *Genesis* (2936 lines), they are quite uniform in length. Taking missing passages into account, *Exodus, Daniel,* and *Christ and Satan* (though not properly a narrative) were all roughly between 700 and 800 lines long. Among the saints' narratives, *Andreas* (1722 lines) and *Elene* (1321 lines) are very much longer than the putative *Judith,* while the shorter *Juliana* (731 lines) and *Guthlac A* (818) are, nonetheless, twice as long, and even *Guthlac B,* at 560 lines, is substantially longer. Of the other major religious poems focused on one figure, the three parts of *Christ* are 439, 426, and 797 lines in length, and *Phoenix* is 677. Just from the viewpoint of probability, it is more likely that *Judith* would fall closer to the average length of poems in its class, that is somewhere around 1100 lines.[23] Although *Judith* has been likened to *Maldon* rather than to religious narratives in genre because of their common celebration of a hero and emphasis on battle, the two poems exhibit such great differences that no convincing evidence emerges for a short *Judith. Judith*'s biblical source, its abundant religious language, its significantly more "schematic" and climactic structure, all are marked differences from *Maldon.* All in all, external evidence suggests the much greater probability that *Judith* would be more equivalent in length to the other obviously religious narratives than to briefer secular and historical heroic poems such as *Maldon,* or the legendary *Finn Fragment.*

Internal and aesthetic arguments toward the fragmentary vs. the virtually complete nature of the *Judith* are more interesting. Cook, Woolf,

---

[21] *Judith*, p. 1; following R. W. Chambers, *Beowulf: An Introduction* (Cambridge, 1932), p. 509.

[22] Woolf suggests that a scribe would automatically repeat the numbers if the poem's beginning were lost (p. 170). First, the second scribe of the Nowell Codex shows that he is a faithful copyist. Second, he might wish to leave an accurate impression about the poem's original length.

[23] Averaging only *Genesis, Exodus, Daniel, Christ and Satan, Andreas, Elene, Juliana, Guthlac* A and B. *Juliana* was actually about 880 lines.

Greenfield, Enzensberger, and Huppé all emphasize the omission in the Old English poem of so many "leading characters" from the Vulgate version. The omissions of "Joachim, Achior, Ozias, Vagao, Nebuchadnezzar" are taken by these critics to imply that the poem could not have been a long epic treatment of the story.[24] But most of the omissions are not difficult to explain. Nebuchadnezzar, the Assyrian King, is mentioned only once (14:16) in the part of the Vulgate covered by the present poem ,12:8-15:14), and Holofernes is also named in the same breath. The Old English poet has no need to mention the King when he focuses on the general. In a longer *Judith,* Nebuchadnezzar could certainly have been named near the beginning as the tyrant and conqueror who sends Holofernes against Israel, but from Chapter 2 on, Holofernes is by far the more important character. This poet could easily have coalesced from the outset the similar aggressors Nebuchadnezzar and Holofernes. In any case, there is little reason to include Nebuchadnezzar in the part we have.

By the same token, Vagao, the eunuch servant of Holofernes, is a fairly prominent character in the part of the Vulgate used in the poem, but the poet has assimilated him into the group of Holofernes' anonymous retainers, and the portion we have seems only to gain from not naming him.[25]

Also not surprising is the poet's omission of the chief nobleman of Bethulia, Ozias, who has only two brief actions in the part of the Vulgate covered by the poem. The second action is inconsequential and much better omitted, for it would change unnecessarily the nature of the battle in the Old English poem to have Ozias send for soldiers from other cities of Israel (15:5-6), a change that few readers, I think, would find an improvement. Ozias's other action described in the Vulgate is a glorious praise of Judith. But if the poet had used it in its original place (13:23-26), it would weaken the exultant speech by Judith on her return, during which she first shows the head of Holofernes and then, immediately and consequentially, calls on her people for their dawn attack on the Assyrians (177-98). On the other hand, if Ozias's speech of praise were placed *after* Judith's appeal, it would again unnecessarily interrupt the pleasing, rapid, and coherent transition to the warriors departing at dawn (199-204). So there are good narrative reasons to eliminate from the poem Ozias's brief role as it appears in the later chapters of the Vulgate. This omission would not necessarily have forced the poet to omit Ozias's name in an earlier part of the poem, but

[24] Huppé's list, p. 137, with misprint corrected.
[25] In the Vulgate, Vagao invites Judith to the feast (12:12) and he is the one who finally dares to enter Holofernes' tent at dawn (14:13). He is not mentioned earlier.

even there his role from the Vulgate could easily have been merged anonymously with the other named and unnamed rulers and elders (*presbyterii; leoda ræswan,* 178a) who act with Ozias at times.[26] Moreover, given the emphasis in the poem on Judith's "folk" as a whole, some of the role of the leaders could have been transferred to the whole people. This would be consistent with the poet's seeming desire to develop Judith in part as a leader of her *folc.*

Furthermore, Ozias's high praise and the similar praise in the Vulgate by Joachim, the High Priest of Jerusalem (15:10–12), who arrives after the spoils of battle and celebrates Judith gloriously with his elders in a typologically suggestive vocabulary, may likewise have been coalesced into one earlier episode of praise—and even attributed to the people as a whole—by a poet deliberately intent on bypassing the manifest opportunities to allegorize and spiritualize Judith as the Church, or Joachim, the High Priest of Jerusalem, as Christ Himself,[27] in order to conserve and keep in the foreground, instead, those elements of the situation that would be more evocative of the tenth century Anglo-Saxon political scene.[28]

Only the character Achior remains, and while his omission poses something of a problem, it is not nearly such a problem that a long poem is "impossible" without him, as Rosemary Woolf suggests.[29] Achior is the gentile ruler of the Ammonites who enrages Holofernes by describing the power of Israel's God, and is sent as a prisoner to Bethulia where the Bethulians console him with the hope of God's help and of conversion (Ch. 6:12–21). In two brief episodes after Judith's return, Achior collapses in fear at the sight of Holofernes' head, praises Judith, and becomes a convert to Israel's God (Ch. 13:27–31; 14:6). Thus, his role is quite long in the earlier part of the story, but very short, although dramatic, in that part of the Vulgate covered by the poem. Some of the reasons offered earlier can help to justify his absence from a longer poem. In terms of the poem's narrative style, Achior's story is highly dramatic and interesting, but essentially digressive from the main plot and, therefore, expendable. Unlike Ozias, he could not *easily* have been used in the earlier part of the poem and then omitted in the last one-quarter,

[26] As on the occasion when Judith first rebukes him for giving a time limit to God (8:9 ff.) and then receives praise from all three rulers for being right (8:28).

[27] Rabanus Maurus, in his standard commentary, explicates the High Priest of Jerusalem as Christ Himself, who here comes to approve the faith and belief of His church, and who has blessed it with His abundant gifts. *Expositio in librum Judith,* PL 109, 579b. The commentary covers 541–92.

[28] That he knows the Vulgate story well enough (as most critics think) to have included this episode is suggested by several precise details, to be discussed later.

[29] Again, *MLR,* 50 (1955), 171.

although I do not think that this would have seemed impossible to the poet.[30] More probably the omission of Achior, like the omission of Joachim, is again another instance of deliberate refusal by the poet to construct or exploit the more obvious allegorical possibilities suggested by his scriptural source. An early medieval poet celebrating the faith and strength of Holy Church in its victory over the Devil[31] would not be inclined to omit, I think, the dramatic conversion of a pagan.[32] An educated poet who neglects such opportunity probably does not wish to emphasize a figurative reading in which Judith connotes mainly the Church. When he omits both the High Priest and the pagan convert, the avoidance of allegorical emphasis is even more striking.

Ælfric tells us, in fact, that one version of *Judith* was set down "as an example to men to defend our land against the assailing army." Ælfric may even have been referring to the present poem, since he implies that the work may be in English poetry, *on Englisc on ure wisan.*[33] In such a poem, inspired by victory or defeat against the Danes, the pagan Assyrians would be parallel to the Danes, but the other pagan Achior, an Ammonite who converts to Israel, would not be parallel to any feasible group on the Anglo-Saxon scene. In terms of cultural context, then, Achior may well have been omitted because he conflicted with the political situation of the times, which the poet wished to exploit in his strongly religious but mainly non-allegorical poem. Again, speculatively one might relate the poem to the Norse attacks of the tenth century, which also produced *Brunanburh* (A.D. 937). In this case, the Assyrians would represent the Norse invaders routed at the battle, and Achior would suggest the Anglo-Danes of Yorkshire, who were beginning to accept Christianity and some of whom probably aided Athelstan against the Irish Norse.[34] But despite the long tradition that glorified the Battle of Brunanburh,[35] the Norse threat in the tenth century seems to have been too restricted and short-lived to have generated the unusual intensity of the *Judith* poet, who one critic thinks "reveals an almost personal hatred for the Assyrians."[36] So Achior, it can be argued, is

[30] He could have implied strongly that Achior would convert if saved, and then omit the actual conversion. But it is more reasonable to think that the poet omitted him altogether, as unnecessary to the *main* plot.

[31] This is a main theme in the interpretations of Huppé and Campbell.

[32] Cf. Rabanus' commentary, *PL* 109, 576C.

[33] "*Libellus de veteri testamento et novo,*" in S. J. Crawford, *The Old English Heptateuch, EETS,* 160 (1922), 48.

[34] F. M. Stenton, *Anglo-Saxon England,* 3rd ed. (Oxford, 1971), pp. 322, 343, 356.

[35] See Daniel Abegg, *Zur Entwicklung der Historischen Dichtung bei den Angelsachsen, Quellen und Forschungen,* 73 (Strassburg, 1894), 27–34.

[36] Brodeur, "A Study of . . . Style," p. 105.

politically irrelevant as well as aesthetically digressive, though admittedly an allegorical emphasis would benefit greatly from his presence. But the *Judith* poet has rejected him and thus lessened the allegorical and heightened the political appropriateness of his work.

This omission of Achior and Joachim illustrates the *Judith* poet's characteristic technique of selecting only major dramatic episodes necessary to the main plot, but it does *not* mean that the poem had to be a short one, as Woolf and others contend. Indeed those who know the Vulgate story well, and then read the Old English, are not nearly as interested, I think, to know how the poet would have handled Joachim, or Achior for that matter, as they are interested to know how the poet might have developed other earlier crucial episodes. These would include the initial power and aggression of Nebuchadnezzar-Holofernes (Ch. 1–3), the fortifying and the ardent repentance of Israel (Ch. 4 and 6), the rage of Holofernes and the siege of Bethulia (Ch. 7), the decision to submit in five days (Ch. 7), Judith's long rebuking of this decision (Ch. 8), her prayers and beautifying (Ch. 9–10), her meeting with the scouts of Holofernes (Ch. 10), her appearance before Holofernes and his captivation by her beauty (Ch. 11). If these episodes were expanded proportionally to their dramatic interest and proportionally to the length of the episodes that do survive—such as the feast of Holofernes, the slaying, the rout of the Assyrians and the plundering—then the poet could readily have created a poem of 1200 to 1300 lines that would have moved rapidly and excitingly to the double climax we now have. Such a poem would also have the balance and irony of a terrifying attack at the beginning positioned against the present rout at the end. The aesthetic pleasure of the beheading, the rout, and the plundering would be considerably greater at the hands of this skillful poet if he had developed over a moderate time the wrath of Holofernes, the fear of Israel, the contrast of Judith's prayers and beautifying, and the suspense of her five-day mission. Furthermore, such a substantial account of the Assyrian attack at the beginning would correct a certain sense of structural misproportion that the poem, at present, seems to me to suffer from in having such a *long* battle and spoiling in so short a poem—141 lines (200b–341a) or close to half the poem (172 lines being half)— although the battle is very pleasing in itself.

Moreover, numerous details in the present poem would be more meaningful in a narrative of the whole story than they are now as parts of a supposed brief heroic poem. The very first sentence, assuming it is not negative, *tweode / gifena in ðys ginnan grunde* [She was doubtful of gifts on this wide earth] would be more meaningful if it came after the audience had seen that Judith was beginning to lose hope because she had been in Holofernes' camp for three days. The next thought, that she received protection *wið þæs hehstan brogan* [against that greatest terror, 4b] would be more meaningful if there had been some considerable display of Holofernes' terror earlier in the poem. In the next sentence, Judith's *trumne geleafan* [firm faith, 6b], for which God aids her, would be much more significant if the audience had experienced her vivid faith in rebuking the leaders of Bethulia (8:10–27) and in praying to God before leaving the city (9:2–19). Much more important than these details, the mention of *þy feorðan dogore* [on the fourth day, 12b], which has puzzled critics,[37] would clearly gain in meaning and suspense if the audience knew that Judith had asked the elders to pray continuously for *five* days to gain God's favor (Ch. 8:32). And both the beheading and the rout would be even more gratifying if they came on the last of five days given to Israel. In the same sentence, the first description of Judith's appearance, *ides ælfscinu* [magically—elvishly—beautiful woman, 14a] is unusually appropriate if the audience has previously heard of the captivation—almost the bewitching—of Holofernes and his companions by the natural and ornamented beauty of Judith when she presents herself, *gleaw on geðonce* [wise in thought, 13b], at his camp. Even the detail of her wisdom echoes a previous episode in the Vulgate where Judith amazes Holofernes' servants, and they declare *Non est talis mulier super terram in aspectu, in pulchritudine, et in sensu verborum* [There is not such a woman on earth in appearance, in beauty, and in sense of words, 11:19]. Thus, several details at the beginning of our fragment imply strongly that something more than a brief introduction preceded them. The poet's continued attention to details of beauty—*torhtan mægð* [splendid woman, 43a], *beorhtan idese* [shining lady, 58b, 340b], *seo beorhte mægð* [the beautiful woman, 254b]—which motivate Holofernes' lust and glorify the heroine, would be even more meaningful if Judith's deliberate cultivation of her beauty and its great effect on the Assyrians had been seen earlier.[38]

Other details about Holofernes would be more effective too if his earlier conquests, siege, and wrath had been directly presented to the audience. When he goes drunk to the tent, "He had reached his cruel end on earth such as he, the harsh lord of men, had earlier been working toward while he lived on earth under the roof of the heavens" (64b–67a). The "end of his glory, success, and strong deeds" (272b–73a), with his officers coughing and gnashing outside his tent, would surely be more ironic if that glory had been vividly rehearsed at the poem's start. The "old enmity" of the Assyrians and the "long suffering" of the He-

---

[37] J. J. Campbell, p. 167.
[38] Vulgate, 10:1–7, 14, 17; 11:19.

brew folk are other images that recur frequently and furnish a sustained political resonance for the original audience of the poem. Judith declares that a gift is given "for the afflictions which you long endured" [*þara læððа þe ge lange drugon,* 158]. The Hebrew soldiers are "those who suffered for a time before the insolence of foreigners, the insult of heathen" [*þa ðe hwile ær / elþeodigra edwit þoledon / hæðenra hosp,* 214b–16a]. The Hebrews awaken the *ealdgeniðlan / medowerige* [the old enemies drunk with mead, 228b–29a]; and repay *hyra fyrngeflitu* [their old struggles, 264a], the *ealde æfðoncan* [old grudges, 265a]; and plunder booty from *hyra ealdfeondum* [their old enemies, 315a] and *ealdhettende* [old foes, 320b]. In a short heroic poem, the action does not seem to warrant the consistently and variously imaged idea of such a long struggle. Therefore, while the suggestive connotations of these phrases might hint at the implication of allegorical warfare between the "ancient enemy," the Devil or his vices, and mankind or the Church, such details also suggest that the original *Judith* was a longer poem that showed the origin and duration of the strife with Holofernes, and they would simultaneously suggest the English wars against the Danes. Both of these effects would tend to diminish further the prominence of an allegorical meaning. Finally, the crowds of Bethulians, women and men, who ecstatically welcome Judith on her return (161b–70) would be more dramatic and thematic in impact if their earlier fear and ardent prayers (Ch. 4) had been directly presented.

Furthermore, the climactic image of Judith, no longer doubting about the reward for which she has long yearned, *Huru æt þam ende ne tweode / þæs leanes þe heo lange gyrnde* (345b–46a), is more appealing if her own previous piety as a widow (Ch. 8:1–8) and her long prayers for aid against Holofernes (Ch. 9) have been pictured by the poet. All these strongly implied continuities with a missing part of the poem strengthen considerably the likelihood of there having been a much more extended treatment of Israel's and Judith's heroic faith in the original longer poem, not really epic in scope or "leisurely," like *Beowulf,* but rapid, vivid, and intense, with its excitement and intensity naturally reaching a climax in the final one-quarter of the poem which has survived.

The proponents of a virtually complete *Judith* claim support for their view from the tradition of Latin writings that treat the biblical story briefly and selectively, and focus on the beheading of Holofernes as the poem does.[39] Chief among works they cite are Ambrose's short chapter

---

[39] Woolf, p. 170; Greenfield, p. 165; mainly Huppé, pp. 137–44, with translations of several passages. J. J. Campbell, pp. 159–60, draws on the same tradition, but does not think the poem is complete.

on Judith in his *Liber de viduis;* two brief sermons of pseudo-Augustine; Jerome's Letter 54 to Furia; short passages of poetry in Prudentius's *Psychomachia,* Dracontius' *De laudibus dei,* Aldhelm's *Carmen de virginitate;* and, most importantly, a short chapter in Aldhelm's prose *De virginitate.*[40] The brevity of these texts, their exclusion of other characters, their focus on the slaying and celebration of Judith herself (rather than Israel) as an heroic exemplum, or as an allegory, it is argued, all are qualities of the poem *Judith.* Furthermore, the traditions of Biblical paraphrase in the Old English *Genesis* and *Daniel,* according to Woolf, and the paraphrase tradition evident in Ælfric's homily on Judith, argues Huppé, are too different aesthetically from *Judith* to represent a tradition that could have generated that poem. Therefore, they conclude, the poem most likely derives from the tradition of brief heroic celebration.

Again, this reasoning seems to be incomplete, for a number of precise details—"the fourth day," "the bed curtain," "the serpent-hall" of Hell, and the "month's time" of the plundering[41]—suggest that the Old English poet was influenced strongly by the Vulgate text itself, although he treats that source very selectively. The Latin works just listed mention none of these details, with the one exception of Aldhelm's mentioning of the bed curtain (*conopeum*) in his prose *De virginitate.* Moreover, most of these exemplary treatments entirely bypass many of the minor narrative episodes that distinguish our poem: the elaborate feast itself, the seizing of the hair and the two sword strokes to Holofernes' neck, the bag for the head, the calling to the men on the walls, the farcical waking of Holofernes, the long plundering of the Assyrians. None of these, for example, are mentioned in Ambrose's chapter on the whole story, Jerome's Epistle 54 counselling widowhood, Prudentius' speech by Chastity, Dracontius' brief poetic sketch or Aldhelm's prose sketch of the whole story.[42] Among the better known brief treatments, only the two short sermons by pseudo-Augustine include these narrative details,

[40] Ambrose, *Liber de viduis,* I. vii, *PL* 16, 245A–47A; pseudo-Augustine, *Sermones* 48 and 49, "De Judith," *PL* 39, 1839–41; Jerome, *Letter 54,* "To Furia, on the preservation of the estate of widowhood," *Letters and Select Works,* trans. W. H. Freemantle, in *Select Library of Nicene and Post-Nicene Fathers,* Vol. 6 (New York, 1912), p. 108; *Prudentius,* ed. H. J. Thomson, Loeb Classical Library (Cambridge, Mass., 1962), p. 282 (lines 58–69). Dracontius, *De laudibus dei,* ed. F. Vollmer, Part 3, lines 480–95 in *MGH, Auctores Antiquissimi,* 14, 105; *Opera Aldhelmi, De virginitate,* ed. R. Ehwald, *MGH, Auctores Antiquissimi,* 15, 316–17.

[41] Lines 12, 47, 119, 324, from Vulgate 12:10, 13:10, 16:21, 15:13. Most critics seem to think that the poet invented Holofernes's punishment, but it is implied in the Song of Judith (16:21). I noticed it before reading Enzensberger (p. 455, n. 43).

[42] Ambrose mentions drunkenness, but no feast, *PL* 16, 247A; Aldhelm mentions the bag for the head in his short sketch in *Carmen de Virginitate,* line 2564.

and it is interesting and significant that these sermons, unlike most of the other works named, have no clear allegorical implications, although they are vividly religious.[43]

Furthermore, while so lacking in close resemblance to the *short* Old English poem, several of these Latin works do provide, though briefly, the essentials for a *long* poem about Judith, alluding to the major episodes that a longer poem would almost surely have included. In his prose chapter (ca. 170 words), for example, Aldhelm manages to mention (in this order) Judith's chastity as a widow, the terrifying attack of Holofernes' thousands, Judith's beautifying and ornamentation, and her return to the citizens with Holofernes' head.[44] The poet who composed *Judith,* while treating so vividly the beheading itself and the rout of the Assyrians, which Aldhelm does not mention, would nonetheless have found in Aldhelm many other seeds to generate an impressive long poem. Huppé prints an interesting illustration from the "Bible of San Paolo, Rome," composed of three panels picturing several episodes of the Judith story. Only the bottom panel portrays events described in the extant Old English poem, the beheading itself and the return with her handmaid and the head which occupy 65 lines of the poem (77b–141a). Hypothesizing a poet who would expand on the two upper panels—the departure from Bethulia and the reception by Holofernes—as he had the first panel (our present *Judith*), we can easily visualize a highly selective but *long* poem. Such graphic tradition, especially given the "pictorial vividness" of *Judith,* is almost as likely a source of inspiration for the poem as the tradition of brief literary celebration, and such a possibility ought to be explored further in a careful searching of illustrations in Anglo-Saxon Bibles.

Another brief Latin work that might provide a model for a *long* poem covering selected major episodes of the whole story is the Song of Judith itself. Apparently this Song was not used in the Anglo-Saxon Divine Office, monastic or secular, since it does not appear among the canticles of any of the Anglo-Saxon psalters that survive.[45] Although the last third of the Song (16:15–21) was added at some later time to the Office to be sung every Thursday at Lauds (except during Advent),[46] and the

---

[43] Modern scholars still attribute these sermons to an unknown African contemporary with Augustine, but they were part of the Augustine canon during the Middle Ages. See *PLS,* II (Paris, 1960), 841ff.

[44] *De virginitate,* Ch. LVII; see my note 40.

[45] James L. Rosier, "The Stowe Canticles," *Anglia,* 82 (1964), 397–432, edits the final set of canticles. For the other printed psalters with canticles, see his *The Vitellius Psalter* (Ithaca, 1962), pp. xii–xiii.

[46] In *Breviarum Romanum,* editio XV (Ratisbon, 1936). I have not traced down the date this partial Song of Judith was added to the Office.

poet probably did not hear in the Office this Song's vivid sketch of the main episodes of the whole story, it is nonetheless likely that he did know the Latin Song of Judith,[47] which is powerful and selective in its technique of construction, naming only Holofernes and Judith, but covering the major events of the whole story: the attack of Holofernes (5–6), the beautifying of Judith (9–11), the slaying of Holofernes in one line (*Amputavit pugione cervicem eius* [She lopped off his neck with a dagger]), and the rout of the Assyrians (12–14), with the other verses of the Song (1–4, 7–8, 15–21) given to praise of God.

Ambrose's brief chapter gives the same graphic encouragement to a poet to use earlier episodes of the story, although he organizes his six paragraphs topically around Judith's fortitude, chaste widowhood, wisdom, and temperance. She alone

> ... was able to recall from the gutters and to defend from the enemy the men broken by siege, shattered with fear, wasted with hunger. . . . Truly, as we read, when Holofernes, fearsome from success in many battles, had forced countless thousands of men within the walls, and armed soldiers were trembling and treating about their final end, she went forth beyond the walls.[48]

Although an Anglo-Saxon poet might not have vivified quite so much as Ambrose does the terror of the defenders, that such a poet would have been interested in the military psychology inherent in such a scene, we may infer from Old English poetry as a whole.

The two sermons of pseudo-Augustine offer even more major episodes, more concretely developed, than Ambrose's chapter. One sermon uses the story of Judith to praise the power of prayer;[49] the other sermon, wholly descriptive until the final line, ("The soul receives from God as great a gift as its faith is able to claim for itself"),[50] names only Holofernes and Judith, and it covers all the major episodes of the story with significantly literal, not allegorical, religious emphasis that is especially apparent in the beautifying of Judith:

> Rising from long prayers, she washes her body; putting on ornaments, she suspended golden hanging jewels and fits on her hands bejewelled

---

[47] He seems to have taken from the Song the image of Holofernes punished in Hell: *Dabit enim ignem et vermes in carnes eorum, / ut urantur et sentiant usque in sempiternum* [he will give fire and worms to their flesh / so that they may burn and suffer always, 21].

[48] *De viduis, PL* 16, 246A.

[49] *Sermo* 48, "De Judith," *PL* 39, 1839 and 1840.

[50] 1841.

rings, gathers to her adorned breast the flowing folds of a royal gown, going to battle with chaste beauty rather than with iron. The weapons of jewels, always hostile to modesty, have learned to strike the enemy.[51]

An Anglo-Saxon poet working from such a source may have de-emphasized the theme of deliberate fraud (though perhaps not, in his contemporary context of fraudulent Danes), but it seems unlikely that he would have omitted the great scene of Judith's beautifying. The pseudo-Augustine sermon goes on to sketch a number of elements that appear in the Anglo-Saxon *Judith:* her departure with a servant, the lust of Holofernes, the elaborate preparation of a nuptial chamber, the drunken stupor, the seizing by the hair, the severing and displaying of the head, and the ignominious rout. And though some episodes of the poem do not appear in the sermon—mainly the waking of Holofernes and the plundering—the sermon well illustrates my main point: a poet inspired by the Latin tradition of brief exemplary celebration would have found here several fetching episodes from the earlier part of the story that he would not have given up easily, and these Latin works would have led him quite naturally to a poem that was long, but selective.

Some critics have suggested that a strong precedent for a short *Judith* appears in the poem *Exodus,* which treats its biblical source with similar selectivity and heroic emphasis, even though *Exodus* is very different from *Judith* in verbal style, and considerably longer.[52] I am suggesting that the same principle of selectivity that produced the present *Exodus* would in fact have produced a long *Judith.* For the Old English *Exodus* is focused on one great martial episode from the biblical source, the destruction of Pharaoh's army. In the biblical Exodus, for all its sensation and suspense, there is no martial or "heroic" episode prior to the one great military event, while in the biblical Judith, on the other hand, the whole earlier story is emphatically martial: the conquests of Nebuchadnezzar himself, the great army of Holofernes that approaches Israel, the fortification of mountain tops and passes by Israel, and the long siege of Bethulia, with the cutting of its water supply. The *"Exodus* kind of poet," a poet who enjoys martial amplification, is not likely to have omitted the great opportunities for martial poetry afforded by the earlier part of the biblical *Judith* story. He could very well omit the exultant Song of Judith (16:1–21)—just as the actual *Exodus* poet omits the similar Song of Moses (Ch. 15)—and still wish to exploit the earlier episodes and themes of the story.

---

[51] 1840, ending *Monilium tela pudori semper adversa, hostem ferire didicerunt.*
[52] Woolf, p. 170; Huppé, p. 137. For Brodeur's view of stylistic differences, see his "A Study of . . . Style," pp. 105–14.

It might be argued here that if the *Judith* poet were motivated as the *Exodus* poet was, then he might be expected to draw on the lengthy description of Pharaoh's defeat that appears in Judith (5:9–14) making some use of the vivid allusions by Judith herself to the great fathers Abraham, Isaac, Jacob, and Moses, as they seem to have been used in the Old English *Exodus* itself.[53] But the *Judith* poet, as I have argued earlier, seems not to have been mainly interested in allegory (as the *Exodus* poet clearly was), and the typologically forceful inclusion of these resonant figures would have run counter to his purposes. In fashioning the longer *Judith* I am hypothesizing here, he would have excluded these typological figures, giving the same literal religious emphasis to the earlier episodes that he seems to me to give to the feast, the slaying, the awaking, the twin rewards of plunder and heaven, though to *some* of his allegorically minded audience the poem would undoubtedly have nonetheless evoked allegorical, as well as literal, religious implications.

One possible source for a long and selective *Judith* that has never been mentioned, so far as I know, is the reading or "lessons" from the Old Testament incorporated into the Divine Office. Most of these "lessons" occurred in the Nocturns or night Office. On Sundays and feasts, the first Nocturn included three "lessons"; the second Nocturn, three "lessons," and the third Nocturn, nine "lessons." On weekdays, the night Office included only one Nocturn with three "lessons."[54] It was mandatory in the Roman, or secular, Office, between Pentecost and Advent, to read the books of "Kings and Paralipomenon, thereafter the books of Solomon, Job, Tobias, Judith, Esther, and Maccabees" at Nocturns,[55] but the time that could be given to these books would vary, depending on the date of Easter and on the number of saint's days that took precedence in different churches. The length of these selective readings was further controlled by the wishes of the one presiding, as well as by the hour of dawn, when Lauds had to begin (the readings were sometimes very long). Thus the readings from a book of the Old Testament, which began anew each Sunday, provided for the frequent possibility that previous books could be left unfinished. There is every reason to think,

[53] See Huppé, *Doctrine and Poetry* (New York, 1959), Ch. VI, pp. 217–23; J. E. Cross and S. I. Tucker, "Allegorical Tradition and the Old English *Exodus,*" *Neophil.,* 44 (1960), 122–27.

[54] Dom Pierre Salmon, *L'Office Divin au moyen age: Histoire de la formation du bréviaire du IXe au XVIe siècle,* Lex Orandi 43 (Paris, 1967), p. 33; I. M. Hanssens, ed., *Amalarii episcopi opera liturgica omnia, Stude e Testi* 138 (Rome, 1948), "Liber Officialis," Libellus IV, cap. 9–11, pp. 442–54. Amalarius of Metz's *Liber Officialis* shows the general structure of the Roman, or secular, Office in the ninth and tenth centuries, but no specific "lessons" that were used in Rome or elsewhere.

[55] *Antiquus ordo Romanus,* PL 66, 1002C.

then, that the author of the poem *Judith,* very likely a secular clerk or monk, would have heard, numerous times, in the "lessons" for Nocturns, a selective reading of Judith that particularly stressed the early episodes, for the simple reason that such reading often would not have time to reach the later, better known episodes.

The specific texts of these Nocturnal "lessons" varied from place to place, and many manuscripts of lectionaries and breviaries lack specific texts or indicate them only briefly or partially, making evidence of specific readings peculiarly scarce. I have discovered no evidence of specific readings in the widely practised Roman Office brought to England by Augustine of Canterbury and Theodore of Tarsus, and observed regularly at least until the great Danish disruptions of 865. Nor have I found any specific texts indicated for this Office that also must have flourished later, at least from the time of Athelstan (924–940), stimulated especially by the Benedictine Revival of A.D. 960–1000. The *Collectar* of Leofric, Bishop of Exeter (1050–1072), while it indicates "lessons" from Job and Tobias, only implies them from Judith.[56] The later *Sarum Breviary,* however, does show six such "lessons" from the Book of Judith, selections from Chapters One to Six, which take the story as far as Holofernes' initial attack.[57] And the *Hereford Breviary* (ca. 1300) indicates that Judith is read in the last week of September, and it provides six selections from Chapters One to Seven, up to the start of Holofernes' siege.[58]

The Benedictine, or Monastic, Office shows no more clearly than the Roman Office the specific amount of reading to be taken from the Book of Judith. However, the Rule of St. Benedict provided about the same numbers of "lessons" at Nocturns as the Roman Office, which indicated the Book of Judith as one of the mandatory sources for Nocturns between Pentecost and Advent. And the *Regularis Concordia* of St. Ethelwold (ca. 970), which made English practice more uniform, follows Benedict's "lessons," though it too gives no specific texts.[59] Neither does the *Portiforium of St. Wulstan* (ca. 1065) name any specific readings

---

[56] *The Leofric Collectar,* eds. E. S. Dewick and W. H. Frere, *HBS,* 45 (London, 1914), cols. 283–86. It does not mention at all the fourth Sunday in September, which was the traditional place for reading *Judith,* so the omission of the name of the book is no evidence that it was not read. Probably it was. *Tobias* is named in its usual place, the second and third Sundays of September.

[57] *Breviarum ad usum insignis ecclesiae Sarum,* eds. Francis Proctor and Christopher Wordsworth, Fasciculus I, ii, Ordo temporalis (Cambridge, 1882), mcccxv.

[58] The *Hereford Breviary,* eds. W. H. Frere and L. E. G. Brown, *HBS,* 26 (London, 1904), I, 450–52.

[59] Dom Thomas Symons, ed., *Regularis Concordia* (London, 1953), pp. xxxi–xxxiii, xli, and cap. i–vi, esp. vi; Justin McCann, ed., *The Rule of St. Benedict,* passim; J. B. L. Tolhurst, *The Monastic Breviary of Hyde Abbey, Winchester,* VI, *HBS,* 80 (London, 1942), "The *Opus Dei* of St. Benedict," pp. 7–14, etc.

from Judith, but the incomplete manuscript strongly implies there were such readings.[60]

The later *Monastic Breviary of Hyde Abbey* (ca. 1300) shows fourteen readings from Judith at Nocturns on Sunday and on two weekdays in the last week of September.[61] These "lessons" are short selections of high points in the narrative from Chapters One to Ten, up to the moment when Judith beautifies herself. The breviary provides readings for only two weekdays, so it is possible that other readings were added on occasion. This breviary probably reflects accurately the disciplined performance of the Office that was re-instituted during the later tenth century in both monasteries and cathedrals, and it suggests how well known the earlier part of the story would have been to the clerk or monk who likely composed the Old English poem.

Finally, consideration must be given to the argument for a presently complete *Judith* which claims that the poem so radically shifts the emphasis of the story from the "triumph of the Hebrew nation" and the "nationalistic spirit" in the Vulgate to celebration of Judith's own chastity and virtue, and so "limits the [nationalistic] implications," as the Latin exempla supposedly do, that it would be largely irrelevant to present any earlier episodes.[62] It should first be observed that the final triumph of the city or nation is actually more glorious in the English poem than in the Vulgate, even though it is not so specifically a *Hebrew* victory. It takes place with Judith off the scene entirely for almost two-fifths of the poem (lines 199–333), further emphasizing a "national" rather than a "personal" quality in the triumph, although it is Judith who makes victory possible.

We should further note that, if the poem is limited to celebration mainly of Judith's own virtue, as critics claim, it is quite strange that the

---

[60] Ed. Dom Anselm Hughes, II, *HBS*, 90 (London, 1960), 40–46. The readings for the time after Pentecost are obviously incomplete. The manuscript (CCCC 391) includes the heading "INCIPIUNT RESPONSORIO DE IUDIT" (scribal errors for "responsoria de Iudith" says the editor), but then the Responds given are not from the Book of Judith but from Proverbs, and the Lessons are from Proverbs. Also in the cases of the other Old Testament books mentioned, Kings, Job, Tobias, and Maccabees, the Lessons are from the same book as the Responds. The heading about Judith, then, clearly implies that to match the Responds from Judith there were lessons from Judith in the pre-Conquest monastic breviary at Worcester and Winchester (see Hughes, pp. vi–vii, on the close relationship of Wulstan's *Portiforium* with Winchester). This is the earliest edited English Breviary.

[61] Ed. J. B. L. Tolhurst, II: *Temporale* (Easter to Advent), *HBS*, 70 (London, 1933), fol. 144v–45v. Tolhurst's collation shows that the same readings were customary at Coldingham (cell of Durham), Muchelney, and Evesham.

[62] Woolf, p. 171; Greenfield, p. 165; Huppé (*Web of Words*, p. 147) defends the patriotic relevance of the poem, but submerges it in the spiritual significance of Judith's beheading.

heroine is not praised specifically for her chastity or loyal widowhood anywhere in the Old English poem, although she is praised abundantly for these traits in every other version of the story I have seen. She is the *eadigan mægð* [blessed maiden, 35a], the *snoteran idese* [wise lady, 55a], the *halige meowle* [holy woman, 56b], *scyppendes mægð* [woman of God, 78a], *ides ellenrof* [courageous lady, 109a], *gleawhydig wif* [prudent wife, 148a], but nowhere does she have the *clænnysse* [chastity] and *wudewanhade* [widowhood] of Ælfric's metrical homily,[63] or the *castitas* and *viduitas* of the Vulgate and Latin versions.

The terms *halige* and *mægð* could of course connote chastity, if it had been clearly established earlier. But chastity and widowhood may not have been stressed because they would not have fitted so well with a likely audience for the poem, the noble Anglo-Saxon households responsible for defending the kingdom, in which the most influential women would have been wives, not virgins or widows. Therefore, the poem clearly stresses the faith, wisdom, courage, holiness, and beauty of Judith but not her chastity.

An important corollary to this de-emphasizing of chastity is the de-emphasis of allegory. Chastity and widowhood are major imageries in the traditional *allegoresis* of Holy Church. To have made them emphatic would have strengthened the allegorical association of Judith with the Church, but their absence works, with the absence of Achior and Joachim, to weaken the implications of allegorical meaning in the present poem. Other details also seem to weaken allegorical emphasis. If Holofernes is to signify mainly the Devil, as he does in the allegorical readings of Campbell and Huppé, it is unsuggestive that his "soul" now goes to Hell for the *first* time, never to return (111b–20b), since we know from other works (*Elene, Juliana, Guthlac*) that Old English poets thought of the Devil as constantly returning to earth.

Allegorical implications are also weakened when Judith keeps the spoils of Holofernes rather than sacrificing them "in a curse of oblivion" as she does in the Vulgate (16:23). To Rabanus, this giving up of Holofernes' "implements of war" signifies Holy Church making acceptable to God souls that have been deluded by the Devil;[64] and sacrificing his bed curtain (*conopeum*) or "net for flies" (*rete muscarum*) is to curse the Devil's "frauds."[65] But in the Old English poem Judith neither brings home the "fly net" (47a) to curse it, nor gives up the spoils. Our poet deliberately avoids these two traditional opportunities for allegorical

[63] Homily on Judith, ed. Bruno Assmann, *Angelsächsische Homilien und Heiligenleben, Bib. angel. Prosa* III (Kassell, 1889), 102–16, lines 200–04, 389–94, 399.
[64] *PL*, 109, 588B.
[65] 588C.

meaning, as well as bypassing an opportunity for Judith to practice a more literal kind of unworldliness in giving up the spoils. Here again he makes his poem more politically appropriate, stressing the realistic importance of booty that we can document vividly from accounts in the *Anglo-Saxon Chronicle,* and even more from the *Chronicle* of the nobleman Æthelweard.[66] Especially if the audience had been invited by the poem to recall its long struggle with the Danes (an argument which I strongly press here), it would have viewed Judith's warfare as literally pious, and the victory as a literal reward for faith, both on earth and in later heaven: *mærðe on moldan rice, swylce eac mede on heofonum* [glory in the worldly kingdom and also reward in heaven, 343], even as Judith is blessed forever in the *literal* Vulgate narrative (*et ideo eris benedicta in æternum,* 15:11).

Furthermore, several other aspects of the standard allegorical tradition seen in Rabanus' commentary (which was incorporated into the *Glossa ordinaria*) are inconsistent with the general tone and mood of the Old English poem. We see that Rabanus does not emphasize Judith's beauty, though the poem does; he does emphasize her chastity, though the poem does not. To Rabanus, the battle itself is a spiritual one (against the devil and sins, not flesh and blood) and the arms are the familiar celestial arms of St. Paul, "the shield of faith, the breastplate of justice, the helmet of salvation, the sword of the word of God,"[67] which are the weapons named in Judith's exhortation of the Bethulians (191b–95a). But in the more realistic battle imagined by the Anglo-Saxon poet, the principal weapons are spears (223b–25a) and arrows (220b–23a), and the arrows do weaken allegorical implications of divine justice because they are generally characterized as the weapons of the devil, as in *Beowulf* (1742b–44b), and *Juliana* (382a–87a), despite the tradition of God's (and Apollo's) divine arrows.[68] In the hands of the *Judith* poet, the arrows create realistic battle but inappropriate allegory.

A long *Judith,* without obvious allegorical emphasis, would be a powerful religious poem and a keenly political one, and Ælfric tells us in fact that a *Judith* was written in order to resist the Danes. The similarity of the general situation in this poem to Anglo-Saxon warfare against the

---

[66] A. Campbell, ed., *The Chronicle of Æthelweard* (London, 1962), under the years 871, 893, etc. The Laud Chronicle, A. D. 933, 997, 1003, etc. Also Asser, *Life of Alfred,* trans. J. A. Giles, *Six Old English Chronicles* (London, 1878), pp. 50, 62, 64–65.

[67] *PL,* 109, 577AB, 578A.

[68] See, e.g., Psalms 7: 14, 37: 3, 76: 18; also Apollo's arrows in the killing of Python. See *Mythographus Vaticanus Primus,* I. 113; *Secundus,* 18; *Tertius,* 8.1, ed. G. H. Bode (Cellis, 1834).

Danes is striking, not only in its battling and plundering, but in its drunken feasting, suggestive of Danes, and its walled fortress (*fæstenne*, 143a; *ginnan byrig*, 149a; *fæsten geates*, 162a; *heanne weall*, 161a, etc.), suggestive of English fortified towns in the tenth century. Proponents of the short poem as virtually complete speak of the unrealistic, unnationalistic quality of the diction;[69] but several clusters of words seem to me to have strongly political and nationalistic associations. The realistic *hæðen* is often applied to the Assyrians (98b, 110a, 179a, 216a), as it often is to the Danes in the *Chronicle*.[70] Although the word *here* is once applied to the Bethulians [army, 161b], it is immediately paralleled with *folc* [the people, 162b]; otherwise this word and most of its compounds are applied exclusively to the Assyrians, a usage that recalls the application of the same vocabulary to the Danes in the *Chronicle*. Judith goes *ut of ðæm herige* (135b); Holofernes is the *herewæða* (126a, 173a); the Assyrians are the *herefolc* (234a, 239a) and most of their "host" (*þæs heriges*, 293a) is destroyed. Assyrians are also the strangers or foreigners (*elðeoda*, 237a) in the *Judith*, while the Bethulians are emphatically a *folc* [folk, people, 143b, 176b], the *sigefolc* (152a), and the *folc Ebrea* (262a), (*mægeneacen folc*, 292a), another discrimination of terms often employed in the *Chronicle* to distinguish the English *folc* from the foreign invaders. More emphatically the Bethulians are the "natives" (*landbuend*, 226a, 314a) defending their "home" (*eðle*, 169a) and "dwelling place" (*folcstede*, 319a), "guardians of the homeland" (*eðelweardas*, 320a) in phrases that embody realistically the Anglo-Saxon ethic of war, as J. E. Cross recently suggests.[71]

Certain minor details of action also suggest a poet realistically in touch with a political situation. Judith does not sit through the drunken feast, as she does in the Vulgate. This obviously heightens her coming to the tent, but by sparing the heroine a long and degrading experience it also allows for more identification between noble women in the poem's likely audience and Judith, the noble woman of the poem (*seo æðele*, 176a, 256a). In the Vulgate, Judith herself takes the head out of the bag (13:19), but in the Old English poem she commands her handmaid to do it (171–73). In the Vulgate and Latin works, Holofernes' head is

---

[69] Woolf, p. 171; Greenfield, p. 165; J. J. Campbell, p. 165, though he thinks the poem was much longer.

[70] In the Parker (A) Chronicle, ed. C. Plummer, *Two of the Saxon Chronicles Parallel* (Oxford, 1892), A.D. 838, 851, etc., but drops out surprisingly from 870 on, at the height of warfare; appears in the poem on Edmund (942). In the Laud (E) Chronicle, appears in 959, in the poem on Eadwig, and in 963, but not thereafter. It has associations, therefore, with historical poetry in the mid-tenth century.

[71] "The Ethic of War in Old English," in *England before the Conquest*, eds. P. Clemoes and K. Hughes (Cambridge, 1971), p. 275.

displayed prominently on the walls, but not in the Old English poem, and so far as I know, this custom, used by William the Bastard, was not commonly practiced by Anglo-Saxons in the tenth century. Again, the omitting of Ozias avoids any possible tincture of shame to noblemen in the audience, by not making a male ruler less courageous than a woman. The Old English poem, then, glorifies a noble woman, emphasizes her faith, prudence, and courage, while offering a religious and political example to the whole audience without demeaning Anglo-Saxon noblemen. And the same, I am sure, was true of the long, almost epic, poem that originally existed.

Tentatively, I suggest that the most appropriate occasion in Anglo-Saxon history for the political and religious exemplum of this poem is the crisis under Æthelred from 990 to 1010. Cook suggested that the poem celebrates in A. D. 856 the second wife of Æthelwulf of Wessex, twelve-year-old Judith, daughter of Charles the Bald,[72] but that occasion itself was not especially glorious, the language of the poem shows no evidence of Early West Saxon, and the tone of the poem seems too intense for that early stage of the Danish Wars. Foster suggested that the poem celebrates Alfred's famous daughter, Queen Æthelflæd of Mercia, about A. D. 917 when she had recaptured the "five boroughs" of Danish Mercia. By that time, however, despite constant battling, there was beginning, according to Stenton, a merger of Danish and English culture and a conversion to Christianity in Mercia, which would seem not to fit the emotional animus of the poem. Æthelflæd was by then a widow, like Judith, but the poem (as I have earlier argued at some length) seems to de-emphasize both widowhood and chasteness, another trait of the Queen, according to William of Malmesbury, who says that after a very hard first childbirth she refused permanently the pleasures that led to such troubles.[73]

On the other hand, in the decade from 990 to 1000 the *Chronicle* and the sermons of Ælfric and Wulfstan all present a great need for the ideals that this poem so forcefully embodies, and there is nothing in the Late West Saxon language of the poem (and its few Anglican forms) to prohibit such a late date, especially if it were the work of an older poet, though it would admittedly be unusually close to the date of the manuscript (ca. 1000). The intensity of ravaging and the collapse of leadership, with actual flight by leaders just before battle, is strikingly reported in the *Chronicle* (MS C)[74] from 980 to 994, intensifying

[72] Cook, *Judith* (Boston, 1888), pp. xxix–xxiii; Foster, *Judith: Studies,* pp. 89–90.
[73] Quoted by Foster, p. 90, n. 2.
[74] Margaret Ashdown, ed., *English and Norse Documents Relating to the Reign of Ethelred the Unready* (Cambridge, 1930).

greatly between 990 and 994, followed by a lull until 997, but four years were enough to have inspired a poem.

The monk Ælfric is not usually political, but in these years he returns often to the need to battle against the heathen in his comments at the end of his *Judges, Maccabees,* and his Epilogue to the *Heptateuch.* In homilies of this and the next decade, he urges King and people to win God's favor by "right action and prayer"; the King to defend his people and give his life for them; the clergy to pray and the nobility to fight.[75] In the homilies of Wulfstan, the theme of *riht geleafa* [right faith] and *soð geleafa* [true faith] constantly recurs as the remedy for political and moral defeat by the "heathen" Danes,[76] and this is just the major theme of *Judith,* stronger than in any other Old English poem: *trumne geleafan* (6b), *soðne geleafan* (89a), *rihtne geleafan* (97a), and *soðne geleafan* (344b). For the disasters so tellingly rehearsed by Wulfstan, the poem *Judith* presents the ideal remedy. The disciplined Nocturns of the Benedictine Revival would have made the story better known than it had been for a century to secular and monastic clergy. The strong political role of monasticism during the Revival,[77] and its nationalism, as seen in the *Regularis Concordia,*[78] also would have encouraged a poetic monk or clerk to inspire his country with a long, selective, heroic religious poem that paralleled his country's situation. Whether or not this reconstruction of the occasion itself is credible, there is abundant evidence that the original poem was long, and strongly political.

[75] Crawford, ed., *The Old English Heptateuch,* pp. 50–51, 414–17; J. C. Pope, ed., *Homilies of Ælfric: A Supplementary Collection,* I, *EETS,* 259 (Oxford, 1967), 373 and 380–81 (lines 46–63). Ælfric emphasizes that the *oratores* are exempt from literal warfare to battle invisible enemies and the *bellatores* should defend the nation ("Old and New Testament," line 1207 f. in *Heptateuch*). This distinction would seem valid for *Judith.*

[76] Dorothy Bethurum, ed., *The Homilies of Wulfstan* (Oxford, 1957), Homily IV. 91; XIII. 67–67; VIIa. 17–18; XII. 4, 49; V. 117; and VII, where *soðan geleafran* recurs about fifteen times.

[77] Dom David Knowles, *The Monastic Order in England,* 2nd ed. (Cambridge, 1963), p. 46.

[78] Symons, *Regularis Concordia,* pp. xlvi and li.

The Lyric Tradition
SECULAR AND RELIGIOUS

12

Toward a Critique of
The Dream of the Rood

ALVIN A. LEE

The Dream of the Rood IN THE VERCELLI MS IS ONE OF THE MOST admired and discussed of Old English poems. Generically a dream vision using the diction of Anglo-Saxon *dryht* poetry, it is at once a heroic battle poem and a starkly effective re-creation of the Christian Passion story. Its evident purpose is to reveal in words to the sons of men that it is through the *wuldres beam* [beam of glory] that they can triumph over *Adomes ealdgewyrhtum* [Adam's ancient works]. Once this victory is behind them, they may become members of the *dryhtnes folc* [Lord's people] who are seated in *singal blis* [endless bliss] at the *symle* [banquet] in the *eðel* [homeland] to which Christ returned following his period of incarnation on earth. The narrative of the poem is deeply involved in the central quest-theme of biblical mythology, the human desire for a return to that *dream* [joy] with God which was forfeited by the disloyalty of the thane Adam when long ago he tasted the forbidden fruit in the guest-hall of Eden.

Since *The Dream of the Rood* is based in part on the crucial tragic episode in Christian myth—the crucifixion of Christ—any attempt to understand it critically as a poem will have to deal with the fact that, as a literary structure, the story of the Passion is a tragedy. More specifically, it is that kind of tragedy in which strong emphasis is placed on the completeness of the hero's achievement. To describe the New Testament accounts of the death of Christ as tragic is not to suggest that they focus on any moral flaw in him as an explanation of the crucifixion. Rather they emphasize the ways in which the sin and wrong-doing of the world, once these are combined with Christ's willingness to be sacrificed, inevitably precipitate his death. But despite the innocence and perfection of the protagonist the primary impact of these accounts of the death on the cross is nonetheless tragic, and evocative of feelings of pity and fear. The overall biblical narrative of course does not end with this tragic episode within its total pattern of meanings and neither does *The Dream of the Rood*. Like other Christian tragedies shaped by New Testament accounts of the death of Christ, the poem is deeply involved in the paradox of victory through apparent defeat. However powerful becomes the poem's imaginative focus on events surrounding the death of Christ, and on the part played in them by the tree who tells the story, there is always another perspective at work whereby the tragedy is seen as an episode in a larger pattern of meaning symbolized by resurrection and redemption. From one perspective the dreamer-poet sees a bleeding tree or body but from another he sees a gold-covered, jewelled *sigebeam* [victory beam]. The first of these points to the dominance of sin and death *her on eorðan* [here on earth], the second to the tree as a *beacen* [beacon] leading his soul away from the world into a kingdom of joyful banqueting.[1]

The critical method used in this article requires some explanation, since it is not in all respects familiar in the field of Old English studies. As all of us know who engage in literary scholarship in this age of sophisticated criticism, any work of literature can be placed in a variety of contexts or relationships for purposes of discussion and interpretation:[2] the rhetorical texture and structure of the poem itself,[3] the poem's his-

---

[1] The edition cited throughout is *The Vercelli Book*, ed. by G. P. Krapp (New York, 1932). It is not possible within the compass of one article, even if one possessed the necessary knowledge and insight, to give a complete account of the art and meaning of so concentrated and fine a poem as *The Dream of the Rood*. What I offer here is a preliminary critical and interpretative commentary on the text itself. In time, this critical prolegomenon may become the basis of a more complete book-length study including the text on the poem, a translation, a full-scale critical commentary, and an annotated bibliography.

[2] For a theoretical discussion of these contexts see my "Old English Poetry, Mediaeval Exegesis and Modern Criticism" in Hugh Keenan, ed., *The Typological Interpretation of Mediaeval Literature*, Studies in the Literary Imagination, Vol. 8, number 1 (Atlanta, 1975).

[3] In recent years much good work of this kind has been done. See the following: J. A. Burrow, "An Approach to *The Dream of the Rood*," *Neophil*, 43 (1959), 123–33, reprinted in *Old English Literature: Twenty-two Analytical Essays*, ed. by Martin Stevens and Jerome Mandel (Lincoln, Nebraska, 1968), pp. 253–67; Faith

torical context or background,[4] its capacity for being read as an exemplary work or potential allegory of human life,[5] its place in a literary tradition,[6] and its function as a religious or anagogic poem pointing beyond both poetry and history. In the commentary that follows no one of these contexts or perspectives is consistently emphasized, though each of them is recognized and the first receives a good deal of attention. At appropriate points in the discussion, parallels between the members of this series and the mediaeval four levels of meaning also are explored: the rhetorical and historical perspectives correspond to the older literal-historical level, the exemplary to the allegorical, the literary or archetypal to the tropological, and the anagogic to the level of the same name in the earlier exegetical tradition. The mediaeval levels are used not as the foreground of the critical discussion but as a series of additional perspectives paralleling those of the main critical activity. In other words, the article is modern criticism, not exegesis, but it is cognizant of, and influenced by, the old ways of thinking about scriptural matters.

H. Patten, "Structure and Meaning in *The Dream of the Rood*," *ES*, 49 (1968), 385–401; Louis H. Leiter, *"The Dream of the Rood:* Patterns of Transformation," in *Old English Poetry: Fifteen Essays,* ed. by Robert P. Creed (Providence, Rhode Island, 1967), pp. 93–127; M. J. Swanton, "Ambiguity and Anticipation in *The Dream of the Rood*," *NM*, 70 (1969), 407–25; O. D. Macrae-Gibson, "Christ the Victor-Vanquished in *The Dream of the Rood*," *NM*, 70 (1969), 667–72; Carol J. Wolf, "Christ as Hero in *The Dream of the Rood*," *NM*, 71 (1970), 202–10; Robert R. Edwards, "Narrative Technique and Distance in *The Dream of the Rood*," *Papers on Language and Literature,* 6 (1970), 291–301; part II of Bernard F. Huppé, *The Web of Words: Structural Analyses of the Old English Poems Vainglory, The Wonder of Creation, The Dream of the Rood, and Judith* (Albany, New York, 1970), pp. 63–112; Constance B. Hieatt, "Dream Frame and Verbal Echo in *The Dream of the Rood*," *NM*, 72 (1971), 251–63.

[4] See Howard R. Patch, "Liturgical Influence in *The Dream of the Rood*," *PMLA*, 34 (1919), 233–57; Margaret Schlauch, *"The Dream of the Rood* as Prosopopoeia," in *Essays and Studies in Honor of Carleton Brown* (New York, 1940), pp. 23–34, reprinted in *Essential Articles for the Study of Old English Poetry,* ed. by Jess B. Bessinger, Jr. and Stanley J. Kahrl (Hamden, Connecticut, 1968), pp. 428–41; Rosemary Woolf, "Doctrinal Influences on *The Dream of the Rood*" *MÆ*, 27 (1958), 137–53; John V. Fleming, *"The Dream of the Rood* and Anglo-Saxon Monasticism," *Traditio,* 22 (1966), 43–72; Robert B. Burlin, "The Ruthwell Cross, *The Dream of the Rood* and the Vita Contemplativa," *SP*, 65 (1968), 23–43; Barbara C. Raw, *"The Dream of the Rood* and Its Connections with Early Christian Art," *MÆ*, 39 (1970), 239–56; N. A. Lee, "The Unity of *The Dream of the Rood*," *Neophil*, 56 (1972), 469–86.

[5] Most of the studies cited in notes 3 and 4 to greater or lesser extent engage in this kind of commentary. Those by Patten, Huppé, Woolf, Fleming, and Burlin are especially illuminating.

[6] For a preliminary discussion of this kind of meaning in *The Dream of the Rood* see the first chapter of *The Guest-Hall of Eden: Four Essays on the Design of Old English Poetry* (New Haven, 1972), especially pp. 60–63. See also Robert Diamond, "Heroic Diction in *The Dream of the Rood*," in *Studies in Honor of John Wilcox,* ed. by A. Dayle Wallace and W. O. Ross (Detroit, 1958), pp. 3–7.

The body of the poem in the Vercelli MS now known as *The Dream of the Rood* is arranged as follows: an introduction (1–3); a description of the dreamer's vision of the tree of glory (4–23); the tree's account of its experiences, including the crucifixion, deposition, and burial of Christ, as well as the burial and rediscovery of the three crosses (24–77); its account of its present position among men (78–94); its message to mankind (95–121); the dreamer's description of his present life and future hope (122–156). Recognition of this organization of material by the poet, however, tells us almost nothing about the structure and texture of the poem, that is, about the fresh, intricate, ways in which the poet reworks the central tragic episode of biblical myth in the trappings and images of the heroic world of the *dryht*. For that we have to let our minds work through the curiously inwrought verbal texture within which the main metaphors take shape, to the point at which we have experienced cumulatively how they do so. In so doing we come to know the ways in which the poem receives its unique structure and meaning.

There are four main subjects in *The Dream of the Rood*. The first of these is the figure of the dreamer, within whose mind and in whose words the whole poem takes place. The second is the speaking tree or cross which appears in visionary form and speaks at length to the dreamer, and by so doing fundamentally alters his life. The third is the *dryhten* [Lord] Christ, described in a rich profusion of epithets which in themselves convey much of the poem's density of metaphorical meaning. The fourth important subject, referred to frequently but not present in the poem as an actual character, is mankind in general. The most accomplished part of the poet's aesthetic achievement, as I hope to show, is the integration, by metaphor, of these four subjects of attention.

The Introduction (1–3)

The poem's initial word is the conventional interjection *Hwæt* (the neuter form of *hwa* [who, what]). It reappears in a non-interjectory way at the beginning of line 2, thus becoming the key in an unobtrusive pattern of anaphora (*Hwæt! Ic swefna . . . , / hwæt me gemætte . . . .*) whose double function is to arrest attention and take the mind into the pattern of words now beginning to unfold. The reader or listener probably will not as yet have mentally posed any question but the combined force of the interjection and of the question implied in the pronoun *hwæt* is to initiate in him a curiosity about "what" it is that is to be told. We note that the poet speaks in the first person, either following in or imitating, in a literary context, the *epos* convention of oral delivery to a live audience: "Lo! I will tell the best of dreams, what came upon me in the middle of the night, after speech-bearers were at rest!" (1–3). The act of telling is a deliberate, conscious response to an experience that came to him, presumably (because of the impersonal force of *hwæt me gemætte*) unsought and unexpected. The anaphora (*Hwæt! ... hwæt ...* [Lo ... what ...]) indicates, then, that something is to happen to the listener because something has happened to the dreamer, who now will tell of it.

The superlative expression for what it is that is to be told, *swefna cyst* "best of dreams," literally, "what is chosen of dreams," is not meant as rhetorical hyperbole but as an accurate description of something presented by the poet as truly "the best." We come to know this in more detail as the poem develops, but experience of the word *cyst* in other Old English poetic contexts indicates clearly and decisively its ideal, often mythical, significance.[7] This "best of dreams" has come to the dreamer *to midre niht* [at midnight, 2] when other men are still and the busy world of "speech-bearers" is hushed. The radiant vision now intruding from heaven into middle-earth through the mind of the poet-dreamer comes at the canonical hour of nocturns when, according to spiritual discipline, the *wacigende* [waking, alert] man is to be vigi-

---

[7] In *Genesis A* (1795) it is used of the *landa cyst* [best of lands] shown by the "King of angels" to Abraham, the *ælgrene* [all green] *rume rice* [broad kingdom] of Canaan in which Bethlehem is found and in which Abraham and his *æfæste men* [men firm in the law] are surrounded by *wlitebeorhte wongas* [radiantly bright plains]. In other words, the *londa cyst* is the Promised Land in which Paradise is to be restored to mankind. In *Daniel* (349) the word is used of the *wedera cyst* [best of weathers], summer-like and with showers of rain, that comes miraculously with an angel into the fiery furnace to save Annanias, Azarias, and Misael. The word recurs in *Christ I* and *II* with equally ideal import, once in reference to holy Jerusalem, the city of God (*cynestola cyst* [best of royal seats, 51], once to designate the service of worship rendered ceaselessly and without wearying to the Ruler of heaven by the seraphim (*folgoþa cyst* [best of services, 390b–91a]), and once (*godwebba cyst* [best of veils, 1134]) to indicate the veil, fashioned in wondrous colors, of the Temple in Jerusalem. This last passage, like *The Dream of the Rood*, describes events taking place at the time of Christ's crucifixion. The veil is split in two as if cut by a sword-edge and all the dumb creation, the *eorðan ealgrene ond uprodor* [the all-green earth and heaven above], laments the actions of the *helfuse men* [men eager for hell] who torment and kill Christ. In *Guthlac B* it is used of the *eðel ... beorht* [bright homeland, 852–54] Eden itself, the *eardwica cyst* [best of earth's dwellings, 853] that is taken away from Adam and Eve and so made *uðgenge* [fugitive, transitory] for their children. In the more mimetic, less mythical art of *Beowulf* the word *cyst* is used of excellent swords (673, 802–03, 1559, 1697), of the great banquet given in Heorot after the slaying of Grendel (1232), and of the people of the heroic world of Heorot (867, 923). From all these references it seems clear that there is a strongly idealized force, poetically current for the adjective *cyst* that makes it a fitting introductory word for the extraordinary vision now about to be told.

lant while the *sleac* [slothful, lax] one sleeps. The midnight hour is canonically and spiritually important because it is then that David rose up to pray (Psalm 118:62), also because Christ said, *"Vigilate ergo quia nescitis quando veniet dominus"* ["Watch, for you do not know when the Lord may come"] (Mark 13:35), signifying that men must always be wakeful in good deeds. It is important also because death comes when least expected, like a thief in the night. In a context of perhaps more immediately poetic relevance than that of the canonical hours, we recall the ways in which the central recurrent cycle of sleeping and waking human life is powerfully exploited in other Old English poems, at the beginning of *Elene,* at crucial points in *Andreas, Guthlac A* and *B,* and in *Beowulf.* It is at night that supernatural forces or dream figures (a radiant cross, angels, demons, and trolls) appear to human beings, seeming to suggest at a large number of crucial points in Old English poetry that ordinary waking experience is imagined to be less real and meaningful than what is revealed in dreams, visions, and nighttime adventures.

The poet's choice of the compound *reordberend* [speech-bearer], a conventional synecdoche identifying man in terms of his faculty of speech, we have, in its context, a richly suggestive indication that this poet does not use formulaic language as tired cliché or for merely alliterative reasons (though the auditory alliterative parallel and the semantic contrast between *reordberend* and *reste* is effective). It is because of the human ability to utter words and to respond to them that the noise and confusion of waking existence can blot out more spiritual concerns, but it is also through his nature as "speech-bearer," as Cædmon learned in his cowshed, that the spiritually receptive man can be addressed by the Word made flesh, that he can understand the meanings of what he hears from heaven, and that he can, as in the cases of both Cædmon and the poem of *The Dream of the Rood,* function as a "speech-bearer" with something to tell mankind in poetry. Because his own mind and soul have been spoken to in a fundamental way, he becomes a functioning poet. Unlike his slumbering fellows, the poet-dreamer is in a condition of spiritual wakefulness in which a highly personal experience of revelation of the Word becomes possible and in which, therefore, a poem with both private lyric associations and archetypally biblical meanings becomes possible.

The Dreamer's Vision of the Tree (4–23)

The dreamer's apparent initial uncertainty about what is happening ("It seemed to me that I saw . . . ."), because of the unexpected and wondrous nature of the tree appearing to him, gives way in the next sentence to direct, more confident, statement: "That beacon was all covered with gold." From then on the description is very direct and sharply visualized. The tree in its extraordinary physicality is simply there, something wondrous borne forth (*lædan*) on the air by an unseen power. Surrounded by light it is called *beama beorhtost*. The phrase is probably not to be understood simply as "brightest of trees," but also as "brightest of beams," thus conveying both the sense of "tree" or "cross" and that of "column" or "beam of light." This second meaning is indicated as well by *beorhtost* [brightest] and *leohte bewunden* [surrounded with light]. With impinges on the dreamer's consciousness, then, is an extraordinary tree which is also a beam of light, the whole symbol serving as a "beacon" or "sign" pointing to the rich spiritual meanings about to be revealed.[8]

Closely related to the light enveloping the tree is the gold "poured" or "sprinkled" (*begoten*, 7) over it, to make it not only a striking sign or beacon but to honour it as a splendid cult object. The fair jewels fixed and gleaming at the surface of the earth and the other five up on the shoulder-span of the cross, probably an iconographic indication of the five wounds of Christ,[9] have the same functions. In addition, the use here (the only one in extant Old English MSS) of the compound *eaxlegespanne* [shoulder-span] appears to be more than an appropriate naturalistic image suggested by the physical shape of a cross fashioned to accommodate the anatomical form of a man's body stretched out. The word *eaxlegespanne,* along with the five jewels, is the first suggestion, an oblique one, of the main rhetorical figure in the poem, that is, the metaphor by which the body of the tree is increasingly identified with that of the Prince it bears in the events of the crucifixion.

The climactic detail in the account of the visual images that initially come to the dreamer is in 9b–10a: *Beheoldon þær engel dryhtnes ealle, /*

---

[8] From other Old English poems we are familiar with the way the appearance of marvellous light is made to symbolize the pushing aside or scattering of a surrounding physical and spiritual darkness, so that illumination of the soul may take place. In *Guthlac B,* as the protagonist's dead body grows cold and his bewildered thane looks on, a light called by the poet *beama beorhtast* [the brightest of beams] and *beacen* [a beacon] rises up from the earth like a fiery tower, while troops of angels sing in triumph (1305 ff.). The vision that comes to Constantine in *Elene* (69 ff.) is very similar to that described here in *The Dream of the Rood;* it is also focussed on the wondrous tree of victory gleaming with gold and jewels, and surrounded by light (94). In *Christ I* the elaborate use of light symbolism to indicate the significance of Christ's coming into the darkened hall of middle-earth is executed with great skill and imagination.

[9] See W. O. Stevens, *The Cross in the Life and Literature of the Anglo-Saxons* (New York, 1904), p. 43, as well as several later interpreters of the poem.

fægere þurh forðgesceaft [All beheld there an angel of the Lord, fair through creation]. The meaning of these two half-lines has been much discussed.[10] Should the word *engel* not be plural to agree with *ealle?* Emendations have been proposed by a whole series of editors but Krapp, and, more recently, Swanton,[11] even though recognizing the possible problems, including the fact that *ealle* seems metrically redundant, have retained the MS reading. My quotation and translation, given above, also (with Krapp and Swanton) follow the manuscript although I think there is a plausible interpretation that would not see the phrase *engel dryhtnes* as referring to Christ himself, as Krapp and others have done, when they base their interpretation on a reference to Christ as an angel in *Soul and Body* I, 27.[12] Though I do not think that the poet is referring to Christ as an angel here, in fairness it should be recognized that the apparent oddity of speaking of Christ as an angel (since by all orthodox teaching he was the Lord and Creator of the angels) does have a tradition behind it, as Robert Burlin has shown in another context.[13] The Old Latin version of Isaiah 9:6 rendered the Septuagint text as *magni concilii angelus* [angel of great council]. Augustine explained the usage as having to do with Christ's role as messenger of the kingdom rather than with his nature. Nonetheless, it seems to me that in the context of this part of *The Dream of the Rood* an appearance of Christ himself, as angel or otherwise, is improbable, and there is good reason to suppose that the poet meant what we actually have in the MS, "an angel of the Lord," that is, an angel of Christ "fair through creation."

First, and important, is the fact that the noun *dryhten* occurs eight other times in the poem (35, 64, 75, 101, 105, 113, 140, 144) and clearly refers to Christ each time. To have him called an angel of the Lord this once, then, would jar with the poem's own usage. Secondly, there is the problem, not insurmountable, of the word *forðgesceaft* whose normal meaning of "created things, creation" (or alternatively "the future world") has to be altered to "decree"[14] if the angel is thought to be Christ, who was not created but coeternal with the Father. A third reason against taking *engel dryhtnes* as Christ, like the first reason, is contextual, but in a different way. At this point in the poem the

---

[10] See Bruce Dickins and Alan S. C. Ross, eds., *The Dream of the Rood* (London, 1963), pp. 21–22; also George P. Krapp, ed., *The Vercelli Book* (New York, 1932), p. 130.

[11] *The Dream of the Rood* (Manchester, 1970), p. 89 and pp. 103–04.

[12] See also *Christ I*, 104.

[13] *The Old English Advent: A Typological Commentary* (New Haven, 1968), pp. 102–03.

[14] See Dickens-Ross, p. 22, n. 10.

imaginative focus is on the gold-covered, jewelled tree which appears on the air as a *sigebeam* [victory-beam, 13] honoured by the whole creation (9b–12). It is a symbol of victory, not a crucifix bearing the unresurrected, dead Christ. As the poem develops it is suggested, moreover, that the tree is itself a dream surrogate for Christ. To have Christ visible to the dreamer, at this point, would considerably weaken the imaginative impact of the main metaphorical idea. The emergence of "the Prince of mankind" into the narrative comes twenty-two lines later, with great effectiveness, because by then a rich texture of meanings has been established for the tree and it has been made ready poetically to recount its highly personal response to the crufixion events.

Finally, there is good scriptural and traditional reason for supposing that the poem refers here to an angel associated with the empty cross of the resurrection.[15] In Matthew 28:1–8 the *angelus Domini* [angel of the Lord] descends from heaven to roll away the stone of Jesus' sepulchre and to announce that he is risen (*surrexit*). In luke 24:23 in a reference to the women's discovery of the empty tomb we read, "And when they found not his body, they came saying, that they had also seen a vision of angels, which said that he was alive." The fourth Gospel reports Mary as seeing two angels in white sitting, the one at the head and the other at the feet, where the body of Jesus had lain (20:12).

According to tradition,[16] the invisible powers were present at the moment of the Passion, exercising their ministry, since an angel appeared to Christ to strengthen him. This tradition presumably is based on the reference to the angel that speaks to Jesus in John 12:29, in the midst of his troubled anticipation of his own imminent death. We recall, also, that through the mystery of the Eucharist, in the part of the ritual known as the *Sursum corda,* Christian man is believed to be lifted up from earth into heaven. He is restored to the angelic creation from which he fell by sin. So transformed he can once more unite his voice with that of the angels and be admitted to the official worship of creation, of which the angels are the representatives.[17] This belief seems to be clearly expressed in our poem by the way holy spirits, men, and the whole great creation in the introductory cosmic vision are said to gaze on the cross of victory now lifted up on the air for the dreamer's gaze, so that he too, as the poem later tells us, may become part of the *dryhtnes folc* [the Lord's folk] who are the society of angels.

In the midst of the description of the light-surrounded tree gazed

---

15 In *Elene* 71 ff., a heavenly *boda* [messenger] or [angel] appears with the "sign of victory" and speaks to Constantine.

16 See Jean Daniélou, *The Bible and the Liturgy* (Notre Dame, 1956), p. 132.

17 Daniélou, p. 135.

on by creatures in heaven and earth the half-line *Ne wæs ðær huru fracodes gealga* [In truth it was not a criminal's gallows there] occurs with startling effect, because so far the dreamer's vision has included only the bright side of the symbolism of the cross. Even though the force of the whole sentence in which the words occur is mainly affirmative, pointing to the various kinds of worshipping creatures, *fracodes gealga* points to that darker, negative side of existence which has not yet been openly mentioned in the poem. The phrase alliterates but contrasts in significance with *fægere* and *forðgesceaft,* thereby setting human criminality and heavenly beauty in sharp antithesis. So alluded to negatively, the as-yet-undeveloped theme of human evil is touched on. It returns in the next unit of the poem's development, beginning at line 13.

Syllic wæs se sigebeam [Wondrous was that victory-beam] repeats and sums up the overall sense of the tree in the first twelve lines of the poem. It has been presented as a bright, unexpectedly revealed image of gold and jewels. Now, in the following reference to the dreamer's sin-stained and badly wounded self, comes a clear indication of an area of earthly existence in which the tree victory has not yet been won. The verb *wæs* serves as a yoking word, almost a zeugma, with the two grammatical subjects *sigebeam* and *ic: Syllic wæs se sigebeam, ond ic synnum fah, / forwunded mid wommum* [Wondrous was that victory-beam, and I stained with sins, / badly wounded with impurities]. In the auditory repetition of *Syllic . . . sigebeam . . . synnum,* however, comes a sharp antitheses of meaning, the wondrousness of divine action and triumph comprehended in the first half-line being set against the sin of the dreamer in what follows. Rhetorically the sentence is a syllepsis in which the simple word *wæs* brings together two constructions, each of which has a different meaning in connection with the yoking word.

The same sentence also begins a subtle complex of thought and feeling that could only be expressed metaphorically—the identification, through the rhetorical device of antonomasia, of the "wondrous" or "strange" tree as a *sigebeam,* a living being that has won a victory, and also the related identification of the Passion of Christ as a battle or act of war against *strange feondas* [strong enemies]. The sentence suggests, moreover, that this particular battle is an ongoing one, because the dreamer, who up until his vision has had no conscious part in the war, is already a wounded and bloodied casualty in it. So far in this conflict, Satan has been the winner but now something *syllic* [strange or extraordinary], signalling a fundamental change, is taking place.

Geseah ic wuldres treow [I saw the tree of Glory]. The force of the conventional epithet for the cross is not simply to designate the tree as the one on which Christ dies but so to name it that it suggests the glory of God's power associated with it, thus explaining why it is *geweorðode* [honoured, or perhaps celebrated], with "garments" or "vestments" and "shining radiantly," "clothed" or "adorned with gold." The diction here, including the hyperbole "gems in honour had covered the Ruler's tree," suggests the devotion, rites, and ceremonies of a cultic observance focussed on the tree and, through the tree, on the Ruler and Wielder who has power or mastery over it. The basis of honouring, celebrating, and vesting the tree with rich trappings is the belief that by it the Lord of the universe has acted decisively and victoriously in middle-earth. But there is another metaphorical strain starting to work here that shortly will be developed powerfully. We have noted that the *sigebeam* is identified as a living being. On one level of metaphor it is also a human body worthy of honour, rich vestments, gold, and jewels. It is covered with the kind of treasures worthy of a warrior who has served his lord well in battle and so received his reward. Also, in the light of the trials of the champions or warriors of Christ in hagiographic writings, it is honoured and venerated in the way a saint's body is.

The adversative word *Hwæðre* [But, 18] signals the beginning of the overt development of the theme of darkness behind the glory, this already having been alluded to, as we have seen, in the negative reference to "a criminal's gallows." The verb *geseon* [to see] (as in *Geseah* [I saw, 14]), denoting the simple physical act of seeing, is used of the dreamer's sense impression of vestments, gold, and jewels on the tree. Now the verb *ongytan* [to perceive, understand, recognize, or know what a thing really is] (as in *ic . . . ongytan meahte,* 18) is used of his understanding of the earlier Passion conflict. Actual details of the crucifixion are referred to directly for the first time but in a startling and unexpected way, that is, through the rhetorical device of catachresis. We have learned that the dreamer thinks of himself as bloodied and wounded by sin, and we might reasonably expect that the wounds of Christ will now be described. We are told instead that the dreamer could perceive through the gold that the tree itself earlier had bled on the right side. This vividly crystallizes the metaphor of the tree as a human body and is the first open indication in the poem that the "best of dreams" has at its metaphorical core an identification of the body of the tree with the divine-human body of its Lord. To realize this is to enter into the lyrical essence of *The Dream of the Rood,* in which the associative processes of poetry are at their strongest and the nonfigurative expressions of logical prose furthest away.

The dreamer's first response to his vision (13b–14a) has been a sense of his own sinfulness. Now again (20b–21a) the images of the dream evoke from him strong emotional reactions; he is "all troubled with sorrows" and "fearful before the fair sight." The sorrow is caused by his realization of the meaning of the bleeding side in the conflict long ago, perhaps also by the sense of his own sinfulness just mentioned. It is based too on his own beginning self-awareness in relation to the fearful reality of the divine-human suffering that has been revealed to him from outside his own ordinary waking experience. The sight is fair but for him it has darker implications, because he has not yet been integrated into the level of reality indicated by the victory-beam.

Geseah ic pæt fuse beacen / wendan wædum and bleom [I saw the eager sign, changing in garments and colours, 21b–22a]. Interestingly, the verb here again is *geseah* [saw], because the altering, ambivalent imagery of the splendid cult object on the one hand and of the Passion conflict on the other is what the dreamer physically "sees." His awareness of the tragic dimensions behind the symbols of divine triumph has its objective cause in the vision itself. "At times" the beacon or sign is made wet and stained with flowing blood; "at times" it is adorned with treasure. In this *hwilum . . . hwilum* anaphora the beacon as sacred sign points to two parts of the Christian story, the original battle at Calvary which ended the earthly life of the Man, and the later ecclesiastical veneration of the cross adorned with treasure in celebration of Christ's victory over sin and death. Without the earlier shedding of blood there would be no jewels on the tree either where it now touches the earth's surface or up at its "shoulder-span."

In the poem's first of several uses of hypermetric lines (20–23) we have a more extended anaphora in the form of four prepositional phrases each of which begins with *mid* [with] and includes a different noun or noun phrase and a different past participle ending in *-ed* (this last device being what the rhetoricians called homoeoteleuton): *ic wæs mid sorgum gedrefed* [I was troubled with sorrow]; *hit wæs mid wætan bestemed* [it was made wet with blood]; *beswyled mid swates gange* [stained with flowing blood]; *mid since gegyrwed* [adorned with treasure]. This is the rhetorical pattern, including within it the less extended *hwilum . . . hwilum* anaphora, which indicates the dreamer's state of mind and feeling. It also describes the tree in its two contradictory but finally reconcilable roles as symbol of suffering and object of honour, as covered with blood and adorned with treasure.

The use of the adjective *fuse* with *beacen* seems to be part of the poem's basic prosopopoeia involving the speaking cross. The word *fus* in Old English is translatable in a wide range of ways: "ready, prepared, prompt, quick, eager, hastening, prone, inclined, willing, ready for death, dying." At the very least, in the context here, it suggests a highly animate, live being. Later in the poem the same word is used as a substantive for the friendly *hilderincas* [battle warriors] who come from afar to the dead *æðelinge* [noble one] Christ, to carry out the deposition and burial rites (57). Also the dreamer, immediately after his vision, is said to be eager to be on the way forth from this world (*afysed on forðwege,* 125).

By the end of line 23 the objective vision of what the dreamer sees in the middle of the night is complete and the poem moves into the story told by "the best of woods." The wondrous jewelled tree borne forth on the air, covered with gold, surrounded by light, and gazed on by many creatures, has been at this point at least partially understood by the dreamer, both *in bono* (as a sign of victory) and *in malo* (as a sign of defeat). He has experienced wonder, a sense of his own sinfulness, and feelings of sorrow and fear. Despite these emotions, he lies there "troubled" or "anxious" for a long time, gazing on the *hælendes treow* [Healer's tree]. In view of his spiritual condition at this point as stained, badly wounded, and afraid, and of the growth in spiritual obedience and commitment that are to follow, it is perhaps pertinent to recall here the psalmist's words: "The fear of the Lord is the beginning of wisdom" (111:10). It is right, also, that the poet at this point should choose the epithet "Healer's tree" to point the way to what is to happen.

The Tree's Account of Its Experiences (24–78)

A "long while" of dream time passes as the dejected dreamer gazes on the tree. This allows him a period in which to experience fully the vision as a set of visual images fraught with meaning—*oððæt* [until] finally he hears it making a sound. The total silence which up until now has characterized the midnight experience is now broken. Here we have a transition (23–27), moreover, in what the dreamer experiences, from the primarily visual to the primarily auditory. Also, instead of the static image of the dreamer lying gazing on the suspended tree, the narrative now is filled with action. (The image of the cross itself has of course not been static, but alternating between its two natures.) In another way this passage marks a transition in the poem. The dreamer-speaker whose reactions to the vision have been central now recedes from attention and does not speak or act again until line 122, although he is addressed directly throughout and is told by the cross what he is to do (95 ff).

In the tree's articulated memories ("That was long ago, I remember that yet, that I was hewn down . . . .") the pronoun *hit* [it] gives way to *ic* [I] and *me* [me]. The events of the crucifixion of Christ are starkly and vividly re-created, beginning with a description of an act of violence in the order of created things. The verbs in the first few lines here convey well the sense of violent aggression, even, in the context, immolation: *ic wæs aheawen* [I was hewn down]; *astyred of stefne minum* [stirred up] *or* [removed from my stem]; *Genaman me* [they seized me]; *geworhton him* [they made for themselves]; *heton* [they ordered]; *Bæron . . . beornas* [Men carried]; *hie . . . asetton* [they set up]; *gefæstnodon me þær feondas genoge* [enemies enough fastened me there]. At the end of this sequence of aggressive acts against a helpless but highly conscious victim we see, from the tree's viewpoint, the sudden, exuberant movement into the poem of the central figure of the Passion story: *Geseah ic þa frean mancynnes / efstan elne mycle þæt he me wolde on gestigan* [Then I saw the Prince of mankind hurrying with great eagerness, because he wanted to mount up on me]. It is a figure of mobilized energy and free will hurrying to the great and decisive battle that will turn the deeds of the aggressors to heaven's purposes.

Having been hewn down at a forest's edge and removed from its trunk by its foes, the tree is made into a *wæfersyne* [spectacle] for them. This image takes us into the negative opposite of the "fair vision" gazed on earlier by the dreamer, holy spirits, men on earth, and this great creation. Specifically, the use of the word *wæfersyne* is part of a central structural paradox in *The Dream of the Rood,* involving the way an ignominious "spectacle" is also a "fair sight."

There is a problem about how to understand line 31b, *heton me heora wergas hebban.* The syntax and overall narrative permit either "they ordered their criminals to raise me up" or "they ordered me to raise up their criminals." The former reading accords better with the immediate chronology of events and requires that the *wæfersyne* be understood as the spectacle of the tree just after it is newly felled. We are accustomed to thinking of the cross as the shameful spectacle of the Passion story but the poet of *The Dream of the Rood* at numerous points is not following biblical details. The tree's suggested sense of outrage at being brutally seized and stared at accords well with the subtle but pervasive metaphorical sense in the poem whereby the crucifixion is imagined and understood by the poet not so much as the killing of Jesus as a violation (to which Jesus submits) by malevolent men of the created order itself, this violation extending, finally and unavoidably, to the body of the King of creation.

The hypermetric lines describing the acts of the enemies and the eager approach of the Prince contain a rush of verbs and nouns depicting two distinct, contrasted kinds of highly purposeful human activity directed toward one end, the death of the *Hælend* [Saviour]. The tree's reaction in the non-hypermetric lines that follow immediately (35–38) is one of controlled restraint:

> Þær ic þa ne dorste   ofer dryhtnes word
> bugan oððe berstan,   þa ic bifian geseah
> eorðan sceatas.   Ealle ic mihte
> feondas gefyllan,   hwæðre ic fæste stod.

> [There then I did not dare   against the Lord's word
> to bow or break,   when I saw
> the earth's surface shake.   I could have felled
> all the foes,   but I stood fast.]

The very evident caesural pauses in lines 36–38 and the antithesis between what the speaker could have done but did not are appropriate to the idea of willed submission and stasis before the divine will now working itself out, in each of the following: the word of the Lord; the shaking of the earth's surface; the enemies against whom the tree stands without counter-attacking.

The idea that the tree might have resisted his Lord's killing but dared not is stated four times (35, 42, 45, 47), the first time in association with the trembling of the earth itself, at the moment when the Prince mounts up on the tree. It is not clear whether the trembling of the earth in this instance is a proleptic reference to the earthquake described by Matthew (27:50–54) as taking place just as Jesus dies or a poetic trope emphasizing the cross's courageous obedience at the same time as another part of creation expresses sympathetic revulsion at what is being done to God. In any case the cumulative effect of the statement of willed submission and the disturbance in nature is to build a tremendous but controlled sense of momentous wrongdoing on the part of the crucifiers. "I could have felled all the foes, but I stood fast." As a loyal thane under oath it could have obeyed its obligation to fight to the death to protect its Prince but its obligation to obey his commands (they are unspoken) transcends this, even though it in no way lessens the sense of tragic, necessary betrayal in the name of loyalty. The tree is in communion with a power beyond ordinary heroism. It is this power that is the cause of its *wyrd* [fate] and its glory alike. Because the Prince of mankind is not only being crucified but is eagerly willing his own death, the tree, along with the *strange feondas* [strong enemies], is a necessary instrument to that end. The centre of the tragedy for both the *hæleð* Christ and the tree is in their isolation from ordinary motives of self-preservation or even self-sacrifice. We twentieth-century readers have to work imaginatively at understanding the ways in which Anglo-Saxon warrior thanes thought about themselves in relation to their *dryhten,* but we can learn enough from the surviving documents to appreciate at least in part how astute and "dead-on" the poet's telling of the Passion story in terms of *dryht* conflicts and loyalties must once have seemed. With his acute sense of what these were he was able to extend their meaning into something which, in the early English Christian view of reality, was a cosmic principle, the willingness of the heavenly *dryhten* to become man and die as a warrior in battle against sin and death, in order to free man and gain for him entry into the *dryht* of heaven.

Ongyrede hine þa geong hæleð, (þæt wæs god ælmihtig), / strang ond stiðmod [The young hero stripped himself, (that was God almighty), strong and unflinching, 39–40a]. It is almost as if the poet, living in the world of the *dryht,* is thinking credally "Perfect God: perfect Man." The young *hæleð* [Hero, Warrior, Man] is the figure of the heroic *dryhten* par excellence, strong, resolute, and eager for battle. But, in another of the poem's fundamental paradoxes, he is the one who reverses the normal pre-battle actions of a warrior, by stripping rather than arming himself, thus symbolically casting off any dependence on conventional *dryht* trappings.[18] As he mounts high on the gallows "brave in the sight of many," we have the poem's second great image of a figure raised up above ordinary human experience, between *feondas* [foes] on earth and the *eðel* [homeland] in heaven. Thus elevated, it is capable of drawing toward it the gaze of men, in precisely the way anticipated by Jesus in his farewell discourses: "And I, if I be lifted up from the earth, will draw all things to me" (John 12:32, Rheims translation of Vulgate). As tragic protagonist he will be killed high on the cross and brought low in death, but that is not the end of the story.

The trembling of the cross as "the Man" embraces it (42) is a startling reminder of the basic metaphor working here, the coming together or union of tree and heroic God being the point of contact between that which is to be redeemed (the whole fallen creation) and the power that will effect the redemption. The movement of the tree (*Bifode ic* [I trembled]), moreover, parallels and intensifies the sympathy of nature indicated by the earlier use of the same verb, *ic bifian geseah eorðan sceatas* [I saw the earth's surface tremble]. We notice also that in this passage describing the actions of the mounting (39–50), the nailing, and the physical dying the poem again proceeds in hypermetric lines, except for the detaching, retrospective two lines in which the tree mentally removes

[18] For a likely explanation of this usage in patristic tradition see R. Woolf, "Doctrinal Influences on *The Dream of the Rood,*" *MÆ,* 27 (1958), 146–47.

himself in time from the narrative actions described: *Rod wæs ic aræred. Ahof ic ricne cyning, / heofona hlaford, hyldan me ne dorste* [As a rood I was raised up, I raised the great King, / the Lord of heaven; I dared not bend, 44–45]. Here too, we notice, is the first use in the poem of the word *rod* [rood, cross, crucifix]. So far *treow* [tree] has appeared most frequently but *beam* [beam], *beacen* [beacon], *gealga* [gallows], *sigebeam* [victory-beam], and *wudu selesta* [best of woods] also have been used. The first occurrence of *rod* here is right poetically, in that this is the moment in the narrative when the tree becomes the cross of the crucifixion and first knows itself as destined to raise up the "mighty King, the Lord of the heavens." Its acceptance of this destiny symbolizes the fusion of divine power and the total obedience of the living creature.

This is the moment (44–49) of the tree's own immolation. We notice that it is this wounding, not the Man's, that is mentioned first: "They drove me through with dark nails."[19] Again there is a transition in time ("The wounds can still be seen on me, open malicious gashes"), so that the past action and the present vision are kept in close alignment. The details pertain to that "earlier strife of wretched men" seen by the dreamer through the gold and jewels. Tree and man together are mocked, abused emotionally as well as physically, and the word *begoten* [poured over] appropriately recurs (compare line 49 with line 7). Now, however, it is used in connection with the blood from the Man's side which pours over the cross. It is this shed blood, as the dreamer knew earlier, that gives meaning to the historically later cultic gold. As the poet completes the account of the wounding of the tree, he also alludes to the actual dying of Jesus rather than ever describing it directly. Aside from the half-line *siððan he hæfde his gast onsended* [after he had sent forth his spirit], it is the tree's feelings and experiences that dominate. It is this fact, realized in the continuous prosopopoeia of this part of the poem, that shows the poet's metaphorical genius. Even so, however, the reference in the one half-line to Jesus' dismissal of his spirit does underscore the effectiveness of the divine will. It is the dying Man himself who sends forth his spirit. It is almost as if, rather than being killed, he makes himself die. The *feondas* [enemies] in a very real sense are background figures throughout, mere instruments of the redemptive purpose.

In what is probably the most moving passage of the poem, at once sensitive lyric and powerful myth, the many hostile happenings experienced by the cross as he sees "the God of hosts sorely stretched out" (50–51) are shown to be part of a drama involving the whole order of

---

[19] For a suggestion that the adjective *deorcan* may mean "red, bloody," see Dickens-Ross, p. 26, n. on line 46.

the world: "Darkness with clouds had surrounded the Ruler's corpse, its clear shining; a shadow went forth, dark beneath the clouds. All creation wept, lamented the King's fall. Christ was on the cross." The light that is temporarily blotted out by darkness is the "clear shining" of the Creator of the universe. The clouds and darkness are signs that death and hell temporarily have the victory. All creation laments the fall of its King. *Crist wæs on rode.* This quietly climactic half-line includes the first use of the name "Christ" in the poem and it comes at the precise moment of death, when "the Man," who is also "the God of hosts" and "the King," is recognized throughout the creation as the Christ.

Immediately following the death of Christ comes the beginning of a sympathetic counter-action on the human level, paralleling the lament of nature and introduced by the adversative *Hwæðere* [But]. Again (59–69) come hypermetric lines characterized by strong action verbs, as "eager ones, come from afar to that noble one," carry out the deposition, the funeral lament, and the burial, and then go sadly away. The specific identity of these human figures is not indicated, though we can probably deduce from the Gospel records (Matthew 27:57–60; Mark 15:42–47; Luke 23:50–56; John 19:38–42) that they are Joseph of Arimathea, Nicodemus (mentioned by name in John only), and the others who take responsibility for the disposition of Christ's body. The mood here is profoundly elegiac and, in sharp contrast to the brutality of the crucifixion scene, the human movements are at once gentle, respectful, and purposeful, the actions of unhappy warriors whose Prince is dead but who is honoured by them before they leave him in the solitude of death: "There they took almighty God, raised him from the heavy torment." "The battle-warriors left me standing covered with blood." "There they laid him limb-weary, stood at his body's head, looked there on heaven's Lord. . . ." "They began to fashion for him an earth-house . . . they cut it from bright rock, placed in it there the Ruler of victories. They began then to sing a song of sorrow, unhappy in that eventide, when they wished to go away in their sorrow from the great Prince. He rested there with few followers."

Again it is through the eyes, thoughts, and feelings of the cross that events are presented to us: "I beheld it all. I was greatly troubled, but I bowed to the hands of men, easy of mind, gladly." This last phrase, *elne mycle,* echoes the line earlier where the Prince of mankind hurried *elne mycle* [gladly, 34] to mount up on the tree, and describes the cross's own eagerness to release Christ from his heavy torment. Before the death the tree "dared not bow" but now, his unwanted work done, he may do so, and does, gladly. The bowing, however, does not mean that the cross is taken down and left to lie on the ground at this point in the action. From three references a little further on (61b–62a, 70–72a, 73b–74) it is clear that it is left "standing" for a while. Literally, then, its bowing here must be an actual physical movement, following which it is again straightened up, but there is perhaps also some metaphorical suggestion of a mental and emotional surrendering of the unwanted burden.

Forleton me þa hilderincas / standan steame bedrifenne; eall ic wæs mid strælum forwundod [The battle-warriors left me standing covered with blood; I was all sore wounded by arrows or shafts, 61b–62]. Literally and obviously the blood on the cross is that of Christ. In accord, however, with the metaphor of the tree as a living, feeling, thinking, and speaking being, and with the dreamer's earlier description of it as having bled on the right side (19a–20a), the blood is also that of the body of the tree with which the body of Christ has been identified. The "arrows" or "shafts" which wound the cross are an integral part of the metaphor of the crucifixion as a battle fought (and paradoxically, not fought, in the sense of there being any physical resistance) by the *geong hæleð* [young Warrior] or [Hero] Christ, with the help of an obedient thane. During this battle both are wounded by the *strange feondas* [strong foes]. The specific metaphor of the arrows and the more general metaphor of the battle itself link the poem with the iconographic tradition reflected in other Old English poems in which sins and temptations are represented as arrows or shafts assailing the body (and the soul) of man. At this point in *The Dream of the Rood* the wounding arrows clearly are the sins of mankind in general, as well as those exemplified in the *strange feondas*. We remember also, however, that the dreamer has earlier contrasted the "victory-beam" with his own sin-stained and badly wounded self (13–14).

Following immediately on the image of the arrows comes one of the poem's finest uses of the battle-as-crucifixion metaphor. By an associative lyrical process the dead Christ, who is also *heofenes dryhten* [heaven's Lord] and so cannot in his divine nature be dead, is presented in a daring catachresis as a "limb-weary" warrior tired after a great battle and laid down to rest a while by his followers, who then stand around his head. But he of course is not just a tired warrior and his battle (*gewinne,* 65) is not just a great battle. The conflict is *ðam miclan gewinne* [that great battle] by which heaven intervenes profoundly in the life of middle-earth and lets man kill "the God of hosts," so that the futile human war inspired by Satan against God will end in defeat for the rebels against heaven.

While "the Lord of heaven" rests, his friends begin to make a *moldern* [earth-house, grave] for him, a sepulchre cut from bright rock, in which they place him, "the Ruler of victories." All this they do, the cross tells us, in the sight of "the slayer" or "murderer" (*on banan gesyhðe,* 66). Though not clearly identified, the slayer referred to is probably the personified cross who, paradoxically, both willingly and unwillingly has temporarily become a tree of death. He had told the dreamer that he looked on at all the post-crucifixion events (58b) and his earlier expressions of the tension of willed obedience at having to be the instrument of death could lead naturally to this self-designation as "the slayer." The other possibility, not in my view very likely, is Satan who in Old English is often called, among other epithets, *se bana.* But such a reading here, implying that Satan was looking on at the preparation of Christ's tomb, seems bizarre, unless (an outside possibility) we are to see in the descent into the *moldern* [grave] some kind of anticipation of the harrowing of hell. But the harrowing as such does not emerge as important in the poem until the very end, 82 lines later. Either of the two readings at least makes sense in the context but the one, in my view, is considerably more plausible than the other. This suggests to me that editorial change of the MS *banan* to *banana* or *banena,* [of the slayers], so that the word refers either to those who crucified Christ (and so would have to be imagined as still present as observers) or to the three crosses, seems unnecessary.[20]

Critically more interesting than this largely editorial problem is the subtle metaphor working here by which, since there is a "slayer," Christ is at once thought to be dead and also, as "the Ruler of victories," only asleep and resting a while after battle. It would be difficult to find a more effective poetic means for conveying the promise of resurrection and triumph while respecting the traditional teaching that Jesus in fact did die. Part of the poet's skill in expressing this paradox can be seen in the way he suggests two perspectives. That the elegiac figures of the friends who conduct the funeral rites have accepted the death of their Lord as final seems likely. On this basis they bury him, sing "a song of sorrow" in the evening-tide, and then, "weary" and "wretched," journey away from their great Prince. It is the rood and the poet who describe the immediate results of the crucifixion as a metaphorical sleep and the "grave" as an "earth-dwelling" into which it is "the Ruler of victories," not just the dead "Man," that is placed.

Reste he ðær mæte weorode [He rested there with few followers, 69b]. Since it seems clear that no human being remains by the tomb throughout the Passiontide night, this may be, as others have noted,[21] a litotes

---

[20] See Krapp's ed., p. 131, n. 66.
[21] See, for example, W. F. Bolton, *An Old English Anthology* (London, 1963), p. 99, n. 69.

or understatement emphasizing the solitariness of Christ's dead body: "He rested there with few followers," meaning "with none at all." Still, in view of the immediately following lines describing the three weeping crosses (we, 70) who kept vigil "after the sound had gone up from the battle warriors" (71b–72a), it is distinctly possible that the reference to "few followers" or "a small troop" is to these three, that is, to the only part of the earthly creation remaining with the corpse of the "fair life-dwelling" of the Creator as it now turns cold in death (72b). Such a reading would still take *mæte weorode* as a litotes but to a different degree, "only three" rather than "none at all." Such a reading, more-over, accords well with the whole imaginative conception of the loyal tree that has informed the poem so far. Another possibility, reconcilable with this second one, is that the reference is to the ministering angels traditionally associated with the tomb of Christ (see above).

The last ignominious experience for the cross (*egeslic wyrd* [a terrible fate, 74]) is its second felling. The first time at the forest's edge it was made a spectacle and taken to a hill. Now it is buried in a deep pit and so thinks of itself as experiencing "a terrible fate," presumably because of natural revulsion at being buried alive. Or is it terrible because in some sense it too is now being killed, or perhaps being treated as dead, having earlier been wounded? (The poem's metaphors are subtle and need not be pinned down too firmly by the logical language of prose paraphrase.) Its last fateful experience in the crucifixion story is terrible also because the burial of the cross terminates the possibility of even the rudimentary act of physical loyalty expressed in the lonely vigil.

On the level of literary structure there is another reason for the burial of the cross. The account of the Passion in *The Dream of the Rood* is a poetic working of the archetypal Christian tragedy. In a tragic structure the theme of inevitable defeat is a major element, even though in both the New Testament Passion and in this poem the tragedy and defeat are treated as an episode in a larger commedic structure involving resurrec-tion and heavenly triumph. The theme of defeat here is focussed not only on the live energy and power of the Christ figure but on the cross as well, as a totally animate and spiritually cognizant representative of the whole fallen creation, including the human part of it. This means that in some way the cross must also be killed and buried. According to tra-ditional teaching, Jesus had to undergo an actual vicarious death, sub-stituting himself for sinful man in order to free him from sin and death. In this poem, then, the cross as vital agent of this redemptive action must undergo a parallel death and burial if it is to be "resurrected" and so become a "beacon" to which men pray and by which they may enter into the mystery of the resurrection. There is no overt recognition in the poem of the long period of historical time (approximately three hundred years) traditionally reckoned for the burial of the crosses before their "resurrection," but the poet may be assuming in his audience knowledge of the kind of legendary lore included in the poem *Elene* (extant in the same manuscript). In any case, the cross's brief account of its being found by *dryhtnes þegnas* [the Lord's retainers], who girt it with gold and silver, returns us in the imagery of the poem to where the splendid cultic object first appeared to the dreamer (though there is no reference at that point to silver, just to gold and jewels).

In a structural sense the tree's narrative of the crucifixion of Christ, presented as a battle ending in a temporary defeat for "the Lord of victories," has now at line 77 been completed. The tale of events long ago has come to the dreamer-poet (and indirectly to us) through the words of the follower who was closest to, even metaphorically identified with, the Prince of mankind. On the basis of this identification, the story cannot end with the cross's burial or even with its physical resurrection and exaltation, any more than the story of Christ ends with his rising from the dead. Those critics who terminate their editions of *The Dream of the Rood* at this point or who assume expansion by a less gifted and astute poet betray an ability to miss the major thrust of *The Dream of the Rood* as a religious poem composed to achieve specific spiritual results. Even the most elementary sense of the way the tragedy of the Passion reaches into post-resurrection church history should rule out the blunder of cutting off the text at this point.

Because of the nature of what follows in the poem this kind of editorial or critical interference with the text can be seen, on a slightly more sophisticated level, as a preference for literature or poetry shorn of explicit *significatio,* that is, as a modern aversion to the common mediaeval habit of seeing and pointing out deeper meanings in the *littera* of important texts. To assume that a Christian poet of the time of *The Dream of the Rood* would say nothing of the wider and deeper significance of the splendid narrative vision about the crucifixion that he has just presented is to betray little knowledge of, or sensitivity to, the way mediaeval Christian poetry works. It is true that the remainder of the poem is less metaphorically subtle and rich, less filled with figures and tropes, and that it is not linked together as a texture of meaning by the same density of associative lyrical expression that we have traced in the earlier part. But it is nonetheless integral and necessary to the mediaeval art and meaning of the poem, because it places the dream vision experiences in the larger typological context provided by the Bible and by credal formulations, and it shows the impact of the vision on the dreamer's own life.

The Cross's Account of Its Present Position Among Men (78–94)

Nu þu miht gehyran, hæleð min se leofa [Now you can hear, my dear man]. In this apostrophe to the dreamer the cross explicitly interprets to him what has so far been told as literal narrative. In a real sense, in the tropological reference of the poem, the dreamer now is to become the hero (*hæleð,* 78) and protagonist, so that the joint heroism of Christ and the tree will be made effective in the context of an individual believer's life. Before this tropological theme becomes fully explicit, however, the allegorical truth and meaning of the cross's story have to be articulated so that its experiences will be seen as exemplary. This allegory is the burden of the next two sections of the poem, lines 78–94 and 95–121.

Iu ic wæs geworden wita heardost [Of old time I was the hardest of punishments . . . , 87]; *Nu ic þe hate. . . .* [Now I command you, 95a]. The present honoured position of the cross, the basis of its authority to command, and the source of its healing power all arise from the deeds of criminals (*bealuwara,* 79) and from the bitter sorrows (*sarra sorga,* 80) it endured long ago. *On me bearn godes / þrowode hwile* [On me the Son of God suffered a while, 83b–84a]. Already the cross has widespread recognition from *menn ofer moldan, ond eall þeos mære gesceaft* [men over the earth, and all this great creation, 82]. This line is a repetition of line 12 and recalls what was said earlier in the dream vision about veneration of the tree on earth and in heaven. It is now *þrymfæst* [fast in glory] and towers up beneath the heavens, able to heal all men who have fear of it (84b–86). This is the second reference in the poem to holy fear or dread, but now a new element of meaning is explicitly added. Earlier (10–21) the dreamer expressed his fear at the "fair sight" but it was not spelled out at that point that this was the spiritual pre-condition for the beginning of redemptive healing. Looking back now in the text from line 85, we can deduce that very early in his visionary experience the dreamer began to respond as he should. His ability to look through the surface of the images, from the "facts" to the spiritual reality and from the *sellic* [wondrous] light and treasure to the mystery behind them, shows him to have been a ready recipient of the spiritual meaning of the crucifixion story.

But the emphasis in lines 78–94 is not on the dreamer directly. Rather it is on mankind in general, those speech-bearers (compare line 89 with line 3) who were silent at the beginning of the poem, and on the way the experiences of the cross have already been widely accepted as exemplary throughout the creation. The cross's power, in other words, has already been partly realized in sacred, post-resurrection history. What is still potential in its allegorical significance, so far as this poem is concerned, is its application to the life of the individual dreamer (and, perhaps, by implication, to the audience). The universality of the cross's applicability and the typicality of the response of creatures to it have yet to be expressed openly in the life of the dreamer whose mind and soul, we remember, are the spiritual arena in which the poem takes place.

It is instructive to observe how the poet prepares for the tropological appropriation of the mystery of the cross by the individual dreamer. Throughout the poem the poet is working with biblical myth but his main imaginative task, so far, has been to recast the story of the Passion in the heroic diction and trappings of the world of the *dryht*. This he has done with great subtlety and power. Now he places that poetic achievement into the larger biblical context. His association of the special mystery of the tree chosen from the forest to bear the Prince of glory in his dying with the special mystery of Mary chosen from all womankind to bear this Prince at his nativity (92–94) is at once a daring poetic simile, a highly effective means of emphasizing the unique glory of the cross, and a narrative link between the story told by the cross and the whole biblical account of God's relation to man.

The Cross's Message to Mankind (95–121)

The highly personal lyrical responses of the speaking cross to the experiences of the Passion recede somewhat in this final dream passage of the poem. Now the cross tells the dreamer what, tropologically or *moraliter* [as to moral action], he is to do; he is to make known his vision to men and reveal to them in words that "it is glory's beam on which God almighty suffered" (97b–98). From the perspective of the listener or reader, the poet-dreamer has in fact been doing this since line one. But now the cross explicates the allegorical import of the vision, by linking the Passion to the fall of man and to the Judgment. In so doing he shows the dreamer how to explain the universal truth of it.

The reference to "mankind's many sins and Adam's ancient deeds" (99–100) extends the cross's significance back through all human history to the point at which the tree of death began to work. The earlier mythical tree is not mentioned in so many words but the reference to Adam's deeds and the immediately following metaphor of Christ tasting death (101) make the allusion unmistakable. Dickins and Ross[22] have cited Vulgate and Old English Gospel uses of the metaphor of tasting

[22] Bolton, p. 32, n. 101.

death but they suggest no significance for its use in the poem. Since the figure of tasting death recurs also in the Judgment passage a little later in the poem (113b–14a), it is important to understand its significance.

The metaphor is used in each of the four gospels and in Hebrews. In Matthew (16:28), Mark (8:39), and Luke (9:27) Christ speaks of the imminence of his second coming, saying that some of his listeners will not taste death before he ushers in his kingdom. The sequence of thought in the poem similarly links the metaphor of tasting death with Christ's coming at Doomsday, the difference being that in the poem the figure is applied to Christ's actual death rather than to the deaths of other men that may not have time to take place. In Hebrews 2:9, though, it is applied to Christ's own death ("that he by the grace of God should taste death for every man") and in John 8:52 the usage ("If a man keep my saying, he shall never taste of death") is close in significance to its second occurrence in the poem because it makes obedience to Christ's commands the precondition of eternal life. In *The Dream of the Rood* the great "Wielder" (*wealdend,* 111) who faces the multitude gathered for judgment asks where the man is who has been willing to taste bitter death for his *dryhtnes naman* [Lord's name], as the Lord himself earlier was willing to die on the *beame* [tree, 110 ff.]. This question throws assembled mankind into confusion as they wonder what to answer, but the assurance is given by the cross to the dreamer that the one who has borne "the best of beacons" on his breast and looked for the kingdom through it need have no fear.

The overall allegorical pattern, then, is this. Shortly after Creation Adam tasted a fatal fruit and was plunged into a kingdom of sin and death. Toward the end of the Incarnation story the Prince of glory tasted death on a forest tree but rose again from the earth-dwelling into which he was placed and ascended into heaven. At the end of time *on domdæge* [at Doomsday, 105] the *dryhten sylfa* [Lord himself] will come with great power to claim as his own the one who "in this fleeting life" has been willing to taste death for the Lord's name.

The Dreamer's Present Life and Future Hope (122–56)

The dreamer-poet's individual tropological response to "the best of dreams" and to the cross's command to him is twofold: the telling of his vision, that is, the composing of the poem, and secondly, the placing of his own eschatological hope in the cross. What has been told by the tree as direct event and explained allegorically by him as truth applicable to all mankind must now, in this part of the poem, be appropriated by the dreamer for his own life and conduct. The literal and rhetorical experience of the dream of the rood, depicting the battle of the crucifixion, has shown the death of Christ to be exemplary and necessary for all men who would go fearless to the Judgment. As this experience has unfolded, the heroic meaning of dying in battle has been redefined in a memorable way. Now, after the objective aspect of the dream vision and its allegory, comes the subjective aspect of meaning, an interiorization of the mystery of the cross in one life. What has happened to God almighty in the battle has been shown as reaching redemptively into the very structure of the created world, through the person of the tree whose experience comprehends all creaturely experience between Creation and Doomsday. The dreamer now eagerly allows the mystery of redemption to reach out and include himself. The scene of the poem's action becomes an interior one, the soul of the *hæleð* addressed by the cross. Here, by thinking daily (136) on the cross's power to rescue him from "this fleeting life," the *hæleð* prepares for eternity.

Two phrases are applied to the dreamer just after the rood has finished speaking which earlier have been applied to Christ himself. The first, *elne mycle* [with great eagerness, 123], describes the dreamer's strong desire to pray to the tree, as his vision ends. It also parallels the *elne mycle* (34) with which "the Prince of mankind" earlier hurried to mount up on the tree (also the alacrity with which the cross relinquishes the body of its dead Lord, 60). We have, then, a parallelism of divine action followed by a human response, with the dreamer eagerly desiring the redemption which the Prince equally eagerly acts to make possible. The second recurrent phrase is *mæte werede* [with few followers] or [alone], probably referring to the midnight solitude of the dreamer on the night of his vision when, he tells us, his spirit is eager to be on the way forth. Or the phrase may refer more generally to his sense of solitude in a world experienced as a place of exile by the one who believes that heaven is his true homeland. Reminding us of the friendless and exiled man in *The Wanderer* who searches for his protector lord, the dreamer tells us that he does not have many powerful friends on earth; unlike the Wanderer, however, as distinct from the voice of the poet narrator in *The Wanderer,* the dreamer knows who his lord is and where he can be found. He knows that the rood is his *mundbyrd* [protector, 130b–31a] and desires this *dryhten* [Lord] who suffered on the gallows-tree to be his *freond* [friend, 144b–46].

There is another interesting parallel between the dreamer in this part of the poem and something described earlier. Mary, according to the cross, was chosen above all womankind. He himself was chosen above all trees. Also, in his newly found zeal he wants to be the most excellent in his veneration of the cross, to surpass all other believers: "It is now the hope of my life that I alone more often than all men may seek that victory-tree, honour it well" (126b–29a). It is one of the peculiar powers of *The Dream of the Rood* as a poem that it expresses vividly by means of highly concrete metaphors of existence a deep human desire for ultimate fulfilment—a tree, a man, a mother, and a dreamer become the Tree, the Man, the Mother of God, and the Worshipper—without in any way reducing the particularity and special nature of each individual poetic image. The myth that sustains and structures the poem is based on a sense of the ideal wholeness of all creation, on a complete theological and imaginative acceptance of the incarnational identification of the Creator-*Dryhten* with his creature-follower. From this myth emerge all the important images of the poem.

Tropology teaches the dreamer what to utter as poet and what hope to rely on daily as worshipper of the *Dryhten*. In addition, toward the end of the poem, an anagogic meaning concerned with last things increasingly emerges. As always with anagogy, so here, it is addressed to a sense of the incompleteness and fleeting nature of life in middle-earth. It draws the mind of the dreamer both upward from the world and out of time and space altogether. Throughout the last section of the poem (122–56) the tropological and anagogic perspectives alternate with each other (they were present earlier but not emphasized), until finally and fittingly anagogy takes over completely.

There is, however, an apparent problem in the way the poet has disposed his materials at the end of his remarkable poem. Why, long after the account of the burial of Christ (65b–67a), and also well after the account of the resurrection and ascension (101–03), do we have at the very conclusion of *The Dream of the Rood* (148b ff.) the first explicit mention of the harrowing of hell, followed immediately by a slightly fuller account than previously of the ascension? That the poet does not bring this material into focus immediately following the account of the burial is not too surprising, since his main narrative interest there is the *egeslic wyrd* [horrid fate] and later glorification of the cross. To have introduced the harrowing motif would have deflected this interest. But this does not explain why the harrowing is left out of the cross's important explanation to the dreamer of the overall Creation to Doomsday pattern into which the sufferings on the cross fit and from which they draw their meaning. There would seem to be a kind of credal and imaginative obligation to remember the crucial harrowing, but we are left to deduce a reason for its being placed at the poem's end, just after the anagogic vision of the *dryhtnes folc* [Lord's folk] seated at the heavenly banquet.

The explanation seems to lie in the evident teaching or evangelical purpose of the poem. Internally in the imaginative fiction of the dream vision, the man addressed by the personified cross as *hæleð min se leofa* [my dear man] is the soul to whom the truths of the crucifixion have been presented and for whom they have been connected allegorically to the whole Christian redemptive scheme. It is he who, once addressed by the shining beacon, has eagerly and happily accepted the content of the faith contained in the Passion story. Tropologically and in charity he is shown as having appropriated the divine revelation for his own soul and life. But tropology includes the whole body of Christ's folk as well as the individual soul. It seeks a communal as well as an individual realization of the truths that are literally and allegorically expressed. And although the main application of the cross's story in the poem is to the life of the dreamer, there are two ways in which the much wider communal reference is shown as important.

First, there are numerous references to mankind in the poem, including those souls in hell who survived the burning and who go in a multitude with Christ into God's kingdom (148 ff.). There is also the reference to the whole of mankind assembled at the Judgment (112). And there are several references to the "holy ones" in heaven. In other words, mankind in middle-earth, hell, and heaven is very much present as the larger human context for the experiences of the tree and the dreamer. Secondly, and even more importantly, these experiences are meant to be seen as paradigmatic and exemplary, even though *The Dream of the Rood* as a poem never uses direct homiletic address to the listener or reader, as numerous other Old English poems do. The overt teaching is directed to the dreamer and he never quite speaks directly to us, nor does he insist on applying the truths to his audience with the conventional *uton* [let us] formula that exhorts spiritual commitment in other poems. Rather like Cynewulf in his signatures, he lets the objective account of the action of the poem, plus his own personal reflection on it and its significance, convey the tropological lesson to the audience.

We are left to ask, then, what is the intended significance for the audience? What does the poet appear to hope for as response from an audience now seeing and hearing in their own cultural and social symbols a powerful recreation of the Passion of Christ, followed by a fictional dreamer's confession of faith and hope, and ending with a reference to the harrowing of hell and the ascension of Christ? In a central way *The Dream of the Rood* is a poem about free will and necessity, about a tree that may disobey its Creator but dare not, because it realizes that it and its Lord must die if mankind encumbered by "Adam's ancient works" is to have a choice between the way of life and the already established way of sin and death. The necessity of the death of the Prince and of the tree's obedience is accepted by each of them, so that mankind may be helped. The dreamer is shown as gladly and eagerly accepting this help. The poem, then, revolves around the ancient paradox of life by means of death. We have been shown how this paradox works itself out for each of Christ, the tree, and the dreamer, and in a more general sense for all those of mankind who show themselves willing to "taste death" for their Lord.

The significance of Christ's descent into the world below, following his death in middle-earth, is that by this descending action he annihilates (buries) the sinful humanity whose form and nature he himself has voluntarily come out of heaven to assume. Like the crosses which are put into a dark pit but later brought out and covered with treasure, he is buried but subsequently rises again, as the firstborn of the new creation. The symbolic death to the things of the "fleeting" world to which men are called by the cross's story is a sacramental initiation into the death and resurrection of Christ, to a spiritual martyrdom that will enable the creature to transcend its fallen condition and be taken into the perfection of the *dryht* of heaven. Early in his dream experience the dreamer knows himself as a "sin-stained" casualty of the war unleashed long ago in middle-earth by Satan, but for him the exemplum of the obedient tree becomes a beacon or sign summoning him away from this earth. By the time the harrowing of hell is described he too knows himself to have been brought forth a new man and placed on the *forðwege* [way forth] to heaven. Like Adam and Eve of old time, and like both the heroic Prince of mankind and the thane-like tree, he has undergone his own spiritual descent or death to the self and so is ready to ascend. But the harrowing and the ascension are the paradigmatic model for what, in the fullest sense, is yet to come, both for the dreamer and for the rest of mankind who still exist in middle-earth.

According to ancient tradition, Adam and Eve and their world were created to replace the defected host of fallen angels. But when they as new creatures also fell, the divine plan was temporarily frustrated. Now in the harrowing and the ascension which end *The Dream of the Rood* we have a brief description of the way in which heaven's ancient plan for the ultimate unity of God and man will be achieved. The *eðel* [homeland] on high mentioned in the last line of the poem has been awaiting restoration to its primal *dream* [joy] ever since some creatures of the *anwealda ælmihtig* [only almighty Ruler] fell into hell and led both mankind and his world away from God's kingdom. With the action of the poem completed by the God-man, in terms of potential anagogic fulfillment for all mankind (*He us onlysde and us life forgeaf, / heofonlicne ham* [He freed us and granted us life, a heavenly home, 147–48a], the action on the human level, into which the poet surrenders his poem, has just begun.

191

13

The Wanderer, The Seafarer, and the Genre of *Planctus*

ROSEMARY WOOLF

The Wanderer AND *The Seafarer*, THOUGH NOW COMMONLY REFERRED to as elegies, may more helpfully be seen to belong to the distinctively mediaeval genre of *planctus* or complaint. The characteristics of this genre that divide it from elegy are firstly that the speaker is invariably fictional and secondly that, whilst the subject of the lament may be a death, it can equally well be any kind of loss that is experienced intensely. The fictional speaker may be either an individual or a representative type. In various western European literatures there survive on the one hand laments of Dido, Orpheus, Guðrun, Eve, Mary Magdalene and, in abundance, the Blessed Virgin, on the other hand, for instance, complaints of an old man or a young woman betrayed by her lover or separated from him.[1]

Our knowledge of the Old English *planctus* is of two kinds: that which derives from extant poems and that which is inferred obliquely from other sources of which the most important is *Beowulf*. Both types of *planctus* existed: complaints of individual speakers are represented by

[1] *The Wanderer* and *The Seafarer* are included in the valuable list of western European *planctus* provided by Peter Dronke, *Poetic Individuality in the Middle Ages* (Oxford, 1970), pp. 27–28.

The Wife's Lament, The Husband's Message, and *Wulf and Eadwacer.*[2] No one would dispute that the latter two are spoken within the context of specific situations. This is made especially plain by the fact that the recipient of the complaint is also a fictional person within the story. In the case of *Wulf and Eadwacer* it would be inappropriately realistic to ask how the lament was conveyed to the person addressed; but it is interesting to note that in the *Husband's Message,* the message is either carved upon a rune staff or is delivered verbally by a messenger.[3] This variation in the form of the *planctus* reminds one of Ovid's adoption of the epistolary form for his series of complaints of unhappy women, a sophisticated device which nevertheless does not always work realistically. *The Wife's Lament,* however, does not quite so unmistakably have a narrative context. Nevertheless, there seem to be too many personal references which are tantalisingly unclear for us to be able to classify it simply as the lament of a women deprived of her husband. It is not, however, addressed to a particular person—in this, of course, resembling the complaints of representative types. Nowadays, when we read these poems on the printed page, we may be inclined to think of ourselves as overhearing an interior soliloquy; but in a period when poetry was read aloud it is much more likely that poets who wrote complaints thought of the audience as being the recipients. For the *Wife's Complaint* they would as it were be a confidant: their relationship to the complaints of the Wanderer and Seafarer is less simply labelled, but is important in that it has a bearing upon the tone of voice heard in these poems at the beginning and the end.

The evidence of these surviving poems is usefully amplified by the allusions to *planctus* in *Beowulf,* which incidentally makes plain that the *planctus* was a varied and flourishing form by the eighth century: a valuable piece of information since most Old English poems are so difficult to date. As has often been suggested, the opening of the Finn Episode may well reflect the existence of a *planctus* spoken by Hildeburg: if it does, it provides a useful illustration of the way in which complaints could be related to heroic stories and could therefore be integrated into narratives if a poet so wished; Chaucer's treatment of the *Heroides* in the *Legend of Good Women* comes to mind as an analogy. A literary tradition of a lament for the death of a hero may also

---

[2] I exclude here poems that are commonly or sometimes described as elegiac, such as *The Ruin,* which, despite its theme, is not a *planctus,* and poems such as *Deor* and *Resignation (The Penitent's Prayer),* which, though they are narrated by an I-speaker, for different reasons present a problem concerning genre. At this stage it seems safest to assume that Old English literature contained a body of poems that were offshoots of the genre of *planctus,* not members of it.

[3] Cf. *Three Old English Elegies,* ed. R. F. Leslie (Manchester, 1961), pp. 12–15.

lie behind the last three moving lines of *Beowulf:* an earlier analogue to this is the lament for Christ in the *Dream of the Rood.* Such laments had already become part of the eastern devotional tradition, but it is easier to suppose that this represents a parallel development from folk-dirge to Christian literary lament than to postulate any direct influence.[4] The end of *Beowulf,* however, is distinguished from the common type of complaint through being eulogistic, and it is therefore possible that, rather than being literary in origin, it reflects historical custom, some funeral address, for instance, at the death of a king.

An equally interesting hint at another type of *planctus* occurs in the account of Hroþgar's composition or narration of various kinds of poetry (lines 2105–14). *Eldo gebunden* [shackled by old age] he lamented the loss of his youth (*ongan . . . gioguðe cwiðan*). The complaint of a typical figure, that of an old man, seems here to have been recited with self-reference by the aged Hroþgar. No doubt Old English *planctus* of this type were far more generalised and decorous than the Middle English analogues which insist upon the disgusting detail of physical senility. The loss of strength (cf. *Beowulf,* line 2113) or the outliving of friends (cf. *Seafarer* 92–93) may have been typical themes rather than those of deafness and a shuffling walk. By the end of the Old English period the disabilities of old age had become a recurrent homiletic theme, deriving directly or indirectly from patristic sources. It would be interesting to know whether there was an entirely native Old English tradition of complaints of an old man and, if so, for how long it remained uninfluenced by Christian didactic literature.

Besides these three brief references to *plantcus* in *Beowulf* there are two famous elegiac passages, one of which is in form a short *planctus,* the other a summary of a *planctus.* The first is the so-called elegy of the last survivor (lines 2247–66). Though there are many differences between these lines and *The Wanderer,* the modern differences of title suggest a distinction that is not there: for the "last survivor" appears to be an exile (*unbliðe hwearf / dæges ond nihtes* [went about sadly by day and by night, 2268b–69a]), while the narrative implications of the poem are that the Wanderer is also a last survivor. The lament of the last survivor is cast in the form of an apostrophe to the earth (this opening is required to adapt the lament to its narrative context); but much of the lament itself is reminiscent of *The Wanderer* and may well give an accurate impression of what were the simpler antecedents of *The Wanderer.*

The second passage is the so-called elegy of the bereaved father. Its

[4] For the eastern tradition see Margaret Alexiou, *The Ritual Lament in Greek Tradition* (Cambridge, 1974).

opening suggests that, unlike the elegy of the last survivor, this is the *planctus* of an individual, for the father mourns for a son who has been hanged. This cannot be a typical situation and scholars have sought to identify the story.[5] The rest of the lament, however, is generalised and, rather interestingly, at its close shows an insight into the psychological responses to bereavement of a kind that, as we shall see, is also to be found in *The Wanderer*. This insight occurs in the narrative summing up, *þuhte him eall to rum, / wongas ond wicstede* [the fields and the dwelling place now seemed to him all too large, 2461b–62a]: the experience that a room or house of a person who has died suddenly seems to become large and empty is surely a common one, though the author of *Beowulf* is perhaps the only English poet to have recorded it.

The abundant references to *planctus* in *Beowulf* show that the genre was current in the eighth century. A slightly earlier date for its currency can be inferred from Bede's famous story of the conversion to Christianity of one of the leading pagan counsellors of King Edwin of Northumbria. According to Bede this counsellor justified his abandonment of the old religion for the reason that Christianity brought a solution to the pagan view of life, which he likened to that of a sparrow which flies from outer wintry darkness through a warm and lighted hall out into wintry darkness again.[6] The source of this image, which is movingly elaborated, is surely a *planctus* concerning the transience of life. Whether a tradition had reached Bede that this image had been used or whether Bede himself turned to the tradition of *planctus* in order to make the counsellor's understanding of the doctrine of the Resurrection articulate is of little consequence, though the latter is perhaps more likely.

The story of the sparrow is also of value in indicating the nature of the first relationship between Christianity and native *planctus*. If this image of the sparrow is indeed pre-Christian in origin, it shows how extraordinarily apt was the Anglo-Saxon imagination for an immediate responsiveness to the Christian doctrine of eternal life. Pagans are not necessarily so acutely aware of the shortness of human life nor of the poignancy of the passing of all that one values. It seems safe to assert that the Church would have fostered a native tradition of *planctus* rather than have attempted to suppress it. Ingeld may have nothing to do with Christ but the Last Survivor in his lonely exile undoubtedly does. It is perhaps paradoxical that Christianity encourages, at least in poetry, a

---

[5] Like the story relating to *The Wife's Lament*, however, it remains unidentified. Klaeber's objection (cf. note to line 2444) to the theory that the father is Jǫrmunrekr is fully convincing.

[6] Cf. *Bede's Ecclesiastical History of the English People*, eds. Bertram Colgrave and R.A.B. Mynors (Oxford, 1969), pp. 182–84.

deep and melancholy response to transience. In later English literature some of the finest poems of Christian authors have been on this subject, and Anglo-Saxon poets would similarly have found that Christianity provided a natural home for traditional laments.

The Church, however, did more than provide fortunate conditions in which a purely native tradition could flourish. With the Old Testament and later didactic works indebted to it, it provided fresh sources upon which Anglo-Saxon poets could draw. Many books of the Bible, including the Psalms, Isaiah, Jeremiah, and Ecclesiasticus, had expressed most powerfully and movingly the idea of the brevity of human life and of all man's achievements. Many such Christian sources have now been identified for *The Wanderer* and *The Seafarer,* and it is clear from these poems that the native and the biblical could be mingled together in a most natural and seemly way.

It is sometimes thought that even if Christianity did contain within the Bible and its later homiletic literature so many imaginatively moving expressions of the theme of transience, there must nevertheless be an obligation upon the Christian poet who writes upon transience to include in his poem some equally moving expression of his trust in eternal life. Such a view would probably be confirmed by a study of the practice of later mediaeval poets. In the "Love Ron" of Thomas of Hales, for instance, which contains in its lament a beautiful use of the *ubi sunt* formula, less than half the poem is occupied with lament;[7] similarly, in Dunbar's "Of Luve Erdly and Divine," which also deals with the superiority of sacred to profane love, the lament for the transience of human love turns midway through the poem to a confident acknowledgement of the unendingness of divine love.[8] Reflection upon the poems of later Christian authors, however, shows this assumption to be wrong. Some seventeenth-century lyrics, for instance, contain at most fleeting or perfunctory reference to the fact that for the Christian transience must yield to eternity. Herrick's "To Daffadills," for instance, contains only a momentary and oblique allusion to a Christian frame of reference, whilst Herbert's "Vertue" and "Life" both end on a Christian note, but in them, as in *The Wanderer,* the imaginative vitality does not extend beyond the lament. In Hopkins's "Spring and Fall" there is no reference to Christianity at all.[9] All these are moving lyrics written by poets who are famous for their explicitly Christian poetry, and this fact makes

[7] *English Lyrics of the XIIIth Century,* ed. Carleton Brown (Oxford, 1932), pp. 68–74.
[8] *Poems,* ed. Mackay Mackenzie (London, 1932), pp. 101–04.
[9] Robert Herrick, *Poetical Works,* ed. L. C. Martin (Oxford, 1956), p. 125; *The Works of George Herbert,* ed. F. E. Hutchinson (Oxford, 1941), pp. 87–88, 94; Gerard Manley Hopkins, *Poems,* ed. Robert Bridges, 2nd ed. by Charles Williams (Oxford, 1930), p. 50.

clear that speculation about a poet's religious convictions—the question of how deep or how well-informed was his faith—is pointless when we have only a single poem to interpret. In this situation an assessment of the equilibrium sought in the poem between a lament for transience and its Christian solution will be an inevitable part of a critical interpretation, but it cannot provide the foundations for any inference about the poet's personal beliefs.

If a Christian poet may write about the experience of transience with little or no interest in the Christian promise of eternal life, this must be especially true of a Christian who writes in the genre of the *planctus,* in which the speaker is by definition someone other than himself. Recollection of this may help in understanding the structure and progress of thought in *The Wanderer* where the question of whether or not the poet felt his Christianity deeply is an irrelevant one that distracts from more pertinent issues. One of the apparently most difficult problems that arise (and certainly a genuine problem for the editor who is compelled by the modern system of punctuation to take a definite view) is that of the number of independent speakers in the poem and which of them is speaking at a number of different points. In a personal response to the poem it seems that the *swa cwæþ* construction at lines 6 and 111 is so conspicuously intrusive that it must serve an important function, whilst paradoxically the question of who is speaking at the beginning of the poem (poet or Wanderer) and at the end (poet, Wanderer, or contemplator of the ruin) seems scarcely to affect one's understanding of the poem. The primary purpose of the *swa cwæþ* construction may therefore be to block off the first and last passages about the consolation of God's mercy from the main body of the poem.[10]

To suggest that these passages are deliberately blocked off is not to imply that they are irrelevant, but that despite their relevancy the poet did not wish them to undercut the power and poignancy of the main part of the *planctus* which they frame. It would furthermore follow that the poet, whilst achieving a logical and lyrical continuity, was not seeking to analyse a subtle psychological continuity of thought. Though there are in the poem moments of sensitive perception, it is no use searching it for an examination of the long, slow movements of the heart which may bring a man to a certain peace and resignation. The very fact that it would only take about ten minutes to read aloud whilst the passage of time within the poem (though past is time recalled) is unchartably long, reveals that the poet is not concerned to show, with any psychological precision, how a person learns: one may contrast it with *The*

10 For a recent discussion of the force of *swa cwæþ* considered from a syntactical point of view see *The Wanderer,* eds. T. P. Dunning and A. J. Bliss (London, 1969), pp. 30–36.

Pearl, where the dreamer's slow and zigzag progress towards acceptance of bereavement and submission to God's will strike a familiar chord.

Once the reader ceases to wonder whether the Wanderer himself was capable of the various degrees of wisdom presented in the poem, it is possible to find a pattern in the poem without resolving the question of who the speaker is at various points, a question which may well be without answer. The reason that it is unanswerable is that at the beginning and end either the Wanderer speaks partially with the voice of the poet-narrator or the poet-narrator speaks partially with the voice of the Wanderer. The authorial voice may be heard clearly but unobtrusively in the use of *us* in the last halfline, *þær us eal seo fæstnung stondeð* [where all our security lies, 115b]. At this point an audience is manifestly addressed and probably this linking of speaker and hearers has a homiletic resonance. Nevertheless the last four lines (of which this half-line is the climax) cannot be interpreted solely as the author's didactic epilogue, for they contain two important indications of the Wanderer's final state of mind. Firstly, of course, they contain the second reference to *ar,* God's mercy, which by implication the Wanderer now seeks (*seceð*) and therefore, according to Christ's promise, will find. Whether this represents a development upon the statement *Oft him anhaga are gebideð* [Often the solitary one experiences, or awaits, God's mercy, 1] depends upon the meaning of *gebidan.*[11] If it means "experience" then the first line as it were sets the seal upon the penultimate one: we know the end at the beginning. If, however, *gebidan* means "wait," a development has surely taken place, for actively to seek God's mercy must represent a spiritual stage beyond passively awaiting it. Moreover if the sense is "await," there is probably some hint that the Wanderer at this stage misunderstands the nature of God's mercy, supposing that it will take the form of his finding a new lord. In that case a wiser understanding of *ar* has been reached at the close of the poem.

The last four lines of *The Wanderer* are thematically related not only to the first five lines but also to the argument of the succeeding twelve lines; indeed at first sight lines 111–12 seem to be mere repetition of the earlier and elaborate statement (probably of classical origin)[12] that it

[11] It does not seem possible to solve the meaning of *gebidan* in *The Wanderer:* as argued above on literary grounds either interpretation is possible, whilst Bruce Mitchell, "Some Syntactical Problems in *The Wanderer,*" *NM,* 69 (1968), 172–75, has convincingly shown that the linguistic evidence shows either meaning to be acceptable.

[12] For the classical-Christian origin of this theme see J. E. Cross, "On the Genre of *The Wanderer,*" *Neophil,* 45 (1961), 65, repr. *Essential Articles for the Study of Old English Poetry,* eds. J. B. Bessinger, Jr. and Stanley J. Kahrl (Hamden, Connecticut, 1968), pp. 517–18.

is a noble and virtuous custom for a man not to reveal his sufferings however intense these may be. The recurrence of this idea may appear ill-placed for it seems a bathetically inadequate response to the awe-inspiring vision of a deserted world, ruined walls representing the last trace of man, and the snow falling perpetually. But the repetition is significant because of a sudden qualification that it is given, ... *nemþe he ær þa bote cunne* [unless he knows the remedy beforehand, 113b]. The *bot* is surely the affirmation in the last line and a half, *Wel bið þam þe him are seceð / frofre to Fæder on heofonum, þær us eal seo fæstnung stondeð* [Well is it for him who seeks favour, consolation from the Father in heaven, where all our security lies, 114b–15], and this relationship should be indicated by punctuation (i.e., a colon after *gefremman* in line 114). This observation resolves the problem that is sometimes raised, namely of how the speaker can so emphatically maintain that a man must keep his sorrows to himself and then reveal them.[13] As we have said before, the theory that with a *planctus* we are listening to man's inner thoughts is not quite happy in a social context in which the poem is recited to an audience. It is more satisfactory to assume that the poet intended an apparent discrepancy between the reticence demanded in lines 11–18 and the poem itself, and delayed the resolution of the discrepancy until his concluding climax.

If *The Wanderer* is interpreted as the lament of a typical figure, namely a last survivor and an exile, the question of whether there may be more than one speaker within the main body of the monologue becomes irrelevant, no matter how subtly it may be investigated.[14] For any argument for two speakers presupposes that the poet is displaying the idiosyncracies of an individual consciousness, so that the reader may properly feel that one individual person could not make the psychological progress towards wisdom that the poem is concerned with. But this type of realistic response is mistaken if the speaker is a typical figure who will describe himself, not through a probing self-knowledge, but rather from the point of view of a thoughtful onlooker: there is no difference of attitude or understanding between the speaker of the *planctus* and the hearer who wisely considers the speaker's plight. Indeed the poet has taken considerable care to prevent an audience identifying themselves

---

[13] There are of course other and plausible explanations such as that of Dunning and Bliss, ed. cit., p. 93.

[14] The most convincing argument for two speakers is that of John C. Pope, "Dramatic Voices in *The Wanderer* and *The Seafarer*," *Franciplegius: Medieval and Linguistic Studies in Honor of Francis Peabody Magoun, Jr.* (New York, 1965), pp. 164–93; repr. *Essential Articles*, pp. 533–70. For a thoughtful and sometimes telling criticism of Professor Pope's arguments see *The Wanderer*, ed. R. F. Leslie (Manchester, 1966), pp. 9–25.

too instinctively and uncritically with the Wanderer's loss. The poet at one point, for instance, describes a common but private experience, namely how a bereaved person for many years (or longer) will dream with special intensity that the dead are alive again: lines 30–50 record this experience and in particular how the awakening from such a dream seems to be a fresh bereavement. The latter is expressed well by the contrast between the warm world of the dream and the wintry scene to which the *wineleas guma* [lordless man, 45b] awakens. Nevertheless the possibility of an intimate sympathy developing between speaker and hearer is prevented through a deliberate act of distancing. This dream is only by implication the Wanderer's, for it is ascribed by the Wanderer to a hypothetical *wineleas guma* and this figure is therefore an imaginary creation who stands anyway at one remove from the audience. This is only one striking instance of a general peculiarity of the poem, which is that the Wanderer most often describes, not how he feels, but how someone in a comparable situation would feel. Over half the poem is set in this form. The intention of the poet must be to distance and generalise, and it is achieved at the deliberate expense of naturalism, for real people do not think in such a stylised way.

In the place of psychological development the poem has a definite thematic patterning and one that is paradoxical in relation to the old issue of the Christian versus pagan or secular elements in the poem: for it is the first part of the poem, which is usually described as heroic, that bears the Christian meaning, whilst it is the second part, which seems to be constructed out of an assemblage of Christian borrowings, that is secular in tone. The secularisation of the passages of Christian origin has been achieved by stripping their normal doctrinal or didactic contexts from them. The *sum*-series in lines 80–84, for instance, is a rhetorical figure and Christian theme; various ways of disposing of the earthly body are listed in a prelude to a demonstration that nevertheless the dead rise up.[15] But as used in *The Wanderer* this theme has nothing to do with the refutation of heretical objections to the doctrine of the resurrection of the body. It stands simply as a melancholy list to remind one that whilst methods of burial may be manifold, dead and buried every man will be.

Similarly the *ubi sunt* passage derives immediately from a Christian sermon tradition in which it serves to emphasive contempt for the world. The preacher asks where various splendours have gone and answers his own rhetorical question by enjoining his audience to visit

---

[15] Cf. J. E. Cross, "On *The Wanderer* lines 80–84, a Study of a Figure and a Theme," *Vetenskaps-Societetens i Lund Årsbok,* 1958–1959, pp. 77–110.

the tomb where dust and bones will provide the true but frightening answer[16]. But in *The Wanderer* there is no suggestion that the *maþþumgyfa* [giver of treasure, 92b] rots in the grave or that the *beorht bune* [bright cup, 94a] may be rusted through. Standing on their own, as they do in *The Wanderer, ubi sunt* questions have the reverse effect. Far from suggesting that their subjects are worthless they confer a deep nostalgic value upon them, and the very fleetingness which the questions call to mind enhances rather than diminishes their preciousness. Such passages following upon the description of the Wanderer's former life in his lord's hall make clear that he has to learn detachment from that life, not because it was worthless and undeserving of his affections, but because it is inevitable that everything that is loved on earth, however precious it may be, must be lost. Such an understanding of life is of course capable of being translated into Christian terms, yet in itself is neither Christian nor unChristian but a straightforward recognition of the nature of things; as expressed, however, in the second half of *The Wanderer* it has resonances of melancholy and wistfulness which make it poetically moving but with more concern for natural feelings than for pure Christian teaching.

The first half of *The Wanderer* has properly been called heroic in that its background is probably the kind of literary-heroic society that is depicted in *Beowulf*. Not only is the background probably literary but also the treatment of the Wanderer himself is literary and stylised. There does not seem to be any historical reason why a man who had lost his lord should not sooner or later in his travels find another (one critic who has considered this question has found too realistic an answer to it, namely that the Wanderer had abandoned his lord in cowardly fashion);[17] certainly there is no reason why the Wanderer should live in a world where the weather is perpetual winter. From outside the poem one can say that the situation is thus depicted because the Wanderer is not an individual, who would experience the normal alternations of loss and gain to which all are accustomed, but the typical figure of an exile living in a typical exile's world. But to dismiss the matter in this way is perhaps to miss the crucial point of how the Wanderer's change of heart comes about. For near the beginning of the poem the Wanderer conceives of himself as a member of a real world where another lord and another meadhall might reasonably be found: in the course of the poem he comes to accept that his lot as wanderer is irreversible. It

[16] Cf. J. E. Cross, *The Dry Bones* Speak—A Theme in Some Old English Homilies," *JEGP*, 56 (1957), 434–39.
[17] For this view see R. W. V. Elliott, "The Wanderer's Conscience," *ES*, 39 (1958), 193–200.

might therefore be not too farfetched to say that the wisdom that the Wanderer acquires is that of coming to understand the Christian truth of which he himself is accidentally a figure, namely that all men are exiles on earth and that the only true home lies, not behind one, but before.[18]

Many quotations assembled by Professor Whitelock with reference to her interpretation of *The Seafarer* show that Anglo-Saxon writers liked to play verbally upon the paradox of a man choosing to become an exile on earth in order more surely to reach his native land thereafter (e.g., *Multo tempore pro aeterna patria exulauerant*).[19] Those to whom Professor Whitelock refers are men who deliberately chose the life of exile or pilgrim: the reason is plainly that they may in fact live the life which allegorically all Christians live. Manifestly, a man who lives in contentment all his life in his lord's hall or in his own home with his wife and children is not likely to feel the truth of the Christian image. The devout therefore change their lives. In *The Wanderer* the poet depicts an exile who has not initially chosen to change his life, but, having this change forced upon him, comes to understand its significance, and through the mouth of an imaginary man, *frod in ferðe* [wise in heart, 90a] expresses the recognition of the permanence of his situation. The very last line of the poem perhaps also captures his understanding of that which he is a figure and of that which the figure promises. It has been ingeniously suggested that *fæstnung* in the last line is a concrete noun and thus reverses the image of the ruin.[20] But the line would provide an even more effective close if the ideas of *frofor* and *fæstnung* are related and are taken to establish a relationship between what the Wanderer originally sought on earth, a lord who would comfort (*frefran*) him and the security of life within the hall, and what he now looks for in heaven.

The Wanderer is an elusive and delicate poem: any interpretation must be based on hints and oblique implications and therefore must be tentative. *The Seafarer* by contrast is a strong and boldy designed poem and therefore well able to withstand firm critical investigation. The problems of interpreting it are in the main similar to those of *The Wanderer,* though the solutions are sometimes different. To begin with

---

[18] For quotations illustrative of this tradition see G. V. Smithers, "The Meaning of *The Seafarer* and *The Wanderer,*" MÆ, 26 (1957), 137–53.

[19] "The Interpretation of *The Seafarer,*" in *The Early Cultures of North-West Europe* (*H. M. Chadwick Memorial Studies*), eds. Sir Cyril Fox and Bruce Dickens (Cambridge, 1950), pp. 268, 271–72; repr. *Essential Articles,* pp. 442–57.

[20] Cf. S. I. Tucker, "Return to *The Wanderer,*" *Essays in Criticism,* 8 (1958), 229–37 and Dunning and Bliss, ed. cit. p. 50.

there is the issue of the number of speakers. In this respect *The Seafarer* has a paradoxical relationship to *The Wanderer*. In the latter, the poet by his *swa cwæþ* construction seems to indicate a change of speaker though there is no sharp difference in tone to suggest that the speaker must have changed, whereas in *The Seafarer* the attitude to seafaring seems to change so abruptly and inexplicably at line 33a that it has seemed necessary to assume a change of speaker although the poet does not indicate one. The failure of the poet to interpose a narrative aside to mark the opening of a new speech must be taken seriously, for the presence of such authorial interjections in *The Wanderer* shows that they were not considered unsuited to the genre (as they presumably were to the more impressionistic emotional style of the *Advent Lyrics*).[21] The significance of this omission is confirmed by the style of the opening line of the poem, *Mæg ic be me sylfum soðgied wrecan* [I can recite a true lay concerning myself]. This is surely the introduction to the whole poem; if the *soðgied* ends at line 33a, what comes after that? There is thus good justification for supposing that there is no break at line 33a and indeed that, as others have pointed out, there is a strong dramatic sweep which carries the reader forward to the climax in lines 64–66.

If there is no change of speaker at line 33a, one must assume that the poet intended the subsequent lines to come as a surprise: the man made wretched by seafaring now chooses to go to sea. But clearly this kind of literary surprise cannot be random: close attention to the text must show it to be justified. The justification for the surprise appears to be that whilst the speaker's attitude to the sea startlingly changes in mid-line, his attitude to the land remains constant throughout. There are all together four passages (two before line 33a and two after) in which it becomes increasingly plain that life on land is to be despised. The first is in lines 12–13 where the Seafarer complains that the man *þe him on foldan fægrost limpeð* [to whom it befalls in the fairest manner on land] does not understand his sufferings on the sea. This statement is at most mutedly pejorative; but it would seem that happiness brings blindness or indifference to the miseries of others, and the poet's method here is markedly different from that of the author of *The Wanderer*, who constantly introduces the thought of other people who will share and understand the Wanderer's desolation.

The next occurrence of the theme is at lines 27–29 where the Seafarer again imagines the prosperous and carefree man, *wlonc ond wingal,*

---

[21] For the dialogue between Joseph and Mary in which no change of speaker is indicated see R. Burlin, *The Old English Advent, A Typological Commentary* (New Haven and London, 1968), pp. 112–14.

living *in burgum,* who again will not understand the sufferings of the man who journeys by sea. Despite the apparently neutral use of the collocation *wlonc ond wingal* in *The Ruin* (line 34), it is difficult to accept that this phrase is free of pejorative connotations in the present text.[22] Whether terms such as *wlonc* [proud] or *wingal* ["drunken" or at best "having abundantly drunk"] are pejorative will depend upon the moral seriousness of the poem in which they occur. But nobody doubts that *The Seafarer* is serious to the point of overt homiletic didacticism, and even in a more obliquely moral work such as *Beowulf,* one could not imagine that even in the triumphal festivities at Heorot Beowulf could be described in these terms. The same idea in *The Seafarer* is repeated in lines 55–56: here it is the *sefteadig secg* who cannot understand the miseries of the exile. *Sefteadig* is an emendation and a nonce word, but the grounds for accepting it in the text are good,[23] whilst the implications of the first element *seft-* are plain: one who is *sefteadig* enjoys a life that is soft or indolent.

The fourth of these passages is the climax: the Seafarer no longer hints that a contented life in the world is worthless but states it explicitly and powerfully:

                    forþon me hatran sind
Dryhtnes dreamas   þonne þis deade lif
læne on londe.

(64b–66a)

It is from this dead life, transient on land, that the Seafarer wishes to escape by embarking on his sea-voyage. The force of the paradoxical collocation *deade lif* has of course often been noticed; but the phrase *laene on londe* is equally pregnant. In other contexts it could of course mean "transitory in this world" (as opposed to the next), but in this context it surely means "on land" (as opposed to on sea). The poet seems in fact to have given an individual twist to the traditional images

---

[22] The evidence about *wlonc* is uncertain: both in Old English secular and religious poetry it may be used of either hero or villain; it is worth noting, however, that in *The Wanderer* (line 80) it seems to suggest simultaneously the value and ultimate uselessness of pride, whilst in *Beowulf* the related noun *wlenco* is invariably used in a depreciatory sense. The pejorative associations of *wingal* are much clearer. If we take together the seven occurrences of *wingal* and the analogous formation *medugal* (excluding *wingal* in *The Seafarer*), the non-pejorative use in *The Ruin* is unique. Particularly notable is the application in *Daniel* of *wingal* to Nebuchadnezzar (line 116) and *medugal* to Belshazzar at his feast (line 702), and of the phrase *modig ond medugal* (a collocation similar to *wlonc ond wingal*) to Holofernes in *Judith* (line 26).

[23] See *The Seafarer,* ed. I. L. Gordon (London, 1960), note to line 56. The alternative emendation to *esteadig* would yield a less obviously pejorative sense.

of man as an exile (as used in *The Wanderer*) and of life as a sea-voyage[24]. According to his stylised figurative pattern the man who lives a life on land is always in a state of security and contentment: he is therefore mindless of the Christian image of man as an exile; indeed the poet's insistence on this point suggests that there is a resolute rejection of it. The sea, however, is always a place of isolation and hardship: the man therefore who chooses to be literally what in Christian terms he is figuratively must forsake the land and live upon the sea.

It will be clear from this argument that there are major differences in tone and situation between *The Wanderer* and *Seafarer*. The latter is a much harsher and more didactic poem. Though the life of sea-faring exile is full of hardship, what alternatives there are may not fittingly be grieved for, nor have they accidentally been lost: they have been deliberately rejected and rejected with contempt. A consequence of this is that when the poet passes in the second half of the poem to his generalised instances of transience, which are borrowed like those in *The Wanderer* from Christian homiletic sources, he does not rid them of their original meaning.[25] The second half of *The Seafarer* is therefore not only of sermon origin but grimly didactic in tone. Fittingly, therefore, the conclusion of *The Seafarer* from line 117 onwards is openly homiletic. There had been a single hint of this in *The Wanderer* in the use of the word *us,* but this preacher's use of *we* is hammered home at the end of *The Seafarer,* occurring six times in eight lines, whilst its first use in conjunction with *Uton* is pure sermon style. Whilst it would be possible to assume that the author spoke in his own voice from line 117 onwards (the arguments against a change of speaker at line 33a would not apply here), it is not necessary to do so. As in *The Wanderer* there is the same possibility of the author speaking partly with the voice of the Seafarer or the Seafarer speaking partly with the voice of the author. The Seafarer's personal voice is heard for the last time in lines 66–67: *Ic gelyfe no / þæt him eorðwelan ece stondað* [I do not believe that earthly prosperity will last forever, 66b–67]. There follow the generalisations about the decay of the world and the inevitability of old age, death, and God's judgment. All these are entirely fitting to the character of the Seafarer, but they could also prepare the way for the Seafarer at the close of the poem to stand aside a little from his dramatic role and to give to the audience a Christian exhortation that takes its force from all that has preceded it.

[24] For evidence of the currency of the latter image see Smithers, p. 150, where he cites texts noted by earlier scholars and adds further instances. To these examples should be added *Christ,* lines 850–66 (already noted by Schücking).

[25] Professor Smithers, p. 142, provides a convenient list of these sermon topics.

This interpretation of *The Seafarer* leaves open the significance of the sea-voyage except insofar as it is the opposite of life on land, in which a man is spiritually dead and subject to transience. It could, for instance, be the life of the voluntary exile, as Professor Whitelock suggested, but it is unlikely to be exclusively so, for a voluntary exile travels over both land and sea and the poet's potent but artificial distinction between them would become obliterated. Since it is also virtually certain that the voyage itself is metaphorical, it could equally take place in a monastery or hermit's cell. Nevertheless the untempered emphasis upon the hardship of the seafaring life seems slightly inapposite if the voyage is a symbol for the religious life. That a religious lives "where no storms come" may be a moving but over-sentimental idea, but that he lives in an especially storm-tossed place (*Stormas þær stanclifu beotan* [there storms beat on rocky cliffs, 23a]) is slightly disconcerting. Alternatively the voyaging could, as Professor Smithers and others have argued, represent death. This interpretation makes good sense of the fluctuations in mood that recur between lines 26–65. The Seafarer both expresses a religious longing akin to St. Paul's declaration, "I desire to die and be with Christ" and yet acknowledges the natural human fear of death, *Timor mortis conturbat me.* Such a reading is also supported by the general impression that the poem is much concerned with death and that its meaning is summed up on the gnomic line, *Dol biþ se þe him his Dryhten ne ondrædeþ: cymeð him se deað unþinged* [foolish is he who dares not fear his Lord: death comes to him unexpected, 106]. It remains certain, however, that *The Seafarer* is not a carefully worked out allegorical poem and that whilst figurative meanings are distinct in outline, they are opaque in detail. Indeed some of the power of the poem resides in its resistance to consistent exposition. It is therefore possible that the poet intended no single meaning for the sea-voyage except insofar as it is anything that is the opposite of life on land. The understanding hearer would provide a referend in terms of his own experience.

An analysis on *The Wanderer* and *Seafarer* as poems belonging to the genre of *planctus* may serve not only as a method of examining each poem individually but also as a means of comparing the two. There is a tendency to consider the poems as companion pieces, bearing perhaps the same relationship to each other as *L'Allegro* and *Il Penseroso.* As *planctus,* however, they are markedly distinct. *The Wanderer* is a genuine *planctus.* Ignoring the modern title we may say that the speaker is a typical figure, that of an exile, and that what he laments is equally clear: in the past the loss of his lord and the miseries of homelessness, and in the present the ever-spreading desolation around him. As is not uncommon in Christian *planctus* (e.g., "An Old Man's Prayer" from *The Harley Lyrics*),[26] the speaker experiences some reconciliation to his loss without the sense of loss becoming attenuated. By contrast *The Seafarer* is a poem that exploits the genre of *planctus*. Whilst the poem may imply, to begin with, that the speaker is again the typical figure of exile, it gradually becomes clear that he is exemplary rather than typical, a subordinate feature of *planctus* thus becoming dominating and exclusive. Furthermore, whilst there is much in the work that could find a place within a *planctus* (even those passages that have most affinity with the theme of *contemptus mundi*), such laments are given a different tone by the fact that the speaker has deliberately chosen a life of earthly deprivation. There is thus no clear way of characterising the speaker and no clear sense of loss.

Of course no value judgments are implied either in the general classification of these poems as *planctus* nor in the distinction that is drawn in these terms between *The Wanderer* and *The Seafarer*. The value of the classification lies in its hindrance to the asking of unuseful questions. For a remarkable characteristic of the poems is that, though differing critical interpretations are imposed upon them, they remain unchanged. Later poetry may be ironic, oblique, and ambiguous or it may be densely metaphorical, and so the text may seem to reflect varying and indeed sometimes self-contradictory meanings. But this is not so with *The Wanderer* and *The Seafarer*. Whoever the speaker, whatever the figurative meaning, they remain grave, sombre formal laments, powerful poems, and in contrast to their themes, immutable.

[26] *Religious Lyrics of the XIVth Century,* ed. Carleton Brown, rev. G. V. Smithers (Oxford, 1952), pp. 3–7.

14

Purpose and the "Poetics" of
The Wanderer and *The Seafarer*

W. F. KLEIN

THE HISTORY OF COMMENTARY ON *The Wanderer* AND *The Seafarer* reveals with particular clarity some important features of the general history of interest in Anglo-Saxon poetics, with the recurring attention to problems of Christian matter and rhetorical manner in these two poems constructing something of a critical epitomé for Anglo-Saxon studies as a whole.[1] My excuse for writing yet another essay on *The Wanderer* and *The Seafarer* is that even the best essays devoted to these poems contain signs of diffidence that leave one with a vague feeling of unease: indeed, John Collins Pope's influential piece published in the Magoun *Festschrift* repeatedly struck this note of qualification even as

---

[1] See especially W. W. Lawrence, "*The Wanderer* and *The Seafarer*," JEGP, 4 (1902), 460–80; Bernard F. Huppé, "*The Wanderer:* Theme and Structure," *JEGP*, 42, (1943), 516–38; Dorothy Whitelock, "The Interpretation of *The Seafarer*," in *The Early Cultures of North-West Europe*, eds. Sir Cyril Fox and Bruce Dickens (Cambridge, 1950), 261–72; Stanley B. Greenfield, "*The Wanderer:* A Reconsideration of Theme and Structure," *JEGP*, 50 (1951), 451–65; "Attitudes and Values in *The Seafarer*," SP, 51 (1954), 15–20; E. G. Stanley, "Old English Poetic Diction and the Interpretation of *The Wanderer, The Seafarer,* and *The Penitent's Prayer*," *Anglia*, 73 (1956), 413–66; R. F. Leslie, *The Wanderer*, "Introduction," (New York, 1966), pp. 1–25; J. E. Cross, "On the Genre of *The Wanderer*," *Neophil*, 45 (1961), 63–75; Edward B. Irving, Jr., "Image and Meaning in The Elegies," in *Old English Poetry: Fifteen Essays*, ed. Robert P. Creed (Providence, 1967), pp. 153–66.

it urged his view of differentiated "speakers" for the poem,[2] and Stanley Greenfield's judicious attack on Pope's argument[3] has been accepted in the main by Pope himself in a recent retraction of his earlier readings of *The Wanderer* and *The Seafarer*.[4]

Part of the difficulty and the diffidence derives from the putative poets that have sometimes been reconstructed for these poems, and the characters that such poets have consequently been assumed to have created. Poets who appear as para-pre-raphaelites with rhetorical tricks borrowed from a degenerate Latin tradition, and with odd *topoi* to fill in the silences, are not convincing Anglo-Saxons, nor are the characters such poets have sometimes been assigned as their creations—tragic quasi-romantics, staving off ruin by compulsively clinging to the rigorous decorums of the heroic code. Perhaps something of this sensibility is there, but for some years now I have been convinced that it cannot be the fundamental thing, though one reason such subtle anachronism has been possible is that the pasts we have studied are capacious enough to contain all our partial recreations. Similarly, a review of seventy-five years of scholarship on these two poems suggests a corporate, coherent, and expanding discovery of poets of large powers, and leads me to suggest still another perspective from which to approach the problem of character in Anglo-Saxon poetry as a whole, and in *The Wanderer* and *The Seafarer* in particular.

An author's conception of human character is related, in part, to the question of purpose in any literary performance.[5] To determine how language should be used, or has been used, it is necessary at some point to determine what it is being used *for*, and in the face of this question, both the modern artist and the modern critic have been profoundly embarrassed.[6] To a contemporary sensibility, character typically manifests

---

[2] John C. Pope, "Dramatic Voices in *The Wanderer* and *The Seafarer*," in *Franciplegius: Medieval and Linguistic Studies in Honor of Francis Peabody Magoun, Jr.*, eds. Jess B. Bessinger, Jr., and Robert P. Creed (New York, 1965), pp. 164–93.

[3] Greenfield, "*Myn, Sylf*, and 'Dramatic Voices in *The Wanderer* and *The Seafarer*,'" *JEGP*, 68 (1969), 212–20.

[4] Pope, "Second thoughts on the Interpretation of *The Seafarer*," *Anglo-Saxon England* 3, eds. Peter Clemoes *et al.* (Cambridge, 1974), pp. 75–86.

[5] For current critical discussions of this large problem of purpose in literary performance see J. Hillis Miller, *The Disappearance of God: Five Nineteenth Century Writers* (Cambridge, 1963) and Hugh Kenner, *The Pound Era* (Berkeley, 1971). Both Miller and Kenner shed valuable light on the particular ethical, literary, and critical milieu of the nineteenth century, within which Anglo-Saxon studies as a coherent discipline originated.

[6] Kenner (p. 23), discussing Henry James and the purpose of literary performance, says, "In his Prefaces he hugs secrets, talking round that overwhelming question, what the story may be *for*."

itself in incoherence and inconsistency because human character is construed as a locus defined by the complexity of sources from which human purpose may spring. The happy man is the one in whom these springs flow in diverse but harmonious order, and modern fictions are populated with characters passing through the varied stimuli of experience, having their springs of purpose touched in diverse and conflicting ways. The complexity of impulse that results from such multiplicity of purpose defines the modern character of capacious and responsive sensitivity to "the human condition."

But, without raising the question of whether such a view of "character" is fundamentally or only accidentally true to what we know of the human, certainly we may question whether or not it is likely to have been the view of "character" held by a tenth-century Anglo-Saxon. In an effort to discover a legitimate alternative view of character that might bring us closer to the truth of the poetry, it occurred to me that contemporary language philosophers have had some success in discovering what persistent conceptions lie behind certain habitual uses of language. Accordingly, I turned to the language itself and studied those Anglo-Saxon words specifically associated with purpose. Not surprisingly, certain features of the order governing the array of "purpose-words" in Anglo-Saxon seem to have a direct bearing on that literature's conception of character, and make particularly keen E. V. Gordon's observation that "the hero of this literature was not merely a courageous man, he was a man who understood the purpose of his courage."[7]

The array of "purpose-words" fell into three distinct groups,[8] each related to the name for the mental faculties[9] of memory, present perception, and what I shall call volitional futurity.[10] For two of these groups the semantic relationship between the generic term and its purposive derivatives is fairly straightforward. The simple meaning of *mynan,* "to remember" (the faculty of memory which makes present to the mind images from the past), is distinguished from its semantic

---

[7] E. V. Gordon, *An Introduction to Old Norse,* 2nd ed., rev. by A. R. Taylor (Oxford, 1957), p. xxx.

[8] Here I draw upon a much larger study of the terms in Anglo-Saxon related to mental states which I am preparing for publication.

[9] On the question of the three faculties, see also James F. Doubleday, "The Three Faculties of the Soul in *The Wanderer," Neophil,* 53 (1969), 189–94. Doubleday suggests an Augustinian parallel; discussion of the three faculties is, of course, ubiquitous in medieval literature. The problem is determining the relationship between the distinguishable views.

[10] For this notion I am indebted to Otto Jespersen, *A Modern English Grammar on Historical Principles: Part IV* (London, 1949). See especially Jespersen's sections on Volitional Future, pp. 244–53.

derivatives of relation and purpose; these semantic complexes are evident in *myne* [love] (which invokes relation), and *gemynegian* [to remind or admonish] (which involves purpose). The relationship between the purpose words in the second group, concerned with the faculty of present perception, are neatly similar. The simple meaning of the generic *þencan* [to think, to consider] (the faculty which makes present to the mind images present to the senses) with the addition of the semantic elements of relation and purpose becomes *geþanc* [gratitude] and *geþeahtian* [to deliberate, to take counsel].

The third group of words, concerned with volitional futurity, proved more difficult and more interesting. Part of the difficulty lies in the fact that the purpose element, ordinarily reserved for a semantic derivation, is present here in the generic term, *willan*. It names the operation of a mental faculty that combines the present power of constructing in the mind images that will become "real" only in the future, and the power of generating motion toward them; in a sense, this faculty involves the power of *choosing* them. I have invoked Jespersen's notion of volitional futurity to describe this faculty because we have no convenient modern synonym, though it combines some of the things we mean by "desire," "will," "choice," "purpose," and "vision." Another difficulty in establishing semantic derivations among the array of "purpose-words" related to the faculty of volitional futurity is that the members of this group are discriminated on different grounds than those related to memory and present perception. The principle of order in the group associated with volitional futurity differentiates *willa, hyge, mod,* and *ellen* (and their derivatives) by discriminating degrees of "intensity," not by distinctions of relation and purpose. By "intensity" here I mean to suggest a quality like "passion" without the loss of cognitive clarity we ordinarily associate with that term, and without implying a source in the soul distinct from that which conceives and chooses the desired object. The common actional metaphors for the operation of this faculty of volitional futurity are "reaching far" and "grasping firmly." Except for the words at the lowest degree of intensity, e.g., *willa,* the terms associated with this faculty fall into the standard "heroic" vocabulary so frequently associated with Anglo-Saxon poetry.

Such an ordering of "purpose-words" suggests a conception of character in which the complex emotions of a twentieth-century protagonist are not the primary consideration. The emphasis is rather on *purpose* and the power to make it coherent through time. The nature of the faculties associated with human purpose, as we are able to infer them from the habitual languages used to denote their operations, indicates that the primary concern was with the human capacity to generate purpose and grasp it firmly rather than to respond powerfully to the provocations of experience.

"Feeling" was not utterly banished; it appears as a condition that results from the complex relation between the images made present to the mind by the three faculties, generating the motion of the character through time. The unhappy man is the one for whom discontinuities appear. The most distressing circumstance occurs when a character cannot imagine a future coherent with his past. The happy man, by contrast, is one for whom the complex relation is one of harmonious order. Such harmony results in a unified and coherent career and manifests the dominance of volition, the distinctively human power, over what "simply happens." T. A. Shippey has called this fundamental value "strength of mind" and suggests that it is a persistent concern in Anglo-Saxon poetry.[11]

It is my impression that the ethical psychology I have just outlined provides a useful way of approaching character in a number of Anglo-Saxon poems and it seems especially helpful in reading *The Wanderer* and *The Seafarer,* for they are poems particularly designed to illustrate the implications of such fundamental discriminations of the sources of human character, and their central concern may be seen as the process of human character itself.

The general form of *The Wanderer* is an argument whose conclusion is drawn in the last line and a half, *Wel bið þam þe him are seceð, / frofre to fæder on heofonum, þær us eal seo fæstnung stondeð* [Well it will be with him who seeks grace, comfort at the Father in Heaven, for there our only confirmation stands, 114b–15].[12] This conclusion brings us full circle from the opening which starkly juxtaposes such an ultimate and future possibility of consolation with a definitive image of pointless and purposeless action. Between these antipodal moments the poem constructs an argument that the only cure for such futility is the purposive direction of one's vision to God.

The rhetorical form of the argument consists of the presentation of three alternative ways of seeking purpose that might shape a coherent career through time. All three prove to be failures. These alternatives are presented under the guise of ethopoeic fictions—imaginary speeches so devised as to characterize the fictitious speaker—in order to draw upon the persuasive resources of that device.[13] Each is presented with a

---

[11] Shippey, *Old English Verse* (London, 1972), p. 66.

[12] I use the Exeter Book text provided in George Philip Krapp and Elliott van Kirk Dobbie, *ASPR,* III (New York, 1936).

[13] See Huppé, pp. 517–18 and Pope, "Dramatic Voices," p. 191, n. 27.

sufficiently distinctive *adfectus*—disposition, state or mood—to distinguish one from the other and from the speaker. But they are not presented as fictions whose interest resides solely in themselves. That the speaker can create such fictions is in itself a manifestation of his ethos. There is a kind of transparency to the surfaces they present to the audience. They are to be recognized both as *convincing* creations and as *creations*. The cultural authority, or ethos, of the speaker derives from the perception that he—quite literally—*under-stands* his ethopoeic fictions even as he makes and manipulates them.

To discern such doubleness in the fundamental device of the poem is typical of the kind of "sophistication" that, for a long time, was proscribed in the study of Anglo-Saxon poems. Furthermore, though use of the Latin rhetorical tradition makes it easy to discuss *ethopoeia*, the use of that device does not necessarily imply the poet's familiarity with that tradition. It reflects, rather, the kind of practical knowledge inevitable for a poet grounded in a tradition of performance distinctly dramatic and oral, encompassing genres as disparate as epic and riddle.

If the rhetorical *form* of *The Wanderer* relies on an array of ethopoeic fictions corresponding closely to the three traditionally conceived faculties of memory, present perception, and volitional futurity, the substance of the argument arises from the way the three encompass the full range of response possible to human resource alone. When these alternatives are exhausted in failure, the only alternative that remains is to turn to the Father. The poet achieves his impact of exhaustiveness by illustrating the failure of each of the three distinctive modes of action that results when purpose is derived solely from images generated by these three faculties of the mind. The body of the poem is carefully divided into three parts corresponding to these alternative modes of action. In the first (lines 6–57), memory is the generative faculty and leads to a futile search that ends in hallucination.[14] In the second (lines 58–87), present perception is the generative faculty and leads to a limiting of intentionality and a dim adumbration of a vacant future. In the third (lines 88–110), future vision is the generative faculty and leads to what John Collins Pope called a "vision of dissolution" that is "almost triumphant" in its sweep.[15]

The first alternative is introduced as the *eardstapa, earfeþa gemyndig* [the wanderer, mindful of hardship, 6]. He is called the *eardstapa*, the "earth-stepper," the "wanderer," because his characteristic action is fruitless search. The generative source of that action is his mental con-

---

[14] Leslie (p. 15) was apparently the first to apply this term to this action.
[15] Pope, "Dramatic Voices," p. 172.

dition, and the key word in identifying that is *gemyndig* [mindful], but mindful in the special sense of being full of images that *memory* provides, certainly not "mindful" in the sense of "cautiously prudent" or "reflectively preoccupied." This first part of the poem, where human purpose is generated by memory, may be divided into four sections that are cumulative in their effect of exhaustiveness.

The first section, down to line 16, generalizes the failure manifest in the career of the *eardstapa,* and closes with an epitomising disjunction:

> Ne mæg werig mod   wryde wiðstondan
> ne se hreo hyge   helpe gefremman.

> (15–16)

[The weary spirit may not stand against fate, nor may the fierce will achieve help.]

These lines might be paraphrased, "Despair cannot affect what will happen, but neither can even fiercely determined purpose achieve satisfaction." The first alternative is obvious; the second and more surprising observation is demonstrated in the career (actual or potential?) surveyed in the second section that follows (lines 17–29a). Such determined purpose is first manifest in physical action. In a brief narrative we learn that the wanderer has sought a new lord since he "covered with earth's darkness his *goldwine.*" Then at line 29b, with a grammatically signalled shift to the third person, the objective failure of that quest is made clear as the third section presents the contrast between the happy past and the sad present:

> Gemon he selesecgas   ond sincþege,
> hu hine on geoguðe   his goldwine
> wenede to wiste.   Wyn eal gedreas.

> (34–36)

[He remembers the companions and the receiving of treasure, how his gold-friend made him accustomed to feasting among the youth. All joy has perished.]

With this rhetorical shift in person we experience the ironic perversion of purposeful activity into mere memory, as the action becomes mental rather than physical. The *eardstapa* has already been characterized as clinging to the image of his place in the company of his lord, and there is no question about the propriety of that choice. What he has chosen is a good thing, and that he clings to it is not a sign of some irrational compulsion. It is the only way he can *wyrde wiðstondan,* [stand against fate], asserting his "will" in the face of "what happens." The problem is the cost.

In the fourth section devoted to the exploration of memory as a source of human purpose, the consequences of this condition are presented in two passages usually set off as separate paragraphs. In the first (lines 37–48), the *eardstapa* attempts to postpone acknowledging the failure of his search by dreaming that he is with his *mondryhten.* But he wakens again to a natural scene devoid of humans. In the second passage he manifests the fervent determination of his *hreo hyge* [fierce will], by clinging to this image in spite of the testimony of his eyes. By clinging to this image he becomes a kind of visionary, but his vision is a vain illusion and mocks him by fleeting away. Even so, he clings to it, and his power of image-bearing choice draws his mind out over the water to the nothing real.

At this point in *The Wanderer* the exploration of purpose focused on images derived from memory is complete. There is a striking reticence here. It is perfectly clear, if we look back from the conclusion of the poem, that all that would be needed to transform the *eardstapa* from a desperate and vain visionary into a Christian longing for his true home would be to turn the energy he has invested in seeking his lost lord to the Father in Heaven. But that would foreshorten the argument into the consideration of only one possible choice, and it would limit the authority of the speaker to that originating in the grasp of blunt doctrine.

Instead, we see him turn to the second alternative source from which an image appropriate to human purpose might arise, present perception. The powers of this faculty, clearly the most modest of the three, are explored in two ways. First, the *eardstapa* is recognized as a cautionary example. In lines 58 to 63 the speaker asks "why his [own] heart should not grow dark," since all hopes for human community seem to reveal the same futility as those of the *eardstapa.* In lines 64 to 72 he illustrates what characterizes the life of such a one whose heart has so darkened. This is, of course, the famous passage compounded of gnomic aphorisms. It is important to realize that this passage does not propose to offer a purpose that might serve as a focus of human volition through time. Consequently, the admonitions it contains are not intended to reveal the manner of the good life. Rather, they are inhibitions, and counsel the avoidance of certain actions that might be possible in more congenial human circumstances but are now to be advisedly modified. One might call them admonitions to cautious prudence. They characterize a manner of life appropriate *oþþæt collenferð cunne gearwe /*

hwider hreþra gehygd hweorfan wille [until the bold one knows clearly where the desire of thoughts will turn, 71–72].

Having so tested the purposive resources of memory and found them poignantly deficient, the second part of *The Wanderer* proceeds to explore the image-making powers of "present perception." As the poem progresses, the rhetorical distance between the speaker and his ethopoeic fiction narrows. Here there is no pretense of quotation like that encountered in the section devoted to the *eardstapa*. The new movement begins with a tentative inferential exploration of the future implied in the present scene.

Ongietan sceal gleaw hæle   hu gæstlic bið,
þonne ealre þisse worulde wela   weste stondeð,
swa nu missenlice   geond þisne middangeard
winde biwaune   weallas standaþ,
hrime bihrorene,   hryðge þa ederas.

(73–77)

[The perceptive man must observe how ghostly it will be when all the wealth of this world stands waste, as now here and there through this middle-earth walls stand blown by the wind, covered with frost, the enclosures clogged with snow.]

The *gleaw hæle* attempts to reach toward a significant future by seeing clearly the implications of the circumstantial present. But the present scene, stripped as it is of human population, forces the mind of the *gleaw hæle,* by a poignantly human logic, to recaptitulate the death of those absent from the scene rather than to discover a future toward which the "desire of thoughts" might turn. The close of this exploration echoes the close of the *eardstapa*'s speech and generalizes the same themes presented there. There is some irony in this, for not only has he failed, like the first seeker, to discover a future toward which volition might properly reach, he seems even farther than the memory-restricted *eardstapa* from being able to so orient human purposiveness. The complex of images which the *eardstapa*'s memory discloses, more nearly adumbrates conditions of life with the heavenly Father than does this presently perceived image of desolation with which the *gleaw hæle* concludes.

It seems legitimate to carry an awareness of this irony to the next part of the poem (lines 88–110) where the third faculty of future vision is explored. The rhetorical distance between the speaker and his ethopoeic fiction which had narrowed in the movement from *eardstapa* to *gleaw hæle* widens here to such an extent that Pope was first prompted to distinguish the *snottor on mode* as a separate and contrasting "dramatic voice" in the poem. The passage has attracted a great deal of attention, and I think its general force has been rightly appraised. It has two aspects, however, that might be attended to profitably here.

First, in keeping with the pervasively rhetorical poetic that I have been describing, the passage—a formally organized discourse or "speech"—displays three distinct parts. The first two epitomize and extend the images of the past and present that have appeared in the preceding sections of the poem. In the *ubi sunt* sequence, the particularity which marked the *eardstapa*'s earlier vision of the past is extended now to include a wider range of objects associated with the aristocratic life. The lines that follow (97–107) likewise describe more elaborately the desolation previously, and more briefly, adumbrated by the *gleaw hæle*. In these concluding parts of the poem the vision is wider and more encompassing than those visions involved by the prior excursions into memory and present perception, and the poetic vision clearly supercedes in kind, as well as in degree, those earlier partial constructions of the ethopoeic speakers:

> Her bið feoh læne, her bið freond læne,
> her bið mon læne, her bið mæg læne,
> eal þis eorþan gestæl idel weorþeð.

> (108–10)

[Here wealth is frail, here friend is frail, here man is frail, here woman is frail. All the domain of earth becomes vacant.]

These lines seem almost the declaration of a man speaking back to the present from the perspective of the future. The apocalyptic exclamation of the last line manifests a willing vision of the future at its greatest reach.

Having first noted the rhetorical positioning of this concluding section, we should next observe the complex relation that it has with the preceding sections of the poem. In contrast to the prior "failures" of memory and present perception, the mental action derived from volitional futurity is recognizable as a kind of success. Here is a human observer whose mental faculties all function with great intensity. He has not been daunted by the losses of the past, the frustrations of the present, nor the terrors of the future. In fact he seems willing to imagine himself squarely in the center of the desolation he envisages. That is a high, perhaps heroic, accomplishment.

Yet it is also a failure, and recognizable as such on the same grounds as the preceding failures, since this heroic self-sufficiency, the very *willfulness* of this desolate vision, renders the grace of another vision even less accessible here than elsewhere. In these concluding lines (111–15), the ultimate power of human vision is located in a final context of failure, for the portrait of the *snottor on mode,* for all his extended vision, echoes the purposive paralysis presented in the poem's *prologomenon.* The memory-bound man idly trailing his hand in the sea gives way to the *snottor on mode* who sits *sundor æt rune* [apart with his secret, 111b], a hero with his *ellen,* to be sure, but with no real future that might draw him into motion. The principle of action in him has been brought to contemplative stasis. In the last line and a half, clearly echoing the first line and a half, the speaker offers, with an authority derived from a truly capacious vision of human possibility and with a devastating modesty and economy, the last and only real alternative, a turning—which is a rhetorically emphasized re-turning— to the Father in Heaven.

The conclusion of *The Wanderer* is understated and succinct, perhaps too succinct, but it rests securely on the clear argument of the whole poem and on the subtle anticipation created by the first line and a half. Without this context it would have far less force. To turn to the closing of *The Seafarer* is to discover a closing that is by comparison wordy, obvious, derivative, and conventional. In principle the conclusions are the same. The good and happy man must derive his sense of purpose from the expectation of joining the Father in Heaven. This principle has a similar corollary in both poems: such consolation is accessible to everyman; he need not be a "hero" in the more public or conventional sense. But the radically different rhetorical force of the closings of *The Wanderer* and *The Seafarer* derives from the observably different poetic forms of the two poems.

The general impact of *The Wanderer,* as I have argued, arises from the poem's essential discrimination of three traditional and fundamentally contrasting modes of manifesting human character. Each is identifiable because of a poetic presentation that incorporates both an indication of the particular mental faculty being explored as a resource for human purpose, and an indication of the inner relation between these three faculties in a carefully organized sequence of scenes where human character is required to act in order to variously demonstrate purposive deficiency.

In *The Seafarer,* the exploration of human resources depends upon the same characterological presuppositions, but it does not lead to the discovery of the same rhetorically organized theme. Rather a recognition of the thematically similar consideration of the mental faculties of memory, present perception and volitional futurity leads to an accomplished and humanly convincing construction of past, present and future coherence. Like *The Wanderer,* the structure of *The Seafarer* derives from three major sections and a conclusion, and each of these sections deal, in obvious ways, with past, present and future human moments. But it is precisely here, in just such general terms, that the limits of similarity are most obvious. For rather than being a sweeping and generalized survey of the ultimate poverty of human resources, *The Seafarer* rests poetically upon a recognition of the power of the individual mind. Consequently, its equally tripartate rhetorical movement is dramatically reversed, proceeding not from the familiar to the strange and terrible, as in *The Wanderer,* but rather from the alien and esoteric to the consolingly familiar.

I divide *The Seafarer* into four major sections, the first two (lines 1–33a and 39–57) marked by the two passages which feature the figure of the spirit as a bird, first struggling against the confines of the soul, and next going forth and returning. The third section (lines 66b–102) is terminated by the shift to the closing exhortations that constitute the fourth and final section (lines 103–24). Since the crucial point of the poem becomes explicit only in this third section, and since it is the part of the poem that seems to me to have been least explored, I will consider it first. The pattern of this third section is not the random association of conventional homiletic and elegiac themes that it first appears, and its order has two rhetorically subtle aspects. It is both a clear sequential argument—logically a series of disjunctions with all but one of the discriminated possibilities negated—and a simultaneously circular exploration of the theme of death. It begins with the apparent suggestion that each man has a variety of alternative futures, and then, with a coyness that must be recognized as wit, it indicates there is only one future with different faces.

Most undergraduate students of English know that "either illness or old age or sword-hate wrests life from the fey and the dying" (lines 70–71), and that "therefore to every man praise of the living is the best word trace" (lines 72–73). But they may not have had it pointed out to them that in the following lines (75–80) the speaker of the poem locates this consolation of enduring fame in two groups of the living, the *ælda bearn* [children of men] and the *englum* [angels] who reside in Heaven. That he locates the traditional heroic fame in these two constituencies is not simply a pious elaboration of a conventional notion. The disjunction sets up, for exploration in the rest of the poem, the two places in which consoling fame may endure.

The possibility of fame enduring among the "children of men" is examined in the lines that follow (80b–102), and the ironic poignancy of this part of the poem derives from the emergent perception that fame will not, in fact, endure among men, for men will not endure. The passage begins, *Dagas sind gewitene* [Those days are gone, 80b], and then notes that there are no kings or kaisers like there were

> þonne hi mæst mid him   mærþa gefremedon
> ond on dryhtlicestum   dome lifdon.
> Gedroren is þeos duguð eal,   dreamas sind gewitene.
>
> (84–86)

[when the greatest achieved glory among themselves and lived according to the lordliest judgment. That troop has all fallen, their joys are gone].

This may well be a common elegaic theme, but it is not a randomly invoked image of the past heroic world. It is specifically that aspect of the past in which earthly fame had its hour, and that particular temporal moment is gone. The presently perceived moment has a rather different character. It lacks utterly the capacity to be an enduring vessel of consoling fame: the weaker dwell in this world and hold it. *Blæd is gehnæged, / eorþan indryhto ealdað ond searað* [Glory is humbled, earthly honor ages and withers, 88b–89]. Rather than singing the praise of the heroic departed, those who now live grow old (91a) and grieve for those "given to the earth" (93b). Only the future remains, and its articulation brings the circle poetically full:

> Ne mæg him þonne se flæschoma,   þonne him þæt feorg losað,
> ne swete forswelgan   ne sar gefelan,
> ne hond onhreran   ne mid hyge þencan.
>
> (94–96)

[The body may not, when its life leaves it, either consume the sweet nor feel the sore; it may not stir its hand nor think with its spirit.]

This part of the poem, presenting images from an imagined future, ironically invokes the ultimate poetic closure of a described burial. Strewn upon the grave, the gold which might have been a manifest sign of glory to the living becomes instead the pointless expression of a brother's grief (97–102).

It is easy to see why the agenda that organizes this part of *The Seafarer* is not easily recognized. A single theme of death and dying is repeated at every stage of its development. But all the varied forms of this theme are couched in terms which specifically relate to the question of whether fame among men is in fact any consolation for death. That enduring fame appears in the history of man only in the distant past suggestively denies such a possibility. Life among men leads only to death, and human fame will yield inevitably to silence. Having disposed so thoroughly of the merely human and hence inadequate alternative, the closing twenty-two lines (103–24) disclose another possibility, that of not merely possessing an enduring fame among the angels, but of actually living in their midst:

> Wyrd biþ swiþre
> meotud meahtigra þonne ænges monnes gehygd.
> Uton we hycgan hwær we ham agen,
> ond þonne geþencan hu we þider cumen.

(115b–18)

[Fate is more violent, God is mightier, than the will of any man. Let us perceive where we have a true home and then consider how we may come there.]

This final section of *The Seafarer* is so tangled in difficult textual and contextual problems that it is not possible in this essay to adequately describe its form. But neither is such formal description necessary to my present purpose of discriminating in the last two parts of the poem a speaker concerned to make his audience aware that their future is death, while displaying a richly adequate sense of the compelling quality of past and present experience. A recognition of this "double vision" of the speaker, who possesses the poetic wit to simultaneously sustain two such coherent lines of development, conducts the poetic force through the rest of the poem. For the first part of *The Seafarer* has seemed the peculiar declaration of a man marked by an intense past experience, recollected from memory in something less than Wordsworthian tranquillity. He has really experienced life at sea and he can speak of it with literal authority. And that is true. The second part of the poem has seemed the peculiar declaration of a man presently marked by some special longing. He perceives the transience of earthly comforts because he knows a compulsive longing which they cannot satisfy. And that is true, too. In comparison with the springs of character suggested in these first two parts by

221

the vivid memory of former seafaring and the present perception of keen and special longing, the third part of *The Seafarer* seems on its surface to connect only with the vacuities of a cut and paste job.

But the special vividness of the first part and the peculiar restlessness of the second—manifestations of the speaker's peculiar sense of the past and present—arise in fact out of his fully adequate sense of the future whose persistent theme is the proximate certainty of death succeeded immediately by the possibility of enduring and true fame. The character that emerges from these three steadily confronted images of past, present and future human resources is a visionary not only because his mind has reached out through time to comprehend the end of time itself, but more importantly, he is a visionary because he is seen as having fully comprehended the potentialities and limitations of human character as they appeared in the first two parts of the poem. He has experienced the sea; he has felt it and known it, discovering in that knowledge that death is an imminent threat, figured in stones, cold, and hunger. It is, he knows, the inevitable conclusion to all voyages. He has also felt a longing so insistent that present comforts—including the comfort of his proper rational perceptions—fail to satisfy it. He sees more clearly than the landsman the nature of the things present to the senses, and he articulates the present perception that the landsman's comforts cannot satisfy a man who knows that human life is process. Even the cuckoo knows the revolution of the seasons. The vision of the speaker is not only linear, incorporating the present, past and future aspects of time, but hierarchical as well. He not only knows how experience *feels,* he knows what it *means.*

A reader fresh from the poem as a whole for the first time senses in the opening lines of *The Seafarer* more than mere mastery of poetic convention: *Mæg ic be me sylfum soðgied wrecan, / siþas secgan* [I can by myself make a true song and tell of travels, 1–2a]. Such a reader will have searched the dictionary and discovered a fascinating system of lexical contrasts with *siþas* [travels, times, deaths, 2], suggesting the promise of an explicit report, in juxtaposition with *giedd* [tale, song, riddle, meter, 2], suggesting the promise of the subtleties of artifice. Likewise, the intimations of energetic intentionality in *wrecan* [drive, advance, fulfill, 1] contrast with the verbal motion of speech suggested in *secgan* [to say, to tell]. To a reader uninitiated in rhetorical *dicta,* the prefixed position of *soð* [truth(ful)] suggests more than poetic convention, and the collocation of first person pronouns (*ic . . . me . . . sylfum,* 1) suggests not a pleonasm at all, but a cunning hint that the reader is being invited to address the problem of identifying the speaker.

A keen-minded reader, innocent of all scholarship on the poem, would probably not adduce the figure of a languid monk armed with paste and scissors. Were such a reader versed in northern lore, he might instead adduce the figure of Oðin who is sometimes described as bearing on his shoulders two ravens named Huginn and Muninn.[16] Their names are cognate with the Anglo-Saxon names for memory and future vision.

[16] For pertinent discussion, see G. V. Smithers, "The Meaning of *The Seafarer* and *The Wanderer*," *MÆ*, 28 (1959), 14–22, and Vivian Salmon, *"The Wanderer* and *The Seafarer*, and the Old English Conception of the Soul," *MLR*, 55 (1960), 1–10.

15

A Reading Context
for *The Wife's Lament*

ALAIN RENOIR

SUBJECT TO THE SCHOLARLY CENSURE FITTINGLY ATTENDANT UPON rash generalizations, one may say that the women of Anglo-Saxon secular poetry endure something more than their rightful share of discomfort. My generalization, of course, does not extend to those women whom the Wife of Bath would lump under the heading of "hooly seintes lyves."[1] There, the opposite principle operates more often than not, so that we may find a Juliana's disposition "greatly cheered" (*miclum geblissad*)[2] at the prospect of her own demise and her quaint optimism fully warranted by the poet's subsequent assurance that in due time "her soul was led straight from her dead body into eternal bliss" (*hyre sawl wearð / alæded of lice to þam langan gefean,* 669b–70b), or a Judith in the enviable position of serving a God who has "granted her honor and fame in the kingdom of earth" (*þe hyre weorðmynde geaf, / mærðe on moldan rice*),[3] or a Blessed Virgin not unexpectedly described as "ever trium-

---

[1] Geoffrey Chaucer, *The Wife of Bath's Prologue,* 690, in *The Works of Geoffrey Chaucer,* ed. Fred Norris Robinson (Boston, 1957).

[2] Cynewulf, *Juliana,* 608b, in George Philip Krapp and Elliott van Kirk Dobbie, eds., *The Exeter Book* (New York, 1936). This and all subsequent translations not otherwise identified are the present writer's.

[3] *Judith,* 342b–43a, in Elliott van Kirk Dobbie, ed., *Beowulf and Judith* (New York, 1953).

phant" (*sio eadge mæg / symle sigores full*)[4]; and the list could be extended at will.

The merest glance at secular poetry, however, suggests that its female protagonists and supporting actresses do not necessarily enjoy the same material and emotional welfare-state as their canonized colleagues. When considered chronologically, in fact, the history of Anglo-Saxon poetry may be said to open with *Widsith* and the mention of a woman on her way to a most unpromising future at the "home of the evil covenant breaker Eormanric" (*ham . . . / . . . Eormanrices, / wraþes wærlogan*),[5] and the following random samples from other poems will argue that this is no isolated case. To wit, the speaker of *Wulf and Eadwacer* devotes all nineteen lines of this profoundly moving poem to bemoaning her ambiguous relationship to one man and especially her tormenting separation from another:

> Wulf, min Wulf   wena me þine
> seoce gedydon,   þine seldcymas,
> murnende mod,   nales meteliste.[6]

[Wulf, my Wulf, my yearnings for thee / have made me sick; thy rare visits, / a woeful heart, and not want of food.]

Elsewhere, the sorrows of Beadohild account for about one-eighth of *Deor*, where we are told that her catastrophic pregnancy tormented her even more than the murder of her brothers:

> Beadohilde ne wæs   hyre broþra deaþ
> on sefan swa sar   swa hyre sylfre þing,
> þæt heo gearolice   ongieten hæfde
> þæt heo eacen wæs;   æfre ne meahte
> þriste geþencan,   hu ymb þæt sceolde.[7]

---

[4] *Christ I*, 87b–88a, in Krapp and Dobbie, *Exeter Book.*

[5] *Widsith*, 7b–9a, in Krapp and Dobbie, *Exeter Book.* Although the date of *Widsith* is by no means certain, George K. Anderson has written that part of it "is the oldest surviving piece of English verse" (*The Literature of the Anglo-Saxons* [Princeton, 1949], p. 59), and Kemp Malone's impressive linguistic argument in favor of the seventh century (*Widsith* [Copenhagen, 1962], p. 112–16) reflects the views of a majority of scholars, as noted by Stanley B. Greenfield (*A Critical History of Old English Literature* [New York, 1965], p. 95), who would personally favor a slightly later alternative. According to Raymond W. Chambers' *Widsith: a Study in Old-English Heroic Legend* (Cambridge, 1912) the "luckless queen" (p. 23) was eventually murdered (p. 28).

[6] *Wulf and Eadwacer*, 13a–15b, in Krapp and Dobbie, *Exeter Book;* trans. Robert K. Gordon, *Anglo-Saxon Poetry* (London and New York, 1926).

[7] *Deor*, 8a–12b, in Krapp and Dobbie, *Exeter Book;* trans. Gordon, *Anglo-Saxon Poetry.*

[Her brothers' death was not so sore upon Beadohild's mind as her own state, when she had clearly seen that she was with child. She could never think with a light heart of what must come of that.]

Even those poems which record stories with presumably joyful endings seem reluctant to dispense unmixed happiness to their women. This point may be illustrated with *The Husband's Message,* which we naturally construe as dealing with a pleasurable incident in the life of the woman to whom it is addressed, since it invites her to rejoin a man from whom she has been separated but who is at last in a position to live up to the loving faith of which they "often spoke in earlier days" (*on ærdagum oft gespræconn*).[8] The text leaves no doubt in our minds, however, that the long days preceding the recorded moment must have seemed painfully uncertain to one whose lover "was driven away from the victory-people by hostility" (*fæhþo adraf / of sigeþeode,* 19b–20a), and we should have to be uncommonly insensitive not to fear for a union which must admittedly be consummated "despite an old threat" (*ofer eald gebeot,* 48a) against both bride and groom. In other words, consideration of the action within its stated context forces us to realize that the flash of hope which we are asked to imagine could conceivably prove nothing more than a momentary respite in an otherwise woeful story. Turning to another poem, we assume Hildegund to be the speaker who so enthusiastically urges Walter of Aquitaine "to give up life or earn lasting fame among men" (*lif forleosan oððe l[. .]gne dom / agan mid eldum*)[9] in the first *Waldere* fragment, and the conclusion of the better-known version preserved in the Latin *Waltharius* prompts our twentieth-century sensitivities to read the Anglo-Saxon lines as a heroic prelude to decades of political stolidity and connubial bliss:

> Illic gratifice magno susceptus honore
> Publica Hiltgundi fecit sponsalia rite
> Omnibus et carus post mortem obitumque parentis
> Ter denis populum rexit feliciter annis.[10]

[There, joyously received with great honor, he duly celebrated his public espousal to Hildegund and, beloved by all, after the death and demise of his father he ruled his people happily for three decades.]

[8] *The Husband's Message,* 53a-b, in Krapp and Dobbie, *Exeter Book.*
[9] *Waldere I,* 10a–11a, in Elliott van Kirk Dobbie, ed., *The Anglo-Saxon Minor Poems* (New York, 1942).
[10] *Waltharius,* 1447–50, ed. Karl Strecker in *Monumenta Germaniae Historica: Poetarum Latinorum Medii Ævi,* VI, I (Weimar, 1951); trans. Francis P. Magoun, Jr., and Hamilton M. Smyser, *Walter of Aquitaine: Materials for the Study of His Legend* (New London, 1950).

Yet, the evidence of the same Latin poem ought to prompt even the most determined optimist to question the quality of the life awaiting her with a man who, as his old friend and recent opponent Hagen points out, has been so maimed as to prove henceforth unable to discharge in the customary manner his duties in the field and in the bedroom:

> Wah! sed quid dicis, quod ritum infringere gentis
> Ad dextro femori gladium agglomerare videris
> Uxorique tuae, si quando ea cura subintrat,
> Perverso amplexu circumdabis euge sinistram?

(1429–32)

[And so help us! what do you say about violating popular custom and being seen girding your sword on your right thigh? And, when that desire steals (over you) (about) putting your left hand—capital!—around your wife in unconventional embrace?]

Furthermore, at least three of the surviving accounts of the legend deal with events posterior to the wedding and show Walter eventually murdering Hildegund while she is lying in bed with a lover.[11] Here as with *The Husband's Message,* the context of the surviving Anglo-Saxon fragments yields no compelling argument for chalking up the poem to the credit of feminine happiness in secular literature.

The foregoing observations apply equally well to *Beowulf.* Considered from a feminine point of view, this overwhelmingly masculine epic comes close to a disaster area. The most important woman therein is Queen Wealhtheow, who enters the narrative on line 612^b and leaves it on line 2174^a. She makes several appearances in between, thus participating in more of the action than anyone except the principal actors, and she is mentioned by name more often than any but six of them, counting Grendel.[12] Consequently, we experience no difficulty in forming a picture of her situation and state of mind, and that picture is at first quite reassuring. With all the grace, cheerfulness, and poise befitting a daughter of the royal Helmings and the wife of a powerful and respected king, Hrothgar's queen seems perfectly free of care as she strolls through

---

[11] Three of the Polish and Latin versions translated in Magoun and Smyser's *Walter of Aquitaine* have Walter thus murder Hildegund (pp. 55, 59, and 61), and Procosius' eighteenth-century *Chronicon* (Magoun and Smyser, p. 62) also suggests that not everything went well between Hildegund and Walter.

[12] Beowulf, Hrothgar, Hygelac, Wiglaf, Wihstan, and Grendel. Ecgtheow, Healf-Dene, and Hrethel are likewise named more often than Wealhtheow, but only as parental identifications for Beowulf, Hrothgar, and Hygelac, and they have no part in the action.

Heorot to bring greetings and drink to young and old alike, while the "laughter of warriors" (*hæleþa hleahtor*)[13] proclaims the general mood of merriment:

> grette goldhroden   guman on healle
>
> . . . .
>
> Ymbeode þa   ides Helminga
> duguþe ond geogoþe   dæl æghwylcne,
> sincfato sealde. . . .
>
> (614ᵃ–22ᵃ)

[Adorned with gold she greeted the men in the hall. . . . The lady of the Helmings went round to each group of retainers and youths, she passed the precious vessels. . . .]

Indeed, her behavior recalls the paradigm preserved in the *Exeter Maxims,* where we are told that a lady, "loved by her people, [must] be both cheerful and . . . generous of heart" (*leof mid hyre leodum, leohtmod wesan, / . . . rumheort beon*).[14] She is clearly "mindful of correct behavior" (*cynna gemyndig,* 613ᵇ), and the resultant mood is the feeling of comfortable security which usually accompanies the conviction that everything is clearly within the framework of a long, respected, and unshakable tradition.

Appearances, however, can be as deceiving in literature as they are in actual life, especially when literature happens to deal with would-be historical events presumably familiar to the intended audience. Thus, we know that Wealhtheow's world must of necessity crumble with the treachery of her husband's nephew, Hrothulf, who is believed to have usurped the throne and probably murdered her sons; and the poet takes pains to keep us aware of the impending catastrophe.[15] In this light, we can see that, although he is not so innocent of chronology as to give Wealhtheow knowledge of events which have not yet occurred, he makes her behave in a way which suggests an awareness of lurking danger and an obsession with the protection of her doomed children. As we see her approaching the spot where Hrothgar and Hrothulf are seated side by side, we are significantly reminded that the two are *still* at peace: *þa gyt wæs hiera sib ætgadere, / æghwylc oðrum trywe* [There was then still peace between them, each true to the other, 1164ᵇ–65ᵃ]. This seem-

---

[13] *Beowulf,* 611ᵃ, in Dobbie, *Beowulf and Judith;* trans. Bartlett J. Whiting, in Whiting *et al.,* eds., *The College Survey of English Literature* (New York, 1948).

[14] *Maxims I,* 85ᵃ–86ᵇ, in Krapp and Dobbie, *Exeter Book.*

[15] Friedrich Klaeber, ed., *Beowulf* (Boston, 1950), p. xxxii, notes four separate allusions to Hrothulf's treachery and discusses its historicity.

ingly gratuitous piece of foreboding information hardly belongs in an account of the joyful celebration of Beowulf's victory over Grendel and has no conceivable bearing on the action, but it goes far in helping us understand why the equally incongruous remarks which Wealhtheow addresses to her husband a few lines later are in effect spoken for his nephew's benefit:

> Ic minne can
> glædne Hroþulf . . . .
> . . . .
> wene ic þæt he mid gode   gyldan wille
> uncran eaferan,   gif he þæt eal gemon,
> hwæt wit to willan   ond to worðmyndum
> umborwesendum ær   arna gefremedon.

> (1180^b–87^b)

[I know . . . my kind Hrothulf. . . . I think that he will repay our sons well, if he remembers all that we two did earlier in the way of kindness for his pleasure and honor when he was a child.]

In juxtaposition to the poet's reminder that all is not well between uncle and nephew,[16] the blatant irrelevancy and ill-timing of her assertion of confidence in Hrothulf's honorable intentions—as well as the alarmingly conditional clause (gif *he* . . . *gemon*) which follows it—alert us to the fact that the gracious and apparently secure lady whom we saw meting out cheer and liquor to all some 565 lines earlier is in fact a very worried mother in a very fragile world.

From the moment Beowulf wins recognition as a powerful warrior capable of protecting others, her every recorded action speaks out her determination to secure his protection for her sons. The high point of a celebration, when all hearts have been gladdened by song and drink, is surely the most opportune moment to request a personal favor, especially when the request is addressed to the guest of honor and comes preceded by a valuable gift which is itself supernumerary to a veritable shower of formal presentations splendid enough to put the recipient in the best of moods. This is precisely the moment which Wealhtheow chooses to seek her sons, whom she finds where Beowulf has conveni-

---

16 One may wish to recall that the technique of making a point through juxtaposition of the information available to the audience and that available to the characters occurs elsewhere in *Beowulf* (see *e.g.,* my "The Heroic Oath in *Beowulf,* the *Chanson de Roland,* and the *Nibelungenlied,*" in Stanley B. Greenfield, ed., *Studies in Old English Literature in Honor of Arthur G. Brodeur* (Eugene, 1963), esp. pp. 245–46).

ently been seated *be þæm gebroðrum twæm* [by the two brothers, 1191ᵇ]. There, she graciously (*estum,* 1194ᵃ) offers him her friendship and adds a magnificent necklace and other priceless tokens of esteem to the official rewards which he has already received. She bids him enjoy them to his heart's content and affectionately addresses him as *Beowulf leofa* [dear Beowulf, 1216ᵇ] as she promises him more treasures if he will watch over her sons' future:

>   ... þyssum cnyhtum wes
> lara liðe;   ic þe þæs lean geman.
>
> . . . .
> . . . .   Ic þe an tela
> sincgestreona.   Beo þu suna minum
> dædum gedefe. . . .
>
>   (1219ᵇ–27ᵃ)

[. . . be kind in counsel to these boys. I will remember you for it with a gift. . . . I wish you many treasures. In your acts be kind to my sons. . . .]

In the light of the materials examined above, one may surely be excused for detecting the hint of a pathetic ring in her attempt at clinching her request with the assertion that the warriors in the hall always do her bidding: *dryhtguman doð swa ic bidde* [warriors do as I command, 1231].

Nor does one find the lot of other women in *Beowulf* unquestionably more enviable than Wealhtheow's. Within the span of time covered by the poem, Princess Freawaru faces the gratifying prospect of marriage to a mighty king, but Beowulf himself does no more than corroborate external evidence with his gloomy prediction that peace between the spouses' respective tribes will hardly last *lytle hwile* [little while, 2030ᵇ][17] and that her husband will become so involved in the feud that *him wiflufan / . . . colran weorðað* [his love for his wife becomes cooler, 2065ᵇ–66ᵇ]. This prediction concerning the princess, incidentally, adds by indirection to the already depressing picture of the queen which has been painted above. Offa's wife, another queen briefly mentioned in the poem, seems so far gone on the unhappy path of paranoiac delusions that she must act *æfter ligetorne* [on account of a pretended insult, 1943ⁿ] and *cwealmbealu cyðan* [make known . . . death, 1940ⁿ] to those unfortunate men whom she believes to have cast their eyes upon her. We can only concur with the poet's opinion that *ne bið swylc cwenlic þeaw* [this is not a womanly custom, 1940ᵇ]. By far the most unfortunate human being in *Beowulf* is certainly Finn's wife, Hildeburh. Through no fault of her own

[17] *E.g., Widsith,* 45ᵃ–49ᵇ; see also Klaeber, *Beowulf,* pp. xxxiv–xxxvi and 202–06.

(*unsynnum*, 1072[b]), she sees her own blood relatives and those of her husband massacre each other with their retainers until she is left totally *beloren leofum æt þam lindplegan, / bearnum and broðrum* [deprived of her loved ones, of her sons and brothers, in battle, 1073[a]–74[a]]. In addition, she must become an active participant in the conclusion of her own tragedy as she orders and supervises the cremation of her son by the side of his uncle:

> Het ða Hildeburh   æt Hnæfes ade
> hire selfre sunu   sweoloðe befæstan,
> banfatu bærnan   ond on bæl don
> eame on eaxle.
>
> (1114[a]–17[a])[18]

[Then Hildeburh ordered her own son committed to the flames on Hnaef's pyre, to place him on the pile by his uncle's side. . . .]

No wonder, then, that this "sad lady" (*geomuru ides*, 1075[b]) should mourn "with sad songs" (*geomrode giddum*, 1118[a]) when she sees the wounds burst open, the blood shoot out, and the heads melt in the blaze that swallows all those whom she has loved. Since we may reasonably assume that the forty-seven lines known as *The Fight at Finnsburg* are a fragment of an otherwise lost version of the events discussed above,[19] we may also infer that at least another Anglo-Saxon poem was in part devoted to the misadventures of a woman. Turning back to *Beowulf*, we note that Queen Hygd herself, though she is *swiðe geong, / wis welþungen* [very young, wise, and accomplished, 1926[b]–27[a]] and seems in possession of an enviable future through her marriage to King Hygelac, eventually faces sorrow through her husband's death on the battlefield at a time when she does not yet feel ready to entrust her own son with a crown which she must therefore offer to a nephew in law:

> bearne ne truwode
> þæt he wið ælfylcum   eþelstolas
> healdan cuðe,   ða wæs Hygelac dead.
>
> (2370[b]–72[b])

---

[18] Some editors (*e.g.*, C. L. Wrenn, *Beowulf with the Finnesburg Fragment* [Boston, 1953], and Francis P. Magoun, Jr., *Béowulf and Judith*, rev. Jess B. Bessinger, Jr. (Cambridge, 1966]) retain the problematic MS reading of 1117[a], *earme on eaxle*, and construe the half-line as introductory to the subsequent sentence. This alternative affects the interpretation of the action but not of its emotional impact upon Hildeburh.

[19] For the relationship between *Finnsburg* and *Beowulf*, see *e.g.*, Greenfield, *Critical History*, pp. 90–92.

[. . . she did not put trust in her son, that he could hold the ancestral seats against foreigners when Hygelac was dead.]

Even these women to whom the poem merely alludes in passing, and not always directly, may put us in mind of various unpleasantnesses. We know absolutely nothing about Beowulf's mother, for example, except that Hrothgar pays her son a compliment by asserting that she is one of whom it may be said that *ealdmetod este wære / bearngebyrdo* [God was kind to her in her childbearing, 945ª–46ᵇ] for having produced a warrior capable of killing Grendel. We need not have delved deep into the mysteries of psychology, however, to imagine something beside constant happiness and comfort in her life with a man who at least once proved capable of mismanaging his personal affairs so dismally that his very own nation *hine . . . / . . . habban ne mihte* [could not keep him, 461ᵇ–62ᵇ]. Elsewhere in the poem, the mention of a song in which a poet tells *welhwylc . . . / þæt he fram Sigemundes secgan hyrde* [everything that he had heard tell about Sigemund's . . . , 874ᵇ–75ᵇ], calls to mind Queen Signy's tragic life, which ended when she threw herself in the same fire which she had helped Sigemund light to kill her detested husband, as quoted here from the *Völsunga Saga: Síðan kysti hón Sigmund Bróður sinn ok Sinfjötla ok gekk inn feldinn ok bað þá vel fara; síðan fekk hón þar bana með Siggeiri konungi ok allri hirð sinni*[20] [Therewith she kissed Sigmund her brother, and Sinfjötli, and went back again into the fire, and there she died with King Siggeir and all his good men].

In view of the evidence presented above, it seems almost appropriate that the only piece of Anglo-Saxon verse normally examined by the general public should be largely devoted to an account of feminine sorrow. The reference is to the runic inscriptions on the Franks Casket at the British Museum, where they have been admired since 1867 by innumerable visitors representing every conceivable nationality, language, profession, age, and social level. The relevant text, on the right side of the Casket, is given here in alphabetic transliteration:

> Her Hos sitæþ   on hærmbergæ,
> agl[.] drigiþ,   swæ hiri Ertae gisgraf
> særden sorgæ   and sefa tornæ.[21]

[Here *hos* (Hos?) sits on the hill of sorrows, endures . . . , as Erte appointed for her, . . . of (or with) sorrow and anguish of heart.]

[20] *Völsunga Saga*, XIII, 19–21, in Ernst Wilken, ed., *Die prosaische Edda im Ausgabe nebst Völsunga-saga und Nornagests-tháttr* (Padderborn, 1877), p. 109; trans. William Morris, *Volsunga Saga* (New York, 1962).

[21] *The Franks Casket*, right side, in Dobbie, *Anglo-Saxon Minor Poems;* trans. Dobbie, p. cxxix, with list of interpretations by previous scholars on p. 205.

Of course, Anglo-Saxon is by no means the only early Germanic literature to have recorded the misadventures and emotions of unlucky women; and a glance at a few familiar texts will illustrate this statement. In the *Hildebrandslied,* the hero who "fled Odoacer's hostility" (*floh . . . Otachres nid*)[22] seems to have felt hard-pressed enough to justify his leaving behind a wife who must henceforth shift for herself and find means of bringing up his yet-ungrown son:

> her furlaet in lante　　　luttila sitten
> prut in bure,　　　barn unwahsan,
> arbeo laosa:　　　her raet ostar hina.
>
> 　　　　(20ª–23ᵇ)[23]

[at home, in his own country, he left behind, wretched, his wife and his ungrown son, bereft of inheritance; he rode eastward hence.]

To turn to modern American idiom, we may say that the poor woman is left holding the bag; and this particular bag is anything but promising, since her little son will grow to manhood only to meet death at his own father's hands. In the Eddic poem known as the *Guðrúnarkviða I,* we see Guthrun sitting in tearless dignity by Sigurth's body as other women recount their own woes in a futile attempt to assuage hers. While one of them recalls how *faþir oc moþir, / fiorir bröþr*[24] [father, mother, and brothers four] were drowned after her husband and sons had fallen in battle, another tells of a veritable hecatomb of husbands, daughters, sisters, and brothers:

> Hefi ec fimm vera
> forspell beþit,
> tveggia dötra,
> þriggia systra,
> átta bröþra,
> þo ec eín lifi.
>
> 　　　　(st. 4)

22 *Das Hildebrandslied*, 18ᵇ, in Werner Burkhard, ed., *Kleines althochdeutsches Lesebuch* (Bern, 1946).

23 Since the word *prut* (21ª) may be construed as an accusative or a genitive (equivalent of *pruti*), Hildebrand abandons *either* his wife at home with his ungrown son *or* his ungrown son in his wife's home (see, *e.g.,* Wilhelm Braune, ed., *Althochdeutsches Lesebuch,* rev. Karl Helm [Halle, 1949], p. 148; and Alfred Jolivet and Fernand Mossé, eds., *Manuel de l'Allemand du Moyen Age* [Paris, 1947], I, 304). I have quoted and translated from an edition whose punctuation favors the genitive construction, but acceptance of the accusative alternative would by no means invalidate my argument.

24 *Guðrúnarkviða I,* st. 7, in Sophus Bugge, *Sœmundar Edda* (Christiania, 1867); trans. Henry A. Bellows, *The Poetic Edda* (New York, 1957).

[Husbands five were from me taken, / (Two daughters then, and sisters three,) / Brothers eight, yet I have lived.]

The catalogue of calamities continues until someone pulls the sheet off Sigurth's corpse, and Guthrun finally breaks down: *Þa grét Gvdrun / Givca dottir* . . . [Then Guthrun, daughter of Gjuki, wept, st. 15]. Her grief provides the subject matter for other Eddic poems as well,[25] and the impression which it must have made on the Germanic mind may be inferred from the fact that it remains a central force in one of the master-pieces of European chivalric literature. Under the name of Kriemhilt, she enters the action of the *Nibelungenlied* with the fifth line, where she is introduced as the loveliest princess ever to grace a royal court:

> Ez wuohs in Búrgónden   ein vil édel magedîn,
>
> . . . .
> Kriemhilt geheizen: si wart ein scœne wîp.
>
> . . . .
> Der minneclîchen meide   triuten wol gezam.
> ir muoten küene recken,   niemen was ir gram.
> âne mâzen schœne   sô was ir edel lîp.
> der juncvrouwen tugende   zierten ándériu wîp.[26]

[There grew up in Burgundy a noble maiden. In no land was there a fairer. Kriemhild was her name. She became a beautiful woman. . . . Bold warriors desired her, and no one disliked her. She was lovely be-yond measure, and her maidenly virtues would have been a credit to any woman.]

From one point of view, the subsequent 2376 stanzas may be read as an account of the process whereby inconsolable grief transforms this de-lightfully innocent maiden into the monster whom Dietrich von Bern will rightfully address as *nu zúo, vâlandinne* . . . [you she-devil, 1748, 4] and who will not hesitate to order her very brother put to death and to carry his head by the hair to Hagen (*bi dem hâre si ez truoc / für den helt von Tronege* [picking it up by the hair, she carried it to the hero from Troneg, 2369, 3–4]) before beheading the latter with her own hand and finally falling under the righteous blows of Hildebrand's aveng-ing sword:

---

[25] *E.g.*, Guthrun's grief is central to *Guðrúnarkviða II* and *Guðrúnarhvöt*, plays an important part in *Sigurþarkviða hin Skamma* and *Brot af Sigurþarkviðu*, and figures in *Atlakviða*.

[26] *Das Nibelungenlied*, ed. Karl Bartsch, rev. Helmut de Boor (Leipzig, 1944), 2, 1–3, 3; trans. Helen M. Mustard, in *Mediaeval Epics* (New York, 1963).

> Hildebrant mit zorne   zuo Kriemhilde spranc.
> er sluoc der küneginne   einen swæren swertes swanc.
> jâ tet ir diu sorge   von Hildebrande wê.
> waz mohte si gehelfen   daz si sô grœzlîchen schrê?

(2376, 1–4)

[In a rage Hildebrand sprang at Kriemhield and delt her a savage sword-swing. She was stricken with terror of him, but what could it help her to shriek so piercingly?]

Other evidence could be invoked, but the instances already cited should go a long way toward justifying the despondent observation about human misery which the concluding stanza of the *Helreið Brynhildar* puts in the mouth of yet another wretched woman:

> Mvno viþ ofstríþ
> allz til lengi
> konor oc karlar
> qvicqvir födaz.[27]

[Ever with grief and all too long / Are men and women born in the world.]

The individual components of the preceding discussion have merely reminded us of facts which belong to the realm of common knowledge. The juxtaposition of these facts, however, has been intended to emphasize the existence of a Germanic tradition of suffering women which we find particularly well attested in the secular poetry of Anglo-Saxon England. As students of Germanic philology will recall, outlines of the works discussed or mentioned above would further suggest that the suffering is most often caused by separation resultant from death or some form of exile. Dangerous though it be to make assumptions about the composers and consumers of a literature which has been largely lost, it seems unlikely that the poets and audiences of Anglo-Saxon England would have been totally unaware of a tradition which has survived in so many insular and continental documents. I should accordingly like to propose that we be permitted to postulate the probability that the former composed and the latter responded to poetry within the context of this tradition. I would not be understood to imply that all Anglo-Saxons

---

[27] *Helreið Brynhildar*, st. 14, in Bugge, *Sœmundar Edda;* trans. Bellows, *Poetic Edda.* For additional evidence of feminine unhappiness, one may turn to, *e.g.*, *Völundarkviða, Helgakviða Hundingsbana I, Oddrúnargrátr,* or *Hamðismál,* also in Bugge's edition.

came equipped with a bibliography of feminine misadventures or even with a first-hand knowledge of a single literary instance thereof but, rather, that enough of them had sufficient first-hand or second-hand experience with this tradition to create certain general expectations and responses. The principle invoked here is the same which applies to ethnic jokes in modern America: though the members of a given audience may never have been directly exposed to this particular brand of entertainment before, enough of them will have heard about it to lead the others tacitly into expecting the humor to be at the expense of some ethnic group and responding accordingly.[28] With these surmises out of the way, I now turn to the controversial Anglo-Saxon poem known as *The Wife's Lament*, which we shall examine briefly within the context of the tradition defined above.

The Wife's Lament has long held a fascination for students of Anglo-Saxon, and the problems it poses may be inferred from the fact that some of the most eminent scholars have tried their hands at interpreting it without being able to reach a consensus on such an apparently clear-cut matter as the number of characters in the poem.[29] In recent years, various interpretations have respectively construed the speaker as a dead woman, a live man, a sorceress-elect, a mistreated wife, a minor heathen deity, and an allegorical voice yearning for the union of Christ and the Church.[30] There would be both foolishness and presumption in proposing yet another meaning for a work which, in addition to having eluded

[28] Adherents to the theory of Anglo-Saxon oral-formulaic composition first advanced in 1953 by Francis P. Magoun, Jr. ("The Oral-Formulaic Character of Anglo-Saxon Narrative Poetry," *Speculum*, 28 [1953], 446–67) may wish to recall Albert B. Lord's statement (*The Singer of Tales* [Cambridge, 1960], p. 29) that oral-formulaic poets insure "the preservation of tradition by the constant re-creation of it" and argue accordingly that the very existence of a given poem is evidence for assuming a general knowledge of its subject matter.

[29] *E.g.*, Edith Rickert ("The Old English Offa Saga," *MP*, 2 [1904–1905], esp. 366–67, notes), and Ernst Sieper (*Die altenglische Elegie* [Strassburg, 1915], p. 223), see respectively two and three participants in the plot.

[30] Rudolph C. Bambas, "Another View of the Old English 'Wife's Lament,'" *JEGP*, 62 (1963), 303–09, sees the speaker as a thane lamenting the loss of his lord; Thomas M. Davis, "Another View of 'The Wife's Lament,'" *PLL*, 1 (1965), 291–305, imagines the speaker accused "perhaps of sorcery" (p. 303); Stanley B. Greenfield, "*The Wife's Lament* Reconsidered," *PMLA*, 68 (1953), 907–12, argues that the speaker is an imprisoned wife cursing the husband responsible for her plight (esp. pp. 907–08); A. N. Doane, "Heathen Form and Christian Function in 'The Wife's Lament,'" *MS*, 28 (1966), 77–91, sees the speaker as a minor female deity lamenting a chief's conversion, pp. 88–89; M. J. Swanton, "*The Wife's Lament* and *The Husband's Message*: a Reconsideration," *Anglia*, 82 (1964), 269–90, esp. 276–87, sees the speaker as a voice yearning for the union of "God and the Church" (p. 276). These and other theories are reviewed by Elinor Lench, "*The Wife's Lament*: A Poem of the Living Dead," *Comitatus*, 1 (1970), 3–23.

countless attempts at imposing a definite interpretation upon its text, has been analyzed by Stanley B. Greenfield,[31] glossed by Kemp Malone,[32] and translated by Burton Raffel.[33] The following examination is accordingly offered as nothing more than a reading within context. Although I find some attraction in the views implied by the subtitle of Elinor Lench's brilliant essay on the subject, "A Poem of the Living Dead,"[34] my reading is intended to apply in various degrees to all major interpretations assuming a feminine speaker. I am not rejecting the masculine alternative for lack of faith in its intrinsic validity, but on purely pragmatic grounds: since this study makes no claim at passing for anything more than the reading of a specific text, it must perforce consider this text as it has come down to us rather than as it ought to have done so, and the masculine alternative requires substantial emendations in the only manuscript version in existence.[35]

Since the remainder of this essay deals with the *Lament* itself, it would obviously be advantageous to print herewith both the entire Anglo-Saxon text and a representative translation. For the sake of brevity, however, I shall instead (a) give the gist of the first forty-one lines, (b) print Malone's translation of the remaining twelve lines because it illustrates problems which have plagued all interpreters, and (c) refer the reader to a standard edition of the original text. The *Lament* is spoken in the first person, and the opening five lines introduce the grieving speaker who states her intention to tell the story of her misery. The next thirty-six lines tell how her lord went away and his relatives used devious means to create ill will between the two of them, with the apparent result that she has been condemned to solitary exile in a dismal grove where she recalls the loving vows which she previously exchanged with him. As she sadly contemplates the wretched earth-cave in which she must now dwell in desperate solitude, she contrasts her fate to that of happier

---

[31] Stanley B. Greenfield's masterful "The Old English Elegies," in Eric G. Stanley, ed., *Continuations and Beginnings: Studies in Old English Literature* (London, 1966), esp. 165–69, must serve as basis for any detailed analysis of the poem.

[32] Kemp Malone, "Two English *Frauenlieder*," in Greenfield, *Studies,* pp. 106–17.

[33] Burton Raffel, trans., *Poems from the Old English* (Lincoln, 1964), pp. 36–37.

[34] Lench's tightly-knit argument ("*The Wife's Lament*: A Poem of the Living Dead," pp. 12–20) considers both internal and external evidence and presents the advantage of explaining out most of the logical difficulties without doing violence to the text.

[35] *E.g.,* Bambas, "Another View," emends endings from the feminine to the masculine and discusses similar undertakings since Benjamin Thorpe's *Codex Exoniensis* (London, 1842). I am of two minds about the brilliant argument whereby Martin Stevens supports the masculine alternative without textual surgery in his "The Narrator of 'The Wife's Lament,'" *NM,* 69 (1968), 72–90.

lovers and bemoans the sorrow that relentlessly gnaws at her heart. Malone's rendition of the remainder follows:

> It may be that by nature the young man [i.e., her husband] is always gloomy-minded, his heart's thought unyielding. Likewise it is his way to have a blithe bearing along with breast-care and a throng of never-ending woes, whether all his world's joy be at his disposal or be it outlawed full widely on far-off folk-land that my friend sits, [be it] under a stonecliff [that he sits], befrosted by storm, a friend heart-weary, flooded with water in the dismal dwelling. That friend of mine experiences great grief of heart, he is mindful too oft of a happier house. Woe shall be to him who is fated out of longing to wait for the dear one.[36]

The distance between the various interpretations to which this passage has been subjected may be illustrated with two excerpts from alternative translations: "Ever may that youth be sad of mood . . . may he be banished very far in a distant land where my friend sits under a rocky slope . . ."[37] and "Ever may the young man be doomed to be sad in soul / . . . . may he be outlawed throughout the full width / Of far governed lands, so that my 'friend' will dwell / Under a stone cliff. . . ."[38] Not only does the tone of these two translations suggest a disagreement with Malone about the speaker's attitude, but the wording also reveals a mutual disagreement concerning the identity of the object of the utterance. In fact, the only undeniable point of agreement between the three translations is the speaker's unhappiness, and this is the point to which I shall address myself herewith.

Regardless of the respective identities of the speaker and the person or persons addressed in the concluding twelve lines, three features of the poem stand out at a glance: (a) the speaker is an unhappy woman, (b) her unhappiness is the result of separation from a man, and (c) her narrative is organized into three clearly distinguishable sections comprising a five-line statement of her wretchedness, a thirty-five-line account of her misadventures, and a twelve-line conclusion in which she either wishes sorrow on a man, presumably the one from whom she has been separated, or merely calls our attention to the sorrowful lot of one or two actual or hypothetical men. Thus the *Lament* unquestionably qualifies for a place within the literary tradition of suffering women which has been discussed in the first part of this essay. More precisely, the speaker's plight calls to mind these other Germanic women whose

---

[36] Malone, "Two English *Frauenlieder*," p. 113.
[37] Gordon, *Anglo-Saxon Poetry*, p. 88.
[38] Lench, *"The Wife's Lament:* A Poem of the Living Dead," p. 23.

misadventures have originated in separation: the speaker of *Wulf and Eadwacer,* for example, who longs for the sight of her Wulf; or Hildebrand's wife, who must remain behind with her helpless child while her husband treads the path of exile; or Brynhild, the speaker of the *Helreið Brynhildar,* whose separation from the man she loved was so unendurable that she had rather see him slain than let another woman keep him.[39]

As in response to Alexander Pope's admonition that "the sound must seem an Echo to the sense," the vocabulary and resultant tone of the poem are likewise suited to the theme and tradition of suffering through separation. The most cursory reading of the Anglo-Saxon text will reveal two half-lines (16[a], 45[a]) and at least thirty-five individual words immediately suggestive of actual suffering (*e.g., modcearu,* sorrow of heart)[40] or something normally associated with the experience or imposition of suffering (*e.g., morþor,* murder, great wickedness, deadly injury); and the tone is established at the outset with the term *geomor* [sorrowful], which concludes the opening line and subsequently recurs three times (17[b], 19[b], 42[b]) in various forms and compounds. Likewise, seventeen individual words and the half-line already mentioned (16[a]) immediately suggest physical separation (*e.g., todælan* [to separate]) or some psychological equivalent thereof (*e.g., miðan* [to dissemble]); and the intensely painful nature of this particular separation is forced upon us by the repetition of various forms and compounds of the term *wræcca* [exile, 5[b], 10[a], 38[b]] and the analogous *fah* [proscribed, 46[b]]. In addition, eighteen individual words immediately suggest passive endurance of whatever action is taking place, and the speaker's attitude toward this endurance is inescapably conveyed by the repetition of the term *langoð* [weariness that arises from unsatisfied desire] and various forms and compounds thereof (14[b], 29[b], 41[a], 53[a]), followed in frequency by *dreogan* [to suffer, 26[b], 45[a], 50[b]].[41] Detailed analysis, which lies outside the scope of this essay, would further show that the information and tone conveyed by these words are greatly reinforced by the masterful organization of the poem and the immediate context within which their impact

---

[39] In *Helreið Brynhildar* (*cf.* n. 27, above) Brynhild complains bitterly of Sigurth's marriage to Guthrun (st. 13), and her vengeful part in the latter's murder is common knowledge, *e.g.,* from the *Nibelungenlied* and *Völsunga Saga.*

[40] Glosses are from *BT.*

[41] *The Wife's Lament,* in Krapp and Dobbie, *Exeter Book.* Words suggestive of suffering occur on 1[b], 2[a], 5[a-b], 7[b], 10[a-b], 14[b], 16[a], 17[b], 19[a-b], 20[b], 22[b], 26[b], 29[b], 31[a], 32[a-b], 38[a-b], 39[a], 40[a], 41[a], 42[b], 44[b], 45[a], 46[b], 49[a], 50[a-b], 51[a], 53[a]; words suggestive of separation occur on 5[b], 6[a-b], 9[a], 10[a], 13[a], 15[b], 16[a], 20[a], 22[a-b], 26[b], 33[a], 35[b], 46[b], 47[a]; words suggestive of passive endurance occur on 3[a], 5[a], 10[b], 14[b], 26[b], 27[a], 29[b], 32[b], 37[b], 38[a], 40[b], 41[a-b], 45[a], 47[b], 50[b], 53[a-b].

is often transferred to otherwise neutral adjacent statements. For those who recall the lessons which *The Wanderer* and *The Seafarer* have taught us about Anglo-Saxon attitudes toward exile and the endurance of hardships, the foregoing survey may be enough to warrant agreement with Roy F. Leslie's view that "the bitterness of separation as seen from her [the speaker's] point of view"[42] stands at the center of the *Lament*.

What lies within the scope of this essay, however, is the fact that the elements discussed above help us read the poem in the context of the same tradition as its subject matter. Analysis has shown similar verbal emphasis on suffering, separation, and passive endurance in *Wulf and Eadwacer,* which also concludes on a foreboding note and whose speaker must sit *reotugu* [tearful, 10ᵇ], just as the speaker of the *Lament* must *sittan* and *wepan* [sit and weep, 37ᵃ, 38ᵃ].[43] Just as the exiled speaker of the *Lament* is *wineleas* [without friends, 10ᵃ] and must endure her man's *fæhðu* [hostility, 26ᵇ], so one of the exiles in the *Hildesbrand-slied* is *friuntlaos* [without friends, 24ᵇ] while another has to flee a great lord's *nid* [hostility, 18ᵇ]; and it is likewise *fæhþo* which has driven away the man who assures the woman in *The Husband's Message* (19ᵇ) that time has come to give up passive endurance and move into action. Passive endurance also lies behind the sorrows which *Deor* attributes to Beadohild, whom the *Völundarkviða* shows recalling why resistance would have been futile against her ravisher: *ec vëtr hanom / vinna máttac* [Nought was my might with such a man].[44] Just as the speaker of the *Lament* complains that her friend's love for her is *onhworfen / . . . swa hit no wære* [changed . . . as it never were, 23ᵇ–24ᵇ], so we recall Beowulf's assertion that Freawaru will soon see her husband's love turn cold (2066ᵇ).

In conclusion, I should like to think of this reading within context as complementary to Malone's statement that, like *Wulf and Eadwacer,* the *Lament* stands "isolated in our inherited poetical corpus of Saxon time."[45] The context which I have chosen for my reading claims no genetic relationship to the story in the poem and must plead guilty to the charge of arbitrariness. Its justification is that it alerts us to certain circumstances, attitudes, and verbal formulas readily associated with the secular women of early Germanic poetry, and thus prompts us to take

---

[42] Roy F. Leslie, ed., *Three Old English Elegies* (Manchester, 1961), p. 3.

[43] I have discussed these points in *"Wulf and Eadwacer: a Noninterpretation,"* in Jess B. Bessinger, Jr., and Robert P. Creed, eds., *Franciplegius: Medieval and Linguistic Studies in Honor of Francis Peabody Magoun, Jr.* (New York, 1965), esp. pp. 153–55.

[44] *Völundarkviða,* st. 41, in Bugge, *Sæmundar Edda;* trans. Bellows, *Poetic Edda.* A more literal translation would be, "I had no strength to withstand him."

[45] Malone, "Two English *Frauenlieder,*" p. 117.

into account some important features which might otherwise pass un-
noticed and to respond emotionally to the poem in a manner perhaps
not altogether different from that of the Anglo-Saxons.[46] Without getting
entangled in the intricate historical arguments which have enabled some
scholars to place the action within certain narrative cycles,[47] the suggested reading context tries to make up in a small way for the isolation in
which *The Wife's Lament* stands and is likely to remain in the foresee-
able future.

[46] As suggested by subject matter and allusions (*e.g.*, in *Beowulf, Widsith, Deor*),
Anglo-Saxon poets must occasionally have assumed their audience's familiarity
with the Germanic tradition in general. I have ignored the very real similarities
which Rickert has noted ("Old English Offa Saga," p. 368) between the *Lament*
and several French and Italian works, because their dates and places of composition rule out their possible influence on Anglo-Saxon England.

[47] *E.g.*, Rickert in her "Old English Offa Saga" and Rudolf H. R. Imelmann in
his *Die altenglische Odoaker-dichtung* (Berlin, 1907).

16

The Enigma of
The Husband's Message

MARGARET E. GOLDSMITH

TO ONE OF THE ENIGMATIC PIECES OF VERSE ON FOLIOS 122 AND 123 of the Exeter Book the editors have given the prosaic title *Riddle 60* (*R60*), to the other, not distinguished from it by the scribe, *The Husband's Message* (*HM*). We therefore come to them nowadays with different expectations, treating the one as an intellectual diversion and the other as a declaration of love. The notion of considering the two as one allegorical poem is, on the face of it, disconcerting and unappealing. Kaske's arguments in favour of a composite Poem of the Cross are not very convincing, in spite of the suggestiveness of some of his evidence.[1] I have been as reluctant as any to link the two pieces, principally because I judged *R60* to be an attractive little poem about a reed, and I found it difficult to believe that Anglo-Saxons were in the habit of carving messages on reeds or even on kelpweed (which dries out).[2] On

---

[1] R. E. Kaske, "A Poem of the Cross in The Exeter Book," *Traditio*, 23 (1967), 41–71. For a decidedly unconvinced assessment of Kaske's thesis, see S. B. Greenfield, *The Interpretation of OE Poems* (London and Boston, 1972), pp. 145–54.

[2] The few editors who have linked the two poems have not regarded *R60* as a "Reed" poem. For references, see *ASPR*, III (New York, 1936), p. lix, and Kaske, pp. 41ff. The immediately preceding poem on fol. 122, apparently on the subject of Tree and Cross, was joined with *R60* and *HM* by Blackburn (1901), but since this riddle also occurs separately as *Riddle 30*, it is obviously independent. The proposition that the runes of *HM* were carved on kelpweed was made by B. Colgrave and B. M. Griffiths, *MLR*, 31 (1936), 545.

the other hand, I have been uneasy, as others are, about the opening of *HM,* which is a bit like a riddle opening, and yet with its initial *Nu ic . . . þe secgan wille* [Now I will tell you] does sound like a continuation of a tale already begun. So I thought it best to make a complete reappraisal of both *R60* and *HM* and to consider also whether Bede (who lived in a great period of riddle-writing) would have associated a reed with the Rood and a cosmic oath.

It may be necessary to emphasize the dignity and seriousness of some *ænigmata* [riddles, obscure allegories] in the Anglo-Saxon period. I have already published something on this subject,[3] but what I said seems to be impugned by Rollinson's contemporary article which argued that *ænigma* meant no more than "conundrum" to Anglo-Saxon poets, his example being the teaser with which Samson enlivened his wedding party.[4] (This riddle, incidentally, is a *problema* in the Latin Bible, not an *ænigma.*)[5] Bede, however, uses the word *ænigmata* of the dark prophecies of the Old Testament, glossing the word himself: *id est obscura dicta* [i.e. obscure sayings]. I refer interested readers to his discussion of *Parabolæ Salomonis,* in which he associates these "obscure sayings" with the parables of Christ, which were not to be understood by the crowds.[6] It can indeed be contended that the *ænigmata* of the Bible are in a unique category, but the distinction between sacred and religious compositions was inevitably blurred when the prophecies were transposed into vernacular poetry.

In the ninety-odd riddles of the Exeter Book, secular and religious subjects are mingled. (Some are edifying, some are obscene—suggesting that the principle *aliud ex alio significare* [to signify one thing by another][7] could be stood on its head by waggish spirits.) The "riddle" which concerns us, the so-called *Riddle 60,* does not include a conven-

[3] M. E. Goldsmith, *The Mode and Meaning of "Beowulf"* (London, 1970), pp. 49ff.

[4] P. Rollinson, "Some Kinds of Meaning in OE Poetry," *Annuale Mediaevale,* 11 (1970), 5–21. Part of Rollinson's argument is quoted by Greenfield, p. 138 f.

[5] Rollinson offers as an instance of a plain "riddle," Samson's "Out of the eater . . . " (Jud. 14:14), distinguishing this conundrum propounded by Samson from the narrative of Samson's act in killing the lion (which has been given Christological significance and is therefore an allegorical or dark saying). It appears to me to weaken Rollinson's case that the plain riddle he cites is *not* called an *ænigma* in the Vulgate (the word *problema* being used each time Samson's conundrum is mentioned). In this essay I normally quote from the Vulgate text of the Bible; biblical translations are from the Douai Bible. I have preferred Douai to Knox because it is usually more literal, and therefore more helpful to the reader who has small Latin.

[6] Bede, *PL,* 91, 939, referring to Matt. 13:11.

[7] See Bede's definition of *allegoria, PL,* 90, 184; *Allegoria est tropus quo aliud significatur quam dicitur* [Allegory is a trope in which something other is signified than what is said]. *Ænigma* is for him a sub-class of *allegoria.*

tional invitation to guess the speaker's identity, but it certainly exploits enigmatic phrasing—how can the "mouthless" speak? Its thematic structure is similar to that of *Riddle 53*,[8] in which a towering tree is described as becoming in age a wounded captive, and of *Riddle 73*, whose speaker-subject "lived where the earth and the sky fed me" until in age he became a weapon in his master's hand.

From these comparisons, it appears that the author of *R60* probably had models to hand in the riddle collections, but should we therefore call his poem a riddle? We know that more important poetry could emerge from the riddle tradition: *The Dream of the Rood* incorporates both the motif of the forest tree hewn from its place to be refashioned by men and the rhetorical device of the speaking wood. Though I should not place *R60* on a level with that great poem, it is far from being just a curiosity. It is, as I believe I can demonstrate, the introduction to *HM*, and in my judgment it is the finest part of the total work, which becomes more and more cerebral as it proceeds.[9]

Let me first deal with the two major objections to joining the two poems. There are two statements about the speaker's origins and early life (*R60* 1–7 and *HM* 2–9). The second seems to be out of place if the same speaker is continuing his story. Moreover, if the speaker of *HM* is a wooden object such as a rune-staff, as many scholars think, the description of a creature growing in the water (*R60* 1–2, 6–7) does not accord with the springing up of a tree. My answer to the first problem is that the second statement (*HM* 2–9) is not about *origins*, but about the *new life* which the creature began after it was cut from its *frumstaþol* [place of origin, root]. My answer to the second is that the speaker of *HM* is not himself a wooden object: he discourses about a tree.

I shall begin my explication with a brief critical analysis of *R60*, following this with a similar analysis of *HM*, before offering some new explanations.

The poem opens with a short description of a place of sand, moving water, and solitude, in which there is a notable juxtaposition of *anæd* [solitary place] with *eard* [homeland, 5]. The ripple and swirl of slack water is all that happens. There is no energy of billows as in *The Seafarer;* though near the *sæweall* [seashore],[10] the place seems calm, like

---

[8] Here and elsewhere I use the numbering of *The Exeter Book* riddles as given by Krapp-Dobbie, *ASPR*, III.

[9] Though I believe that there is no division between *R60* and *HM*, I have kept the separate line-numbering of the standard editions, for convenience of reference. Where the editions differ, I give the *ASPR* numbering.

[10] R. F. Leslie, "The Integrity of *Riddle 60*," *JEGP*, 67 (1968), 452–53, compares *Beowulf* (1924) for *sæweall* in the sense "shore" (rather than "cliff").

an estuary or pool. The atmosphere evoked is like that of the "pale-brown map of sandbanks / Barely submerged" where "It seems nothing will occur" in Charles Tomlinson's poem *Rower*.[11]

But the Anglo-Saxon poet's scene is even more "a plotless tale" than Tomlinson's empty seascape. There is not even a sense of tidal freshness, nothing but dawn succeeding dawn and the creature passive in the embrace of the brown water.[12] How could a creature in such a solitary spot conceive of *speaking?* He who is addressing us has no voice of his own: this is the mystery and the theme of this part of the poem.

The *meodu* [mead, 9] here, as in *Beowulf* (604), may be a synecdoche for the shared pleasures of people in company. It conjures up the singing and talking that are missing from the solitary habitation on the shore, where none can ever *wordum wrixlan* [exchange words, 10]. To make the voiceless speak or sing is the achievement of creative art, and for this we need the intrusion of the man with his knife, cutting the creature from its first habitat and remaking it into a new thing with his own impress upon it, a new creature capable of playing the part the man has designed for it. All the purposive energy in the poem flows from the man, but such is the imagined perspective here that he only appears in the possessive case (13). He has no name; he is present only as a strong hand pressing, together with a knife point (12). The creature itself now has a purpose and a power which emanated from the man's *ingeþonc* [mind, 13], inner, unknowable, and yet capable of inventing the tool and the process which imparts some of his own life to the passive creature. Now the creature, re-made, can act like a human servant in addressing another mind and in conveying the thought of his master.

But the miracle goes beyond this transformation. The messenger has become more strangely powerful than even a human servant, as the last lines enigmatically tell us. He can speak directly to the mind of the man or woman who receives the message. He and the writer join to communicate a thought. He and the reader work together to understand that

---

[11] C. Tomlinson, *Written on Water* (Oxford, 1972), p. 6.

[12] The notion of the "embrace" of the lapping water may have been suggested by the first line of the short Latin riddle on *Arundo* [Reed], Symphosius No. 2 (*CCSL*, 133A, p. 623). I quote it here in full:

> Dulcis amica ripæ semper vicina profundis
> Suave cano Musis, nigro perfusa colore
> Nuntia sum linguæ digitis signata magistris.

[Sweet darling of the banks, always close to the depths,
Sweetly I sing for the Muses; when drenched with black
I am the tongue's messenger by guiding fingers pressed.]

communication. On each occasion, he can say, in effect, "these words are *ours*." The poet combines speaker-object and reader in *for unc anum twam* [for us two alone, 15] and speaker-object and sender in *uncre wordcwidas* [our sayings in words, 17].[13] There is an ambiguity in *abeodan bealdlice* (16), which generally means "announce *boldly*" (as when a spokesman comes to parley), but in this special context also has the sense "declare *instantly*," since the written communication passes in the space of a glance. With economy and, I think, with charm, the poet has evoked a world of silence and a world of voices, and he has brought the power of the silent voice into the midst of the company.

I have so far avoided the difficult question of the identity of the speaker. Of the three contenders for the role, the reed, the rune-staff, and the Cross, the last two require very special pleading.[14] Intrinsically, we must decide whether to give weight to the waterside scene, which will not allow an ordinary tree as the speaker-object, or to give weight to the secret passing of the message, for which a rune-staff (or even a wooden cross) would be a tangible focus of attention. I concur with Leslie here: his argument in favour of a reed pen as speaker is very strong.[15] Only metaphorically can the pen "speak" over mead, but the idea of a skillful guiding hand working with a point to make a private communication certainly suggests writing of some sort. Extrinsically, there is further support for this identification in the similarity to Symphosius's Latin riddle *Arundo*,[16] and in the existence of other riddles on the theme and the wonder of writing.[17] As for the Cross as the subject, I do not think it would occur to any reader who was not working backwards from *HM,* in which a tree certainly figures. In sum, the Reed-pen, as the writer's instrument, most satisfactorily fills the requirements.

---

[13] Leslie, *JEGP,* 67 (1968), p. 455, uses this phrase in line 17 as evidence that *R60* is *not* the opening of *HM,* because he cannot accept that the other person indicated by *uncre* [of us two] is the woman addressed in *HM.* I shall explain away this difficulty in my interpretation of *HM.* On *R60* generally, I differ from Leslie only in points of detail, regarding the literal sense.

[14] I have already referred (n. 2) to the various attempts to associate a rune-staff with something growing in the water. Kaske's argument that the Tree of the Cross grew in or near the waters of Paradise is ingenious but highly conjectural, and it does not take any account of the detail of *R60.*

[15] See n. 13.

[16] See n. 12 for this riddle. Other editions use the variant spelling *Harundo.* An alternative Latin word for the kind of reed used as a pen is *calamus,* which sometimes suggests a stiffer stem than *(h)arundo.* OE has the equivalent *hreod* for both, and *hreod-writ* for the pen.

[17] The Exeter Book includes other riddles on writing and making a book (Nos. 26, 51), and there are several more from Anglo-Saxon authors in the Latin collections: notably, Aldhelm Nos. 32, 59; Eusebius Nos. 31, 32, 35; Tatwine Nos. 5, 6; (all in *CCSL,* 133).

I now come to *The Husband's Message,* which follows on in the manuscript after a scribal section mark (similar to those we find dividing *HM* itself into three sections). For discussion, the three sections may be called: preamble (1–12), summons (13–25), promise (26–53). There is a hole in the manuscript which breaks into lines 1–7 of the preamble and lines 36–40 of the summons.

The most notable fact about the preamble is that the first-person speaker apparently *is* or *is talking about* something in the nature of a tree. This matter has up till now been unresolved,[18] because only the word *treocyn* [tree-kind] is legible in 2a, and we cannot be sure whether the missing words included *ymb* [about, concerning]; if they did, the speaker proposes to talk "about" the "tree." Those editors who favour a human speaker here insist on a fullstop after *treocyn[ne],*[19] which makes line 2b very odd indeed: *ic tudre aweox* [(?) I grew up from a child—*or* from a shoot]. Things are not much better if we take out the fullstop and try to join this phrase to *treocyn.* I would say this is the first and the most significant of several signs in this poem that we are dealing with no ordinary messenger. Even Polonius would hardly have expected to hold the royal attention with a report that started "I grew up from childhood"—unless there followed some mention of household or region, with bearing on the message. But in *HM* the sentence cannot tell us anything more of this "childhood," for the next phrase *in mec* [in *or* on me] requires us to look ahead to the verb *sceal . . . settan* [must . . . set] (the new subject being lost in the hole in the parchment). The editors and critics try to make the best of it. Leslie says, "As it stands, the statement 'I grew up from childhood' may appear unnecessary, but the whole introductory passage has a highly formal tone."[20] Greenfield, backing Leslie's reading, elaborates: "Then the *human* speaker, having indicated his readiness to say something about the piece of wood he is carrying, goes into a presentation of his *own* pedigree and credentials."[21] Pedigree? Having pursued a steady course from childhood to manhood may possibly testify to perseverance; it can hardly instill confidence about the man's good breeding or his credibility. And the next sentence, to which Leslie would reasonably restore as subject *æld[a bearn]* [a son of men, 3] seems, if anything, to mark off the speaker from mankind. In my view, the poet is being deliberately enig-

---

[18] See Leslie, *Three OE Elegies* (Manchester, 1961), p. 13 f., and Greenfield, pp. 150–52.

[19] Leslie *et al.* punctuate with a fullstop before *ic* (2b). Krapp-Dobbie, *ASPR,* III, p. 225, do not break the line in this way.

[20] Leslie, *Elegies,* p. 59, n. 2.

[21] Greenfield, p. 151.

matic in writing *ic tudre aweox* (2b), choosing a word (*tudor*) which might fit either a plant or a human being.[22]

The phrase *in mec* (3) and the verb *settan* (4) continue the ambiguity inherent in the first two lines. The words might refer to some process like carving, if the speaker were non-human, or metaphorically signify "place in my charge" (so Leslie).[23] The gap in the manuscript affects the next four lines also, but it emerges plainly enough that the messenger has often voyaged in a boat across the seas. At this point, those who wish to identify the speaker as a special staff or token, or the Cross, have to gloss over an awkward passage. I do not find difficulty, as some have done, in the speaker's references to his "lord"—it is natural enough in the language of a personified servant. But we have a real problem if we try to envisage a token *carved wtih runes which convey a unique message of love.* Such a token could not have journeyed *ful oft* (5) in its master's service. So, when we look at this enigmatic preamble section fair and square, we have to admit that some phrases point to a human personality and others to a vegetable speaker. To my mind, the Pen, which communicates through the words it "utters" on the page, fills this human/non-human role peculiarly well. As often in riddle poetry, the subject is not to be thought of as a single individual of its kind, but as a class of creatures which may serve various uses. As Pen, the speaker "voyages" whenever the writings done at his lord's command are disseminated across the world. "Now," as part of this service, he is passing on a message composed overseas to you, the present reader. I assume, then, that the same speaker here continues the account of his new active life and begins his message concerning the "tree." There is little in this part of the poem to suggest that there are *carved runes* on either the speaker-object or the "tree" he is talking about. The message a reed-pen would bring must obviously be set on a page; it is surely *within the words of the poem,* perhaps reinforced by symbols engraved (cp. *agrof,* 13) on the *beam* [tree, post, staff, ship, etc.].[24]

The message is, in brief, "Trust my lord, remember the promises between you in earlier days and take ship for the south, where your exiled prince is waiting for you, true to his vows."

But, before this message begins, the speaker rather strangely says, "I dare promise that you will find there glorious faith." The strangeness lies

---

[22] I ask the reader's indulgence for not pursuing the matter further at this stage.

[23] Leslie, p. 59, n. 3–4. Leslie's line-divisions in the damaged passage do not coincide with Krapp-Dobbie; I have used Krapp-Dobbie numbering.

[24] It is possible that the poet hints at the idea of a carved staff so as to draw an analogy with a runic token, but he does not in fact associate the runes at the end of the poem with the *beam* which is "engraved."

in the choice of *tirfæst* [assured in glory] with *treow* [faith]. The modern word "honorable" used by some translators here is not a true equivalent of *tirfæst*, which often has religious associations; the phrase *tirfæst treow*, as Kershaw noticed,[25] occurs in The Paris Psalter as part of the Anglo-Saxon rendering of Psalm 100:6. In itself, the similarity with the psalm-verse could be fortuitous, but it is a small point to be noted as we read.

The second section of *HM*, as marked by the scribe, calls attention with the word *Hwæt* (13) to the command of the man *se þisne beam agrof* [who (?)engraved this (?)wood, 13]. The form of words implies that the messenger is now indicating a wooden token, but the words are (perhaps deliberately) quite imprecise. The woman addressed is given no name or specific title; where we might have expected "princess" we read *sinchroden* [treasure-adorned, 14]. The promises which the lady is bidden to remember were made "long ago" *on ærdagum* (16). They were made while the two still lived in the same land and were loving to one another.[26] It is notable that the stylistic elaboration of lines 17–19 emphasizes the dwelling in one land more than the sharing of love, and this emphasis leads to *Hine fæhþo adraf of sigeþeode* [feud drove him from his victorious people, 19–20]. This sentence tells against any interpretation of *HM* as a real-life message brought to a royal lady: even as part of a dramatic fiction, it says either too much or too little. A lady still in the dark about why she was deserted would hardly be content with this laconic statement, and, conversely, if she did know about that past feud, it ought to go into a "Remember . . ." construction, or into a subordinate clause of time. Moreover, the message is imperative rather than wooing. The lady is told to put to sea when the cuckoo's voice is heard. The word *læra[n]* (21) does not ordinarily mean "persuade" (so Leslie), and lines 24–25 are a command rather than an exhortation: "Do not allow any living man to keep you from the journey."

The third section, beginning at line 26, promises that the lady will find her lord waiting and much else to delight her in his rich kingdom. She is bidden to go on board the ship and voyage south to the place where she will find him. Concerning "south" (27) (as concerning

---

[25] N. Kershaw, *Anglo-Saxon and Norse Poems* (Cambridge, 1922), p. 176. See *The Paris Psalter, ASPR*, V (1933), p. 71. Kershaw's suggestion is that the Psalm translator was drawing upon *HM*; but he would hardly have done so if he had thought, as she does, that *HM* was a secular poem. There may also be wordplay on *treow* "truth" and "tree"; the possible double reference of the word was noticed by Leslie (p. 18), though he dismissed the thought.

[26] Though the phrase *freondscipe fremman* might refer to a physical relationship, it does not commonly do so. (*BT* gives "foster friendship" for this line.)

fæhðo above), my feeling is that it is curiously unspecific. Why is she not told the name of the country her lover now rules?

Line 30 is metrically irregular, leaving *worulde willa* [desire (?) of the world] to contrast with the supreme joy the absent lord has said he will have if God grants that he and she shall jointly be treasure-givers to men, in later days. Some editors, on the strength of the scribe's deletion of a few letters (now illegible) before *worulde,* insert *on* to give "*in* the world" and add the innocuous *gelimpan* [happen].[27] Critics have argued whether or not the phrase in the next line *þæs þe he me sægde* [as he said to me, 31b] is consistent with a non-human speaker. The phrase is disconcerting if the reader has been imagining a rune-staff as the messenger, but I see no problem with a personified pen taking down his master's words.

We have now reached the second damaged part of the text (35b–39), but the general sense is clear. The messenger asserts that his lord now has abundant gold, a fair land, and faithful men: [*geon*]*d elþeode eþel healde* [among foreign people(s) he rules his homeland, 37].[28] As we observed in line 18, stylistic elaboration here emphasizes the land. The phrase with *elþeode* [foreign people(s)] appears otiose unless it serves the function of pointing the paradox of an *eþel* [fatherland] among strangers.[29]

Line 39b introduces the contrasting situation of the lord when he was "here"; under compulsion he thrust off his boat and had to voyage on the wide sea alone, *forðsiþes georn* [eager for departure, 42]. Again, it is hard to make a credible "real-life" incident out of this exiling of the lord. How could he, the lover who was separating from his betrothed, be *forðsiðes georn* [eager to depart]?[30]

Nu se mon hafað wean oferwunnen (43b–44) is rendered "Now the man has overcome woe" by Greenfield,[31] but this translation has very little metaphorical force, whereas the Old English word belongs quite positively in the field of battle, and the possibly plural *wean* covers pains, afflictions, and evils. The message continues with an idiomatic expres-

---

[27] See Leslie, n. 30, p. 62, for the MS reading here. Leslie himself inserts *on* and *gelimpan.*

[28] Only the final "d" is legible in the word before *elþeode,* but a preposition is called for and *geond* is generally accepted.

[29] Leslie speaks of "the contrast between *elþeode* 'a foreign people' and *eþel* 'a homeland,' in this case by adoption, as in *Genesis* 927, 962" (p. 63). (In *Genesis* the "homeland by adoption" is Adam's Earth, after his expulsion from Paradise.)

[30] Greenfield tacitly drops the awkward phrase when translating these lines (p. 148).

[31] Greenfield, p. 148. The form *wean* may be singular or plural here: Leslie's glossary opts for the plural.

sion *nis him wilna gad* [he has no lack of good things, 44], twice used in *Beowulf*[32] in a promise of unbounded rewards to follow upon victory in combat. This lord could wish for nothing further—"if he possessed you, king's daughter" (47). The importance of this vital *if*-clause is marked by a rhetorical series of good things which anyone might desire —horses, treasures, pleasures of the meadhall, princely possessions— all these things so placed as to claim, "He has nothing to wish for, if he has you."[33]

We have now reached the mystifying climax of the poem. Kaske asserts, "Not until the runic passage . . . is the identity of this wooden messenger stated unambiguously—though still after the manner of the riddles, cryptically and in runes."[34] The "unambiguous" statement he discerns depends essentially upon the disputed reading *genyre* (49a), which he takes as a form of *genyrwe*, "I contract *or* constrain"; hence, in context, "I constrain into unity." Aside from the paleographical dispute, there are both semantic and syntactic difficulties if we read *genyre*. First, as to the authenticity of the reading: I have made a close examination of the manuscript in the light of Kaske's observations, and in my opinion the damaged letter in its present state may be read as "c," "n," or the lower half of "h," with almost equal justification.[35] On grounds of syntax and general sense, there can be no doubt that the order of probability is *gehyre, gecyre, genyre*. The phrase *aþe benemnan* (50), apparently dependent on the disputed verb, occurs both in *Beowulf* (1097, 3069) and in The Paris Psalter, where it glosses God's *juravi* [I have sworn] in Psalm 88:3.[36] In all the instances the oath is a declaration which any

---

[32] *Beowulf*, lines 660 and 949 f.

[33] See Kaske, p. 57, and Greenfield, p. 23 f.

[34] Kaske, p. 71; cp. Greenfield, p. 149.

[35] Leslie, p. 66, objects to the *ASPR* reading *gecyre* and substitutes *gehyre*. Kaske's article "The reading *genyre* in *The Husband's Message*, line 49," *M Æ*, 33 (1964), 204–06, offers an ultra-violet photograph as positive evidence for *genyre*. Greenfield is "not entirely convinced" by the photograph (Greenfield, p. 173). Kaske rightly observes that there is now no trace of the upper part of an "h" (*contra* Leslie), but he erroneously states that there is no "roughening" of the surface in the blotched area. More importantly, he fails to state that part of the top of the preceding letter "e" has also vanished. I am not able to determine what agent was at work here, but some of the ink has certainly gone. This means that "h" is not positively ruled out. We must also note the fact that the supposed "n" is abnormal in having no "wedge" to start it and in having a thickening where the two strokes join. (This latter characteristic gives it something of the appearance of a "spurred" "c," but the vertical is to my eye unnaturally straight for the back of a "c.") If by some as yet untried process it can be proved that the scribe wrote "n," I should regard it as a mechanical error for "h" (cp. fol. 75ʳ, line 8, where such an error has occurred)

[36] *ASPR*, V, p. 56; cp. Ps. 94:11, *ASPR*, V, p. 67. See also n. 47, below.

witnesses would *hear*. The natural sense of the verbal phrase in *HM* (49–50) "I hear . . . declare by oath" has of late been rejected by interpreters of the poem because of their preoccupation with *carved* (not *penned*) runes or with the Cross. But, with the Reed as messenger, we have only to assume that he, as Pen, records what all those present *hear* (with him) when the great oath is uttered. (Those readers who still prefer the reading *gecyre,* or Kaske's *genyre,* will need to assume instead that the Pen "converts" (*gecyre*) or "binds together" (*genyre*) the *runic symbols.*)

I think there is now a general consensus that *sigel-rad, ear-wyn,* and *monn* are the right verbal equivalents of the runes, but I do not recall that anyone has given the poet credit for exploiting the semantic possibilities which his choice of rune-compounds gives him. "The sun's course" is not a simple synonym for "sky"; we hardly need the reminder of *sigel suðan fus* in *Beowulf* (1966) to associate the course of the sun with the south, the direction of the lover's voyage, the region of his new realm. And, since *ear* can mean both "earth" and "sea," we may be asked to bear both meanings in mind. The "man" can be no other than the lord of the kingdom, and I believe with Elliott that the five runes epitomize the substance of the message.[37]

Who is this lord? From the poem we learn that after the time of the vows and promises he was forced to go alone to the south, where among foreigners he has become a rich and powerful ruler. Let me match this summary with a passage from Bede:

> Christus, relicta terra sua, et cognatione sua, et domo patris sui, populo scilicet Judæorum, apud exteros locupletatur, in populo gentium præpollens.

> [Christ, *having left his country, and his kindred,* and his father's house (that is to say, the people of the Jews), *is made rich among foreigners,* being more powerful among the Gentile people.][38]

[37] R. W. V. Elliott, "The Runes in *The Husband's Message,*" *JEGP,* 54 (1955), 3, takes the runes to epitomize the message, rendering the symbols "southward journey," "sea-joy," and "day" *or* "man." (Other scholars have since pointed out that the final rune matches M-runes in the Exeter Book, not D–hence "day" may be ruled out.) As a literal interpretation of the runes, this seems to me right, but it by no means exhausts the meanings the runes suggest. In his book *Runes* (Manchester, 1959), p. 73, Elliott offers a "somewhat expanded" translation: "Follow the *sun's path* south across the *ocean* to find *joy* with the *man* who is waiting for you." (It is not clear how this will join on to *aþe benemnan.*) He notes that *ear* also means "earth," "soil" and in *The Runic Poem* "the grave," but he does not use these facts in his argument.

[38] Bede, *In Pentateuchum Commentarii, PL,* 91, 230. The second quotation is from *In Genesim, CCSL,* 118A, p. 173. The association of the tropological theme with the Reed will be shown below (cp. n. 59).

The phrases Bede is echoing here come from Genesis 12:1–3, in which Abraham is promised blessing for himself and all his descendants if he leaves his homeland. Abraham then begins his journey to the promised land, "going on still *towards the south*" (Gen. 12:9). Bede, as we see, reads the passage typologically, as an allegorical prophecy of Christ's foundation of a spiritual kingdom, in which he becomes rich in souls. But this is by no means the only spiritual meaning the exegete can extract from God's command to journey to the land in the south. Bede also takes God's command as addressed to each one of us *ad celestem patriam iter facere* [to journey to the heavenly fatherland] leaving the world and temporal pleasures behind for "the region of the south";

> Meridiana quippe plaga . . . fervorem dilectionis mystice demonstrat, qua corda electorum, ne in rerum infimarum appetitu ac desideriis torpeant, sole iustitiæ desuper, videlicet Christo inlucente, semper accenduntur.

> [The *region of the south* indeed mystically betokens the heat of *love* in which the hearts of the chosen are ever fired *by the sun of righteousness* from above, that is to say, *by Christ* shining upon them, lest they should grow inactive amid their appetite and longings for lower things.][39]

Bede's commentary thus not only gives us an explanation of the king's rich kingdom in the south among foreign peoples, but also links it with *sigel-rad* [the sun's course] and the journey of the lover. And there is further pertinent matter in this passage: from the same source comes a quotation from Psalm 44 (Vulgate numbering). Bede elaborates this exhortation to leave "the world" by speaking of the divine call in this way:

> . . . dicente nobis, id est ecclesiæ suæ, Patre Nostro Qui Est in Coelis, "Audi, filia, et inclina aurem tuam, et obliviscere populum tuum et domum patris tui."

> [. . . Our Father who is in Heaven saying *to us*, that is, *to His Church*, "*Hearken, O daughter*, and incline thine ear; forget also thine own people, and thy father's house."]

I note here how readily the biblical scholar has moved from the typological to the moral and anagogical significances of the texts concerning

---

[39] Introducing this psalm, Augustine says: *Cantatur enim de sanctis nuptiis de sponso et sponsa, de rege et plebe, de Salvatore et de his qui salvandi sunt* [In truth, it is sung about the holy nuptials of the Bridegroom and the Bride, about the King and the people, about the Saviour and those who are to be saved.] (*Enarr. in Psalmos, CCSL*, 38, p. 493).

the journey to the south. The ideas in *HM* are, I believe, a distillation from these and other allegorical interpretations of associated biblical texts. Bede's quotation of *Audi, filia* [Hearken, O daughter] brings to mind a complex of Bride imagery, for the theme of Psalm 44, as interpreted, is the marriage of *Ecclesia* and Christ the King. Both Swanton and Kaske have realized that the lady of *HM* is *Ecclesia*,[40] but they have not pursued the hint of *wordbeotunga . . . on ærdagum* [promises . . . in earlier days, *HM* 15–16] which takes us to the prophetic books of Genesis, Isaias, and Ezechiel, as well as the Psalms, for the making and renewal of the promises of the Lord to his chosen; both in Genesis 22:16–18 and in Psalm 88:4 the divine promise is sealed with an oath. In the light of the Bedan passages I have quoted, there is surely sound reason to expect that the problem phrases of *HM* will yield good sense in Bedan terms? (I have preferred to quote Bede, as the most likely of the great biblical scholars to have been available to the Anglo-Saxon poet, but most of the material we are concerned with is part of a much older exegetical tradition.)

Returning, then, to the meaning of the "engraved" *beam* (*HM* 13) which apparently comes from the messenger's lord, we shall at first be inclined to identify it, as Kaske does, either as the Cross, or as a "figure" of the Cross. However, I think we should not discount the intuition of many scholars that the messenger is indicating a rune-staff. How can we reconcile these notions? If *HM* is an example of "multiple allegory" based on scriptural images, as I think it must be, we should not expect to find an imaginary non-scriptural object at its centre. We have to look in the Bible for something resembling a rune-staff. Amongst the prophecies of the future Kingdom there is in fact a rod inscribed with letters, and I would guess—though the poet's language is too imprecise to allow of certainty—that the reader is being invited to think of this rod, which is interpreted as the sceptre of Christ the King, being a symbol of the unity of the Church under his rule. The rod was made by Ezechiel under God's direction by the joining of two sticks, on each of which the prophet had "written" the names of the tribes of north and south, and the joined rod was proffered as a sign to God's people that they would be gathered into one nation "and one king shall be king over them all" (Ezech. 37:22). The symbolism of this rod is explained by Jerome, not

---

[40] M. J. Swanton, *"The Wife's Lament* and *The Husband's Message:* A Reconsideration," *Anglia,* 82 (1964), 269–90, esp. 277f.; Kaske, p. 57. Kaske does in fact quote Psalm 44 within a quotation from Bede, *In Cant.* (*PL,* 91, 1188), but merely to draw attention to the phrase "daughter of the king," comparing *þeodnes dohtor* [king's daughter] (*HM* 47a), Kaske, p. 58, n. 45. See also n. 46, below.

only in his commentary on Ezechiel, but also in his explication of the prophecies of the Kingdom made by Isaias, and he is followed by other exegetes in this.[41] In this way, the sign made by Ezechiel to the warring tribes of Israel has become associated with the spreading of the Gospel of the Kingdom, as envisaged in Chapter 11 of Isaias. It is likely that the poet was thinking of this chapter of Isaias (as well as of Ezechiel's vision of the Kingdom "towards the south") when he was composing *HM:* the lines about the messenger's voyages (*HM* 4–9) could aptly refer to the spreading by the Pen of the written Word of God, perhaps with allusion to the prophecy "for the earth is filled with the knowledge of the Lord, as the covering waters of the sea" (Isa. 11:9). What I am suggesting about the *beam* (13) is that the king's messenger, travelling the world to proclaim the Kingdom, could appropriately point to the inscribed staff he "carries" as a sign of the Lord's promise to unite the nations of north and south. I do not know whether we can assume that our poet would have associated this inscribed "sceptre" with the Cross, so allowing into the riddling line the other possible meanings of *agrof* [fashioned, pierced, etc., 13] which Kaske has proposed and documented.[42]

If the drift of my thinking about the prophecies of the Kingdom is right, we may need to look again at *treocyn* (2) and *tirfæst treow* (12). *Treocyn* is a very odd word, and there seems no reason whatever why the messenger should speak of *"this species* of tree" unless there is some cryptic meaning. The first point I would make is that *cyn* means "kindred," "lineage," "people," as well as "kind," and there are several ways in which the compound might riddlingly refer to Christ and the Church. If the quoted chapter of Isaias is in our minds, we may think of the famous opening verse of that chapter: *Et egredietur virga de radice Jesse* [And there shall come forth a rod out of the root of Jesse], and render the riddling phrase in *HM* (2a) "about the lineage of the Tree," with reference to the Tree of Jesse. Alternatively, *treocyn* could mean "the people of the Cross," suggesting a possible wordplay in *tirfæst treow* (12), if we recall that the Anglo-Saxon translator of Psalm 95:9, *Dominus regnavit a ligno* [the Lord hath reigned from the tree], uses similar wording: *from treowe becwom tirfæst rice* [from the tree came the glorious kingdom].[43] I have already stated my conviction that Psalm 44 (the epithalamium) is an important conceptual source for

41 Jerome, *In Hiezechielem, CCSL,* 75, p. 521, and *In Esaiam, CCSL,* 73, p. 155.
42 Kaske, p. 43.
43 Cp *ASPR,* V, p. 68. The phrase *a ligno* does not occur in the Vulgate text, but both Augustine and Cassiodorus regard it as authentic. I have added it to the Douai translation.

HM, and I note here the coincidence that the *titulus* [superscription] of that psalm includes "For the sons of Core" which Augustine, followed by Ps.-Bede, interprets as "For the sons of the Cross."[44]

I now turn again to the other problem phrases in the poem. The feud [*fæhðo,* 19] which separated the lovers can be referred to the alienation of God and man which the prophets frequently speak of in the language of marital separation (e.g., Osee 2:16, 19–20; Jer. 31:22; Isa. 54:1–6). The repeated promises of the Lord (*HM* 15) were first made when God appeared on the earth and talked with Abraham (cp. *HM* 17–19). At that time the chosen lived in amity with God, but their later history is one of increasing alienation, which culminates in the rejection of Christ by his own people (cp. *HM* 19a–20a).[45]

The Lord's call to his beloved to take ship when the cuckoo's voice is heard has been fully discussed by Kaske, who rightly associates the harbinger of summer with the reunion of the lovers celebrated in The Song of Songs (2:12).[46] The bird's song announces that winter is past (2:11), and the puzzle here, as in *The Seafarer,* is that the cuckoo is called *geomor* [sad]. I would add to the debate about this one small point: that Alcuin, interpreting the "winter" that is past as "the coldness of infidelity" which covered the world up to the Incarnation, hears the *vox turturis* [the voice of the turtle-dove] as calling "Do penance: for the kingdom of heaven is at hand" (cp. Matt. 4:17).[47] A call to repentance perhaps hinted in *geomor* would be appropriate both for *HM* and for the voyage which the Seafarer feels drawn to embark upon.

In the context of a "voyage" which is essentially a spiritual movement towards perfection of life and union with God, the "living man" (*HM* 25) who might hinder the voyager is anyone who would urge the claims of "the world." The "voyager" will remember Paul's words: *Mortui enim estis, et vita vestra est abscondita cum Christo in Deo* [For you are dead; and your life is hid with Christ in God, Col. 3:3]. In the poem the "living man" is contrasted with the living Lord who summons the

---

[44] Augustine, *CCSL,* 38, p. 493.

[45] Abraham's "friendship" with God and God's appearances "in the same land" are recorded in Genesis (e.g., 17:22, 18:1), and notably in 22:16, where the Angel of the Lord who makes the Promise is identified by the exegetes with Christ. Note also Ep. Jac. 2:23: *et amicus Dei appellatus est* [and he was called the friend of God]. Kaske, p. 53, refers the "friendship" (*HM* 19) to the original bond between God and man before the Fall, but the context of the "old promises" makes reference to the blessing of Abraham and his people more appropriate.

[46] Kaske, p. 58. Earlier, Swanton had realized the typological importance of The Song of Songs for the Bride imagery of our poem, though he did not use the other O. T. "marriage" prophecies. He also declared that the oath of *HM* (48–53) must be God's oath, but without positive evidence (cp. *Anglia,* 82, pp. 277 and 289).

[47] Alcuin, *Compendium in Cant. Cant., PL,* 100, 647.

believer to "the land of the living" (cp. Ps. 141:6). The implied antithesis here is similar to the play upon *dryhten* [lord] in *The Seafarer*
(41–43), which contrasts the secular and religious meanings of the
word.

The destination of the voyage, the Kingdom of God, is frequently
imaged as a court where the King rewards his followers. In Psalm 44
the divine King is described as a great warrior, with sword and sceptre
and scented garments; at his right hand stands his gold-adorned Queen.
In *HM* the lady is promised that in the kingdom in the south she can be
a queen dispensing *nægled beagas* [nailed *or* studded circlets, 35] which
presumably are the martyrs' crowns.[48] The King's riches are said to
comprise burnished gold, a fair land, and faithful men (35–39a).
Though the gold might merely suggest the splendour of the Kingdom,
it possibly implies that the Lord's riches are counted in burnished souls
(cp. the Bedan passage quoted above,[49] in which Christ is said to be
"made rich among foreigners, being more powerful among the Gentile
people").[50] The Lord amidst this shining company is contrasted by the
poet with the solitary Christ on earth, rejected by His people (cp. *HM*
39b–43a).

This train of thought requires that *nacan ut aþrong* [he thrust out his
boat, 40] should be a metaphor for the Passion, as indeed Kaske has
already suggested, adducing a passage from Bede which, in my view, is
very important for the interpretation of *HM*.[51] I therefore repeat the
passage here. Bede is educing allegorical meaning from a verse which
tells how the Lord entered into a boat, and his disciples followed him
(cp. Matt. 8:23):

> Mare quod Dominus . . . transire desiderat præsentis sæculi tenebrosus
> accipitur æstus. Navicula quam ascendunt nulla melius quam dominicæ

[48] Cp. Ps. 44:4, 7, 9–10. For the "dividing of the spoils" by the Queen, cp. Ps.
67:13. Both Augustine and Cassiodorus take the "spoils" to be souls rescued from
the Devil (cp. *CCSL*, 39, p. 879).

[49] Cp. n. 38, above.

[50] For the connection of *aurum* [gold] with holy souls in biblical exegesis (and,
incidentally, the journey from north to south as one towards spiritual perfection),
cp. Gregory, *Moralia in Job*, *PL*, 76, 440, on the text *Ab Aquilone aurum veniet*
[Gold will come out of the north] (Job 37:22). (Douai has "Cold cometh out of
the north.") To make sense of the Latin before him, Gregory allegorizes the "gold"
as follows: *Quid per Aquilonem, nisi peccati frigore constricta gentilitas desig-
natur? . . . Quid vero auri nomine, nisi animæ fideles exprimuntur?* [What is
designated by the North, unless it be the Gentiles bound by the cold of sin . . .
What indeed is expressed by the noun "gold" unless it be the faithful souls?] The
association of brightness with holiness and the dullness of impure or unpolished
metal with sin is commonplace.

[51] Kaske, p. 55. The passage quoted is from Bede *In Matt.*, *PL*, 92, 42.

passionis arbor intellegitur, de qua alibi dicitur, Si quis vult post me venire tollat crucem suam, et sequatur me.

[The sea which the Lord . . . wished to cross is taken as the gloomy tur-moil of this present world. The little boat which they climbed into is to be understood as nothing more than *the tree of the Lord's Passion,* of which it is said in another place, If any man will come after me, let him take up his cross and follow me.]

The equivalence Bede makes here between following the Lord by climbing into a small boat and following him by taking up one's cross is precisely the key we need to interpret the central image of *HM*. (Bede is not being extraordinarily fanciful in seeing the Cross as a boat: the same idea is implied in Augustine's comment, *Lignum Christi per mare te traicit* [The tree (wood) of Christ transports you across the sea] in his discourse on Psalm 95:12, and Gregory, elucidating Ezechiel, also speaks of the Cross which *nos ad terram viventium ligno portat* [carries us by wood to the land of the living] across the sea.)[52] I would say, therefore, that *HM* is *partially* "a poem of the Cross," and much of Kaske's argument can be vindicated. But, because Kaske identifies the *messenger* with the Cross, the interpretation he offers must break down at this point: the messenger cannot also *be* the boat. But the dominical call, to "Take up your cross and follow Me," rings true as the heart of the message and is quite properly spoken by the Reed-pen (recording Holy Scripture, the word of God).

This is not an unsupported assertion. The clinching evidence for the unity of *R60* and *HM,* the Reed-pen bringing the Lord's Message, lies in the opening verse of that Psalm of the King and his Bride which Bede quoted when he was thinking of the fire of divine love and the mystical meaning of the journey to the south.[53] Psalm 44:1 reads:

Eructavit cor meum verbum bonum; dico ego opera mea regi. Lingua mea calamus scribæ velociter scribentis.

[My heart hath uttered a good word: I speak my works to the king. *My tongue is the pen of a scrivener* that writeth swiftly.]

(Douai)

"My tongue is the pen of a writer." *Here, I have no doubt, is the germinal text for the theme of* R60-HM. The exegetes take *mea* [my] to

---

[52] Augustine, *CCSL,* 39, p. 1350. The sea is *sæculum* [the world]. Gregory, *In Hiezech., CCSL,* 142, p. 74. Gregory also supports his argument in this place by quoting *Dominus regnavit a ligno* (cp. n. 43).

[53] Cp. n. 38, above.

refer to God, inspirer of Holy Scripture. Augustine explains that His tongue is called a *calamus* [reed, reed-pen] because His words are not ephemeral like spoken utterances, but are enduring like written words. Thus Psalm 44 provides the idea of the reed-pen as a speaker about the King and his beloved, and it is composed, we recall, for "the sons of the Cross."[54] The remaining phrase in the long *titulus* which heads this Psalm is *In finem, pro iis qui commutabuntur* [Unto the end, for them that shall be changed], and in what follows I propose to show how both these ideas are cryptically present in *R60* and *HM* when the poems are joined.

If we now separate in our minds the "engraved" staff of *HM* (13) from the runes which conclude the poem, and focus instead upon the Reed-messenger and the oath, we can, I believe, read the apocalyptic message.

Holy Scripture does include a divine oath uttered in the presence of a reed: the runes employed here can mysteriously suggest various aspects of the biblical message. As with *treocyn* (2), different though related meanings can be read into them. The substance of the oath remains unchanged whichever reading we prefer, but in my judgement there is now very little reason to keep the unusual form *genyre*. (The upholders of *genyre* can still, if they wish, fit its possible sense of "bind together" into the context of the Reed-pen's message, with reference to the united witness of the whole creation to the divine oath.) The *Anglo-Saxon Poetic Records* reading *gecyre* would give us the meaning "I convert" (see Bosworth-Toller for its religious use), implying that the Reed-pen brings the once-heathen runic symbols into God's service, to be reinterpreted as part of the divine message. But simpler sense is made by reading *gehyre* [I shall hear] and referring to the presence of the *calamus* [reed] when Christ utters the oath at His Second Coming. On the literal level, the reed-messenger tells us that he will hear *heaven* and *earth* (and *sea*) and the *man* declaring the oath that the living lord will fulfill his promises. Allegorically, the runes *sigel-rad* and *ear-wyn* proclaim that the oath involves the *sun's journey*, the *joy* beyond the *sea* and the *joy* beyond the *grave*, in allusion to the Passion and Resurrection of Christ. Speaking to the reader and the Church (*nobis, id est Ecclesia sua* [to us, that is, His Church]), the runes declare the message of joy awaiting those who take the *southward journey* to the *happy land*.

The oath in which the earlier divine oaths are confirmed can be no other than the oath recorded in The Book of the Apocalypse (cp. *in*

---

[54] Cp. n. 44, above. The poet's use of Ps. 44 may also, incidentally, explain why he speaks of God and the king separately, when the king is Christ (cp. Ps. 44:3).

finem [unto the end]). The Seventh Angel of this vision, who has "a face like the sun," was, for Bede and his contemporaries, Christ himself. The Angel, standing with his feet upon *earth* and *sea,* raises his hand to heaven and swears *per viventem in sæcula sæculorum* [by Him that liveth for ever and ever] (cp. *be him lifgendum, HM* 52) that "time shall be no longer" and "the mystery of God shall be finished" (Apoc. 10:6–7). Bede explains the significance of this oath as follows:

Angelus per viventem in sæcula jurat dum Christus in nomine Patris veniens incommutabili sua dicta veritate confirmat: *Coelum,* inquiens, *et terra transibunt, verba autem mea non transibunt.*

[The Angel swears "by Him who lives for ever" at the time when Christ coming in the name of the Father confirms His words with immutable truth: saying "Heaven and earth will pass away, but My words will never pass away."][55]

Bede's reference to the immutable words of God will recall to us Augustine's explanation of *Lingua mea calamus scribæ* [My tongue is the pen of a writer] which I quoted earlier. The Reed-pen records the divine oath, in the presence of the witnesses, heaven, earth, and sea, and thus we have at the close of *HM* an allusion to the scriptural guarantee of the truth of this message, which most fittingly brings together the beginning and end of redemptive history, the *eald gebeot* [old promise] of Genesis, and the prophesied coming of Christ at the end of the world.

The *calamus* [reed] who "hears" the Angel's oath is given into John's hand (Apoc. 11:1), not—as one would have expected—to be used as a pen to write down the vision, but to be used as a measuring-rod. The reconciling imagination of the exegetes equates this with the similar *calamus mensuræ* [measuring reed] of the earlier prophetic vision of the new Kingdom "towards the south" given to Ezechiel (Ezech. 40:3). The Man who holds the *calamus* before Ezechiel is likewise identified with Christ. Jerome tells us that the reed *designat gratiam prophetalem* [signifies the gift of prophecy] and adds "concerning which it is written in the 44th Psalm, *Lingua mea calamus scribæ.*"[56] So the poet who composed *HM* could be following an exegetical tradition which associates the Reed both with the immutable words of God spoken through the

---

[55] Bede, *In Apoc., PL,* 161. It is of some interest that a Reed is also present when Christ speaks His last words upon the Cross: *Consummatum est* [It is consummated] (Jo. 19:29–30). This allows symbolic association of the Reed = Scripture with the fulfilment of the scriptural prophecies in His death (cp. Bede *In Marc., CCSL,* 120, p. 635).

[56] Jerome, *In Hiezechielem, CCSL,* 75, p. 553.

prophets and with the "measuring" of souls. This latter association remains latent in the poem and gives the theme its personal application to the reader.

The semantic leap from reed-pen to measuring-rod is no problem for the commentators, who detect a hidden connection between the two. Gregory, for example, explains that the Redeemer holds a *calamus* [pen, yardstick] in His hand to signify that His words are given to be communicated through the learned study of doctors, and that in these studies there is a kind of hidden judgement, since some will profit from their reading and some will not. Like Bede, he quotes: *"Quia vobis datum est nosse mysterium regni cœlorum, illis autem non"* ["Because it is given unto you to know the mysteries of the kingdom of heaven, but to them it is not given," Matt. 13:11]. Therefore, Gregory concludes, the *calamus* [reed, reed-pen] is certainly a *calamus mensuræ* [measuring reed], since in His sacred eloquence His dispensations are hidden.[57] I need not further labour the point that the Reed is in every way the proper "messenger" in this poem of the Kingdom. By choosing the Reed as his speaker, the poet also covertly offers a kind of self-justification for the *ænigma* form he is using, the dark allegory.

We are now in a position to summarize the complex meanings of this highly-wrought, deliberately enigmatic poem. The speaker throughout is the Reed, symbolizing primarily Holy Writ, the word of God. The Reed's own life, dramatically severed from its place of origin and given a more than human power in the new life, is a similitude of the central theme of the poem that man, born in "the world," must be re-born in the life of the spirit and then follow Christ to His Kingdom. (We recall here the last piece of the *titulus* to Psalm 44, "for them that shall be changed.") Corporately, individuals become the Church, *Ecclesia*, setting out upon her "voyage"; the corporate journey will end when the Reed hears Christ declaring that the mystery of God is finished. In its eschatological role, the Reed becomes a "measuring rod," separating the just and the unjust according as they have accepted or rejected the words of God given to mankind in the Scriptures. Thus the life-story of the Reed, which frames the inner story of the exiled King's love, has its own important symbolic statement to make, in the transmuting of the frail creature into a rod of power. Essentially, this is "a poem of the Reed" (rather than "a poem of the Cross"), since *the poem itself is a paradigm for the work of propagating the hidden truths of the gospel,*

---

[57] Gregory, *CCSL*, 142, p. 217. He returns on p. 219 to the idea that the *calamus mensuræ* is Holy Scripture, since, he says, "whoever reads it is measured as to how far he has advanced in spiritual virtue," etc. See also n. 38 above.

in doing which the scholarly writer himself is given a strength and power beyond his native capabilities, and is himself "measured."

Within this frame, as in Psalm 44, the Reed-pen tells us of the King whose betrothed Queen is summoned to him. She must make the journey of faith, clinging to the hope warranted by the Cross. The poet, following exegetical tradition, uses the conceit of *The Cross as a boat* which will bear up the believer during the dangerous voyage. In this striking way, the call to a Christian life is dramatized as a summons to take ship to the south.

In the light of all this, I come back to some textual problems. The expressions relating to the tree, wood, ship, and so on, can now perhaps be regarded as deliberately vague and ambiguous, because they must suggest Tree, (?) sceptre, Cross, and boat. *Ofer meodu* (*R60* 9) probably has a double sense; in addition to the meaning "in the meadhall" it can also carry the meaning "surpassing mead" (i.e., a drink of honey),[58] since (in the Psalmist's words) the testimony and the judgements of the Lord are "sweeter also than honey and the honeycomb" (Ps. 18:11).

Ic tudre aweox (*HM* 2) has been the greatest stumbling-block to interpreters of the poem. It is probably intended to be so, requiring a scriptural key to reveal its meaning. The relevant verse is in Paul's famous disquisition on love (I Cor. 13), in which *love is contrasted with prophecies,* which will fail "when that which is perfect is come" (I Cor. 13:10). The immediately following verse (I Cor. 13:11) unexpectedly and obscurely begins "When I was a child . . . ":

Cum essem parvulus, loquebar ut parvulus, sapiebam ut parvulus, cogitabam ut parvulus; quando autem factus sum vir, evacuavi quæ erant parvuli.

[When I was a child, I spoke as a child, I understood as a child, I thought as a child. But when I became a man, I put away the things of a child.]

This verse in context is taken to mean that Paul has grown in spiritual understanding sufficiently to be conscious that his understanding is still relatively immature, still partial. He continues:

---

[58] Kaske is halfway to this interpretation when he offers, among other paraphrases of *R60* (8–9), "that I who am mouthless should ever bring forth utterance surpassing mead," and suggests that "the words of spiritual assurance" (in his view, spoken by the Cross) "are more sweet and intoxicating than mead itself" (p. 68). Note that Ps. 18:5 also praises the sun, "coming as a Bridegroom" which could be a conceptual source for *sigel-rad* (*HM,* 49).

Videmus nunc per speculum in ænigmate; tunc autem facie ad faciem.

[We see now through a glass in a dark manner; but then face to face.]

This text is constantly quoted by exegetes faced with the obscurities of scripture. (Gregory has recourse to it four times as he wrestles with Ezechiel's mysterious prophecies.) The Latin phrase, *in ænigmate,* "in a dark manner," could also be translated "in an allegory," and the scriptural verse and its context could not fail to be known to a writer of religious riddle-poetry. If *HM* is a dark allegory of divine love, "spoken" by the Reed representing the word of God, the unexplained "I grew up from a child" (*HM* 2) must surely be a direct allusion to Paul's words? The Reed-pen, like Paul, is to proclaim the fulfillment of prophecy in the New Testament relevation of divine love: he has grown in understanding, but his words can still only partially reveal the holy mystery: he must still speak *in ænigmate.*

In order to say many things by allusion, the poet sacrifices surface clarity, and the relatively simple descriptive writing of the opening scene (the so-called *R60*) gives way to a demanding, deceptive style in which several meanings are hidden. It is a kind of writing modern readers may find ingenious rather than inspiring, but I believe that this poet was not simply elaborating a psalm to show his cleverness: he was composing a poem about the principles which governed his own life. One last patristic quotation, this time from Ambrose, may help us to understand what the poet means, in his cryptic fashion, to say:

Harundines fluvios amant, et nos labentia mundi caduca delectant. Tamen hanc harundinem si quis de terræ vellat plantariis et superfluis exuat, exspolians se veterem hominem cum actibus eius et scribæ velociter scribentis manu temperet, incipit non harundo esse sed calamus, qui præcepta cælestium scripturarum penetralibus mentis imprimat, tabulis cordis inscribat.

[Reeds love running waters, and we delight in the fleeting, passing things of this world. Nevertheless, if anyone plucks this reed from the reed-bed and takes off what is not needed, stripping himself of the "old man with his deeds"; and if he trims himself by the hand of "the Writer writing quickly," he begins to be—not a reed—but a pen, which prints the precepts of the heavenly scriptures in the inmost parts of the mind, and inscribes them on the tablets of the heart.][59]

---

[59] Ambrose, *Exp. evang. Luc., CSEL,* 32, p. 224.

17

The Design of the
Old English *Deor*

JAMES L. BOREN

DESPITE THE LARGE NUMBER OF STUDIES DEVOTED IN WHOLE OR IN
part to *Deor,* there seems at this juncture no general agreement concerning the genre of the poem or the context in which this enigmatic work is
to be read. The poem has been most often considered as one of a number
of OE elegies and, more specifically, as a form of dramatic monologue,[1]
but, more recently, *Deor* has been interpreted as a charm,[2] a begging
poem,[3] and a form of *consolatio.*[4] It is, perhaps, inevitable that the

---

[1] P. J. Frankis, "*Deor* and *Wulf and Eadwacer:* Some Conjectures," *MÆ,* 31
(1962), 161–75, has most ingeniously pursued this line of interpretation.

[2] Morton W. Bloomfield, "The Form of *Deor,*" *PMLA,* 79 (1964), 534–41, rpt.
in *Old English Literature: Twenty-two Analytical Essays,* eds. Martin Stevens and
Jerome Mandel (Lincoln, 1968), pp. 212–28. For objections to Bloomfield's thesis,
see Burton Raffel, "Scholars, Scholarship, and the Old English *Deor,*" *NDEJ,* 8
(1972), 3–10.

[3] Norman E. Eliason, "Two OE Scop Poems," *PMLA,* 81 (1966), 185–92, and
"*Deor*—a Begging Poem?" in *Medieval Literature and Civilization: Studies in
Memory of G. N. Garmonsway,* eds. D. A. Pearsall and R. A. Waldron (London,
1969), pp. 55–61.

[4] Diverse textual interpretations have recently supported a reading of the poem
as a form of *consolatio.* Murray F. Markland, "Boethius, Alfred and *Deor,*" *MP,*
66 (1968), 1–4, suggests that the poem's structure derives from Boethius and, in
part, from an error in Alfred's translation of Boethius. Whitney F. Bolton, "Boethius, Alfred, and *Deor* Again," *MP,* 69 (1972), 222–27, agrees with Markland's
identification of genre while differing significantly with him on particular points
of interpretation. Leslie Whitbread, "The Pattern of Misfortune in *Deor* and

obscurity of the poem's allusions and the uniqueness of its form should give rise to varying interpretations, but these widely divergent generic hypotheses suggest that some reconsideration of the assumptions and methodologies of *Deor* criticism might be in order. The text of the poem, however obscure, should function as a restraint upon generic speculation, and the validity of any overall interpretation must finally depend upon the extent to which it offers some aesthetic rationale for the totality of the work. In the case of *Deor,* any valid interpretation of the poem must account for all of the following artistic constituents: the pattern of legendary and historical allusions, the gnomic statement of lines 28–34, the personal fiction of lines 35–41, and the refrain.[5] Enough has been written concerning each of these constituents to make possible a meaningful synthesis of critical opinion supportive of the hypothesis that there is in *Deor* an intrinsic governing design, the discernment of which will account for the disparate elements of this poem, delimit the possible contexts (generic and cultural) in which the poem may be read without distortion, and suggest in some ways the basis for its continuing aesthetic appeal.

The distinctive form of *Deor*—six stanzas clearly delineated in the manuscript by capitalization, end punctuation, and refrain—suggests the possibility of a significant pattern of differentiation and order, in which the five occurrences of the refrain within the first 28 lines of the poem serve to focus attention upon and encourage discrimination between those legendary and historical allusions which have been treated too frequently as serial elements in a homogenous catalogue of misfortunes.[6] The Weland-Beadohild story came intact to the poet, and he

---

Other Old English Poems," *Neophil,* 54 (1970), 167–83, considers the treatment of the theme of misfortune in the OE elegies in order to establish the general influence of the *Consolation of Philosophy* on these distinctive poems.

[5] Bloomfield, for example, proceeds on the assumption that the first five stanzas of *Deor* are essentially irrelevant to the meaning of the poem, since "The chief problems of the overall interpretation of the poem lie in the meaning of 1) the refrain and particularly the word *þisses* and 2) the last stanza which purports to be autobiographical and uses the word I (*ic*)" ("The Form of *Deor,*" p. 537). This hypothesis excludes one-half of the poem from critical consideration.

[6] Markland makes explicit an assumption implicit in much *Deor* criticism when he contends that "The first five stanzas are short and simple, each having essentially the same form and performing the same function as each of the others. Each stanza adds an example but does not change or add to the idea presented in the first stanza. Any one stanza could, in this respect, stand for all five stanzas, or any number more of examples might be added" ("Boethius, Alfred, and *Deor,*" p. 4). I follow Bolton's suggestion that "It would be better if we could do away with the theory that the five stanzas all illustrate the same theme and are merely an agglomerate of exempla and find instead a meaningful pattern of differentiation and number" ("Boethius, Alfred, and *Deor* Again," p. 224).

chose to render apart episodes which the reader, if the allusions were understood at all, must have known to be elements of one story. It may be supposed that the reader is meant to account artistically for the deliberate isolation of each allusion through the use of the refrain. If we proceed on this assumption, a consideration of this pattern of differentiation will show the poet to have had a sense both of total design and structural balance.

Not counting the occurrences of the refrain, six lines are devoted to the opening account of Weland's misfortunes; five lines describe the plight of Beadohild; three lines allude to the story of Mæðhild and Geat; and, at nearly the mid-point in the poem, Theodoric's thirty years in the city of the Mærings is remembered in only two lines. The following account of Eormanric's tyranny continues for six lines, and the final stanza consists of fourteen lines divided evenly into seven lines of philosophical generalization and seven lines of "personal" reflection. The effect of this variation in stanza length is to focus attention upon the Theodoric stanza as the sections progressively narrow from six lines to only two and then widen to an account of six lines and the concluding long stanza. This view of the centrality of the Theodoric stanza is further supported by the recognition of the poet's skillful use of rhetorical variation in the first five stanzas.

Stanzas I and II begin with references to the subject figures (Weland and Beadohild respectively), while stanza III varies the pattern, the poet telling us that

> We þæt Mæðhilde   mone gefrugnon . . .
>
> [We learned that, Mæðhild's moans . . .];[7]

and stanza V similarly begins

> We geascodan   Eormanrices . . .
>
> [We learned of Eormanric's . . .].

But stanza IV continues the verbal pattern of stanzas I and II:

> Ðeodric ahte   þritig wintra . . .
>
> [Theodoric ruled for thirty years . . .],

---

[7] All quotations of *Deor* are from *The Exeter Book*, eds. George Philip Krapp and Elliott van Kirk Dobbie, *ASPR*, III (New York, 1936). Here I accept Kemp Malone's emendation of *monge* to *mone* (see "On *Deor* 14–17," *MP*, 40 [1942], 1–18, rpt. in *Studies in Heroic Legend and in Current Speech* by Kemp Malone, eds. Stefán Einarsson and Norman E. Eliason [Copenhagen, 1959], pp. 142–57.) Translations are my own.

and is thus framed by the variations of stanzas III and V. Our sense of the poem's design in the first five sections is thus prompted both aurally and visually in the sequence

> Weland . . .
> > [refrain]
> Beadohild . . .
> > [refrain]
> We . . .
> > [refrain]
> Theodoric . . .
> > [refrain]
> We . . .
> > [refrain].

The subtle accomplishment of this rhetorical variation is to make the Theodoric stanza verbally parallel to the first two stanzas (and thus to encourage our perception of other linking elements) and at the same time to have the stanza function as a focal point signalling a new development in the poem.

It may be argued further that this view of the first five stanzas will support a reading of the total poem in terms of the following tri-partite scheme:

1. Stanzas I-III (17 lines) consisting of allusions to legendary private misfortunes;

2. Stanzas IV-V (10 lines) consisting of allusions to historical, public misfortunes;

3. Stanza VI (15 lines) consisting of philosophical reflection upon the nature of misfortune and its meaning for the individual.

It can be seen that the three figures which dominate these sections through structural position and thematic significance are Weland, Theodoric, and Deor.

The first stanza of *Deor* tells us that Weland experienced persecution, sorrow, longing, and woe *siþþan hine Niðhad on nede legde, / swoncre seonobende on syllan monn* [after Niðhad laid fetters on him, / supple sinew-bonds on the better man]; and it can hardly be an accident that, from the legendary traditions available to an Anglo-Saxon poet, the *Deor*-poet chose to begin this poem with a description of the plight of Weland, the Daedalus of Germanic legend, who fell from prosperity but was revenged and freed through art. It was a grim but triumphant artist

267

who fashioned a drinking cup from the skull of his persecutor's son and flew from bondage with magic feathered wings; and something of the poet's attitude toward the Weland story may be suggested by his description of the smith as an *anhydig eorl* [strong-minded noble] and a *syllan monn* [better man]. From this perspective, the stanza is not intended simply as an account of the misfortune which befell a legendary figure but is specifically an allusion to the suffering of an artist and to that artist's triumph over adversity through his resolution of mind and skill in artifice. It is this story which prompts the poet to interject the refrain:

> Þæs ofereode,   þisses swa mæg:

> [With respect to that, it passed away; so can this!];

and, although *þisses* introduces the idea of an undefined current misfortune, it is possible to know what happened in the past: misfortune was overcome through thought and craft.

To accept the thesis that the first five stanzas of *Deor* are essentially alike, multiplying examples but not adding to the idea of the first stanza, is to ignore the thematically significant distinction made between Weland in stanza I, described as *anhydig* [strong-minded], and Beadohild in stanza II, of whom the poet says:

>   æfre ne meahte
> þriste geþencan,   hu ymb þæt sceolde

[never could she boldly think how her situation should turn out].

The account of Beadohild is a portrait of passivity in misfortune, and her inability to "boldly think" is in stark contrast to Weland's reaction. Overwhelmed by grief, she cannot see beyond herself and comprehend the enormity of the slaughter of her brothers:

> Beadohilde ne wæs   hyre broþra deaþ
> on sefan swa sar   swa hyre sylfre þing

[Her brothers' death was not to Beadohild so grievous in spirit as her own affair].

It seems likely that the poet saw one possible consequence of adversity to be a debilitating egocentricity,[8] and this limitation of Beadohild's

---

[8] T. A. Shippey, *Old English Verse* (London, 1972), p. 76, suggests that "the point is that when one experiences grief personally it seems too immediate and overmastering to be controlled, outweighing even the deaths of brothers."

vision suggests, in turn, a new dimension to the refrain attached to this stanza. The misfortune of Beadohild did, in fact, pass away, but little did she see and little did she effect that change.

It is possible to see the subsequent obscure account of Mæðhild and Geat as developing themes introduced in the stories of Weland and Beadohild, for the Norwegian and Icelandic ballads which have been suggested as analogues of the *Deor*-poet's version contain elements which make this allusion particularly appropriate at this point in the poem.[9] In the first stanza of *Deor,* the poet alluded to a man who overcame misfortune by means of his art, and, in the second stanza, the allusion was to a woman who could foresee no end to her troubles. In both instances the oppressor was human. If Malone is right in his identification and reconstruction of the Mæðhild-Geat story, in this, the third stanza, the poet may be seen to combine elements from the first two stories: Mæðhild is a woman who laments her inevitable misfortune; Geat is a man who counters misfortune with the power of his art. The important variation is in the nature of the oppression, for the Mæðhild-Geat story introduces the idea of supernatural agency in the misfortunes of mankind. In this reading, Geat is clearly parallel to Weland, Mæðhild is parallel to Beadohild, and the change in the nature of the oppression adumbrates a change in the focus of the poem.

Whether the Theodoric of stanza IV is identified as Wolfdietrich or Theodoric the Great, it has generally been assumed that this stanza continues the tales of misfortunes endured. But, while the first three stanzas are concerned with the victims of misfortune, the fifth stanza clearly alludes to a tyrant who inflicted great suffering on others, and, as P. J. Frankis has correctly observed, "there are no grounds for assuming that the fourth section must agree in form with the first three rather than with the fifth."[10] It can be argued that the fourth stanza ought to be read as alluding to the Ostrogothic Theodoric, the man remembered as the persecutor of Symmachus, Pope John, and, most importantly, Boethius. The rhetorical connections with the first three stanza would then

[9] The ballad analogues proposed by Kemp Malone are concisely summarized in Kemp Malone, ed., *Deor,* 4th ed., rev. (New York, 1966), pp. 8–9. The analogues are alike in referring to a woman lamenting what she sees as inevitable disaster and to a man's skill in harping which counters supernatural malevolence. Malone offers the following translation of stanza III: "We learned that, [namely] Mæðhild's moans, [they] became numberless, [the moans] of Geat's lady, so that that distressing love robbed her of all sleep." He suggests that "The distressing love was that of a water-demon or merman for Geat's wife, who feared for her life and lay abed lamenting instead of sleeping" (*Deor,* p. 9). See Norman E. Eliason, "The Story of Geat and Mæðhild in *Deor,*" *SP,* 62 (1965), 495–509, for a quite different translation and interpretation of this stanza.
[10] *"Deor* and *Wulf and Eadwacer,"* p. 164.

enable us to see the allusions in terms of the following thematic development:

Stanza I—Weland, the persecuted artist;

Stanza II—Beadohild, the antitype of the artist;

Stanza III—Mæðhild as the antitype and Geat as the type of the artist;

Stanza IV—Theodoric, a famous persecutor of an artist.

The concern with Theodoric and Eormanric as tyrants can be seen to represent an intellectual development in the poem from a concentration on the sorrows of misfortune in stanzas I-III to a concern with some sources of misfortune in stanzas IV-V. In this regard, an allusion to a tyrant famous for his persecution of Boethius is especially appropriate to the pivotal section of the poem, for the *Consolation of Philosophy* offers a philosophical pattern analogous to the one being presented in *Deor*.[11] The *Consolation* likewise begins with a concern for the sorrows of misfortune, and it is only after Philosophy expels those muses who encourage Boethius in the perpetuation of his grief that he begins his process of recovery through memory. The recovery of Boethius is represented as being a movement of the intellect from obsessive concern with the particularities of private experience to a comprehension of those philosophical generalizations which offer the only opportunity for understanding and thus enduring the misfortunes of this world. It is possible to see the structural centrality of the Theodoric stanza as having the thematic function of making clear a subtle philosophical progression in the poem, with the poet first proposing the artist as the exemplar of rational man, then exploring the active and passive aspects of individual reactions to adversity, and, finally, moving from the limitations of a subjective reaction to misfortune to a consideration of the sources of misfortune, a prerequisite to the achievement of wisdom represented in the gnomic statement of stanza VI.

Our sense of this thematic development in the first five stanzas is reinforced by the recognition of a shift from a passive reaction to the story of Theodoric—*þæt wæs monegum cuþ* [that was known to many] —to an expression of active interest concerning the story of Eormanric: *We geascodan Eormanrices / wylfenne geþoht* [We learned of Eor-

---

[11] Bolton suggests a much more direct Boethian influence, seeing the first five stanzas as specifically illustrative of the five false goals discussed by Philosophy in Book III of the *Consolation of Philosophy* ("Boethius, Alfred, and *Deor* Again," pp. 224–25).

manric's wolfish thought]—*geascodan* suggesting learning through inquiry or because of active interest. A similar change from a passive to an active attitude is implied by the poet's tacit expression of sympathy for Weland (a "better man") and his later overt judgment of Eormanric —"that was a grim king"—and even the generalized description of Eormanric's victims may be seen to convey an implicit judgment:

> Sæt secg monig   sorgum gebunden,
> wean on wenan,   wyscte geneahhe
> þæt þæs cynerices   ofercumen wære.

[Many a man sat bound by sorrows, in expectation of misery, wished constantly that the reign were ended.]

The *seonobende* [sinew-bonds] of Weland yielded to his craft,[12] but to be *sorgum gebunden* [bound by sorrows] is to be as Beadohild and Mæðhild, not as Weland or Geat. The poet may be implying that, although the lesson of Boethius' imprisonment at the command of Theodoric is *monegum cuþ* [known to many], *secg monig* [many a man] still passively sits, awaiting the passing of misfortune.

In the final stanza, the thematic design of these legendary and historical allusions becomes clear in the poet's conjoining of gnomic wisdom and his account of personal distress:

> Siteð sorgcearig,   sælum bidæled
> on sefan sweorceð,   sylfum þinceð
> þæt sy endeleas   earfoða dæl,
> mæg þonne geþencan,   þæt geond þas woruld
> witig dryhten   wendeþ geneahhe,
> eorle monegum   are gesceawað,
> wislicne blæd,   sumum weana dæl.
> Þæt ic be me sylfum   secgan wille,
> þæt ic hwile wæs   Heodeninga scop,
> dryhtne dyre.   Me wæs Deor noma.
> Ahte ic fela wintra   folgað tilne,
> holdne hlaford,   oþþæt Heorrenda nu,
> leoðcræftig monn   londryht geþah,
> þæt me eorla hleo   ær gesealde.
> Þæs ofereode,   þisses swa mæg![13]

(28–42)

---

[12] *Seonobende* can be read as referring either to leather restraints or the hamstringing of Weland without changing the thematic meaning here.

[13] I follow Kemp Malone in reading lines 28–34 as one sentence and modify the punctuation of this passage accordingly.

[If a sorrowful man sits, deprived of joy, in spirit becomes gloomy, thinks in himself that a multitude of troubles might be endless, then he may consider that, throughout this world, God in his wisdom turns constantly, shows honor—certain fame—to many nobles, a multitude of miseries to some. I will say concerning myself that I was for a time the *scop* of the Heodenings, dear to the Lord. Deor was my name. I held for many years the good position, served the kind lord, until Heorrenda, a man skilled in song, received the estate that the earl, the protector, gave before to me.]

In the context of the poem as a whole, the poet's historical fiction (*Me wæs Deor noma*) has often been seen as simply serving to emphasize the theme of stoic endurance in adversity, and, in the more limited context of the concluding stanza, the personal story of Deor has seemed less important than the poet's description of God as dispenser of *are* and *wea* ["honor" and "misery"].[14] But it is possible to argue that our perception of the aesthetic coherence of this poem depends upon a recognition of the importance of the personal fiction and its inseparability from the philosophical generalization of lines 28-34. It is possible to contend that the *Deor*-poet's assumption of a fictive personality is a carefully considered strategy which allows for a dramatic presentation of the discovery of wisdom in experience through the powers of memory. If the story of Deor is taken as the imaginative beginning of the poem rather than as some felicitous after-thought, one way of describing the rationale underlying the design of the poem as I have so far described it would be in terms of the following hypothetical reconstruction.

In the poet's imagination, Deor is an artist who once enjoyed honor and worldly prosperity until Heorrenda, "the most famous minstrel of Old-Germanic story,"[15] replaced him as *scop* of the Heodenings and received for his skill in song the reward which had been Deor's. Contending with this calamity, Deor seeks consolation in song, and, unable at first to speak directly of his own grief, he thinks instead of an artist like himself, the legendary Weland, who suffered great misfortune. It is in alluding to this story that Deor first suggests to himself some possibility of escape from misery through the agency of art, but he knows at the same time that not all men are like Weland. Some, perhaps even he, will be like Beadohild in their passivity, intellectual distraction, and lack of perspective on their own misfortune. The legendary story of Mæðhild and Geat is then recalled, and there is the suggestion of an increase in Deor's powers as he remembers a story which in its details

---

[14] Malone prints lines 35–42 as a separate stanza in his edition and suggests that the personal fiction may be "a species of postscript" (*Deor*, p. 16).
[15] Malone, *Deor*, p. 16.

represents a synthesis of the meaning which he has seen in the Weland and Beadohild stories. From his stock of traditional tales, Deor remembers those which relate to his own misfortune, and, as he moves from legendary to historical figures, he comes closer to acknowledging his own "historical" downfall. The story of Theodoric suggests a first attempt by Deor to comprehend his own misery by understanding the sources of misery, just as Boethius, the most famous of Theodoric's victims, attempted to overcome misfortune through understanding the nature of changing fortune. Moving from legendary particularities to historical generalities (the victims of Eormanric are spoken of only in general terms), Deor becomes able to abstract from the experiences of the past a liberating wisdom; recognition of the universal principles inherent in individual experience breaks the constraining bonds of emotion, and Deor is at last able to speak of his own misfortune. Like Weland, Deor is released through art.[16]

Read in this way, the poem portrays the unfolding drama of a man acknowledging and reconciling himself to misfortune, and the structure of the poem reinforces our perception of each of the first five stanzas as representing stages in the process of self-discovery which culminates in the "autobiographical" revelations of the concluding stanza. Through a recapitulation and synthesis of earlier details, the *Deor*-poet succeeds in integrating the final stanza into the thematic design developed in the first five stanzas, thus reinforcing the idea that wisdom derives from experience. The first two lines of the concluding stanza (*Siteð sorgcearig, sælum bedæled, / on sefan sweorceð, sylfum þinceð*) echo the descriptions of Eormanric's victims (*Sæt secg monig sorgum gebunden*) and of Beadohild (*on sefan swa sar swa hyre sylfre þing*), and, in realizing that it is the will of a wise God that some men be given *weana dæl* [a share of miseries], the poet's language recalls the story of Weland (who often experienced *wean*) and also the account of Eormanric's subjects (who sat in expectation of *wean*). These same two earlier stories are recalled again in the "autobiographical" second half of the stanza in the phrase *ahte ic fela wintra*, which associates Deor's prosperity with the winter-cold torment of Weland and the thirty-year rule of Theodoric.[17] While these two parallel patterns of repetition serve to link the philosophical

---

[16] Although Bolton is arguing a quite different thesis, his suggestions that the *Deor*-poet "asserts the adequacy of the medium [poetry] to comprehend and order a situation characterized by disorder and instability" ("Boethius, Alfred, and *Deor* Again," p. 226) illuminates one aspect of the poem. Note as well Shippey's comment that "Treating the present as if it were already legendary is a practical demonstration of the controlling power of the mind" (*Old English Verse*, p. 78).

[17] For a different interpretation of this verbal linking, see Whitbread, "The Pattern of Misfortune," p. 169.

and personal sections of the stanza, the description of a period of personal prosperity in language which recalls past misfortunes suggests as well an application of the wisdom which Deor has abstracted from the experiences of the past: prosperity and privation are alike in being manifestations of God's will and the reality of this world.

If the aesthetic rationale for the order and selection of legendary and historical allusions is to be understood in terms of the historical fiction of the poet Deor, it seems possible that the refrain as well is governed by the same thematic design.[18] I have already suggested, in the instance of the first two stanzas, that the refrain may subtly modify or extend the meaning of the story to which it is attached, but, in addition, the refrain can be seen to function in at least three important ways: the separation of the stories by the refrain functions as an objectification of the persona's fragmented imagination; at the same time, the verbal repetition establishes continuity between superficially disparate allusions and suggests the possibility of integration of these stanzas on other than a verbal level; and, finally, the change of the referent for *þæs* in the last occurrence of the refrain confirms our sense of the thematic achievement of the concluding stanza.

If the stanzaic movement of the poem is from intellectual chaos to intellectual order, the refrain might be seen as serving to reinforce our perception of this design, for, in employing the refrain to separate the familiar story of Weland and Beadohild into two distinct stanzas, the poet succeeds in suggesting the intellectual fragmentation of experience and the disruption of memory which is one consequence of an emotional reaction to disaster. As each successive allusion occurs to the poet, it occurs not as an element in a coherent and continuous narrative but as an anecdote rendered discrete by the very refrain which suggests an attempt to discern some coherence, some continuity of meaning, in the misfortunes remembered.

That the poet sees personal understanding as not just following upon the attainment of wisdom but inseparable from it is suggested by the absence of a refrain between the philosophical generalization and the personal history of the final stanza. And, following upon the synthesis of wisdom and experience in the concluding stanza, the final occurrence of the refrain confirms our sense of the thematic design of the poem through the poet's change of the referent for *þæs*.[19] While the refrain in

---

[18] The most commonly held view is that the refrain "serves primarily to point the moral of the example to which it is attached" (Malone, *Deor*, p. 17).

[19] Murray F. Markland, *"Deor: Þæs ofereode; þisses swa mæg,"* AN&Q, 11 (1972), 36, observes that "Modern readers seem always to have read the *þæs* of the sixth stanza as a generalizing demonstrative including all the misfortunes

its first five occurrences demonstrates Deor's vision of his own misfortune as having meaning only with reference to other misfortunes, the acknowledgment of God as the source of all change, good and bad, enables Deor not only to see that misfortune will not last but that it is the nature of the world that fortune also will have an end. The wisdom of the concluding refrain represents the reconciliation of an individual to the reality of his world.[20]

If we seek some context in which the poem, interpreted in this way, might have been read and understood, we may only have to look to the manuscript in which *Deor* has survived, for T. A. Shippey has suggested that

> There is some justification for treating much Old English poetry, and especially the "elegiac" group, as "wisdom literature," nowadays an unfamiliar literary category, but in its day a large and successful one. Many poems in the Exeter Book qualify for such treatment in two ways, first by offering advice, the fruit of wisdom, second by describing the process of acquiring wisdom. . . . Not many of the poems collected in [the Exeter Book] are narrative or even descriptive. Instead the compiler has brought together a very considerable block of admonitory, reflective verse, in which the "elegies" are planted without any mark of distinction, and from which they differ only through their deliberate illusions of personality.[21]

Shippey sees *Deor* as "embodying the Old English philosophy of wisdom with its stress on the strengthening and controlling of the mind" (p. 78), and contends that

> All the "elegies" depend on some . . . alternation of involvement and detachment, and share as a basic theme the ability of the mind to control itself and resist its surroundings. The group as a whole exemplifies the great strength of a traditional literature—the ability to use common thoughts and images as a springboard, so that poets need only small additions to create great effects without baffling their audiences.[22]

---

previously mentioned. In this stanza, however, we should see that the poet contrasts his former happy state which *has* passed, with his present state which *will* pass. The referent of *þisses* is clearly his present state, his own and current misfortune, but the referent of *þæs* is not any or all of the misfortunes listed in the other stanzas; the referent of *þæs* is that former state of happiness."

[20] Shippey says of this change in the referent for *þæs* in the concluding refrain: "The speaker recognizes change in both directions, and so draws even a slightly more Stoic moral from his own history than from anyone else's" (*Old English Verse*, p. 78).

[21] *Old English Verse*, p. 67.

[22] *Old English Verse*, pp. 78–79.

The Design of the Old English *Deor*

A detailed analysis of *Deor* is beyond the scope of Shippey's discussion, but his overall interpretation of the poem within the context of OE "wisdom literature" is substantially confirmed by my own reading of the poem. The diversity and disposition of the poem's artistic constituents may be understood without generic speculation, but to interpret the poem's subtleties of structure and allusion in terms of a governing aesthetic design does not preclude generic identification. The design of *Deor* which I have attempted to describe should allow us to see the poem simultaneously as an example of OE "wisdom literature" and as an intrinsically explicable work of art.

Biblical Narrative
THE OLD TESTAMENT

18

The Fall of Angels and Man in the Old English *Genesis B*

THOMAS D. HILL

THE OLD ENGLISH *Genesis B* IS IN SOME WAYS ONE OF THE MOST PUZ-
zling poems in the corpus of Old English poetry. The poem is, as has
been recognized from the time of Sievers, a translation of an Old Saxon
original and in addition to being the only Old English poem (as far as
we know) translated from another medieval vernacular language, it is
also apparently unique in its presentation of significant aspects of the
narrative of the fall of man.[1] The crucial biblical texts are themselves so
spare that virtually every poet or dramatist who attempted to retell the
narrative found himself impelled to elaborate upon the biblical account,
but the version of the story of the fall in *Genesis B* differs quite markedly
from its biblical exemplar. There are thus both differences of detail—
Adam and Eve are tempted by a demon in the likeness of an angel rather
than by a serpent, and must choose between the (biblical) tree of life
and a tree of death[2] which has no counterpart in the Bible; and more

---

[1] For discussion of *Genesis B* in comparison with various other Latin and vernacular versions of the narrative of the fall of man see J. M. Evans, *Paradise Lost
and the Genesis Tradition* (Oxford, 1968) pp. 151–67 *et passim.*

[2] This contrast between a tree of life and a tree of death (*Genesis B,* 460–81) is
apparently a prominent feature of gnostic speculation concerning man's primal
state. For discussion and references see Henri-Charles Puech, "The Prince of Darkness in His Kingdom," in *Satan* (New York, 1951) p. 129. This work is based
upon a volume of *Études Carmelitaines* (1949). See also Tertullian, *Aduersus*

importantly, crucial features of the Old Testament narrative seem to be obscured. According to the third chapter of Genesis, Eve is primarily motivated by her desire to be "as God, knowing good and evil" while in *Genesis B* the poet alters this aspect of the narrative and depicts Eve as deceived by the devil. Far from rebelling against the commands of God, Eve believes she is fulfilling the will of God and saving Adam from God's wrath. The poet explicitly says that Eve, in tempting Adam to eat the fruit, acted in good faith. *Heo dyde hit þeah þurh holdne hyge, / nyste þæt þær hearma swa fela, / fyrenearfeða, fylgean sceolde / monna cynne* [She did this though with good intent, she did not know that so much sorrow and grievous sin should result to the human race, 708–10].[3]

This aspect of the poem has always attracted a good deal of attention and a number of critics have discussed this problem fairly recently. J. M. Evans has argued that the seemingly heterodox aspects of *Genesis B* are derived from Christian-Latin literary tradition, notably Cyprian's *Heptateuchos,* and that the poet was fundamentally concerned with exonerating Adam and Eve.[4] Rosemary Woolf has discussed the problem of the exoneration of Eve in *Genesis B* and suggested that Eve was not to be excused since she listened to the devil "with a willful credulity springing from nascent vanity."[5] John F. Vickrey has discussed the poet's description of Adam as a *selfsceaft guma;* he glosses the hapax legomenon *selfsceaft* as "self-fated" in the sense that Adam was created free to choose his destiny and goes on to argue that the poet's presentation of the fall of Adam and Eve reflects the traditional allegorization of the fall in which Adam represents reason, Eve bodily sense, and the serpent temptation.[6] Although I would agree with the substance of Vickrey's discussion of the poem, I would argue that his suggestions are relevant to the pattern of the narrative of *Genesis B* as a whole; and I

Marcionem, II, 12, *CCSL,* 1, 489, (*Pl* 2, 325). Tertullian speaks of the *arborem agnitionis, mortis et vitae* [tree of knowledge, of death and of life], a formulation which although orthodox is one which could be misconstrued. Gnostic (dualist) imagery though not, apparently, gnostic thought was current in Anglo-Saxon England; see Rudolf Willard, "Two Apocrypha in Old English Homilies," *Beiträge zur Englischen Philologie,* 30 (Leipzig, 1935), 30.

[3] All quotations of Anglo-Saxon poetry are from *ASPR,* 6 vols., eds. George P. Krapp and Elliott van Kirk Dobbie (New York, 1931–53) by line numbers.

[4] *Genesis B* and its Background," Parts I and II, *RES,* 14 (1963), 1–16, 113–23.

[5] "The Fall of Man in *Genesis B* and the *Mystère d'Adam,*" *Studies in Old English Literature in Honor of Arthur G. Brodeur,* ed. Stanley B. Greenfield (Eugene, Oregon, 1963), pp. 187–99. The phrase I quote is from p. 196.

[6] " 'Selfsceaft' in *Genesis B,*" *Anglia,* 83 (1965), 154–71. Vickrey has written two other important papers on *Genesis B,* "The Vision of Eve in *Genesis B,*" *Speculum,* 44 (1969), 86–102, and the "*Micel Wundor* of *Genesis B,*" *SP,* 67 (1971), 245–54.

would like to review his arguments and then discuss the fall of Adam and Eve as one episode within a larger structure. Probably the simplest place to begin is with Vickrey's discussion of the hapax legomenon *selfsceaft,* concerning which he remarks:

> . . . because *Genesis B* was a close interdialectal translation from Old Saxon it is probably justifiable to assume that the Old Saxon poem had **self-giskefti(e) gumo* at this point. As *metodi-giskaft* and *wurd(i)-giskefti* signify "dispensation from God or fate" (or, loosely, "fate"), so the analogous *selfsceaft* signifies "dispensation by oneself" or "self-fate, self-destiny."
>
> A passage in Ælfric is apposite: "Næs him [Adam] gesceapen fram Gode, ne he næs genedd, þæt he sceolde Godes bebod tobrecan, ac God hine let frigne, and sealde him agene cyre, swa he wære gehyrsum, swa he wære ungehyrsum." If Adam's transgression "was not ordained him from God, nor was he compelled to break God's commandment" it was ordained by himself: Adam could be said to have been **self-gesceapen* in that if he had free will, then what befell him was of his own determining.[7]

This discussion of *selfsceaft* seems fundamentally sound; and the argument is strengthened by the fact that while *selfsceaft* is a hapax legomenon in Old English, and the corresponding Old Saxon form **self-giskeftie* is unattested, a cognate form bearing approximately the same meaning Professor Vickrey suggests is attested in Old Icelandic. In the *Atlamál in graenlenzco* after the death of Gunnar and Hogni, Atli addresses Guðrun as follows: *Morginn er nú, Guðrun, mist hefir þú þér hollra, / sums ertu siálfscapa, at hafi suá gengit*[8] [It is now morning, Guðrun, you have lost dear ones; you are somewhat responsible that it has turned out this way]. The usual translation of *sums ertu siálfskapa,* "you are responsible to some degree," or "somewhat to blame," corresponds to Professor Vickrey's gloss of *selfsceaft.* Again, the phrase *sjálfskapa víti,* which means "evil for which one is responsible for oneself," is attested in older and modern Icelandic prose.[9]

But apart from the problem of the meaning of *selfsceaft,* I would like to take up Vickrey's larger argument that the depiction of the fall of

---

[7] Vickrey, p. 158. The passage from Ælfric I translate as follows: It was not ordained for him (i.e. Adam), nor was he compelled that he had to break God's command; but God left him free, whether he would be obedient or disobedient.

[8] *Edda,* ed. Gustav Neckel, rev. Hans Kuhn (Heidelburg, 1962), stanza 68, p. 257.

[9] See for example Hugo Gering, *Vollständiges Wörterbuch zu den Liedern der Edda* (Halle, 1903), **sjálf-skapa,* and Richard Cleasby and Gudbrand Vigfusson, *An Icelandic-English Dictionary,* ed. William A. Craigie (Oxford, 1957), *sjálf-skapa.*

Adam and Eve reflects the traditional allegorical understanding of the fall in which Adam represents reason, Eve sense, and the fallen angel temptation.[10] An immediate problem involves the kind of symbolic meaning which the narrative might bear. One possibility is what Charles Singleton has defined as "allegory of this for that"[11] in which the protagonists of a given narrative are simply figures representing given meanings. Vickrey's comment "that Adam represented reason and Eve the animal bodily sense—almost that Adam *was* reason and Eve *was* sense"[12]—comes close to suggesting that the narrative of *Genesis B* involves this kind of allegory. Though Vickrey qualifies this statement very carefully, the essential problem remains; and I would suggest that one possible resolution of the question is that the symbolic dimension of the Old English poet's depiction of the fall is implicit in the relationship of the characters within the narrative, rather than in his depiction of the characters themselves. That is, Adam is Adam, Eve is Eve, and the fallen angel who tempts them is himself, but the *relationship* of these figures suggests the familiar allegorical pattern in which Adam represents reason, the fallen angel represents temptation, and Eve, who mediates between these two figures, represents the body or rather the body as it exists in human consciousness as sense.

Apart from this attempt to define more clearly the kind of symbolic meaning the narrative articulates, it seems to me that other aspects of Vickrey's important argument can be developed further. The point is that this allegorization suggests a fundamentally hierarchical understanding of the fall. That is, if Adam represents reason, Eve sense, and the serpent temptation, the fall involves a subversion of hierarchy rather than Promethean overreaching as the biblical text itself would suggest. In terms of the allegory, the crucial and irreparable moment at which man is lost is not the moment at which Eve accepts the serpent's suggestion, but rather the moment when Adam yields to Eve's persuasion. When this subversion of hierarchical order is achieved, the fall has occurred, but the burden of guilt rests with Adam rather than Eve.[13]

---

[10] Vickrey cites a number of instances of this commonplace (note 33, p. 164); in my comments on the hierarchical nature of this mode of understanding the fall I am indebted to the discussion of this problem in D. W. Robertson, Jr., *A Preface to Chaucer* (Princeton, 1963), pp. 70–75, *et passim*.

[11] Charles S. Singleton, *Commedia: Elements of Structure* (Cambridge, Mass., 1965), p. 89.

[12] Vickrey, p. 165.

[13] In this context note Augustine's remarks concerning the relative culpability of Adam and Eve: *Sicut enim Aaron erranti populo ad idolum fabricandum non consensit inductus, sed cessit obstrictus nec Salomonem credibile est errore putasse idolis esse seruiendum, sed blanditiis femineis ad illa sacrilegia fuisse conpulsum: ita credendum est illum virum [i.e. Adam] suae feminae, uni unum, hominem*

Again, since the fall involves in these terms the subversion of a hierarchical order, it is the fact of the subversion rather than the precise nature of the sin involved which is important. This allegorization of the fall is in effect a model for all human sin. In one sense, each time a man sins sense has subverted reason. And the crucial passage in *Genesis B* which describes the fall of Adam reflects, I believe, precisely such an understanding of the nature of the fall.

> Heo spræc ða to Adame   idesa sceonost
> ful þiclice,   oð þam þegne ongan
> his hige hweorfan,   þæt he þam gehate getruwode
> þe him þæt wif   wordum sægde.
> Heo dyde hit þeah þurh holdne hyge,   nyste þæt þær hearma swa fela,
> fyrenearfeða,   fylgean sceolde
> monna cynne,   þæs heo on mod genam
> þæt heo þæs laðan bodan   larum hyrde,
> ac wende þæt heo hyldo   heofoncyninges
> worhte mid þam wordum   þe heo þam were swelce
> tacen oðiewde   and treowe gehet,
> oðþæt Adame   innan breostum
> his hige hwyrfde   and his heorte ongann
> wendan to hire willan.   He æt þam wife onfeng
> helle and hinnsið . . . .

(704–18)

[She spoke then to Adam, the fairest of women, continually, until the mind of that man began to change until he believed the promise which

---

homini, coniugem coniugi, ad Dei legem transgrediendam, non tamquam uerum loquenti credidisse seductum, sed sociali necessitudine paruisse. Non enim frustra dixit apostolus: Et Adam non est seductus, mulier autem seducta est, *nisi quia illa quod ei serpens locutus est, tamquam uerum esset, accepit, ille autem ab unico noluit consortio dirimi, nec in communione peccati; nec ideo minus reus, si sciens prudensque peccavit. De civ Dei,* XIV·11, *CCSL,* 48, 433 (*PL* 41, 419). [For as Aaron was not induced to agree with the people when they blindly wished him to make an idol, and yet yielded to constraint; and as it is not credible that Solomon was so blind as to suppose that idols should be worshipped, but was drawn over to such sacrilege by the blandishments of women; so we cannot believe that Adam was deceived and supposed the devil's word to be truth, and therefore transgressed God's law, but that he by the drawings of kindred yielded to the woman, the husband to the wife, the one human being to the only other human being. For not without significance did the apostle say "And Adam was not deceived, but the woman being deceived was in the transgression," but he speaks thus, because the woman accepted as true what the serpent told her, but the man could not bear to be severed from his only companion, even though this involved a partnership in sin. He was not on this account less culpable, but sinned with his eyes open.] I have used the Modern Library translation of this passage, which Vickrey mentions (p. 167) but does not quote.

his wife told him. She did this though with good intent; she did not know that, as a result, so many sorrows and evils should result to the race of men when she accepted in her mind that she should obey the teachings of the evil messenger. But she thought that she would obtain the favor of the king of heaven by those words so that she showed such a sign to that man and promised good faith until Adam in his breast changed his thought and his heart began to accede to her will. He took from the woman Hell and death . . . .]

Eve is in effect subjectively innocent—she acted *þurh holdne hyge*— and this depiction of her relationship to Adam suggests the relationship of sense to reason in the medieval Christian "model" of the human personality in that the former is unavoidably accessible to temptation. A man can decide to forego an illicit good, but he cannot help being aware that it is attractive. Again, Vickrey remarks in passing that the clause in which the poet states that Adam *þam gehate getruwode / þe him þæt wif wordum sægde* (706–07), is inconsistent with the suggestions elsewhere in the poem that Adam represents reason. But the point is that Adam (reason) should have followed his own judgment rather than trusting the promises of Eve (sense). And the crucial phrase *oðþæt Adame innan breostum / his hyge hwyrfde and his heorte ongann / wendan to hire willan* suggests the subversion of reason by sense rather more precisely than has been recognized. Adam yields *innan breostum* and his *heorte* accepts Eve's desire; in terms of early medieval physiology the heart is thought of as the physiological seat of the reason. According to Isidore, *splene ridimus, felle irascimur, corde sapimus, iecore amamus* [We laugh from the spleen; we become angry from the gall-bladder; we think from the heart; we love from the liver.][14]; and the Irish-Latin compilation the *Liber de Numeris* expresses a similar view of the physiological basis of psychology: *homo habet in corde intellectum . . . in splene risum, in felle iram, in iecore amorem* [A man has intellect in the heart . . . laughter in the spleen, anger in the gall-bladder, and love in the liver].[15] In Old English poetry this conception is attested in *Maxims I*, in which the poet remarks that *snyttro in breostum / þær bið þæs monnes modgeþoncas* [wisdom is in the breast, where a man's thoughts are, 122–23]. Thus the poet's explanation that Adam's "heart" yielded to Eve's persuasion is more precisely meaningful than critics have sug-

[14] *Etymologiae*, ed. W. M. Lindsay (Oxford, 1911), XI, i, 127.
[15] There is no edition of the full text of the *Liber de Numeris*. The passage I quote is from the study of R. E. McNally, *Der irische Liber de numeris: Eine Quellenanalyze des pseudo-Isidorischen Liber de numeris*, Inaugural—Dissertation, (Munich, 1957), p. 34.

gested, and indicates that Adam's reason is affected in the process of the fall.[16]

One further point about the presentation of the fall of man in *Genesis B* is the question of the nature of the sin involved. Vickrey points out that the poet does not specify precisely what the sin of Adam and Eve is, but suggests that the audience probably would have inferred that their sin was in fact pride.[17] While Vickrey's suggestion is reasonable enough, I would emphasize that this hierarchical mode of viewing the fall does not necessarily involve any particular sin. It is, rather, like Gregory's identification of the four sequential stages of sin as suggestion, delectation, consent, and *defensionis audacia* [the presumption of resistance; i.e. hardened wickedness],[18] a model of the psychological and spiritual process of sin in general. In terms of the allegorical pattern in which Adam is associated with reason, Eve sense, and the serpent temptation, temptation deceives the sensual aspect of the human personality, which in turn "persuades" the rational aspect to accede to its will. But neither the literal narrative of the poem nor the allegorical pattern which the literal narrative suggests specifies what particular sin the fall involves. Both narrative and allegory are rather concerned with the subversion of hierarchical order which is involved in the commission of any sin.

There is, however, a larger problem which to my knowledge has yet to be seriously discussed in the critical literature on the poem, and it is a very basic one. Assuming that the narrative of the fall of Adam and Eve does in fact reflect this traditional allegory, the question still arises as to why the poet chose to depict the fall in these terms. The text of Genesis does provide a perfectly coherent account of the fall of Adam and Eve: the biblical account of the fall with its emphasis on Promethean overreaching is certainly no less subtle and is more intellectually coherent than this allegorization of it. One could argue that the poet simply chose

---

[16] Cf. in this connection lines 530–31 and lines 825–26. The conception that the heart rather than the brain is the seat of reason is ultimately Aristotelian in origin. On this topic see Charles Singer, *A Short History of Anatomy and Physiology from the Greeks to Harvey* (New York, 1956), pp. 19–20. Plato, however, had maintained that the cognitive faculty is situated in the brain, and this belief is perhaps attested in the Old English dialogue *Adrian and Ritheus: Saga me hwær byð mannes mod. Ic þe secge, on þam heafde and gæð ut þurh þone muð.* [Tell me where is a man's intelligence? I tell you (it is) in the head and emerges from the mouth.] (See *The Dialogue of Salomon and Saturnus*, ed. J. M. Kemble [London, 1848] p. 202; the text I have quoted is according to the forthcoming edition which J. E. Cross and I are preparing.) At any rate, the current and authoritative view was that one reasoned with his heart.

[17] Vickrey, p. 168–69.

[18] *Moralia in Job*, IV, xxvii, 49; *PL*, 75, 661.

to reorder the narrative of the fall in terms of a traditional allegorization of it, but the question can be answered less arbitrarily.

Genesis B is of course a fragment, but we have enough of the poem so that we can discern something of the dialectical structure of the work as a whole. The text, as it is preserved, begins with God's instructions to Adam and Eve, and the poet then narrates the fall of the angels who, after they have been cast down to Hell, plot the temptation of Adam and Eve. And it is at this point that the narrative of the fall of Adam and Eve begins, with which most critics have been primarily concerned. But the narrative of *Genesis B* involves the fall of Lucifer and his angels as well as the fall of man. And it is obvious from simply glancing at the description of the fall of the angels in *Genesis B* that the Promethean overreaching, which according to the Old Testament was Eve's primary motivation for yielding to the persuasion of the serpent, is here attributed to Satan and his angels. That Satan was motivated by pride and that he wished "to live according to himself"[19] is of course a commonplace in Christian theological literature of this period and later, but the poet's emphasis on Satan's overreaching is marked. Satan is frequently characterized as proud and unwilling to serve God;[20] and the poet remarks at the conclusion of his narrative of the fall of the rebellious angels that their punishment was a consequence of their pride.

> Fynd ongeaton
> þæt hie hæfdon gewrixled   wita unrim
> þurh heora miclan mod   and þurh miht godes
> and þurh ofermetto   ealra swiðost.

> (334–37)

[The devils perceived that they had obtained a countless number of torments because of their great pride and because of the power of God and because of their arrogance most of all.]

I would suggest then that the pattern of the dialectical structure of the poem as a whole is as follows: the poet was concerned with the fall, but

[19] Augustine, *De civitate Dei*, XIV, 3, *CCSL*, 48, 418, (*PL*, 41, 406—07).

[20] The fact that Satan's rhetoric in this part of the poem is very markedly "Germanic" has frequently been noted, but the implications of the fact that it is Satan who speaks like the leader of a rebellious Germanic warband has received less attention. That Milton is implicitly criticizing the classical tradition by depicting his devils as classical rhetoricians and by associating them with classical mythography is widely recognized in contemporary Milton criticism. I wonder whether the *Genesis B* poet might not be attempting to make a similar point in depicting Satan as a rebellious Germanic warrior?

the biblical narrative of the fall was understood morally in terms of Promethean overreaching and allegorically in terms of subversion of hierarchy. While these two modes of understanding the fall are not necessarily contradictory, it is difficult to see how a literary artist could construct a narrative which would reflect both a "Promethean" and "hierarchical" view of the fall. The poet, I suggest, resolved the aesthetic problem which the two modes presented him by depicting the fall of the angels in terms of Promethean overreaching, and the fall of man in terms of the subversion of hierarchical order.

This resolution of the difficulty created by various modes of understanding the fall involves the assumption that the fall of the rebellious angels is an event which is intrinsically relevant to man's own history. In one sense every time a man sins out of pride—out of a desire to be sufficient unto himself—he recapitulates the fall of the angels, and this is a point which the poet emphasizes. After Satan has completed the speech in which he asserts his own autonomy, the poet remarks:

> Þa hit se allwalda   eall gehyrde,
> þæt his engyl ongan   ofermede micel
> ahebban wið his hearran   and spræc healic word
> dollice wið drihten sinne,   sceolde he þa dæd ongyldan,
> worc þæs gewinnes gedælan,   and sceolde his wite habban,
> ealra morðra mæst.   Swa deð monna gehwilc
> þe wið his waldend   winnan ongynneð
> mid mane wið   þone mæran drihten.
>
> (292–99a)

[At that time the ruler of all heard everything—that His angel began, with great pride, to exalt himself against his superior and spoke arrogant words, foolishly against his Lord. He had to pay for that deed, endure grief for that strife, and had to bear suffering, the greatest of all evils. So does each man who begins to strive against God, criminally against the glorious Lord.]

The gnomic injunction with which this passage concludes explicitly associates the fall of angels and the fall of man, and the poet's emphasis on this association is significant for the larger structure of *Genesis B*. Satan's fall is not an isolated event, since it foreshadows the fall of Adam and of the "fall" of any of his descendents who *winnan ongynneð / mid mane wið þone mæran drihten*. [begin to struggle, criminally, against the glorious Lord].[21]

---

[21] This conception is quite widely attested. Thus Gregory, for example, comments on the fact that Satan's fall is in effect an *exemplum* on the danger of pride. *De quo idcirco tam mira in quibus fuit, et quae amisit insinuat ut territo homini*

If these suggestions seem tenable, then the intellectual structure of *Genesis B* is comparable to that of the *Dream of the Rood*. In both poems the fundamental event with which the poem is concerned is polysemous in that it bears more than one significance in traditional Christian exegesis. The fall thus involves both Promethean overreaching and subversion of hierarchical order, and the crucifixion involves both Christ's humiliation and defeat as a man and His triumph and vindication as God, since it was only through the Cross that He could redeem the world. In the *Dream of the Rood* the poet resolves this difficulty by having the cross itself speak for the suffering human aspect of Christ's nature and by depicting Christ Himself in terms of His Divine Nature as a *geong hæleð, (þæt wæs god ælmihtig) strang ond stiðmod* [young man (that was God almighty) strong and valiant, 39–40].[22] Similarly in *Genesis B* the poet depicts the fall of the angels in terms of Promethean

---

ostendat quid ipse si superbiat de elationis suae culpa passurus sit si feriendo illi parcere noluit, quem creando in gloriam tantae claritatis elevavit. Consideret ergo homo quid elatus in terra mereatur, si et praelatus angelis angelus, in caelo prosternitur [But He (i.e. God) mentions these wondrous things of him, in what he had, and in what he lost, expressly to show to awestruck man, what, if guilty himself of pride, he is likely to suffer from the sin of his haughtiness; if He would not abstain from smiting him, whom He exalted at his creation to the glory of such great brightness. Let man then consider what he deserves for his pride on earth, if even an Angel, placed above other Angels, is cast down in heaven, *Moralia in Job*, XXXII, xxiii, 49; *PL*, 76, 666. I have used the Library of the Fathers translation.] Gregory's remarks are paralleled in Old English poetry in *Christ and Satan* in which the poet remarks that Satan's fall should teach us all to beware of *oferhygd*.

> Forþan sceal gehycgan   hæleða æghwylc
> þæt he ne abælige   bearn waldendes.
> Læte him to bysne   hu þa blacan feond
> for oferhygdum   ealle forwurdon.
>
> (193–96)

[Therefore, each man ought to think that he not offend God's Son. Let how the black devils were wholly destroyed for pride be a sign to him.]

[22] See Rosemary Woolf, "Doctrinal Influences on *The Dream of the Rood*," *MÆ*, 27 (1958), 137–53. Note in this connection O. B. Hardison's remarks on the aesthetic significance of Amalarius' allegorization of the "seating of the Bishop" as an image of Christ in glory which is juxtaposed with the "historical" allegorization of the remainder of the Mass as a reenactment of the crucifixion and resurrection of Christ. ". . . a remarkable eschatalogical effect is produced. Instead of being limited to a single plane, the action of the Mass moves forward on two visible planes or stages. The first is the presbyterium. It is the plane of eternity, from which the ascended Christ looks down on suffering humanity. The second is the altar. It is the plane or stage of history upon which, amid the mobs of Jerusalem and the sorrowing disciples, the incarnate Christ is crucified and dies. These two planes intersect at the moment of sacrifice in a manner which transcends the normal limits of allegory" (*Christian Rite and Christian Drama in the Middle Ages* [Baltimore, 1965], pp. 54–55).

overreaching and that of man in terms of subversion of hierarchy, and thus succeeds in presenting both traditional modes of understanding the fall in the scope of a single narrative. But this parallel between the *Dream of the Rood* and *Genesis B* is obviously not exact, since in the former poem, the poet is concerned with depicting two aspects of the same event simultaneously while in *Genesis B* the fall of Satan and that of Adam are separated by an interval of time. Again, the various aspects of the crucifixion which are depicted in the *Dream of the Rood* seem in some ways to suggest various levels of the traditional four-fold system of biblical exegesis—specifically the historical and the allegorical levels, while the relationship of the two narratives of the fall in *Genesis B* seems closer to that kind of typological relationship which exists between two narratives that prefigure the same event. Part of the significance of a series of events which are all types of a given moment of salvation history lies in the fact that each event defines a different aspect of the event which is prefigured. And it is this dimension of typological history which perhaps suggested the kind of structure which the Old English poet imposed upon his version of the narrative of the fall. The fall of Satan and the fall of Adam suggest different aspects of the fall as it is still experienced—in terms of a Christian understanding of history at any rate—in our own experience.

But the poet's achievement is, I believe, greater than this discussion of it might suggest. One of the fundamental principles of Anglo-Saxon art and literature is that of interlace—the interweaving of the various elements of a pattern within the design as a whole.[23] And the principle of interlace in both art and literature involves what might almost be described as a dialectical tension—the eye follows the pattern but the opposition between its various elements is not resolved. One could argue that the structure of *Genesis B* resembles in some ways an interlace pattern. Both modes of understanding the fall are valid, but they reflect quite different aspects of that event. The poet however, rather than simply presenting either one or the other, juxtaposed the moral and allegorical understanding of the fall, and by this juxtaposition achieved a structure of considerable complexity.

I would like to conclude this essay with a final suggestion which cannot be either proven or conclusively ruled out of consideration. One of the common assumptions of medieval literary scholarship is that the vernacular religious poetry of the early middle ages, which was presumably intended for a relatively unlearned audience, is generally less

[23] For discussion of interlace in connection with Old English poetry, see John Leyerle, "The Interlace Structure of *Beowulf*," *UTQ*, 37 (1967–68), 1–17.

intellectually sophisticated than contemporary Latin literature. Certainly this is an apparently reasonable assumption, and yet I wonder whether it is as valid as is generally assumed. That is, the vernacular, precisely because it was a relatively obscure medium, had certain advantages over the more widely accessible medium of Latin. The poet who wrote *Genesis B* was in no sense heterodox—at least as far as we can tell from the poem—but he certainly does treat the events of the fall with an intellectual and imaginative freedom which is somewhat surprising, and the poem certainly could be misconstrued. One can see how a learned poet writing in the vernacular, which would be accessible only to a relatively small group of friends and countrymen, might well feel less inhibited than if he were writing, potentially at least, for all Europe. Again, the vernacular is by definition a less formal, less serious medium than Latin. I do not want to exaggerate my point; certainly the assumption that much vernacular poetry was intended for a relatively unsophisticated audience is sound. Nor do I wish to concern myself with the problem of intellectual freedom in early medieval Europe—though it is worth remembering that even as learned and intellectually responsible an author as Bede was accused of heresy. The tendency to feel less inhibited in a more private, less formal context is after all a universal one. One of the current and persistent rumors about the various developments in contemporary Roman Catholic thought is that the radical Dutch theologians enjoy a measure of freedom which their French and German colleagues do not, simply because the conservatives who might object are unable to read Dutch. And I wonder whether the intellectual freedom which the *Genesis B* poet exhibits reflects the fact that he is writing for a circle of sophiticated and sympathetic readers in the relative privacy of the vernacular.

19

More Scriptural Echoes
in the Old English *Exodus*

JOSEPH B. TRAHERN, JR.

IN HIS EDITION OF THE OLD ENGLISH *Exodus,* EDWARD B. IRVING, JR. remarks that "if we say that the basic source of the poem lies in the 13th and 14th chapters of the book of Exodus, there is no question that the source next in importance is the rest of the Vulgate itself."[1] Though the research on the poem in the past twenty years has provided many useful insights through the liturgy, the baptismal rite, exegetical tradition, etymology, and related ancillary material, Irving's assertion remains, I think, basically valid, and in fact more clearly documented than before.[2] In a recent essay intended primarily to update the intro-

---

[1] Edward B. Irving, Jr., *The Old English* Exodus (Yale Studies in English 122, New Haven, 1953; rpt. Archon Books, 1970), p. 17 (cited hereafter as Irving, ed.). To supplement the reprint, Irving provides a thorough set of "New Notes on the Old English *Exodus,*" *Anglia,* 90 (1972), 289–324 (cited hereafter as Irving, "New Notes"); and he offers a useful supplemental introduction to the poem in *"Exodus* Retraced," in *Old English Studies in Honour of John C. Pope,* ed. Robert B. Burlin and Edward B. Irving, Jr. (Toronto, 1974), pp. 203–23 (cited hereafter as Irving, "Exodus Retraced"). Citations of and references to the text of the Old English *Exodus* are to Irving's edition, as modified by the two supplemental articles. A major modification which should be singled out is Irving's rejection of his earlier rearrangement of the text and his return to the manuscript order, with consequent renumbering of lines.

[2] See the bibliographical references in "New Notes" and the notes to *"Exodus* Retraced."

ductory material of his reprinted edition, Irving points particularly to the influence of the Psalms and the book of Wisdom upon the poem. The concluding chapters of the latter, he notes, "demonstrate the operation of divine wisdom and justice in sacred history, particularly in the Exodus."[3] It is well-known, moreover, that the eleventh chapter of Hebrews offers, from a New Testament perspective, the same sort of synopsis of Old Testament history to illustrate the operation of faith. And another book of sapiential lore well-known to the Old English, Ecclesiasticus, offers a similar synoptic view of sacred history by way of its lengthy catalogue of illustrious men. My intention here is to examine four brief passages in the Old English *Exodus* which can be appreciated more fully in the light shed upon them by the three books of scripture just mentioned, and to demonstrate that in each instance the poet has selected details from these apparently disparate books of the Bible in precisely the narrative or dramatic context in which he employs them in the poem.

I

Hwæt, we feor and neah   gefrigen habað
ofer middangeard   Moyses domas,
(wræclico wordriht   wera cneorissum—
in uprodor   eadigra gehwam
æfter bealusiðe   bote lifes,
lifgendra gehwam   langsumne ræd)
hæleðum secgan!   Gehyre se ðe wille!

(*Exodus*, 1–6)

[Lo, we have heard men speak of the judgments of Moses, far and near throughout the world—a marvelous law in words for the generations of men—a recompense of life in heaven for each of the blessed after the baleful journey, a long-lasting counsel for each of the living. Let him hear who will!][4]

The opening lines of *Exodus* are still the subject of considerable conjecture. Robert T. Farrell considers the passage "an involved and rather difficult sentence, which none the less clearly sets forth the theme to be developed, Moses' commands (*domas*). They constitute a wonderful spoken, or oral, law (*wordriht*) for the races of men, and offer an 'amendment for life' (*bote lifes*) for those in heaven, and a long-lasting

---

[3] Irving, "*Exodus* Retraced," pp. 206–07.
[4] The modern English renderings of quotations from Old English are my own. The English translations for quotations from the Vulgate are from the Douai version.

counsel for the living."[5] Irving's interpretation is roughly similar, though less assured: "the general meaning of this introductory passage is fairly clear, but the syntax presents a puzzling problem . . . The whole passage from 3 to 6 represents loosely the message given by Moses; within that passage the phrases may be taken in several ways. *Domas, wordriht, bote lifes* and *langsumne ræd* seem to be loosely parallel, with the last two representing distinctions or qualifications."[6] The essential elements of both these interpretations can, I think, be reinforced through the examination of a similar collocation of almost identical distinctions in the description of Moses which opens chapter 45 of Ecclesiasticus—a description from which other echoes can be heard as the *Exodus* poet begins to frame his narrative. Ecclesiasticus 45:6 states that God *dedit illi* [Moses] *coram præcepta et legem vitæ et disciplinæ* [gave him commandments before his face and a law of life and instruction], a statement which corresponds both in sequence and in sense to *wordriht, bote lifes*, and *langsumne ræd*. The collocation of *præcepta* and *coram* (which often means "by word of mouth") lends support to Farrell's assertion that *wordriht* is associated with oral law and to Irving's contention that *bote lifes* and *langsumne ræd* are specific qualifications of the first term. There are other, less specific echoes in the poem of the opening of Ecclesiasticus 45 which indicate not so much direct borrowing as a consciousness of a pre-existing structural synopsis of Moses' career which could be followed in shaping an introduction to a detailed account of the Red Sea journey. Ecclesiasticus 45 opens, for example, with *Dilectus Deo et hominibus Moyses, cuius memoria in benedictione est* [Moses was beloved of God and men, whose memory is held in benediction]. The sense of the latter clause is, of course, conveyed in the conventional, formulaic opening of the poem, following which the Old English poet offers a statement which roughly parallels the first clause, beginning *he wæs leof Gode* [he was dear to God, 12], then expanding upon a series of Moses' virtues, which would have the effect of demonstrating that he was likewise beloved of men—*leoda aldor, horsc and hreðergleaw, herges wisa, freom folctoga* [chief of the people, quick-witted and wise, leader of the army, bold people-leader, 12–14]. Other parallels can be noted,[7] but I would not assert confidently that they are deliberate. The point which can be made, however, is that in choosing to preface his poem about a limited aspect of Moses' career with a broader statement about his hero, the poet makes at least passing use of a similar synopsis which adds further scriptural authority to his endeavor.

[5] Robert T. Farrell, "A Reading of OE. *Exodus*," *RES.* n.s. 20 (1969), 406.

[6] Irving, ed., p. 67. For references to other interpretations of these lines see the notes to them in Irving, ed., and "New Notes."

[7] For example, compare *Ecclesiasticus* 45:24 and *Exodus* 8–11.

More Scriptural Echoes in the Old English *Exodus*

II

Heofon þider becom.

(*Exodus*, 46b)

[Heaven came thither.]

Heofon in this verse has been emended frequently, but without much success. Irving defends the manuscript reading by equating heaven with God.[8] Robinson supports it more convincingly as "a more or less literal descriptive statement added to heighten the awesomeness of the divine punishment," citing "a striking detail from one of the later Old Testament accounts of God's wrath being visited on His chosen's enemy: *inclinavit cælos et descendit*" [he bowed the heavens, and came down.] (II Kings 22:10 and Psalm 17:10).[9] A more convincing parallel is, however, one which appears in the same context as that in which it is employed in the poem. Wisdom 18:14–16 describes vividly the descent of God's word, in the person of the avenging angel, to slaughter the first-born of Egypt:

> Cum enim quietum silentium contineret omnia,
> et nox in suo cursu medium iter haberet,
> omnipotens sermo tuus de cælo, a regalibus sedibus,
> durus debellator in mediam exterminii terram prosilivit,
> gladius acutus insimulatum imperium tuum portans
> et stans replevit omnia morte
> et usque ad cælum attingebat stans in terra.

> [For, while all things were in quiet silence,
> and the night was in the midst of her course,
> thy almighty word leapt down from heaven from thy royal throne,
> as a fierce conqueror into the midst of the land of destruction,
> with a sharp sword, carrying thy unfeigned commandment.
> And he stood and filled all things with death;
> And standing on the earth reached even to heaven.]

Irving has noted "possible parallels" between Wisdom 18:4 and *Exodus* 49–53 and between Wisdom 18:12 and *Exodus* 40–41.[10] The passage

---

[8] See notes to 46b in Irving, ed. and "New Notes."

[9] Fred C. Robinson, "Notes on the Old English *Exodus*," *Anglia*, 80 (1962), 364–65. For other views, see "New Notes" on line 46.

[10] Irving, "*Exodus* Retraced," p. 222, n. 23. Other parallels are discussed in greater detail at p. 207.

under discussion here comes immediately after the passages cited by Irving from Wisdom and between his parallel citations from *Exodus*. It displays, I think, the poet's ability to effect, with remarkable economy, the heaven's coming to earth in the imposing form of the avenging angel who stands upon the earth and at the same time reaches heaven.[11]

III

> . . . nymðe hwylc þæs snottor   in sefan weorðe
> þæt he ana mæge   ealle geriman
> stanas on eorðan,   steorran on heofonum
> sæbeorga sand,   sealte yða;
> ac hie gesittað   be sæm tweonum
> oð Egipte   ingeðeode[12]
> land Cananea,   leode þine,
> freobearn fæder,   folca selost.

(*Exodus*, 439–46)

[. . . unless someone should become so wise in his heart that he alone might number all the stones on the earth, the stars in the heavens, the sand on the seashore, the salt waves; but they, thy people, the noble children of the patriarch, the best of peoples, shall inhabit Canaan land between the two seas, up to the Egyptian people.]

The details cited above from the speech of the *stefn of heofonum* [voice from the heavens] to Abraham are a conflation of at least three biblical passages. The principal one is, of course, Genesis 22: 11–12 and 16–18. There God promises Abraham that, as a reward for his obedience, he will multiply Abraham's seed as the stars of heaven, and as the sand by the sea shore. The statement that only the man who can number the dust of the earth can number Abraham's seed comes, as Irving has noted,[13] from Genesis 13:16: *Faciamque semen tuum sicut pulverem terræ: si quis potest hominum numerare pulverem terræ, semen quoque tuum numerare poterit* [And I will make thy seed as the dust of the earth: if any man be able to number the dust of the earth, he shall be able to number thy seed also]. There is, however, yet a third biblical text

---

[11] The passage at issue from *Wisdom* was incorporated dramatically into portions of the Christmas liturgy. See Allen Cabaniss, *Liturgy and Literature* (University, Alabama, 1970), pp. 53–57.

[12] I am accepting, with Irving, the emendation of MS *incaðeode* here, though not fully convinced that it is necessary. Neither reading is prejudicial to the point being investigated here.

[13] Irving, ed., p. 92

which combines several of these motifs and which, alone of the three, describes the promise of God in the third person, as does the poem, and adds the detail of Abraham's race inheriting "between the two seas." It is the catalogue of illustrious men, which begins in chapter 44 of Ecclesiasticus and which includes Noah, Abraham, and, as we have seen already, Moses. Of Abraham it says:

> ideo iureiurando dedit illi gloriam in gente sua,
> crescere illum quasi terræ cumulum
> et ut stellas exaltare semen eius
> et hereditare illos a mari usque ad mare
> et a flumine usque ad terminos terrae.

(Ecclesiasticus 44: 22–23)

[Therefore, by an oath he gave him glory in his posterity, that he should increase as the dust of the earth, and that he would exalt his seed as the stars, and they should inherit from sea to sea and from the river to the ends of the earth.]

The presence here of the phrase *hereditare illos a mari usque ad mare,* together with the details already noted, provides, I think, conclusive evidence that the poet was following the description of God's promise from Ecclesiasticus. If this is the case, it contributes new evidence to the study of the controversial *be sæm tweonum* of line 443.

The phrase *be sæm tweonum* has been the basis of a number of hypotheses concerning both the origin of the phrase and the influence of *Exodus* on other Old English poetry. It occurs twice in the poem, here and at line 563. Mürkens quite correctly cites Exodus 23:31 as the source for the second occurrence, where the context is completely different—God's series of commandments and promises to the Israelites in the wilderness.[14] Rau's explanation, that the phrase originated in the continental home of the Anglo-Saxons (the two seas being the North Sea and the Baltic) wins at least partial acceptance from Irving, who says that "its widespread occurrence points to the probability that it was a native expression rather than a borrowed phrase. If we accept it as traditional, we have here an astonishing example of the skill with which the poet managed to apply such native phrases accurately to a new context."[15] Klaeber was tempted to trace back to *Exodus* the use of the

---

[14] Gerhard Mürkens, "Untersuchungen über das altenglische Exoduslied," *Bonner Beiträge zur Anglistik,* 2 (1899), 76–77.

[15] Irving, ed., p. 92, citing Max Rau, *Germanische Altertümer in der Angelsächsischen Exodus* (Leipzig, 1889), p. 17.

phrase in *Beowulf, Guthlac,* and the *Paris Psalter.*[16] It is, of course, quite possible that *be sæm tweonum* entered the formulaic word-hoard while the English were still on the continent, and that the two seas which inspired its first use were precisely those suggested. My point here is that three of the uses which constitute a substantial portion of its so-called widespread occurrence in Old English poetry are highly predictable and literal renderings of a scriptural phrase which was probably likewise formulaic (it is, I think, a reasonable inference that the author of Ecclesiasticus knew the phrase from Exodus or the Psalms). And in each of these instances, *be sæm tweonum* is employed to render *a mari usque ad mare* in precisely the same context in poem and scripture, the *Paris Psalter* text translating Psalm 71:8, *Exodus* 563 rendering the Vulgate Exodus 23:31, and, as we now see, *Exodus* 443 rendering Ecclesiasticus 44:23.

IV

He us ma onlyhð
nu us boceras   beteran secgað
lengran lyftwynna.

(Exodus, 530–32)

In a convincing defense of the manuscript reading *lyftwynna,* Robinson translates "He will grant more to us, scholars now tell us, better things, more lasting joys of heaven."[17] I think I detect here an echo, not of the sapiential books, but of chapter 11 of Hebrews, which, as noted earlier, operates in the same fashion from a New Testament perspective, and whose influence on other parts of the poem has been pointed out before.[18] In Hebrews 11:13–16, following an account of how Abraham, through faith, was granted the privilege of fathering the Hebrew race, we are told that his descendants died with the faith:

... non acceptis repromissionibus, sed a longe eas aspicientes et salutantes et confitentes quia peregrini et hospites sunt super terram. Qui enim hæc dicunt significant se patriam inquirere. Et, si quidem ipsius meminissent de qua exierunt, habebant utique tempus revertendi. Nunc autem *meliorem* appetunt, *id est cælestem* [italics added].

[... not having received the promises, but beholding them afar off, and saluting them and confessing that they are pilgrims and strangers on the

---

[16] Fr. Klaeber, "Concerning the Relation between *Exodus* and *Beowulf,*" *MLN,* 33 (1918), 221.
[17] Robinson, pp. 370–72.
[18] See Irving's "New Notes" to lines 362 and 380 ff.

earth. For they that say these things do signify that they seek a country. And truly, if they had been mindful of that from whence they came out, they had doubtless time to return. But now they desire *a better, that is to say, a heavenly country.*]

If the manuscript reading is retained, we have here a striking syntactic parallel between *beteran . . . lengran lyftwynna* and *meliorem . . . id est cælestem,* offered in the same sort of synthesizing context in both the Epistle and the Old English poem. The message is that those patriarchal pilgrims saw the transitoriness of the earth, but that their successful journey typifies for us the promise of a better, heavenly homeland at the end of the voyage. It is in this sense that the words of Moses at the bank of the Red Sea become *ece rædas* [eternal counsels, 516], which, when we use the *gastes cægon* [keys of the spirit, 525], reveal themselves as the message expounded by later *boceras* such as the author of Hebrews and the exegetes who attest to the typological significance of the crossing of the Red Sea.[19]

---

[19] For details concerning the exegetical treatment of the typology of the Red Sea journey, perceptively related to the Old English poem, see James W. Earl, "Christian Tradition in the Old English 'Exodus'," *NM,* 71 (1970), 541–70, esp. 552–54.

The Runic Tradition
CYNEWULF'S SIGNED POEMS

20

The Diction of the
Old English *Christ*

ROBERT E. DIAMOND

CERTAIN ASSUMPTIONS ABOUT THE FIRST 1664 LINES OF POETRY OF
the Exeter Book, traditionally called *Christ,* have come to be accepted
by the majority of scholars in recent years: (1) that the poem is to be
divided into three shorter poems, *Christ I, Christ II,* and *Christ III;*
(2) that *Christ I* ends with line 439, *Christ II* ends with line 866, and
Christ III ends with line 1664; (3) that the lines that have sometimes
been called lines 1665–1693 of *Christ* are rather the first twenty-nine
lines of *Guthlac.* Since Franz Dietrich[1] first described these lines as a
single poem, to which he gave the title *Christ,* a number of scholars
have considered the question of the unity and authorship of this work,
and the majority have decided against unity, seeing these lines as three
separate poems, one on Advent, one on the Ascension, and one on the
Last Judgment.

Of all the studies on this subject, only one provides any very sound
basis for rejecting the unity of *Christ:* Brother Augustine Philip's "The
Exeter Scribe and the Unity of the *Crist.*"[2] He concludes from an
examination of the way the MS is marked that the maker of the book
regarded these lines as three separate and distinct poems.

[1] "Cynevulfs Crist," *Zeitschrift für deutsches Altertum,* 9 (1853), 193–214.
[2] *PMLA,* 55 (1940), 903–09.

That these pieces are juxtaposed in the MS by no means implies that they constitute a single unit, since this is the order in which they would naturally have been arranged by the compiler of the Exeter Book. On the other hand, if the *Christ* had been composed as a single poem, it is most unlikely that the poet would have treated the Advent, Ascension, and Last Judgment without enlarging upon the themes of the Passion and the Resurrection. The very title, *Christ,* it should not be forgotten, is one devised by modern scholars for a combination of three poems which are distinguished unmistakably in the MS. For this hypothetical combination, one is forced to conclude, the MS itself affords not the slightest evidence.[3]

Aside from the MS evidence, the best reason that has been brought forward for rejecting the unity of *Christ* is the position of the runic signature in *Christ II.* The runic signature with which Cynewulf signed that poem comes near the end of the poem, and in each of the other three signed poems of Cynewulf, *Elene, Juliana,* and *Fates of the Apostles,* the runic signature comes near the end of the poem. To maintain that *Christ* is one unified poem by one author is to place the runic signature, which begins in line 797 and ends in line 807, before the middle of a 1664-line poem, a position totally different from the position of the signatures in the other signed poems.

Most of the scholars have based their rejection of unity on a rather impressionistic analysis of style and theme. Others have sought to apply more exact tests to the problem. For example, Franz Schwarz[4] makes an elaborate metrical analysis of the text. He tabulates the frequency of the various types and subtypes of verses and the frequency of their use in the first or second half-line, the frequency of anacrusis and hypermetric verses, the use of single and double alliteration, and the use of rhyme. This detailed system has the basic fault of focusing on metrical criteria in a poetic vacuum. That is to say, Schwarz's system is entirely mechanical, having little or no regard for poetic technique or diction. Using this system of analysis, surely, if one took any long poem and selected just the right section, one could apply these metrical tests and demonstrate that it could not have been written by the poet who wrote some other section of the same poem.

Eduard Sievers also uses a metrical test, pointing out[5] that *Christ III* (which he thinks begins with line 779, thus including the runic signature) and *Elene* both have a great many hypermetric verses, whereas *Christ I* and *Christ II* (which he thinks ends with line 778) have almost no hypermetric verses. Thus he misplaces the runic signature in *Christ,*

---

[3] Philip, p. 909.

[4] *Cynewulfs Anteil am Christ*, Diss. Königsburg, 1905.

[5] "Zur Rhythmik des germanischen Alliterationsverses," III, *Beiträge zur Geschichte der deutschen Sprache und Literatur,* 12 (1887), 455–56.

enabling him to ascribe *Christ III* to Cynewulf and associate it more closely with *Elene,* a signed poem, as both are rich in hypermetric verses. This seems a peculiar basis for rejecting unity, for, although *Christ I* and *Christ II* have very few hypermetric verses, the same is true of *Juliana* and *Fates of the Apostles,* both signed poems. Surely, any attempt to draw conclusions from the frequency of hypermetric verses in a given poem or poems seems doomed to failure. We simply do not know why *Dream of the Rood* and *Judith,* for example, have a great many hypermetric verses, some poems, such as *Beowulf,* have scattered patches of them, and some poems have none at all.

Just as focusing on metrical considerations without regard to diction seems unlikely to furnish any answers about authorship, the converse is also true: checking on the frequency of lexical items without regard to their metrical use also seems unlikely to establish authorship of an Old English poem. A. Brandl, in a review[6] of the Cook edition of *Christ,*[7] rejects unity on the basis of a lexical check of epithets found in *Christ II* and *Christ III.* Brandl seems to be another in a long list of scholars who have arrived at what is probably the right answer by using questionable methods.

If impressionistic stylistic criticism, a count of frequency of verse types, and listing lexical frequency seem to be unreliable criteria for determining authorship, is there any methodology that can be applied to this problem? What is wanted is some method that will give us insight into the practice of the poet's art, the way he puts words together to make correct verses in a meaningful context.

The application of principles of scientific analysis, breaking a complex structure down into its elements, can go too far. For example, when the scientific method was first applied to the analysis of language, speech was broken down into its smallest units, phones, or speech sounds, and a generation of linguists worked out the possibilities of phonetics. But later linguists discerned the need to come up one level of complexity to the phoneme, that is, to describe how phones cluster in phonemes, to relate speech sounds to meaningful utterance. So, in applying scientific principles to an analysis of Old Germanic poetics, merely listing verse types or lexical items is breaking the structure down too far, below the level where the poetic process takes place.

Recent studies have indicated that Old Germanic poetry was traditional in style, relying on poetic formulas handed down from an age when poetry was delivered orally. The oral-formulaic analysis of Homeric, Serbian, and Old English poetry by Milman Parry, Albert Lord,

---

[6] *Archiv,* 111 (1903), 447–49.
[7] Cook, *Christ* (Boston, 1900).

F. P. Magoun, Jr., and others has given students of Old English poetic style a new awareness of how the poets must have worked.[8] During a period of some kind of apprenticeship, such as we know that the Serbian oral singers went through, a poet acquired a large stock of poetic formulas, with substitutions, enabling him to express just about any idea in the kind of verses that his poetic tradition used. An Anglo-Saxon poet must have known hundreds of formulas that would fit the Anglo-Saxon alliterative line, which was composed of alliterating pairs of verses, each of which, in turn, consisted of two measures.

The oral-formulaic analysis of Old English poetry is dependent upon the metrical analysis of Old English poetry known as the Sievers Five Types,[9] which designates the verses A-, B-, C-, D-, or E-verses, on the basis of frequency. This system of scansion is widely accepted and has been further refined by John C. Pope, who discerned that the B- and C-verses consisted of a light first measure and a heavy second measure that contained any alliterating syllables, even double alliteration.[10] The Pope corollary to the Sievers theory, then, enables us to see that there are fewer kinds of measures than of verses. That is, some kinds of measures can serve, for example, as the second measure of a C-verse, the second measure of a D-verse, or as the first measure of an E-verse. Thus it is possible to affirm that the poetic formula occupies the space of a measure. For example, *brad-sweord* (inflected) might be a formula that would give the second measure of a C-verse, thus: *mid brad-sweorde*. As the second measure of a D-verse is usually the equivalent of the second measure of a B- or C-verse, this formula could also give the second measure of a D-verse, thus: *slog brad-sweorde*. Similarly, a phrase might be a formula that would give the second measure of a B-verse or of a D-verse, such as the phrase *agen bearn,* which can be used in the B-verse *his agen bearn* or in the D-verse *Godes agen bearn*. The poetic formula, then, seems to be the essential unit of composition in Old English poetry. It is a word or group of words that expresses the idea the poet wants and fills a measure or a verse in the alliterative line. The poetic formula, which operates in the metrical dimension at the same time as it operates in the semantic dimension, seems to be the equivalent in Old English poetry of the phoneme in linguistics, the basic unit associated with meaning. Thus, mere tabulation of the frequency of verse types or of lexical units does not give us an adequate basis for

[8] Francis P. Magoun, Jr., includes a selective bibliography of works by Parry and Lord in "Oral-Formulaic Character of Anglo-Saxon Narrative Poetry," *Speculum,* 28 (1953), 446, n. 2, 3.

[9] *Altgermanische Metrik* (Halle, 1893).

[10] *The Rhythm of Beowulf* (New Haven, 1942), pp. 38–79.

analyzing poetic style, for each poet had his own stock of formulaic diction, and, to know him, we must take account of his diction. This is not to say that each poet had his own exclusive stock of formulas. On the contrary, the poets shared a common stock of traditional poetic formulas. But each poet may well have developed his own slightly personalized diction.

If we can establish some index of the diction of Cynewulf, we may be able to apply it to *Christ I* and *Christ III* to determine whether they may also be by Cynewulf. Aside from one nine-line hymn which Bede tells us is by Cædmon, we cannot safely ascribe any Old English poem to any author whose name we know, except Cynewulf. In the four signed poems of Cynewulf, *Elene, Juliana, Christ II,* and *Fates of the Apostles,* we have a unique phenomenon in Old English literature: a group of poems, amounting to about 2600 lines, which we can confidently assign to one poet. If we seek to determine the nature of the diction of Cynewulf in some way that is neither subjective nor excessively mechanical, the best indicator would seem to be the occurrence of repeated poetic formulas. Checking every verse in the four signed poems against the entire Cynewulf corpus, we find a set of figures that we may call the incidence of Cynewulf formulas, the Cynewulf norm. If we then check every verse in *Christ I* and *Christ III* against the entire Cynewulf corpus, we may be enabled to see the relationship between the diction of those two poems and the Cynewulf norm.

It must be emphasized that simply finding a similarity in phrasing is not finding a repeated poetic formula. The check cannot be done in a metrical vacuum: the formulas must be analyzed as providing verses or measures of verses. A good example is a prepositional phrase, which is most useful to the poet, for it enables him to make, for example, a noun that he may wish to introduce into his poem into a regular A-verse. Instead of saying, for example, simply *menn*, which is the word he wants to express, he can say *menn ofer moldan* [men on earth], which means very little more than just "men." The more nearly empty and meaningless the prepositional phrase is, the greater its utility, for it enables him to fill out an A-verse without saying something that he does not mean. The preposition provides the necessary second syllable of the first measure of an A-verse (in this case, the second and third syllables), and the object of the preposition makes the second measure of the A-verse. This verse, *menn ofer moldan,* has the additional advantage of having double alliteration. It somewhat limits its utility, however, for it cannot be used in the off-verse (second half-line), because it was customary to use double alliteration only in the on-verse (first half-line).

Another example may serve to illustrate how an analysis of poetic formulas proceeds. The phrase *heortan gehygdum* [the thoughts of the heart] is a formula that makes an A-verse. The inflected noun *heortan*, together with the prefix *ge-*, makes the first measure, and the inflected stem *-hygdum* makes the second measure. This formula has double alliteration, with which the poets strove to embellish their on-verses, although not every on-verse has it. But it could not be used in the off-verse. There is a variant of it, however, *heortan geþohtas*, which has exactly the same meaning and can be used in the off-verse, because it has single alliteration. Although the second word of the verse is different, this phrase is clearly related to the verse with double alliteration. We may say that these two verses belong to a common formulaic system.

Sometimes one word of a formula will be varied simply in order to enable the poet to say the same thing in verses that have different alliteration, for he must arrange his verses in alliterating pairs. For example, *foldan mægðe* and *eorðan mægðe* have exactly the same meaning, "the peoples of the earth." One is an A-verse with single alliteration on *f*, the other an A-verse with single alliteration on a vowel. It may be appropriate here to point out that a rather outdated kind of criticism of Old English poetry would make much out the poet's choice of *eorðan* or *foldan* (both meaning "earth") and would seek to find stylistic reasons for the choice. This is the wrong track. It seems pretty clear that the exigencies of alliteration determined the choice. Some of the techniques of criticism that have been applied to modern literature thus seem not to be valid for an analysis of Old Germanic poetry.

Bearing in mind, then, the nature of Anglo-Saxon alliterative verse and giving scrupulous attention to metrics, we check every verse in the four signed poems against the entire Cynewulf corpus to find the Cynewulf norm. Such a check (made by means of an unpublished Cynewulf concordance) shows that 45.7 percent of the verses in *Elene* contain poetic formulas, i.e., Cynewulf formulas. For *Juliana,* the figure is 41.4 percent. For *Christ II*, it is 36.6 percent, and for *Fates of the Apostles,* it is 36.4 percent. The variation from 36 to 45 percent is a variation of only 9 percent. Of course, if we check every Cynewulf verse against every verse in the entire corpus of Old English poetry, the figures will run higher, but our concern is to find some indication of the Cynewulf norm, and we have it: from 36 to 45 percent.

The next step is to check the two poems of questionable authorship, *Christ I* and *Christ III*, against every verse in the four signed poems of Cynewulf. If the figures are in or near the 36 to 45 range that seems to be the Cynewulf norm, it may well be that they must be regarded as possibly by Cynewulf. Such a check, however, gives us the figure 20.3 percent for *Christ I* and 19.9 percent for *Christ III*. The figures are significantly below the 36 to 45 range of the Cynewulf norm. Hence we may assume with some confidence that *Christ I* and *Christ III* are not by Cynewulf. The figures for the two poems cluster closely together, varying less than half of one percent, although *Christ III* is almost twice as long as *Christ I*. This affinity raises the interesting speculation that perhaps they may be the work of the same poet, who may have sought to provide Cynewulf's poem, *Christ II,* with a setting, much as an artisan might provide a setting for a gem. It is only a speculation, however, for the figures cannot lead us very far.

Some of the figures on repeated formulas in the Cynewulf poems, along with some of the supporting evidence, have already been published.[11] All the supporting evidence appears in my unpublished doctoral dissertation.[12] Unfortunately, space in these pages does not permit giving all the supporting evidence for the percentage figures given above. Instead, it has seemed even more illuminating to give a sampling of formulas in *Christ I* and *Christ III*, along with related verses in the four signed poems, to suggest some idea of how Anglo-Saxon poets worked. In addition, instances from elsewhere in the corpus of Old English poetry are included in parentheses. The abbreviation *Ele* will be used for *Elene, Jln* for *Juliana, Chr* for *Christ,* and *FAp* for *Fates of the Apostles.*

CHRIST I

Chr 62 *siðe geseceð,* an A-verse with double alliteration, is shown to be a formula by the following evidence: *Jln* 452, *FAp* 32 *siðe gesohte* (also *Beowulf* 1951, *Andreas* 175, 845, *Genesis* 2516). *Chr* 146 *siþe gesecan* is another example of this formula. The forms *geseceð, gesecan,* and *gesohte* have the same metrical value: in each, the prefix *ge-* provides the last syllable of the first measure, and *-seceð / -secan / -sohte* provides the entire second measure of the A-verse.

Chr 65 *cwædon þe to frofre* is a normal A-verse, with *c* alliteration. Again, the prepositional phrase fills out the A-verse. Evidence: an A3-verse, *Chr* 758 *habbað we us to frofre,* and two A-verses, with double alliteration, *Ele* 502 *folca to frofre* and *Ele* 1142 *folcum to frofre.* Also *Chr* 1421 *folcum to frofre.* (Cf. also *Andreas* 606, *Menelogium* 228,

11 *PQ*, 38 (1959), 234–41.
12 "The Diction of the Signed Poems of Cynewulf," Diss. Harvard, 1953.

Beowulf 14, *Exodus* 88. For a variant, with *m* alliteration, cf. *Menelogium* 57, *Lord's Prayer II* 33, *Psalm* 50,148 *mannum to frofre*. For other A-verses ending with the prepositional phrase *to frofre,* cf. *Genesis* 1108, 2176, 2219, *Daniel* 338, *Judith* 296, *Andreas* 311, *Order of the World* 97.

Chr 71 *geond wuldres þrym* is a B-verse with *w* alliteration. Evidence: *Chr* 740 *gesawan wuldres þrym, Jln* 641 *and wuldres þrym. Chr.* 83 *nu þu wuldres þrym* is another example. (Cf. also *Guthlac* 1364 *in wuldres þrym.*)

Chr 81 *wenan þurfon.* Evidence: *Ele* 1103 *wenan þorfte* (also *Beowulf* 157). The change of number and tense of the verb does not alter the metrical type.

Chr 105 *ofer middangeard.* Evidence: *Chr* 698, *Ele* 434, 917 (also *Andreas,* 224, 345, 701, 1323, 1372, 1718, *Exodus* 2, 48, 286, *Daniel* 105, *Phoenix* 4, *Psalms* 58,13, 137,6, 144,12). Also *Chr* 1046. Variants of the formula are *Chr* 452, 787, *Ele* 6, 774 *in middangeard* (also *Andreas* 1502, *Phoenix* 640, *Christ and Satan* 438, 474); *Chr* 644, *Ele* 16, 1176 *geond middangeard, Jln* 3 *se geond middangeard* (also *Christ and Satan* 271, 582, *Guthlac* 501, *Phoenix* 119).

Chr 143 *þætte sunu meotudes,* a C-verse. Evidence: *Ele* 474 *hu hie sunu meotudes, Ele* 686 *þurh sunu meotodes, Ele* 1318 *ond to suna metudes,* also C-verses (also two C-verses, *Christ and Satan* 142, 527); two D-verses, with double alliteration, *Ele* 461, 564 *soð sunu meotudes* (also *Daniel* 401).

Chr 161 *weoroda wuldorcyning,* a D-verse, with double alliteration. (The verse is repeated in *Genesis* 2, *Exodus* 548, *Daniel* 308, *Meters of Boethius* 20,162). The second measure is the equivalent of the second measure of a B-verse. Evidence: B-verses, *Jln* 238 *symle heo wuldorcyning, Jln* 428 *þurh wuldorcyning.* Also a B-verse, *Chr* 1022 *þonne wuldorcyning.*

Another example of variation of a word in a formula, thus changing the alliteration without changing the meaning, is *Chr* 188 *womma lease* (also found in *Judgment Day I* 94). Evidence: *Ele* 497, *Jln* 188 *synna lease,* with *s* alliteration; this verse also appears in *Chr* 1640; *Jln* 566, 583 *leahtra lease,* with double alliteration (also *Guthlac* 947, 1189). All these variants mean "sinless."

Chr 207 *in me frofre gæst,* a B-verse, a typically Christian formula, the second measure meaning "spirit of consolation." Evidence: *Ele* 1036 *siððan frofre gast* (also *Andreas* 906, 1684, *Guthlac* 136, 936, *Judith* 83); also D-verses, with double alliteration, *Chr* 728, *Ele* 1105, *Jln* 724 *fæder, frofre gæst.*

CHRIST III

Chr 867 *foldbuende,* a compound that gives a D-verse. Evidence: *Ele* 1013, *Chr* 1177 (also *Beowulf* 309, 1355, *Guthlac* 64, *Descent into Hell* 101, 105, *Azarias* 24, *Creed* 21, *Riddle* 1,13, *Meters of Boethius* 8,4, 17,2). A variant, with vowel alliteration, is *Chr* 1323 *eorðbuendra,* not found in the Cynewulf poems (but widely attested elsewhere: *Genesis* 221, 1000, 1636, 1685, 1754, 2618, *Exodus* 84, *Daniel* 564, *Christ and Satan* 1, *Finnsburg* 32, *Creed* 21, *Riddle,* 29,8, *Psalms* 82,14, 93,10, 95,4, 100,6, 118,130, *Meters of Boethius* 10,25, 12,18, 19,13, 29,71). A variant with *þ* alliteration is *Chr* 1172 *þeodbuendra, Chr* 616, 1371 *þeodbuendum.* (Two other variants are *landbuende,* with *l* alliteration, found in *Beowulf* 95, *Judith* 226, 315, *Widsith* 132, *Gifts of Men* 29, *Order of the World* 80, *Riddle* 95,11, and *weoroldbuende,* with *w* alliteration, found in *Judith* 82, *Meters of Boethius* 27,27, 29,81.) All these formulas have the same meaning, "human beings."

Chr 903 *beorhte blican,* a regular A-verse, with double alliteration. Evidence: *Chr* 701 *beorhte bliceð* (also *Phoenix* 599, *Andreas* 789, *Genesis* 1822, *Riddle* 34,9). A variant of the formula, with *h* alliteration, is *Chr* 1012 *hlutre blicað.* Another variant, with *l* alliteration, is *Chr* 1238 *leohte blicaþ.* All these variants have the same meaning, "shine brightly." Closely akin to this formula is another A-verse, with double alliteration on *sc, Chr* 1088 *scire scineð* (also *Andreas* 836), and a variant, with *s* alliteration, *Chr* 1102 *swegle scineð.*

Chr 903 *þonne bearn godes,* a C-verse. Evidence: *Ele* 813 *nu ic þe, bearn godes, Ele* 963, 1126 *þurh bearn godes,* also C-verses. Also found in *Chr* 147 *hwonne bearn godes,* and in *Chr* 1072 *fore bearn godes* (also C-verses in *Andreas* 1028, 1613, *Christ and Satan* 620). *Chr* 774 *biddan bearn godes* and *Jln* 666 *biddað bearn godes* make use of the formula in the second measure of D-verses.

Chr 924 *forht on ferðe.* Evidence: *Jln* 328 *forhte on ferþe* (also *Beowulf* 754, *Phoenix* 504). The prepositional phrase *on ferhþe* [in mind] makes the content word *forht(e)* [fearful] into an A-verse, without really adding anything to the meaning: "fearful in mind" means little more than simply "fearful," but the prepositional phrase is needed for scansion and is desirable for double alliteration. (A variant, with the same meaning, but with single alliteration, and thus capable of being used in the off-verse, is *Daniel* 724 *forht on mode, Andreas* 448 *forhte on mode.*)

Chr 976, 1059 *hat, heorogifre* [hot and fiercely ravenous] a formula describing the fires of hell, as might be expected in *Christ III,* a poem on the Last Judgment. Evidence: *Jln* 586, where it rather inaccurately describes the cauldron heated to put the saint to death.

Chr 991 *brecað brade gesceaft,* a D-verse, with double alliteration on *b.* Evidence: *Chr* 672 *secgan side gesceaft,* a D-verse, with double alliteration on *s.* The formula, which gives the second measure of a D-verse, means "vast creation." Varying the adjective does not change the meaning, but only alters the alliteration. This formula appears as the second measure of B-verses also: *Chr* 59, 356 *þas sidan gesceaft, Chr* 239 *þe þas sidan gesceaft, Chr* 1087 *þæt ofer side gesceaft.* A variant of the formula, with double alliteration on *sc,* is found in *Jln* 728 *þurh þa sciran gesceaft.* Another B-verse second measure, with identical meaning, but with single alliteration on *b,* is *Ele* 1088 *in ða beorhtan gesceaft.* (Checking the entire corpus of Old English poetry turns up variant second measures: *leohte gesceaft,* a variant of *sciran gesceaft* and *beorhtan gesceaft; ruman gesceaft,* a variant of *sidan gesceaft* and *brade gesceaft; wlitige gesceaft* and *fægran gesceaft,* variants of one another; also *ealle gesceaft, halgan gesceaft, mære gesceaft, læne gesceaft,* and *dumban gesceaft,* all filling the second measure of a B-verse, a widely used formula in Christian poetry. Formulas that we might tend to associate exclusively with Christian poetry also turn up in heroic poetry, e.g., *Beowulf* 1622 *ond þas lænan gesceaft* [transitory creation], a Christian tag.)

Chr 1031 *leoðum onfon* looks like a mismetered verse. A clue to what went wrong may be furnished by *Chr* 1068 *leoþum onfengen,* which looks like a formula (although there is no supporting evidence) expressing the idea, literally, "receive limbs," i.e., "be clothed with flesh," "become incarnate." The noun *leoðum* receives resolved stress, and the prefix *on-* fills out the first measure of an A-verse, but the second measure demands a disyllabic form of *-fon,* such as *-fengon, -fenge, -fengen,* or *-fangen.* This formula may go back to a time when the contract verb *fon* was still disyllabic in all its forms, although the idea would seem to be a Christian concept.

Chr 1092 *womwyrcende,* a D-verse consisting of a compound, with double alliteration on *w.* Evidence: *Ele* 395, 943 *synwyrcende, Chr* 841 *synwyrcenda, Ele* 761, *Jln* 445 *scyldwyrcende.* These variants provide *s* and *sc* alliteration. (Another variant is *Psalm* 72,2 *fyrenwyrcende, Psalm* 70,3 *firenwyrcendra.*) A variant, with double alliteration on *f,* is *Chr* 1117 *firenfremmendra.* A variant of that, with single alliteration on *m,* is *Ele* 906 *manfremmende.* All these variants of the formula have the same meaning, "sinful" or "sinners."

Chr 1145 *cyðde cræftes meaht.* Evidence: *Ele* 558 *cyðdon cræftes miht.* (Cf. also a B-verse, *Andreas* 585 *þurh his cræftes miht.*) The phrase *cræftes meaht* is redundant, for *cræft* and *meaht* have roughly the same meaning, "strength," making the phrase rather difficult to translate literally. Neither *cræft* nor *meaht* alone and uninflected could combine with *cyðde / cyðdon* to make a regular verse, but putting them together in a genitive phrase enables them to fill the second measure of a B- or D-verse. This is an excellent example of metrical demands taking precedence over meaning.

Chr 1196 *hæleþa cynne,* an A-verse, of which the second measure is an inflected form of *cynn.* Evidence: *Ele* 188, 1203 *hæleða cynnes* (also *Andreas* 545, 567, 907, *Guthlac* 683, *Whale* 40). The first measure, the genitive plural of a word meaning "man," can be substituted in order to vary the alliteration, without changing the meaning. A variant, with *f* alliteration, is *Ele* 897, *Jln* 509, *Chr* 610 *fira cynne* (also *Guthlac* 864, 988, 1250, *Andreas* 590, *Phoenix* 492, 535, *Order of the World* 14). A variant, with *g* alliteration is *Jln* 719 *gumena cynnes* (also *Beowulf* 1058, *Andreas* 582, *Guthlac* 1362). A variant, with vowel alliteration, is *Jln* 727 *ælda cynna, Ele* 521 ilda cynnes, *Chr* 780 *ælda cynnes* (also *Phoenix* 546). A variant, with *m* alliteration, is *Jln* 470, *Chr* 956 *monna cynnes, Chr* 425 *monna cynne* (also *Beowulf* 701, 712, 1725, *Genesis* 193, 425, 710, 750, *Phoenix* 358, *Widsith* 16, *Andreas* 1374, *Gifts of Men* 104, *Psalm* 77,25). All these formulas mean "the human race."

Chr 1357 *hyge staðeladon,* a D-verse, consisting of a monosyllabic (or disyllabic with resolved stress) word meaning "spirit" in the first measure and a form of *staðolian* in the second measure; the first two syllables of *staðolian* receive resolved stress. Evidence: *Ele* 1093 *hyge staðolian* (also *Psalm* 61,11). A variant, with *f* alliteration, is *Ele* 427 *ferhð staðelien, Jln* 270, 364 *ferð staþelian.* A variant, with *m* alliteration, is *Jln* 222 *mod staþelige* (also found in *Andreas* 82 *mod staþolige* and *Guthlac* 1110 *ongan þa his mod staþelian,* a hypermetric verse, of which the second measure is the equivalent of a normal D-verse).

Chr 1594 *lacende leg,* an E-verse, with double alliteration; the first measure consists of a present participle, and the second measure is a monosyllabic noun; it means "leaping fire." Evidence: *Ele* 580, 1110. A variant, with *w* alliteration, is *Chr* 1250 *weallendne lig* [raging fire]. Another variant, with *h* alliteration, is *Chr* 973 *hiþende leg* [ravaging fire]. (Cf. also a variant, with *s* alliteration, *Beowulf* 3145 *swogende leg* [roaring fire] and a variant, with *b* alliteration, *Judgment Day I* 117 *byrnende lig* [burning fire]). Although the participles vary slightly in meaning, they are all appropriate to any fire description.

21

The Art of Cynewulf's
Runic Signatures

DOLORES WARWICK FRESE

THE CYNEWULFIAN RUNIC SIGNATURE HAS BEEN UNIVERSALLY AC-
knowledged as an erudite, clever, and successful means of perpetuating
the poet's name in an age when poetry was largely anonymous.[1] It is
true that when Cynewulf came to construct his art of words, clerical
copyists—especially those connected with the Alcuinian "diaspora"—
had instituted something of a rage for the insertion of runic inscription
into their manuscripts, and it was already a centuries-old custom in other

---

[1] Ear̃lier critics of the four runically signed poems tended to view the signatures as a purely acrostical device whose employment was entirely prayerful; cf.
Frederick Tupper, Jr., "The Cynewulfian Runes of the Religious Poems," *MLN*,
27 (1912), 131–37; Kenneth Sisam, "Cynewulf and His Poetry" (Sir Israel
Gollancz Memorial Lecture), *Proceedings of the British Academy* (London, 1932),
pp. 303–31; Ralph W. V. Elliott, "Cynewulf's Runes in *Christ II* and *Elene*," *ES*,
34 (1953), 49–57, and Elliott, "Cynewulf's Runes in *Juliana* and *Fates of the
Apostles*," *ES*, 34 (1953), 193–204; Claes Schaar, *Critical Studies in the Cynewulf
Group* (Lund, 1949). Later critics have suggested that Cynewulf's signed poetry
possibly displays more complex intentions and structures—intellectual, rhetorical,
magical—than had heretofore been acknowledged; cf. Rosemary Woolf, Introduction to *Juliana* (London, 1955), p. 9; Lucien Musset, *Introduction à la Runol-
ogie* (Paris, 1965), p. 199; James L. Boren, "Form and Meaning in Cynewulf's
Fates of the Apostles," *PLL*, 5 (Spring, 1969), 115–21. None of these, however,
argues for a poetic complexity integrating each signature to its preceding poem,
which is the subject of this essay.

arts to runically engrave the signature of the artificer upon the product of his art.[2] Typically contained in a formula of donation, dedication, consecration, or supplication, runic signatures were variously applied to such movables as arms, jewels, coins, and drinking horns—as well as to more stationary objects like baptismal fonts, bell towers, and funerary monuments. Cynewulf, however, was doing more than importing into his poetry a common runic device employed by precedent artisans; he was striving for more than nominal immortality. Had Cynewulf wanted merely to guarantee the survival of his name as author of each signed poem, or even to assure a helpful specificity in the prayers he asks for at the conclusion of each of these works, there is no reason why a single runic signature, appended to each poem somewhat in the nature of a trademark, would not have sufficed.

The individual rune signs did, of course, each have their fixed meaning and happily the substantives indicated by each of the twenty-nine Old English runic characters are glossed for us in the Anglo-Saxon "Runic Poem."[3] The word that each rune "stood for" then, if not "sun clear" to the eighth- and ninth-century audience as Tupper claimed,[4] was surely a relatively fixed nominal commodity with which the poet perhaps wittily played, but never promiscuously exchanged for any poetically convenient word that happened to begin with the same character. Thus, while there has been debate over the years concerning possible alternative readings suggested by certain of the runes that spell the name CYN(E)WULF[5] the univocal critical impression of the signature sections has been one of tiresomely repetitious similitude.

[2] Musset, pp. 144, 156–61, 323–25. Musset, it should be noted, distinguishes Cynewulf's "très subtils exercices sur le fuþorc" [extremely subtle exercises on the fuþorc, p. 199] from the wordy proliferation of runic contrivances that flourished during the ecclesiastical "diaspora" of Alcuin's period—cryptographic exercises that ranged from runic numbering of manuscript leaves (in alphabetical order!) and the colophonic signing of scribal names (in Latin!) to formulaic farewells, latinate moral apothegms and the like. Of these latter, Musset justly observes, "Ces distractions de *scriptorium* n'offrent qu'un médiocre intérêt" [These distractions of the scriptorium offer only mediocre interest, p. 198].

[3] Included in Bruce Dickens, ed., *Runic and Heroic Poems of the Old Teutonic Peoples* (Cambridge, 1915). Cf. also Sisam, pp. 316–17, for other Old English manuscript attestations to rune names, all of which agree with the "Runic Poem" equivalences.

[4] Tupper, p. 132.

[5] Elliott, "Runes in *Christ II* and *Elene*," pp. 49–53, and "Runes in *Juliana* and *Fates*," pp. 193–99, provides a fair review of variant readings suggested by Arntz, Keller, Sievers, Trautmann, Gollancz, Wrenn, Wright *et al.*, and argues, persuasively, I believe, that it is safest to retain the meanings assigned to the runes in the "Runic Poem," especially since those meanings—particularly the much debated *Ur*, meaning "bison"—can be demonstrated to signify "male strength" in earlier Germanic associations and as such fits quite naturally into Cynewulf's verse,

And after all, what variety or originality ought we expect of four pieces of poetry that needs must include, each within the space of five to thirteen lines, the words *Cen* [torch], *Yr* [bow], *Ned* [need], *Eoh* [horse], *Wyn* [joy], *Ur* [bison], *Lagu* [water], and *Feoh* [fortune]? The problem—which was Cynewulf's poetic problem—is obvious. His solution, I believe, is somewhat subtler, and deserves our attention. Cynewulf constructs four *different* signatures, each spelling out his name. In each instance, his choice of poetic encouchment for the runes seems to grow out of his poetic concern in the poem he is signing. The signature sections, carefully scrutinized, seem to provide a kind of glossary of major ideas and images in each work and appear to be elaborate verbal networks that link by name the fact of the poet to the fact of the preceding poem. In an age not entirely severed from the idea of "word magic," such a use of runic device as a means of mastery and power over the matter of the poem would seem to be a notion worth investigating. This essay proposes, as a first step in that direction, to present some discoveries concerning the ingenious art of Cynewulf's wordweaving in the four concluding sections of those works he designates as his own in such signal fashion.[6]

In each of the four signed poems—*Juliana, Fates of the Apostles, Christ II,* and *Elene*—Cynewulf signals the beginning of his deliberately personal presence in the piece by a clear grammatical shift to the personal pronoun: *Is me þearf micel* [I have great need, *Juliana,* 695b]; *Nu ic þonne bidde* [Now I pray you, *Fates,* 88a]; *Huru ic wene me* [Nonetheless I expect for myself, *Christ II,* 789b]; *Þus ic frod ond fus* [Now, I, old and ready for death, *Elene,* 1236a].[7]

---

making unnecessary the rather dubious substitutions of *ure* [our], *unne* [legal grant], and the like. Elliott convincingly suggests that "the poet could achieve his double purpose—a coherent poetic narrative embodying the runes spelling his name—only by using the relevant runes in their accepted senses" (p. 193), since "in Anglo-Saxon usage there appears to be no evidence that the common Germanic habit of letting a single rune stand only for its name and what it symbolized was in any way modified" (p. 52).

[6] In an essay on "The Runes in *The Husband's Message*," *JEGP,* 54 (1953), 1–8, Elliott constructs an argument for the five runes in that poem as "the actual message supposed to have been carved into the wood and sent to the wife . . ." suggesting that "the poem may properly be deemed an explanation of the terse runic message in greatly expanded form" (p. 5). Elliott's thesis, then, though not suggesting that the runic section has been built out of its poetic matrix, as I venture here, does involve a similar argument for the contiguity of imagery between the poem and its runes.

[7] Throughout this essay, all citations to the Old English text of *Fates of the Apostles* and *Elene* are from *The Vercelli Book, ASPR,* II, ed. George Philip Krapp (New York, 1932); citations to the text of *Juliana* and *Christ* are from *The Exeter Book, ASPR,* III, eds., George Philip Krapp and Elliott van K. Dobbie (New York, 1936).

It is at this point in each poem that the poet begins to identify himself (not at the appearance of the first rune sign), and consequently here that we should look to find the beginnings of whatever poetic individuality each signature section may bear. By attending too narrowly to similarities in each of these signature sections—each signs the name of the poet in runes; each acknowledges his sinfulness; each petitions the reader for prayers—we may have missed the pleasurable skill with which Cynewulf fashions a unique and impressively artful signature each time out of materials specific to the preceding poetry.

JULIANA

In *Juliana*, the opening of the runic signature section is conventional, even obvious, in the way it relates the signed conclusion to the body of the poem:

> Is me þearf micel
> þæt seo halge me   helpe gefremme,
>
> (695b–96)

[I have great need that this holy maid help me].

But the poetry is quickly furthered and complicated as the bid for prayers continues. The urgency is focused on a particular time, a time

> þonne me gedælað   deorast ealra,
> sibbe toslitað   sinhiwan tu,
> micle modlufan.   Min sceal of lice
> sawul on siðfæt,
>
> (697–700a)

[when the dearest of all shall divide me, rend the relationship, when the wedded couple sever their kinship, their mighty love, my soul shall be off on its way from my body . . .].

Cynewulf chooses to present the time of death, the time when the soul leaves the body, in terms of a broken relationship, and that relationship the "dearest of all," an undone union between two closely related in love. In doing this, he neatly recapitulates, in four superficially conventional lines, the entire life-death dilemma of his heroine whose choice of Christ and everlasting life necessitates her breaking with bridegroom and father, either of which might be a logical referent for the *deorast ealra* of the signature. This sense of echoic suggestion at the

315

end of the poem, that reiterates while it reshapes the poem's idea of cherished connection, has been prepared for earlier by the repeated use of the *seo dyreste* and *seo sweteste* forms of address used by the father toward his daughter in urging the marriage, and by the *Min se swetesta* remarks of the bartered bridegroom, Heliseus, to Juliana.

The next lines in the signature section are characterized by this same technique of bifurcation; much as Cynewulf initially manipulated the image of separation, so he now doubles and splits the stock poetic meditation on the moment of departure from the earth:

> eardes uncyðgu; of sceal ic þissum,
> secan oþerne ærgewyrhtum,
> gongan iudædum. Geomor hweorfeð
>
> (701–03)

[from this one I shall seek another unknown dwelling place, according to my acts of old, proceeding on deeds that are done. Sad shall I go . . .].

The tonal sadness here attaches the passage specifically and exclusively to the sinful poet, deliberately heightening the disparity between his anxiety about the afterlife and the contrastively eager spirit of his heroine as she commits the identical act of contemplation:

> Ða wearð þære halgan hyht geniwad
> ond þæs mægdnes mod miclum geblissad,
> siþþan heo gehyrde hæleð eahtian
> inwitrune, þæt hyre endestæf
> of gewindagum weorþan sceolde,
>
> (607–11)

[Then was the hope of the holy one freshened, and the mood of the maiden greatly gladdened, when she heard the men craftily counsel that the days of her struggle should come to an end].

But in either case—sinner or saint—the *ærgewyrhtum gongan iudæ-dum,* the former deeds of the individual, shape the vision of the eternity one is contemplating. In the terror of the poet we are aesthetically returned to the serenity of the saint. This characteristic movement backwards into the poem as the signature lines continue their forward thrust sets up a sustained tension in the next set of images, giving particular density and intensity to the actual runic occurrence. The nouns *cyning* [the king] and *syllend* [the lord] and the verb *deman* [to judge], occur-

ring respectively in lines 704, 705, and 707, with the qualifying vocabularies of *reþe* [angry], *sigora* [victorious (of victories)], and *wille lifes
to leane* [(what) he will deem according to their deeds, as a life's reward], are the poet's references to Christ. But they are inescapably
evocative of Heliseus, described earlier as *yrre gebolgen* [swollen with
anger, 58b], *hildeþremman* [(one of two) war lords, 64a], a man urged to
judge Juliana according to his own inclinations of reward or punishment:

> Dem þu hi to deaþe,   gif þe gedafen þince,
> swa to life læt,   swa þe leofre sy.

> (87–88)

[Doom her to death if it suits you, or leave her alive, whichever seems
better to you.]

In similar fashion, when the signature section presents the terror of a
repentance too long delayed, *Wæs an tid to læt* [it (the time) was too
late, 712b], a salvific opportunity neglected while the sinful man still
enjoyed a sound earthly base of operation *onsund on earde* [secure on
earth, 715a],—the poetic statement is enriched by the verbal force of
gravity exerted on these Cynewulfian words by those last words of
Juliana as she converted her executioners with reminders that they had
no way of knowing when it might be too late,

> Forþon ge sylfe neton
> utgong heonan,   ende lifes.

> (660b–61)

[And so you yourselves do not know your going hence, your life's end]

and reminded them, with a particularly terrestial image, that they would
do well to soundly establish their spiritual foundations:

> þæt ge eower hus
> gefæstnige, ...
> . . . .
> . . . .   to þam lifgendan
> stane stiðhydge   staþol fæstniað,

> (648b–49a, 653b–54)

[so that you make your houses fast . . . stouthearted ones, set the foundations firmly upon the living stone].

In all of this there is a subtle but apparent binding of the sinful poet to the saintly heroine of his poem. While the dissimilarities of her worthiness and his unworthiness are superficially stressed, the magic of words is being invoked with great craft to align his needs with her powers. This undercurrent of almost unheard but powerfully felt insistence on the alignment is achieved through a manipulation of language that provides the adhesive force for connecting and controlling two such disparate realities. The signature concludes with a return to the explicit linking of petitioning sinner to powerful saint with which it began:

> Þonne arna biþearf,
> þæt me seo halge   wið þone hyhstan cyning
> geþingige.

(715b–17a)

[Thus there is need of mercies, that the holy maid plead my case for me before the highest king.]

But the reintroduction of the poet's need that the saint intercede for him is expanded now to include the request that *monna gehwone / gumena cynnes* [each man of the race of men, 718b–19a]—and especially *þe þis gied wræce* [he who recites or reads this poem, 719b]— might remember the poet's name:

>   bi noman minum
> gemyne modig,   ond meotud bidde
> þæt me heofona helm   helpe gefremme,
> meahta waldend,

(720b–23a)

[be most mindful of me in terms of my name, and pray that the Helmsman of Heaven, the Ruler of Might, may lend me help].

By positioning his poem's conclusion in these terms the poet achieves an internal poise, poetically and prayerfully, that is superb. A direct identification of himself with the saint would, of course, be unthinkably presumptious, and as we have seen, Cynewulf skillfully avoids doing this. But *Cyn(n)* [people] and *gumena cynnes* [mankind] are verbally and metaphorically inseparable. Cynewulf the poet is setting himself up, quite consciously, as spokesman and representative of sinful mankind. Yet he redeems himself, in a sense, via his poetry, positioning the "everyman" to whom his plea is addressed in direct equivalence to the saint, through the verbal texture of the passage which links them as intercessors of equal status. But such an identification via verbal formula has already been poetically complicated by the fact that the devil, earlier in the poem, had himself piteously petitioned Juliana for mercy through God's friendship:

> Ic þec halsige, hlæfdige min,
> Iuliana, fore godes sibbum,

(539–40)

[I implore you, my lady Juliana, for the love of God].

By keeping in such close touch with the language of the poem itself, the signature section suggests the consideration that man, in his fallen nature, contains the ambivalent potential for heaven's bliss or hell's damnation at the same time, and by the same words, wherein Cynewulf clearly opts for the alignment of the sinful man with the saint. It is a subtle alignment, operating out of the sustained alignment of the entire signature passage with the poem's previous materials. Its efficacy, as prayer or poetry, would be utterly ruined by the toppling weight of obviousness. The poet avoids such a tumbling of his elaborate poetic structure by an almost airy lightness in the concluding lines. The parting words of the poet are of a piece with the parting words of the saint. Cynewulf designates God as *æþelinga wyn* [the joy of men, 730b] and prays that we may find his face *milde gemeten on þa mæran tid. Amen* [mild of mien on that great day. Amen, 731]. The benignity of the language is calculated to recall for the reader Juliana's own "Peace and Love" remarks, uttered to the crowd immediately before her own anticipated meeting with God: *Sibb sy mid eowic, / symle soþ lufu* [Peace be with you, true love forever, 668b–69a].

These apparently superficial pieties have been structurally conditioned to support each other, and they gain in depth when we appreciate the craft of the poet who wrought to actualize in his "word work" some of the submerged ambiguities of the human and the poetic conditions that occupied him here.

FATES OF THE APOSTLES

In Cynewulf's *Fates of the Apostles,* the concluding section (88–122) has generally been regarded as extrinsic to the poem, a rather crudely "tacked on affair" exhibiting little continuity with the wholeness of *Fates.*[8] Without claiming any over-elaborate aesthetic achievement in

[8] Cf. Boren, p. 115, for a fair summary of the univocally negative critical response to the poetry of *Fates.*

this poem, I would argue that it is precisely in the signature lines that Cynewulf executes a carefully plotted relation of his name to his work that is at least quite clever, and not entirely unpleasing in its poetic architecture. The signature portion where Cynewulf runically enters his own name, then subtly incorporates each nameless reader into the poem—*Ah utu we þe geornor to gode cleopigan* [ever ought we the more eagerly cry out to God, 115]—contains no single thought cluster that does not have a direct poetic ancestor or offspring elsewhere in the text. This weaving back and forth, the re-embroidered quality of verbal texture that one senses in surface and depth structure, creates a vigor of re-enforcement and a delicacy of elaboration that is not poetically unworthy.

If the connection of signature to prior poem in the foregoing discussion of *Juliana* has seemed to employ a recondite methodology, Cynewulf himself invites us in the signature to *Fates* to discover *hwa þas fitte fegde* (98), to learn not only by whom, but *"how* this song was made." The onset of the signature, with its invitation to the reader to participate in the compositional act, *Nu ic þonne bidde beorn se ðe lufige* [now I ask that the man who loves this, 88], returns us to the onset of the poem with its equally conscious reference to itself, *Hwæt Ic þysne sang* [Lo, I sang this, 1a]. Furthermore, these opening phrases of the signature cause the reader to touch the text in a peculiarly live way; *beorn se ðe lufige / þysses giddes begang* [the man that loves the course of this song, 88b–89a]. Their reappearance, shortly thereafter, in virtually identical form, *mann se ðe lufige / þisses galdres begang* [the man that loves the spell of this song, 107b–08a], testifies to the poet's central concern that the reader's involvement in the compositional act be strengthened as a way of appreciating the poet's own needs. Regardless of whether the verbal recurrence here represents deliberate Cynewulfian intent to repeat, or scribal insertion of alternate epilogue possibilities,[9] the involvement of the reader/listener in a sympathetic relationship with the poet is clearly intentional to the poetry. From that point of involvement, the pleas for prayer and remembrance, two urgent concerns of this poetry, converge with utmost efficiency. Thus the *halgan heap* [blessed band, 90a] whose adventures have been recorded by the poet are enlisted as allies in the battle for immortality which prayer and poetry both express. By employing a similar verbal pattern for apostolic and poetic activity, Cynewulf relates the reader, the poet, and the entire Christian brotherhood in a kind of poetic communion of saints. The reference to the reader

---

[9] For a discussion of various possibilities that have been advanced concerning the "double epilogue" problem of *Fates,* see Schaar, pp. 102–04.

þæt he geomrum me / þone halgan heap helpe bidde [that he pray the holy company succor me in my sadness, 89b–90a], repeated in the later *þæt he geoce me* [that he help me, 108b] as well as the *helpe bidde / friðes ond fultomes* [ask help, peace, and guidance, 90b–91a] reemerging several lines later in *ond frofre fricle* [and ask for aid, 109a], all conspire to intensify this poetic effect of insistent personal supplication. It might be easy enough to dismiss such repetition as toilsome uninventiveness at its worst were there not such pointed reference back into the narrative moments of the prior poetry as the poet stresses and restresses, with the same rhythmic insistence, the *eardwic uncuð, ana gesecan* [the unknown dwelling I shall seek out alone, 93], the *an elles forð* and *Wic sindon uncuð* [I shall go elsewhere alone; the place is unknown, 110a and 112b]. In referring so repeatedly to his own journey to the "unknown country" which he must "seek out alone," he reminds us of the foregoing poem's concern with the apostles' journeying out, also alone, also for unknown lands: the earthly and the heavenly journeys are bound together by the words. Similarly, the earthly body that must be left behind—*lætan me on laste, lic, eorðan dæl* [to leave the body, the bit of earth, behind me, 94]—repeats the sense of separation of soul from body explicated in the twin martyrdom of Simon and Thaddeus:

> þa gedæled wearð
> lif wið lice, ond þas lænan gestreon,
> idle æhtwelan, ealle forhogodan.

(82b–84)

[Then was the life cut free from the body, and those (bodily) treasures on loan, the worthless wealth, all scorned.]

Here the poet seeks to construct, through his words, a guarantee of immortality to be shared with his holy heroes, much as he employed the device in the *Juliana* signature. Here, as there, the distance between the serenity of the saint and the anxiety of the sinner is stressed, even as the two are being yoked talismanically by the repetition of actual word and phrase clusters. Thus the dread of decay, conveyed by the poet's vision of his body as *wælreaf wunigean weormum to hroðre* [spoils of the slain, remaining as a treat for the worms, 95] distinguishes, as it associates, with the earlier typical description of death for the apostolic saint, *þonon wuldres leoht / sawle gesohte sigores to leane* [thence his soul sought the light of glory as a reward for victory, 61b–62].

This signature, more so than any of the other three, insists repeatedly and explicitly on its own powers to communicate concealed intelligence

321

to the aware or initiate reader. Line 96 assures such discovery: *her mæg findan forþances gleaw* [here the keen-minded man can find]; lines 105b–06 repeat the guarantee: *Nu ðu cunnon miht / hwa on þam wordum wæs werum oncyðig* [Now may you know who was made known to men in these words]. Having thus connected himself verbally with the apostles' journeyings, Cynewulf now cleverly and obliquely associates himself with their final triumphs. The poem has repeatedly presented the apostles after death as enjoying eternal reward. There are *swegle dreamas* [joys of heaven, 32b], *lifwela leofra* [dearer riches, 49a] and all *Hafað nu ece lif / mid wuldorcining, wiges to leane* [now have eternal life with the King of Glory as a reward of the combat, 73b–74]. Now the signature section puts the poet in a direct verbal relationship to that same reward-dealing Ruler of Bright Creation. Cynewulf gnomically states at the outset of his signature that ᚠ (Fortune or Wealth) "comes at the end." As the eye is pulled down to the typographical end of the poem we see that the terminal position, the "last word" as it were, is given to God himself. Moreover, the identical verb form, *standeð*, is used to link the poet's rune—which-is-his-name-which-is-himself—*þær on ende standeþ* [it stands there at the end, 98b] with the Creator's praise: *Nu a his lof standeþ* [Now his praise endures forever, 120b]. The creature, whose deeds are the praise of the creator, will arrive, at the end of his work, at reward and immortality. The fates of apostles and poets are joined on the single richly runic occurrence. It is a deliberately ᚠ fortuitous connection. This characteristic Cynewulfian device of simultaneous linking and differentiating through the doubled use of a single word is seen too in the apposition of worldly possession and spiritual possession: concerning the former, *eorlas þæs on eorðan brucaþ* [earls enjoy this on earth, 99a] whereas the latter, positioned on the same verb, *brucaþ,* is seen as an absolute survival tool for the proper *way out* of this world:

> Wic sindon uncuð,
> eard ond eðel,   swa bið ælcum menn
> nemþe he godcundes   gastes bruce.

> (112b–14)

[The places are unknown, dwelling and homeland, so be it to each of men unless he enjoy godly grace.]

So too, the impossibility of enjoying earthly wealth forever is affirmed as an absolute: *Ne moton hie awa ætsomne* [They (men and their treasures—here one thinks invariably of the fool and his money which are soon parted) may not be together forever, 99b]. But the notion of in-variable parting is played skillfully against the notion of everlasting con-nection, a notion brilliantly foregrounded in the poet's choice of the twinned exemplars of eternally linked fortunes—Simon and Thaddeus described earlier: *Him wearð bam samod / an endedæg* [a single death-day brought both of them together, 78b–79a].

In a final interesting word link, describing the plight of the Torch and Bow (ᚺ and ᚱ runes which I take, with Elliott, to signify man's transient earthly light and life),[10] Cynewulf figures them forth as constrained in *nihtes nearowe* [the narrows of the night, 104a] a particularly imprison-ing image that recalls the *nearwe searwe* [oppressive skill, 13b] of Nero earlier in the poem which caused the deaths of Peter and Paul. But even as that *nearwe searwe* led to the apostlehood becoming *wide geweorðod* [widely honored, 15a], so too the poetic *cyninges þeodom* [service of the king, 105a] offers to the poet the possibility of fame and immortality at the same time that it imposes a narrow constraint upon him. In the coherence of the runic signature of *Fates of the Apostles*, Cynewulf clearly hopes to relate himself and his poetry to the *halgan heape* [holy fellowship, 9a] who have already been granted the enduring life beyond time where all is *ece ond edgiong* [eternal and renewed in youth, 122a].

ELENE

Cynewulf's distinct art of creating signature sections from the mate-rials of the preceding poem is equally apparent in the conclusion to *Elene* where verbal surfaces and deeper imaginative structures of narrative and signature thread over and under one another like the warp and woof of Eastern weaving. Such patterned design forcefully shapes the opening of the signature where Cynewulf introduces his personal presence into the text—*Þus ic frod ond fus þurh þæt fæcne hus* [thus, I, old and ready to leave this fraudulent house (body), 1236]—and immediately observes *Nysse ic gearwe / be ðære rode riht* [I did not exactly know the truth about the cross, 1239b–40a]. It is a typically synthetic verbal play whereby Cynewulf connects himself signally to the adult conversions of Constantine, Helena, Symon, and Judas, the four major figures of the poem, all of whom, like Cynewulf, grow from scant to deep knowledge of the cross in the course of poetic events. Furthermore, the single word *frod*, which has occasioned a certain amount of fruitless speculation as to Cynewulf's advanced age at the time of composition, is probably bet-

[10] Elliott, "Runes in *Juliana* and *Fates*," p. 196.

ter understood as a word deliberately employed to associate the poet with the *frod fyrngewritu* [wise old writings, 431a] referred to by Judas when he tells his fellow Jews "the truth about the cross" as he learned it from his father, Symon, *guma gehðum frod* [a man wise with sorrow, 531a] who in turn had been instructed about the salvific cross by his father, Sachius, *frod fyrnwiota* [a wise prophet, 438a]. Such deliberate verbal filiation, which places the poet in a genealogy of those charged with the story of the cross, is consonant with the Cynewulfian technique evident elsewhere in the poem. When Cynewulf ventures autobiographical information about the compositional act, *wordcræftum wæf ond wundrum læs* [wove wordcraft and wondrously gathered, 1237] he describes a process of reordering his thoughts in the straits of the night— *þragum þreodude ond geþanc reodode / nihtes nearwe* [thought through and at times reordered (my) thought in the narrows of the night, 1238–39a]. The language, which curiously recalls the opening lines of the *Dream of the Rood* (*hwæt me gemætte to midre nihte* [what appeared to me in the middle of the night]), is subtly evocative of the nighttime anxieties and resolutions of Constantine with which the *Elene* begins. At the same time, such consciously employed "wordcraft" binds the poet to the person of Judas who is characterized in the poem as *wordes cræftig* [skilled in words, 419a] and *wordcræftes wis* [wise in wordcraft, 592a]. Judas too, like Cynewulf, has reordered his thoughts about the cross in a latterday fashion, confessing *ðæt soþ to late seolf gecneowe* [I myself perceived that truth too late, 708], and likewise through a peculiarly nocturnal constraint . . . *duguða leas / siomode in sorgum VII nihta fyrst* [bereft of blessing he dwelt in sorrows for the space of seven nights, 693b–94]. Having cast these opening phrases of the signature section in terms that posit so fine an ambiance between the Cynewulfian, the Constantinian and the Judeccan histories out of which the *Elene* is woven, the poetry deliberately extends this sense of connection between biographical and hagiographical impulse.

Ic wæs weorcum fah,
synnum asæled,   sorgum gewæled,
bitrum gebunden,   bisgum beþrungen,
ær me lare onlag   þurh leohtne had
gamelum to geoce,   gife unscynde
mægencyning amæt   ond on gemynd begeat,
torht ontynde,   tidum gerymde,
bancofan onband,   breostlocan onwand,
leoðucræft onleac.   Þæs ic lustum breac,
willum in worlde.

(1242b–51a)

[I was darkened with deeds, snared by sins, tormented with troubles, bitterly bound, circled with sorrows, before the mighty King meted out knowledge, enlightened me, in wondrous wise, glorious grace to console me in my age, and infused in my mind the kindled clearness, made wider the while, unbound my body, loosened my heartlocks, unfastened my songcraft. I have used it with joy, with love through my lifetime.]

Now clearly the poet here is describing, with post-Caedmonian confessional fullness, his reception of the grace of songcraft after a prior experience of embattled anxiety. But it is interesting that the language manages at the same time to evoke Constantine, *Modsorge wæg / Romwara cyning* [The King of the Romans bore heart-sorrow, 61b–62a]: *wæs afyrhted, / egsan geaclad* [was afraid, troubled with terrors, 56b–57a] prior to his own luminous experience of crucial revelation. Indeed, the Cynewulfian conclusion that extends the joy of the gift over the rest of his lifetime is close in spirit and letter to the summary remarks concerning Constantine's entry into new life via baptism:

> ... se leodfruma
> fulwihte onfeng   ond þæt forð geheold
> on his dagana tid,   dryhtne to willan.

(191a–93)

[. . . the prince received (the gift of) baptism, and fostered it henceforth for the rest of his life according to God's will.]

Nevertheless, with verbal technique that we can now recognize as characteristic, Cynewulf continues to connect himself not only to the victorious Constantine, but equally to the anxiously constrained Judas. The cross as ultimate triumph is established in the narrative of *Elene;* it is the victory token of the biographical signature section as well. And yet, as that signature tells us, Cynewulf achieved this poem, as well as his enlarged salvific insights, only after years of painful ponderings that are uncannily close to the ponderings of Judas *ymb þæt halige treo* [about that holy tree, 442b]. Indeed, those excruciating reflections of Judas that comprise one of the extended dramatic tensions of *Elene,* flow like an undercurrent through the concluding Cynewulfian statement that we now sense to be only quasi-personal, or, more accurately, more-than-merely-personal:

> oft, nales æne,   hæfde ingemynd
> ær ic þæt wundor   onwrigen hæfde

325

ymb þone beorhtan beam,   swa ic on bocum fand,
wyrda gangum,   on gewritum cyðan
be ðam sigebeacne.

(1252–56a)

[Not once but often I had in mind that shining tree before I had explained the wonder about the bright wood, as I found in books in the course of events, revealed in writings about the victory beacon.]

Even in the most narrowly constrained section of the signature—those lines containing the invariable rune signs themselves—Cynewulf manages to introduce certain clef-words that provide associative access to the earlier narrative parts of *Elene*. Thus *nearusorge dreah* and *enge rune* [endured narrowing sorrow; severe secret, 1260b–61a], phrases Cynewulf uses to describe the poet-as-everyman in his doomed earthly limitations, resound with echoes of the unconverted Judas in his *nearwe . . . engan hofe* [narrow . . . straitened cell, 711a–12a]. Indeed, the very word *nydcleofan,* also used in line 711 in connection with Judas' incarceration, reappears like some verbal wayfarer in line 1275 of the signature, to describe the transient life of man in terms of a wind that rises up furiously, fares forth, and then is returned to the punishing still of a *nydcleofan,* or narrow prison cell—in this case, the grave.

Such typical reflections on the brevity of the temporal moment comprise a significant portion of the *Elene* signature, and the familiar theme is couched in fairly conventional language:

Nu synt geardagas
æfter fyrstmearce   forð gewitene,
lifwynne geliden,   swa ᚱ toglideð,
flodas gefysde.

(1266b–69a)

[Now is the past, after an interval, sped forth, the joys of life fled, as water flows away, hastening the floods.]

Still, it is interesting to note that the essence of brevity and temporality hang together here on the rune sign for water, ᚱ , and on the signal word *fyrstmearc*. But the word and water have already been joined earlier in the poem (1033) to describe Judas at the moment of his baptism; his baptism, in turn, touches the earlier christening of King Constantine: such a collocation of Christian "living waters" (waters that of course

326

include the Christian poet) affords a subtly felicitous redemptive contact
with the traditional elegiac tone being sounded.

So too that part of the signature that figuratively describes man's
proud but passing prowess on earth:

> þær him M fore
> milpaðas mæt,   modig þrægde
> wirum gewlenced.

(1261b–63a)

[when the horse formerly ran, measured the milepaths, pranced proudly,
decked with precious metal.]

The passage is a poignant one, quickened as it is with the sudden
contrast of ᚹ *is geswiðrad* [delight is diminished, 1263b] that immediately follows. In one sense, the image seems almost conventional, the
language perhaps interchangeable with any number of other meditations
in Anglo-Saxon poetry on the transitory nature of man's human moment
and the ultimate withering of the world. Still, the reader experiences a
subtle excitement playing about the words here as they construe the
image of the proudly mounted man with verbal specifics calculated to
recall for us that earlier picture of Constantine, his horse ornamented
with a bridle made for him by Elene, fashioned from the precious metal
of the nails with which Christ was crucified (1127–1200). The consistent, inventive poetic of the Cynewulfian signature section is operating
again through the subtleties of wordcraft to fuse the specific author and
specific subject of the poem to an elaborately imaged idea of man in his
most universal guise. This inseparability of poet and poem is a peculiarly
aesthetic coefficient of the later Yeatsian "dancer and dance," and it
suggests a greater complexity of art in these runic structures than we
have been accustomed to look for.

CHRIST II

The question of unity that vexes every reader of the *Christ* is resurrected afresh by the poetic methodology of Cynewulfian composition for
the signatures that I have been inferring here. If, indeed, the language
of the signature section consciously plots referential verbal paths to essential contact points in the poem to which it intentionally means to
attach itself, a close scrutiny of the language of the signature section of

Christ II may well be a heretofore unopened door on a problem by no means definitively resolved.[11] The question of linguistic and imagistic texturing is, of course, particularly complicated in the three-part *Christ* by the obviously derivative quality of shapely but conventional language used in each of the three texts—univocally liturgical imageries drawn variously from the Ascension homiletics of Gregory which structure *Christ II,* the Advent Antiphonic usages of *Christ I,* and the hortatory Apocalyptic language of *Christ III*.[12] A further complicating datum in any discussion of the unity or discretion of the three poetries is the peculiar location of the signature section of *Christ:* if we logically assume, on the basis of the other three signed poems, that the signature poses a compositional terminus, then *Christ II* would certainly seem to be a separate poem, accidentally joined in manuscript to two other separate poems because of their common Christocentric subject.[13]

A small thorn remains in the otherwise comfortable flesh of such a theory. Aside from dismissing a certain impressionistic coherence sensed among the three panels of the triptych by such serious scholars of the poem as Cook, Dietrich, Mather, Gerould, and Moore,[14] who sought variously over the past century to objectify their subjective impressions of a deliberate unity, the argument for three entirely discrete compositions requires that we ignore a salient fact about the verbal artificing of this signature: until the literal "last word" in the last line of the poem, *þa he heofonum astag* [when he rose up to heaven, 866b], nowhere do the ideas and images that vivify this signature section invoke the prior poetry that deals with the central Ascension event of *Christ II.* This

[11] The general tenor of recent criticism is best invoked by John Collins Pope in his 1964 Preface to the Reproduction of Albert S. Cook's Edition of *The Christ of Cynewulf* (Archon Books, Hamden, Connecticut): Pope says, "Times have changed. The poem that Cook so lovingly described as a three-part whole is now generally regarded as three separate poems, of which only the second, with its runic signature, can safely be attributed to Cynewulf" (p. iii). One concern of this essay is the qualified modification of such apparent critical univocality. There are many hypothetical questions still unresolved in the unity problem, and such an assured air of critical resolution seems to me not in the best interest of the *Christ.*

[12] For a comprehensive review of suggested sources for each of the three sections of *Christ,* cf. especially Schaar, pp. 35–39, 71–73, and 106. Schaar's work precedes *The Advent Lyrics of the Exeter Book,* ed., Jackson J. Campbell (Princeton, 1959).

[13] Brother Augustine Philip, "The Exeter Scribe and the Unity of the *Christ,*" *PMLA,* 55 (1940), 903–09, develops this argument at length. Elsewhere in this volume, Robert E. Diamond, "The Diction of the Old English *Christ,*" assumes it. Schaar, pp. 104–08, gives a careful accounting of scholars' treating of the problem of the Christ trilogy from Dietrich's initial detailed study in 1853 through Kenneth Mildenberger's iconographic argument for unity in his "Unity of Cynewulf's *Christ* in the Light of Iconography," *Speculum,* 23 (July, 1948), 426–32.

[14] Cf. Schaar, pp. 104–08.

would seem to be a singular state of poetic affairs in light of the clear compositional methodology of constructing the signatures that has operated in the other three signed poems. Furthermore, the poetic of the signature of *Christ II* appears to have in fact been rigorously arranged in a way that causes the reader to move backwards into the Advent and Nativity themes of *Christ I* and forward into the Judgment and Doom considerations of *Christ III*.

It is true, of course, that *Christ II* itself makes use of certain Incarnational and Judgmental references; the first ten lines, following their Gregorian source, recall specifics of the birth in Bethlehem, and there are equally explicit Doomsday reflections at the conclusion of the poem. Nonetheless, we might consider the possibility that such deliberate referential constructions, bracketing, as it were, a poem whose chief subject is Christ's Ascension, could imply the poet's intention to draw a reader's mind precisely to the fact that the work had been consciously artificed to occupy its present medial position between *Christ I* and *Christ III*. In any case, what emerges from this possibly deliberate construction of rhythmically regular movement—forward to the third section, backward to the first—is a peculiar fulcrum feeling carefully wrought about the second and signed portion of the poem. This, I suspect, is partially what critics have responded to when they have "sensed" a unity among the poems, even where careful lexical, stylistic, and dictional indications toward an apparently contrary hypothesis of multiple authorship have been ventured.[15] The suggestion by Moore[16] that we need to separate the question of unity from the question of authorship may not be the conundrum it might superficially appear to be.

Indeed, my suggestion here is that we consider the following as probable:[17] Cynewulf had available to himself two extant poems dealing with the salvific events of Incarnation and Parousia. (Perhaps the two poems were those of a single author—perhaps the author of one or both of them was Cynewulf himself at an earlier point in his poetic career—none of these auctorial suppositions needs to have been the case.) Deciding to compose a poetry which would both touch and yoke the *terminus a quo* (Incarnation) and *terminus ad quem* (Judgment) of Christian salvation history, a poet intimate with the scriptures and liturgies of the

---

[15] Cf. Schaar and Diamond, who refers to many of these studies as "the long list of scholars who have arrived at what is probably the right answer by using questionable methods."

[16] Samuel Moore, "The Old English *Christ: Is It a Unit?*", *JEGP*, 14 (1915), 550–67.

[17] Cook, in his discussion of the Unity of Christ, refers (p. xviii) to Sievers' suggested possibility that *Christ I* and *Christ II* might belong to a different period of composition from *Christ III*, all three being the work of the one poet.

Church would not be unaware that the Church herself deliberately signifies such connection. Thus the second coming of Christ as Judge comprises the Gospel reading for both the last Sunday after Pentecost and the first Sunday of Advent, causing the beginning and end of the liturgical cycle to converge on a given occasion within a single text. Neither, it seems to me, would a poet as liturgically sensitive as Cynewulf obviously was be unaware that, regardless of the movable feast of Easter around which the ecclesiastical calendar is arranged, the weeks of the liturgical year divide in half on the occasion of the feast of the Ascension, celebrated forty days after Easter and immediately prior to Pentecost Sunday. The subsequent Sundays after Pentecost (which cannot number more than twenty-eight nor less than twenty-three, depending on the dating of Easter) adjust correspondingly with a variable number of Sundays after the Epiphany to fulfill the entire liturgical circuit which was (and is) considered to be a yearly synchronic reenactment of the diachronics of human redemption. Here, I venture, we can plausibly infer a compelling unitive liturgical rationale for a three part *Christ* poem that surprisingly ignores such signal Christian events as the Crucifixion and Resurrection, to place the Ascension of Christ at the exact poetic midpoint between His first and His second coming.[18]

The ecclesiastical year begins with Advent; it concludes on the liturgically apocalyptic last Sunday after Pentecost; and it locates the Ascension exactly midway between these two points. By this arrangement of

---

[18] Mildenberger, p. 426, referring to Dietrich's sense of theological unity—the threefold "coming" evident to Dietrich in the materials of the Advent, Ascension and Judgment poetries—observes, "This trilogy was composed of the themes of Advent, Ascension, and Judgment, corresponding roughly to the divisions in the manuscript. Attractive as this [Dietrich's] proposal seemed some foundation for it had to be found in contemporary or antecedent church philosophy before it could be persuasively argued; proof of a local and current eighth century association of the three dominant themes was necessary. Neither Dietrich nor his supporters have produced such evidence." Cook, too, p. xvii, refers to Dietrich's argument, dismissing the designation of the Ascension as a "coming" of Christ back to Heaven, and calling it "not less strained" to designate the Ascension "as the middle point of the life of Christ, the Nativity and the Last Judgment marking the beginning and end."

My suggestion here of the clear liturgical basis of such a threefold arrangement, with a medial position for the Ascension, seems to me to provide quite securely for the association demanded by Mildenberger of the three dominant themes in the eighth century; indeed the association in the liturgy endures in the twentieth century. Hopefully, too, my suggestion of the liturgical rationale eases Cook's legitimate "sense of strain" at Dietrich's locating the Ascension at a biographical midpoint between Christ's Incarnation and Judgment, and makes unnecessary the argument for three "comings" in order to establish an intentional connection of the three parts of *Christ*.

the Church year, the *Proprium de Tempora* [Proper of the Time] signifies and stresses the twofold necessity of Christ's coming and dwelling
on earth, to be followed by the ongoing apostolic work of the Church
continued by her members after Christ's departure from earth, a departure and division dramatically signalled on Ascension Thursday by the
extinguishing of the Paschal candle.

Attention to the verbal specifics of the *Christ II* signature tends to
confirm this hypothesis of a deliberately woven Cynewulfian construction of triptychal coherence intended to explicitly unify the stylistically
various parts of the *Christ*. The signature section opens with a reference
to the "Judgment at hand where we shall be requited according to the
works of our lives on earth," (*Is þam dome neah / þæt we gelice sceolon
leanum hleotan, / swa we wideteorh weorcum hlodun / geond sidne
grund,* 782b–85a). Though conventionally phrased, these lines push us
forward to the judgmental sensibility to be apotheosized in *Christ III,*
where the works of our lives on earth will be "opened," much like the
graves of the dead, *Opene weorþað / ofer middangeard monna dæde*
[The deeds of men will be opened on the earth, 1045b–46]. This forward
thrust toward Judgment in the *Christ II* signature immediately returns
back to the Advent sensibility of *Christ I* for its next verbal moment.
While maintaining a dense poetic connection with the "opening on
earth" image that has been deposited as a physical and spiritual emblem
for the ending of the world, the poet now uses the same notion of an
"opening on earth" as the physical and spiritual emblem of Christ's
incarnational flowering: *hu æt ærestan eadmod astag / in middangeard
mægna goldhord, / in fæmnan fæðm freobearn godes, / halig of heahþu*
[how the treasure house of might first humbly sprang up on earth in the
womb of a woman, God's freeborn Son, holy from on high, 786–89a].
The athleticism of the language here (*astag* [sprang up]) subtly evokes
the Incarnational *forma hlyp* [first leap, 720] of the Six Leaps of Christ
elaborated earlier in *Christ II* (720–38); it also reminds us, by such
evocation, that the "sixth leap" was that of Christ's Ascension into
Heaven, the central event poeticized in *Christ II*. Furthermore, this language of "leaping," while explicated in *Christ II* (712–719) as deriving
from an image in the Song of Solomon (Canticles 2:8), also echoes
another scriptural and liturgical usage found, not surprisingly, in the
Antiphon for Vespers and Lauds for the Fourth Sunday of Advent, and
reappearing in the Introit for the Mass of the Sunday within the Octave
of Christmas, and the first Antiphon for Vespers of that feast: *Dum
medium silentium tenerent omnia, et nox in suo cursu medium iter ha-
beret, omnipotens sermo tuus, Domine de caelis a regalibus sedibus venit*

331

[While all things were in quiet silence, and the night was in the midst of her course, Your Almighty Word leapt down from heaven, from Your royal throne, O Lord].[19]

From the comforting humanity invoked in the scripturally recalled Nativity, the signature moves forward inexorably to the dread anxiety of the anticipated judging Divinity. The poet expects and dreads a doom the sterner when the Prince of angels comes again (*Huru ic wene me / ond eac ondræde dom ðy rebran, / ðonne eft cymeð engla þeoden . . . ,* 789b–91).

This liturgically replicative alternation between comfort and dread is sustained in the poetry of the signature as the lines containing the rune signs themselves present a concatenation of flood imagery, suggestive of birth, life, and redemption, which gradually evaporates in the consuming imagery of judgmental destruction and doom. ᚾ *wæs longe / ᚢ flodum bilocen, lifwynna dæl, / ᚣ on foldan. Þonne frætwe sculon / byrnan on bæle* [For a long time ᚾ (Manly strength) was at hightide, lakelike, / the portion of lifejoys, wealth in the world, 805b–08a]. Then, the poet suggests, the treasures of the world are to be burned in the blaze, a blaze which will "rush fiercely around the wide world" (*repe scripeð / geond woruld wide,* 809b–10a).

This rhythmic management of alternating comfort and anxiety continues in the subsequent consoling incarnational alignment of man and God, both verbally characterized as "world dwellers" (cp. 817–18 and 821–23), a consolation immediately revised by the terrifyingly separatist vision of sinners in the hands of that same God, returned to the earth once more, and angry now: *þonne eft cymeð / reðe ond ryhtwis* [when he comes again, angry and righteous, 824b–25a]. As the signature section concludes, these terse alternations give way to swollen alternations of hot and fiery images of dread and judgment, followed by cool and

[19] This particular passage from Wisdom, 18:14–15, is the text chosen by William McGarry, S.J., *He Cometh* (New York, 1941), p. 40, to illustrate the scriptural process of "accommodation," the using of Old Testament sources to embellish and elucidate New Testament events. "The process supposes the fulfilment of the Old Testament in the New; it justifies itself on the principle that little is contained in the Old Testament promise (mighty though it is), while the whole Godhood is contained in the New Testament fulfillment." McGarry (p. 41) goes on to quote the verse from Wisdom and observe, "Here the liturgy drops the following: 'as a fierce conqueror in the midst of a land of destruction,' for the original context (Wis. 18:14) belongs to a description of the avenging angel of Egypt's first-born at the first Pasch, and the words do not suit the spirit of Advent. In the original again, the *word* is the avenging angel; in the accommodation it is the Word of God." This process of scriptural "accommodation," practiced from the earliest days of the church, suggests too the poetic option to freely rearrange scriptural materials for specific liturgical ends that seems to have informed the poet(s) of *Christ I, II,* and *III.*

refreshing images of God's continued guidance and redemptive grace offered to mankind on earth. Thus, the *fyrbaðe* [firebath, 830b], the *þeodegsa* [widespread fear, 833b], the *egsa mara / þonne from frumgesceape gefrægen wurde / æfre on eorðan* [terror greater than any ever heard of on earth since the beginning of creation, 838b–40a], and the *gryrebrogan* of the *gæsnan tid* [furious terror of the ghastly time, 848b–49a], are quite literally "cooled," poetically quenched by the *cald wæter* [cold water, 851a] and the *laguflode,* [floodtide, 850b], the *frecne stream* [daring stream, 853b], and the *windge holmas* [windtossed waves, 855b] that lead to the assuring final assertion that God will continue to send us help as he formerly sent his "spiritual son" (*godes gæstsunu,* 860a),

> ond us giefe sealde
> þæt we oncnawan magun   ofer ceoles bord
> hwær we sælan sceolon   sundhengestas,
> ealde yðmearas,   ancrum fæste.

(860b–63)

[and gave us grace that we may know, from the ship's deck, where we must tie up with anchors fast our sea horses, old wave mares].

The compositional methodology I have inferred for the construction of the four signature sections of the signed Cynewulf poems raises questions that are not within the scope of this essay to answer. For example, insofar as the deliberate connection of the signature to the prior poem by a subtle use of the poem's own verbal network now seems a plausible inference, to that extent we must entertain the further, and surprising, possibility that perhaps these signature portions alone are all that is authentically "Cynewulfian" in the signed poem.[20] Such a possibility is tantalizingly implied by the necessarily suppositious, but nonetheless entirely arguable, suggestion that the signature section of *Christ II* has in fact been consciously and deliberately artificed to establish that poem as a poetic fixture of unity between pre-existing texts, yoking the precedent Advent focus of *Christ I* and the subsequent apocalyptic focus of *Christ III*. Such a centrist location of *Christ II* is focally supported by that peculiarly liturgical sensibility that has always been recognized as lying at

[20] Sandra J. Harmatiuk, on the basis of discoveries reported in her unpublished doctoral dissertation, "A Statistical Approach to Some Aspects of Style in the Signed Poems of Cynewulf: A Computer-Assisted Study" (University of Notre Dame, 1975), has ventured a preliminary opinion that the poet who composed *Juliana* was not the same poet who composed the other signed poems.

the heart of the *Christ* and variously shaping the vocabulary of image and idea in each of its three sections. Undoubtedly, stylistic studies now underway and those still to be undertaken will provide tentative answers to these questions, and in the best tradition of critical *aeternitatem,* generate new questions in turn.

What does seem unarguable at this point is the fact that a poet, who signed himself CYN(E)WULF, through the elaborate human exercise of art in each of these four runic signatures, reached, with faith and good works, toward an existence beyond the temporal human sentence. It is, literally and figuratively, the only salvation for a poet to whom words are deeds.

Wisdom Literature
MAXIM, RIDDLE, AND GNOME

22

Maxims II:
Gnome and Poem

STANLEY B. GREENFIELD
RICHARD EVERT

THE EARLIEST SURVIVING CRITICAL ASSESSMENT OF THE COTTON TI-
berius B. i. *Maxims II* is the remark, added by George Hickes to his
1703 Latin translation, that the poem is a work of which the "elegantia,
splendor et proprietas Latine exhiberi non possunt" [elegance, brilliance,
and special quality cannot be shown in Latin].[1] Hickes's successors, unfortunately, have been considerably less impressed with the literary value
of the poem; for although they have often treated it (and its inevitable
companion, the Exeter *Maxims I*) as a cultural artifact, few have shown
any interest in it as a poem, except as a basis for generalizations about
"gnomology." Yet *Maxims II* appears in many Old English readers, and
experience in teaching the poem reveals that, despite the disinterest of
critics, beginning students of Old English respond enthusiastically to its
poetry. Perhaps a literary interpretation of the poem can explain both
the enthusiasm of students and Hickes's respectful assessment and, at
the same time, serve as a tribute to the inspirational teaching and scholarship of John McGalliard.

Commentary on *Maxims II* has, generally, denied any aesthetic unity
to the poem, and in so doing has itself achieved a unity rare in Old

---

[1] Quoted in Blanche Colton Williams, *Gnomic Poetry in Anglo-Saxon* (New
York, 1914), p. 104.

English criticism. Indeed, many of the poem's critics have discerned the hand of a monkish reviser at work upon heathen material. Typical of this view is the remark with which Blanche Colton Williams concludes her reading: "That the pattern is torn and corrupt, that the heathen foundation is patched with Christian embroidery,—that there is absence of integrity must be plain from the preceding brief analysis."[2] Despite the general rejection of theories of interpolation and the open-mindedness to the possibility of complex thematic development which have characterized post-World War II Old English scholarship, critics tend to see *Maxims II* as a rather loose pastiche. One recent critic refers to the poem as a "catalogue" and a "handbook."[3] Another, who applies a "stream of consciousness" analysis to the poem by explaining the arrangement of the lines as the result of phonic or conceptual associations in the *scop's* mind, assesses the technique he has ascribed to the poet as "a rambling style which covers a great deal of ground, yet never reaches any particular goal. This is not, perhaps, a good pattern for a poem, but it is an adequate one, and is far more satisfactory than the total absence of form which many critics feel to be characteristic of these poems [i.e., *Maxims I* and *Maxims II*]."[4] The very titles given over the years to our poem, *Versus Gnomici, Denksprüche, Cotton Gnomes,* and *Maxims II,*[5] demonstrate the persistence of the critical commonplaces that the poem is a compilation, not a creation, and that it is best viewed as being of a piece with a certain portion of the Exeter Book.

Because critics have seen *Maxims I* and *Maxims II* as mere collections of gnomes, discussion of the genre of these poems has been limited largely to attempts to define the individual gnome. The most comprehensive modern definition is that of the Chadwicks, who begin by quoting Aristotle: "A gnome is a statement not relating to particulars, as e.g. the

---

[2] Williams, p. 110. See also Alois Brandl, "Englische Literatur," *Grundriss der Germanischen Philologie,* ed. Hermann Paul, 2nd ed., Vol. II, part 1 (Strassburg, 1901–09), 960.

[3] Paul Beekman Taylor, "Heroic Ritual in the Old English Maxims," *NM,* 70 (1969), 387 and 388, respectively. See also Elliott van Kirk Dobbie, ed., *The Anglo-Saxon Minor Poems,* Vol. VI of *ASPR* (New York, 1942), lxvi, where *Maxims II* is described as "characterized by lack of unity in content and arrangement, and . . . a purely mechanical juxtaposition of ideas gathered from a great diversity of sources."

[4] R. MacGregor Dawson, "The Structure of the Old English Gnomic Poems," *JEGP,* 61 (1962), 22. The principle of association is endorsed by Gerd Wolfgang Weber, *Wyrd: Studien zum Schicksalsbegriff der altenglischen und altnordischen Literatur* (Berlin, 1969), p. 111, who points out that this view was also proposed by Max Rieger, "Über Cynevulf," *ZfdPh,* 1 (1869), 332.

[5] C. W. M. Grein, ed., *Bibliothek der Angelsächsischen Poesie,* Vol. II (Göttingen, 1858), 346; Richard P. Wülker, ed., *Bibliothek der Angelsächsischen Poesie,* Vol. I (Kassel, 1883), 338; Williams, p. 126; Dobbie, p. 55; respectively.

character of Iphicrates, but to universals; yet not to all universals indiscriminately, as e.g. that straight is the opposite of crooked, but to all such as are the objects of (human) action and are to be chosen or avoided in our doings."[6] The Chadwicks are quick to note that the modern usage of *gnome* embraces several classes of statements not covered by Aristotle's definition. Accordingly they divide gnomes into two major types: I, gnomes which deal with human choice and judgment, i.e., Aristotelian gnomes, and II, gnomes of observation, i.e., all gnomes which are not of type I. The topics of type II gnomes are divided into three subclasses: "(a) human activities or experiences in which no choice or judgment is involved, (b) the operations of Fate (death) and the gods, (c) all other gnomes belonging to this type. . . ."[7] The open-endedness of subclass (c), which is meant to include gnomes which discuss the processes of nature, reflects the difficulty of classifying the individual statement as to subject. Yet the Chadwicks insisted on the importance of the broad distinction between gnomes which dealt with human choice and those which dealt with matters beyond human choice, even though, as they point out in reference to *Maxims II*, both types may be expressed with the same verbal formulae.[8] Blanche Colton Williams defined *gnome* as "a sententious saying; in particular, it may be proverbial, figurative, moral."[9] Similarly, Kenneth Jackson states: "A 'gnome' is a sententious statement about universals, as well about the world of nature ('nature gnome') as about the affairs of men ('human gnome'). . . ."[10] The definitions of Williams and Jackson are probably about as close as one can get to a clear definition of the individual gnomic statement. Yet it is interesting to note the dissatisfaction with Williams's definition expressed in a 1916 review of her book by J. W. Rankin, who remarked, "certainly an inclusive definition, but necessarily so if it is to take in sayings such as *Forst sceal freosan, Winter byð cealdost,* and the like; which indeed are sententious only on the assumption that much more is meant than meets the ear."[11] We would like to suggest that a collocation of gnomes, such as *Maxims II,* can create a meaning which is greater than the sum of individual gnomes which meet the ear. If this is so, then an

---

[6] *Rhetoric,* II.21 as quoted by H. Munro Chadwick and Nora K. Chadwick, *The Ancient Literatures of Europe,* Vol. I of *The Growth of Literature* (Cambridge, England, 1932), p. 377.

[7] The Chadwicks, p. 377.

[8] The Chadwicks, p. 378.

[9] Williams, p. 3.

[10] Kenneth Jackson, *Studies in Early Celtic Nature Poetry* (Cambridge, England, 1935), p. 127.

[11] J. W. Rankin, rev. of *Gnomic Poetry in Anglo-Saxon* by Blanche Colton Williams, *JEGP,* 15 (1916), 163.

understanding of what a particular gnomic poem is must be sought in the investigation of the interaction between the individual gnome and its specific context.

In a recent essay Patrizia Lendinara takes the position that *Maxims II* is not a gnomic poem at all, but a hymn to creation like the Old English *Order of the World.*[12] While our own reading of the poem differs from hers significantly, we endorse her concern for *Maxims II* as a unified entity and believe the poem subtly develops the idea that true wisdom ultimately reveals the limitations of human knowledge. These limitations, implicit throughout the poem, are made explicit in the final section in the poet's statement that men cannot know the nature of the heavenly kingdom. This development, coupled with a movement from consideration of the *visibilia* of the earthly experience to the *invisibilia* of the heavenly, gives the poem its unity. The handling of its traditional verbal, rhythmic, and syntactic counters gives it that *elegantia, splendor,* and *proprietas* that Hickes observed in it. It shall be our concern in what follows to examine more closely this unity and quality of presentation.

The poem begins with the statement, *Cyning sceal rice healdan,*[13] a verse that sets the dominant syntactic form and tone and alerts the listener or reader to the poetic genre. We suspect that the generic suggestion was a signal to the audience to prepare to exercise its critical intelligence on this piece of wisdom literature.[14] Note the alternative meanings: "A king ought to rule (or preserve) a kingdom" (i.e., a king ought to rule it rather than abuse or neglect it), or "A king shall rule a kingdom" (i.e., it is the nature of a king to rule a kingdom), or "A king must rule a kingdom" (i.e., each kingdom must be ruled by some king). The crux of the verse lies, of course, in the verb *sceal*. Does that term have a prescriptive or descriptive sense? Are we being told what kings ought to do or what they, in fact, do? We shall return later to this problem.

The poem continues with a purely descriptive reference to cities.

> Ceastra beoð feorran gesyne,
> orðanc enta geweorc, þa þe on þysse eorðan syndon,
> wrætlic weallstana geweorc.

> (1b–3a)

---

[12] Patrizia Lendinara, "I *Versi Gnomici* Anglosassoni," *Annali, Sezione Germanica* (Naples), 14 (1971), 134–36; cf. Weber, p. 109.

[13] The text of *Maxims II* given here is essentially that of Dobbie, pp. 55–57, although we have occasionally altered his punctuation and, where noted below, his readings of individual words.

[14] T. A. Shippey, although he does not treat *Maxims II* as wisdom literature, urges the importance of this category for Old English criticism in his *Old English Verse* (London, 1972), pp. 67–68. See also Morton W. Bloomfield, "Understanding Old English Poetry," *Annuale Mediaevale,* 9 (1968), 16–25.

[Cities, the skillful work of giants, those (cities) which are on this earth, the marvellous work of wall-stones, are visible from afar.]

Ceastra is given two variations and a modifying relative clause, and, given the terse style of the major portion of the poem, this relatively expansive treatment well expresses the cities' impressive extension both in space and time. The poet conveys the physical magnitude of the cities not by saying they are large, but by telling us that they are "visible from afar," much as the gold-roofed Heorot gleamed over many lands. By this device the poet does not merely observe; he begins to establish the essential perspective of the poem: human knowledge and observation are limited. For though he tells us what we can know about the cities, he also suggests that we cannot entirely comprehend them. Although their physical magnitude may be perceived, other aspects may not. The double variation of *ceastra* tells us that they are the work of giants, i.e., built by a craft not possessed by men and, therefore, *wrætlic,* something at which men must marvel. The poet intensifies this sense of wonder in line 2b, where the relative clause, by qualifying *ceastra* as those cities which are on *this* earth, intimates that there are cities which may be farther off yet, a suggestion which prepares us for the final mention of the *sigefolca gesetu,* the extraterrestrial locale which cannot be described.[15] The cities on this earth are monuments of the mysterious past, just as the heavenly kingdom lies ahead for each of us in the veiled future.

Having established a context in which observable phenomena offer the possibility of the unobservable, the poet moves to a generalized characterization of the earthly world by means of a list of superlatives.

<pre>
                            Wind byð on lyfte swiftust,
þunar byð þragum hludast,   —þrymmas syndan Cristes myccle—
wyrd byð swiðost: winter byð cealdost,
lencten hrimigost   (he byð lengest ceald),
sumor sunwlitegost   (swegel byð hatost),
hærfest hreðeadegost,   hæleðum bringeð
geres wæstmas,   þa þe him God sendeð.
Soð bið switolost,   sinc byð deorost,
gold gumena gehwam,   and gomol snoterost,
fyrngearum frod,   se þe ær feala gebideð.
</pre>

(3b–12)

[Wind is in the sky the swiftest, thunder is at times the loudest—the glories of Christ are many—*wyrd* is most powerful: winter is the coldest, spring the frostiest (it is cold for the longest time), summer the most

15 A similar suggestion is made by Richard Hamer, *A Choice of Anglo-Saxon Verse* (London, 1970), p. 110 n.

radiant with sun (the sun is the hottest), autumn the most glorious, it brings to men the fruits of the year, which God sends to them. Truth is the most evident, treasure is dearest, gold (dearest) to each of men, and the old one the wisest, experienced on account of his former years, he who has experienced much.]

The most noteworthy fact about the poet's use of the superlative in these lines is the way in which he fails to make explicit a context within which a given quality is superlative. Clarity in the use of the superlative requires that the object to which a superlative quality is attributed be identified as a member of a class of objects within which it is superlative in the sense specified. We say, for example, "Johnny is the tallest boy in my class," or "Johnny is the tallest boy in town," not merely "Johnny is tallest." Except for line 3b, the poet does not specify such contexts, although in some instances the context is fairly clear. Thunder, for example, must be the loudest *of noises* at times *in the world,* winter the coldest *of the seasons in the year,* the old one the wisest *of men,* etc. But of what class of things is truth the most evident, or, in particular, of what is *wyrd* the *swiðost?* The poet's omission of a clarifying context achieves a dual effect: on the one hand, this omission gives to each statement a maximum generality, making it applicable to all conditions *on þysse eorðan;* on the other hand, it produces a riddling quality, especially in lines 4b–5a, where the relationship between *wyrd's* strength and the powers (or glories) of Christ is difficult to determine.

Scholars have long puzzled over this relationship. The difficulty arises both from their lack of understanding of the precise connotations of *wyrd* and from the poet's failure to specify a context within which *wyrd* is *swiðost.* As a result they have felt that *wyrd* and Christ were being compared or contrasted. Williams, for example, assumed that *wyrd* is a supernatural entity of the same order as Christ, and she saw a clear conflict in lines 4b–5a, "Christ and Fate being put in opposition to each other, the predominance of the latter testifying to remote heathen origin."[16] The most persuasive recent scholarship, however, rejects her view on the ground that it misunderstands both the meaning of *wyrd* and the implied limitations under which, to the perceptions of the Anglo-Saxon audience, *wyrd* would be expected to operate. Gerd Weber argues that other references in the poem to the power of God make it clear that to the poet's mind God is the strongest force in the universe.[17] Timmer observes cogently that even if line 4b were an interpolation, surely the interpolator would have struck out the reference to *wyrd* in line 5a, if he

16 Williams, p. 107.
17 Weber, pp. 108 and 111–13.

had felt it to be a kind of rival deity. Timmer's own view is that "the adapter probably read in the word: however great the powers of Christ may be, the order of events as ordained by God's Providence is mightiest."[18] Although Timmer rejects the idea that *wyrd* refers to a personal deity, he still sees it and Christ as being placed in comparison. Yet it seems a strange comparison, a kind of theological hair-splitting, to see the powers of Christ as somehow subordinate to God's providence.[19] It seems fair enough to assume that the Anglo-Saxon Christian audience would have automatically supplied a limiting context to *wyrd byð swiðost* which would eliminate any diminution of respect for the powers of Christ. Weber, moreover, argues that the audience's associations of the Resurrection with *þrymmas syndan Cristes myccle* would place *wyrd* in a subordinate context:

In „þrymmas syndan Cristes myccle" schwingt die Bedeutung ‚gloria' zweifellos mit, denn Christi Ruhm besteht ja zuvörderst in seinen Wundertaten und in der Überwindung des Todes als deren Grösster. Ganz folgerichtig wird der Gedankengang von dieser Ruhmtat Christi zu dem menschlichen Dasein als zu einem zum Tode hinführenden Sein geleitet: Der Mensch unterliegt der ‚wyrd'; der Tod, die Vergänglichkeit ist *in der Welt* am stärksten, von Christus jedoch überwunden worden. Der „Gegensatz" besteht nicht in einem Vergleich der absoluten Macht der ‚wyrd' mit der absoluten Macht Christi als zweier paralleler *ausserweltlicher* Mächte, sondern der Gedanke an Christi Rettertat lenkt das Bewusstsein des Dichters auf den Gegenstand dieser Rettertat, die irdische Vergänglichkeit, der der Mensch völlig unterliegt.[20]

[Without a doubt the meaning *gloria* is implied in *þrymmas syndan Cristes myccle,* for indeed Christ's glory consists primarily in his miracles and in the overcoming of death as the greatest of these. Consequently one's train of thought is led from this glory of Christ to human life as an existence leading to death: Man is subject to *wyrd;* death, transitoriness is the strongest *in the world,* but has been overcome by Christ. The "contrast" consists not in a comparison of the absolute power of *Wyrd* with the absolute power of Christ as two parallel *supernatural* powers, but the thought of Christ's act of deliverance leads the poet's conscious-

[18] Benno J. Timmer, "Wyrd in Anglo-Saxon Prose and Poetry," *Neophil,* 26 (1941), 219–20.

[19] Alois Brandl, who sees *wyrd* as a supernatural being, explores the passage as an example of the gradual transition from heathen to Christian thinking in "Vom kosmologischen Denken des heidnisch-christlichen Germanentums: der früh-ags. Schicksalsspruch der Handschrift Tiberius B. 13 [sic] und seine Verwandtheit mit Boethius," *Sitzungsberichte der preussischen Akademie der Wissenschaften. Phil.-hist. Klasse,* 16 (1937), 116–25.

[20] Weber, p. 112.

ness to the opposite of this act of deliverance, the earthly transitoriness to which man is utterly subject.]

Weber has substituted for the comparison between the power of Christ and the power of *wyrd* the comparison between man as subject to earthly transitoriness and Christ as triumphant over it.

But is it necessary to see a comparison or contrast here, even though the verses are juxtaposed? *Þrymmas,* it should be noted, is the only principal in this section to which no superlative is ascribed. We would, therefore, construe line 4b as a parenthetical remark, as our punctuation and translation above indicate, translating *myccle* as "many."[21] Such a reading not only eliminates the unsatisfactory (or at least disturbing) notion of comparison from the passage, but also suggests that those principals encompassing the parenthesis are manifestations of Christ's glory; and although this reading is adopted by neither Lendinara nor Weber, it squares well with their view of the poem as "Schöpfungspreis." The wind and thunder, then, are two of the many glories of Christ, and *wyrd* likewise is one of them. For *wyrd* in the context of this poem would seem to have the meaning it held for Alfred in his translation of Boethius's *Consolation of Philosophy,* Bk. IV, pr. 6, where he writes: *Ac þæt þæt we wyrd hatað, þæt bið Godes weorc þæt he ælce dæg wyrcð, ægþer ge þæs (ðe) we gesioð ge þæs þe us ungesewenlic bið. . . . Sio wyrd . . . dælð eallum gesceaftum anwlitan and stowa and tida and gemetgunga. . . .*[22] [But what we call *wyrd,* that is God's work that he does each day, both what we see and what is invisible to us. . . . That *wyrd* . . . deals out to all creatures forms and places and times and measures. . . .] The following enumeration of the seasons, progressing from the coldest to the most bounteous, illustrates, then, this most powerful emanation of Christ-God *in this world,* and suggests again the limitations of what man sees and what man does, in his specific dependence upon God's grace.

The poet then uses superlative gnomes to introduce the measure of values in the world of human experience, with his "Truth is most evident (to the understanding),[23] treasure, gold, is the dearest to each of men, and an old man is the wisest. . . ." *Gomol* is given a variation in line 12a and a modifying relative clause in 12b which emphasize the

---

21 *BT* s.v. *micel,* II.

22 Walter J. Sedgefield, *King Alfred's Old English Version of Boethius* (Oxford, 1899), p. 128, lines 18–23. We have expanded Sedgefield's "þ" and "ȝ" to *þæt* and *and.* Brandl (see note 19), pp. 123–25, discusses this passage's possible connection with Boethius.

23 The MS has *swicolost* in line 10a. For the emendation to *switolost* see Williams, p. 148, and for other proposed readings see Dobbie, p. 175.

connection between experience and wisdom. The *fyrngearum* of line 12a is of particular interest because the poet has just given us a year in his characterization of the four seasons, and perhaps we can see in *fyrngearum frod* a connection between wisdom and the experience of the limitations placed upon man by forces beyond his control. The wise man is the one who has experienced *wyrd* many times.

Having introduced his poem with gnomes referring to the rulers and cities of this world, to the glories of the Ruler of the heavens and his disposition of cyclical time, and to the measure of human values and understanding, the poet presents in line 13 a pair of somewhat puzzling gnomes: *Wea bið wundrum clibbor. Wolcnu scriðað* [Woe is wondrously clinging. Clouds glide]. E. V. K. Dobbie, in an uncharacteristic lapse of editorial judgment, emended *wea* to *weax,* finding the MS reading "hardly defensible."[24] Certainly the metaphoric clinging quality of woe is all too familiar; here, the suggestive contrast to the gliding nature of clouds implies, perhaps, a contrast between human experience and the processes of nature. While man may suffer long-lasting woe, the clouds above him move effortlessly on their way. That the poet places these provocative verses immediately before the section of *sceal*-gnomes might indicate that he wishes us to look for further traces of such a contrast in the passage ahead.

The students of gnomic poetry noted above all agree in making a distinction between gnomic statements about human moral obligations and those about non-ethical human activities and processes of nature. Yet the group of gnomes in lines 14–54a completely ignores this distinction in an important way, that is, by use of the same verbal formula. This parallelism largely gives the poem its uniqueness; certainly no comparably uniform series of gnomes occurs in *Maxims I.* Perhaps the *proprietas* which Hickes saw in the poem lies in this use of the *sceal*-gnome. In each independent clause in lines 14–54a *sceal* operates as an auxiliary with a complementary infinitive or with "to be" understood. With minor variations, e.g., ellipsis of *sceal,* the syntactic paradigm is: subject + *sceal* + adverbial phrase (usually denoting location) ± / variation or modification of subject / ± / infinitive + complement /. Such syntactic regularity creates the expectation of a concomitant semantic consistency in the meaning of *sceal* in each of its occurrences. Yet many of the poem's translators have not cared to render each instance of *sceal* with the same word. Richard Hamer, for example, translates *Til sceal on eðle / domes wyrcean* (20b–21a) as "The good on earth / *must* work for glory," while translating *Daroð sceal on handa*

24 Dobbie, p. 175.

(21b) as "Dart *shall* be in hand."[25] Kenneth Jackson reads "A bird *shall* swoop in the sky above" for *Fugel uppe sceal / lacan on lyfte* (38b–39a) and "A king *must* distribute rings in the hall" for *Cyning sceal on healle / beagas dælan* (lines 28b–29a).[26] The Chadwicks, who, as we noted above, argued strongly for a distinction between gnomes of moral exhortation and other gnomes, sought to maintain that distinction in translation. Commenting upon lines 14–15,

> Geongne æþeling sceolan   gode gesiðas
> byldan to beaduwe   and to beahgife,

they suggest: "This may be translated according to Type I: 'Good knights ought to encourage a young prince to warfare and generosity'; but also—and perhaps most probably—according to Type II *a:* 'It is characteristic of good knights to encourage', etc."[27] Thus, despite the pressure for a uniform meaning for *sceal* generated by the syntactic regularity of the passage, many scholars have believed that *sceal* has different meanings in the several gnomes.

But if there *is* a single meaning for *sceal* that would make good sense in all the gnomes in this passage, such would seem more suitable to the poem's design. Paul Beekman Taylor has made such a proposal in an article in which he deals with Old English gnomic poetry in general, without treating *Maxims I* and *Maxims II* as separate works. He argues that "the *sceal*-maxims . . . embody expressions about what *should* be, how things should function. As such, the *sceal*-maxims comprise a sort of handbook on ritual: descriptions, on the one hand, of the rituals of nature which, being of God's provenance, are out of man's control, and, on the other hand, descriptions of the rituals of men which are heroic obligations."[28] Many of the *sceal*-gnomes in *Maxims II*, lines 14–54a, lend themselves easily to an interpretation denoting some nuance of obligation, fitness, or propriety. Several lines, however, are not readily adaptable to this view. It seems unlikely that *Þeof sceal gangan þystrum wederum* (42a) should be translated "The thief ought to go about in dark weather." Clearly, from a thief's point of view he ought to, but we should not, without clear and convincing evidence, ascribe that point of view to the poet. We also doubt that the following lines are a statement of "how things should function":

---

[25] Hamer (see note 15), p. 111. The emphasis is ours.

[26] Jackson (see note 10), p. 129. The emphasis is ours.

[27] The Chadwicks, p. 378, and see also the note on that page in which they defend their reading of "knights" for *gesiðas*.

[28] Taylor (see note 3), p. 388.

fyrd [sceal] wið fyrde,   feond wið oðrum,
lað wið laþe   ymb land sacan,
synne stælan.

(52–54a)

P. L. Henry makes a more attractive generalization in his extended discussion of the force of *sceal*-gnomes in *The Early English and Celtic Lyric:*

> It will appear from the foregoing analysis of the Exeter, Cotton, and other gnomic material that gnomic *sceal* typically expresses the notions of customary action or state, inherent quality and characteristic property, passing over on the one hand to ideal or hortatory action, (state), expressing on the other that sense of certainty which current dialectical varieties of the future (with *will*) bring out and which is also a feature of that future in Shakespearian English.[29]

Henry elsewhere distinguishes the senses of moral exhortation and of constraint in *sceal*-gnomes;[30] but most important is his view that *sceal* "typically expresses the notions of customary action or state, inherent quality and characteristic property." Employing this definition, we might render *Wulf sceal on bearowe* (18b), for example, several ways: "It is characteristic of the wolf to be in a grove," or "It is customary that the wolf is in a grove"; but we can best duplicate the terseness of *Maxims II* with the translation "The wolf is typically in a grove," and we employ this locution in the translations given below of the various gnomes in lines 14–54a.

Geongne æþeling sceolan   gode gesiðas
byldan to beaduwe   and to beahgife.
Ellen sceal on eorle,   ecg sceal wið hellme
hilde gebidan.   Hafuc sceal on glofe
wilde gewunian.   Wulf sceal on bearowe,
earm anhaga.   Eofor sceal on holte,
toðmægenes trum.   Til sceal on eðle
domes wyrcean.   Daroð sceal on handa,
gar golde fah.   Gim sceal on hringe
standan steap and geap.   Stream sceal on yðum
mecgan mereflode.   Mæst sceal on ceole,
segelgyrd seomian.   Sweord sceal on bearme,
drihtlic isern.   Draca sceal on hlæwe,

---

[29] P. L. Henry, *The Early English and Celtic Lyric* (London, 1966), p. 103.
[30] Henry, pp. 94–96.

frod, frætwum wlanc.   Fisc sceal on wætere
cynren cennan.

(14–28a)[31]

[Good companions typically exhort a young prince to battle and to ring-giving.[32] Courage is typically in a warrior. The edge typically experiences battle against the helmet. The hawk typically remains wild on the glove. The wolf, a wretched recluse, is typically in a grove. The boar, strong of tusk-might, is typically in a forest. The good man typically strives after glory in his homeland. The spear, a missile adorned with gold, is typically in the hand. The gem typically stands projecting and curved on a ring. The river typically mixes in the waves with the sea-flood. The mast is typically on a ship, the sailyard (typically) stands (there). The sword, noble iron, is typically in the lap. The dragon, old, exulting in orna-ments, is typically in a barrow. The fish typically produces its offspring in the water.]

As noted above, the independent clauses in this passage conform to a single syntactic paradigm, and with line 16b is established another important pattern: the *b*-verse begins a clause which is completed by the following *a*-verse. Williams, who saw this passage as "an exercise in verse technic," argued, following the work of Hugo Müller, that the *b*-verses represented prose gnomes, which were the source material for the poem, and the *a*-verses adapted these prose gnomes into the neces-sary alliterative pattern, while also serving as poetic "adornment."[33] Few scholars today would accept such dissection. We can, moreover, see this pattern as a valid stylistic accomplishment. The *a*-verses in the passage, with the exception of lines 14a, 15a, and 16a, are of three general types: (1) a complementary infinitive with some other grammatical element; (2) substantival variation of the subject of the preceding *b*-verse; (3) adjectival modification of that subject. This pattern is con-tinued with but one possible exception, line 33a, until the hypermetric lines beginning with line 42. Once this pattern is established in the lis-tener's mind, each *b*-verse brings with it both a sense of incompleteness, a need for resolution, and an uncertainty as to which of the three methods of resolution will occur in the following *a*-verse. Similarly, a rhythmic pattern unfolds in lines 16b–41. Each *b*-verse, except lines 30b, 38b, and

[31] We reject Dobbie's emendation of MS *mecgan* to *mencgan* as do Frederic G. Cassidy and Richard N. Ringler, eds., *Bright's Old English Grammar and Reader*, 3rd ed. (New York, 1971), p. 374.

[32] The sense of moral obligation in this gnome comes not from *sceolan*, but from the adjective *gode*, the only such attributive modification of a subject in the poem. *Til*, perhaps, carries a similar ethical force in lines 20b–21a.

[33] Williams, pp. 108–09.

41b (which effects a transition to the hypermetric passage), is a Sievers Type A, while much greater variety occurs in the *a*-verses. Type D occurs in lines 19a, 22a, 23a, 24a, 27a, 37a, and 38a; Type E in lines 20a and 32a; Type C in 40a.[34] By the alternation of these types of verses the poet creates an interest in the unfolding of each sentence's syntax and rhythm. The technique of beginning a new independent clause in the *b*-verse and ending it in an *a*-verse serves, moreover, to link together by alliteration clauses which have no apparent connection in content. Thus the poet imposes upon a set of semantically disconnected statements a pattern within which syntactic and rhythmic expectations create a highly satisfying sense of aesthetic order in the multiform diversity of the experiences of life.

One feature of this passage which we wish to note is the consistent concern with location. This emphasis begins in the passage quoted above and continues until the hypermetric lines:

	Cyning sceal on healle
beagas dælan.	Bera sceal on hæðe,
eald and egesfull.	Ea of dune sceal
flodgræg feran.	Fyrd sceal ætsomne,
tirfæstra getrum.	Treow sceal on eorle,
wisdom on were.	Wudu sceal on foldan
blædum blowan.	Beorh sceal on eorþan
grene standan.	God sceal on heofenum,
dæda demend.	Duru sceal on healle,
rum recedes muð.	Rand sceal on scylde,
fæst fingra gebeorh.	Fugel uppe sceal
lacan on lyfte.	Leax sceal on wæle
mid sceote scriðan.	Scur sceal on heofenum
winde geblanden	in þas woruld cuman.

(28b–41)

[The king typically dispenses rings in the hall. The bear, old and dreadful, is typically on a heath. The river typically flows downwards floodgray. The army, a band of ones fast in glory, is typically together. Fidelity is typically in a warrior, wisdom in a man. The forest typically flowers with blossoms on the earth. The hill typically stands green on the earth. God, the judge of deeds, is typically in the heavens. The door, the spacious mouth of a building, is typically on a hall. The shieldboss, a firm protection for the fingers, is typically on a shield. The bird typically sports upwards in the sky. The salmon typically glides in a pool with the trout. The shower typically comes into this world from the heavens mixed with wind.]

34 If one reads *sceot*, "quick, ready," then the verse is Type A with anacrusis.

None of the poems which make up *Maxims I* shows this concern with placing things in their typical location. Moreover, the locational referents are frequently earth (lines 33b, 34b, and 41b) and heaven, or the heavens (lines 35b and 40b). The audience is thus reminded of the earlier qualification of the cities as *þa þe on þysse eorðan syndon* and prepared for the final distinction in the poem's concluding lines between heaven and earth.

The aesthetic patterns described above are broken by several hypermetric lines:

> Þeof sceal gangan þystrum wederum.   Þyrs sceal on fenne gewunian,
> ana innan lande.   Ides sceal dyrne cræfte,
> fæmne, hire freond gesecean,   gif heo nelle on folce geþeon
> þæt hi man beagum gebicge.

(42–45a)

[The thief typically goes about in dark weather. The troll dwells typically in a fen, alone in the land. The woman, a maiden, typically visits her lover by secret craft, if she does not wish it to succeed among her people that a man buy her with rings.]

The statement about the thief introduces a hitherto unheard discordant note. Thieves, it is clear, go about in dark weather to avoid being seen by others, even as the *þyrs* lives alone within the land, in the fen. The poet's next sentence has been something of a crux, but it is clear at least that the poet says that the woman visits her lover by means of secret craft. A woman, presumably, is expected to follow the marriage customs of her people, i.e., to allow herself to be bought with rings, but she may, if she wishes, frustrate the expectations of her people by secretly stealing away to her lover, just as the thief moves about concealed by darkness from the eyes of others. This passage about the thief, the *þyrs,* and the young woman, by suggesting a hiddenness and secrecy in the movements of some even on this earth, prepares us for the ultimate limitation of knowledge the poem will present. The poet even uses the word *dyrne* here, the same word he uses in the concluding lines of the poem to convey the unknowability of the life after death.

Following the hypermetric section, the "normal" aesthetic patterns reappear:

> Brim sceal sealte weallan,
> lyfthelm and laguflod   ymb ealra landa gehwylc;
> flowan firgenstreamas.   Feoh sceal on eorðan
> tydran and tyman.   Tungol sceal on heofenum
> beorhte scinan,   swa him bebead Meotud.

(45b–49)

[The sea, the mist and waters around each of all lands, typically wells with salt; the mountain streams (typically) flow.[35] Cattle typically teem and propagate on the earth. The sun typically shines brightly in the heavens, as the Lord commanded it.]

Here, again, are references to heaven and earth. Dawson, accounting for the position of gnomes by positing phonic or conceptual associations in the mind of the poet, applies his critical approach to the repetition of *on heofenum*. After noting the three occurrences of that expression (35b, 40b, and 48b), he asserts: "The meanings differ slightly, but the sounds are the same. The composer possibly had the three *on heofenum* lines in his repertoire and the one called to mind the others."[36] The weakness of this view, and of Dawson's approach in general, is that while pursuing what may have been in the poet's mind, it misses what is in the poem. The subtle contrasting of heaven and earth is a further preparation for the poem's concluding contrast of the unknowability of the state of heaven with the relative knowability of conditions on this earth.

Next come lines which have been called by some critics a summary of everything that has gone before:

> God sceal wið yfele,   geogoð sceal wið yldo,
> lif sceal wið deaþe,   leoht sceal wið þystrum,
> fyrd wið fyrde,   feond wið oðrum,
> lað wið laþe   ymb land sacan,
> synne stælan.

(50–54a)

[Good typically against evil, youth typically against age, life typically against death, light typically against darkness, army against army, enemy against others, foe against foe contend around the land, advance feud.[37]]

T. D. Hill, who sees Ecclesiasticus 23:15 as the source for the above lines, argues that "The first forty-nine lines are a playful collocation of natural imagery and sapiential statement . . . ; the poet summarizes these lines by paraphrasing Ecclesiasticus on 'natural' disorder and then concludes by asserting that ultimately God will impose order on *þysse*

---

[35] The crux of lines 45b-47a, as noted by Dobbie, p. 176, is whether *lyfthelm* and *laguflod* are to be construed with *weallan* or *flowan*. Williams, pp. 150–51, construes them with *flowan*, stating that the terms refer to fresh water as opposed to salt water. We see a contrast between the flowing of the *firgenstreamas* and the welling of the *brim*, and we suggest that line 46 is a more suitable variation of *brim* than of *firgenstreamas*.

[36] Dawson (see note 4), p. 22.

[37] For different readings of line 54a see Dobbie, p. 176.

worulde gewinn."[38] It seems inaccurate, however, to consider the lines in question a *summary* of the earlier part of the poem. Although some idea of strife is implied in the preceding references to weapons and warriors, it is only an implied *part* of the subject matter of the poem.

Then the following lines occur:

> A sceal snotor hycgean
> ymb þysse worulde gewinn,   wearh hangian,
> fægere ongildan   þæt he ær facen dyde
> manna cynne.
>
> (54b–57a)

[Ever ought the wise man to think upon the strife of this world, (ever ought) the criminal to hang, justly repay that he formerly committed a crime against the race of men.]

Here, as our translation suggests, is where *sceal* shifts its meaning to "ought," as a result of the initial *A*.[39] Context indeed seems to call for a concluding statement, and a moral exhortation is most appropriate here. The wise man is urged to ponder earthly strife as presented in the immediately preceding lines. The poet then declares the moral desirability of justice in this world when he remarks that the criminal ought always to hang. This reflection, too, seems derived from the poet's account of strife and, perhaps, his reference to the *þeof* and the misconduct of the *ides*. The existence of such conflict creates the need for justice in this world.

From the consideration of earthly justice the poet moves to a mention of judgment in God's kingdom. We have already heard that God, the judge of deeds, is in the heavens, but we now receive a greater elaboration of this idea:

> Meotod ana wat
> hwyder seo sawul sceal   syððan hweorfan
> and ealle þa gastas   þe for Gode hweorfað
> æfter deaðdæge,   domes bidað
> on fæder fæðme.   Is seo forðgesceaft
> digol and dyrne.   Drihten ana wat,
> nergende fæder.   Næni eft cymeð
> hider under hrofas   þe þæt her for soð

---

[38] T. D. Hill, "Notes on the Old English 'Maxims' I and II," *N&Q,* 215 (1970), 446.

[39] Cf. Henry, p. 100.

> mannum secge   hwylc sy Meotodes gesceaft,
> sigefolca gesetu,   þær he sylfa wunað.

(57b–66)

[God alone knows where that soul (of the criminal) must afterwards journey and all those souls which journey before God after the day of death, await judgment in the embrace of the father. That future state is hidden and secret. The Lord alone, the saving Father, knows (it). None comes again hither under the roofs who might here in truth say to men what sort of thing is God's domain, the seats of the victorious peoples, where he himself dwells.]

These concluding lines have often been seen as a scribal addition. Henry, however, has noted a connection between these lines and the rest of the poem: "Note how naturally the final section . . . on the whereabouts of the soul after death grows from the reference to capital punishment in 55b; and how its formula *Meotod (drihten) ana wat . . .*, posing ignorance, systematically complements the *sceal, byð* type (of observation and experience, i.e. knowledge), in the earlier parts of the poem."[40] We would go further and say that this final statement of the limitations of man's knowledge integrates the entire poem. We traced in the poem's opening lines some implied statements about the limitations of man's knowledge and experience. Men are, for example, unable to comprehend fully the origins of earthly cities and the skill that went into their construction. In the final lines the seats of the victorious peoples, where God himself dwells, lie even further beyond man's ken. While the opening lines, through the list of superlatives, seek to give a characterization of this world in time and place, the concluding lines state that the world after death is secret and hidden and that none can characterize it. The distinction between this world and the other implied in the beginning of the poem, a distinction which is furthered in the *sceal*-section by references to earth and heaven, is, in the final lines, explicitly expounded upon. The section of *sceal*-gnomes, furthermore, assigns to each thing named a typical location. The concluding lines assign the soul to its necessary destination. Though the poet gives discrete pieces of information about natural and human phenomena, he can only say at the end that one cannot *her for soð / mannum secg[an] hwylc sy Meotodes gesceaft*. There is in this final remark a wistful note about man's unfulfilled curiosity which accords well with the importance placed upon wisdom in the earlier lines.

[40] Henry, pp. 99–100.

J. W. Rankin closed his review of Williams's book with the observation that her introduction did not "throw much light upon these dark sayings." He then asked, "What was the purpose of the author or compiler of these collections? Was there any method in his incoherence when he wrote in apparently hit-or-miss fashion what must in large part have been obvious truisms?"[41] We hope that our reading of *Maxims II* is a constructive step toward answering those questions. The author's intention, we believe, was to write a poem. He may have brought together commonplace ideas and used the common poetic conventions of his time, but he wrought language and a poem which pleases. He wrote a poem which advocates wisdom, not only by explicitly recommending it, but by showing, through the form of the individual statements of knowledge, what wisdom is. And he unified the poem thematically through his development of the idea that man's knowledge is indeed limited.

One venerable critical view of *Maxims II* is vindicated by this reading of the poem. Over a century ago John Earle suggested that the compiler of Cotton Tiberius B. i. intended *The Menologium* and *Maxims II* to serve as a preface to the text of the *Anglo-Saxon Chronicle* which follows.[42] The evidence of capital letters and the spacing between the two poems and the *Chronicle* strongly suggests this.[43] Each of these works is, to some degree, a list: *The Menologium* lists the important holidays of the year; *Maxims II* is a "list" of bits of knowledge; the *Chronicle* is an attempt to list important events: what happened, when and where. Perhaps the compiler of the manuscript felt that the extremely linear historical view of the *Chronicle* ought to be balanced by *The Menologium*'s presentation of the year as a cycle of important holidays, i.e., a recurring recapitulation of the most significant events of history. Perhaps also the compiler saw a kind of propriety in prefacing an ambitious intellectual endeavor such as the *Chronicle* with *Maxims II,* a poem on the limitations of knowledge.[44]

[41] Rankin (see note 11), p. 165.

[42] John Earle, *Two of the Saxon Chronicles Parallel* (Oxford, 1865), pp. xxix–xxxvi.

[43] Dobbie, pp. lx–lxi. Despite the MS evidence, he denies any connection between *Maxims II* and the *Chronicle*.

[44] J. K. Bollard, "The Cotton Maxims," *Neophil,* 57 (1973), 179–87, which considers the aesthetic structure, came to our attention after our essay had been submitted, but his reading differs substantially from our own.

23

Artful Ambiguities in the Old English "Book-Moth" Riddle

FRED C. ROBINSON

IN RECENT YEARS SEVERAL SCHOLARS HAVE IDENTIFIED INTENTIONAL verbal ambiguities in Old English verse, thus challenging effectively an earlier assumption that Anglo-Saxon poets did not indulge in this stylistic device.[1] The present paper suggests that in the well-known "Book-Moth" Riddle of the Exeter Book (Krapp-Dobbie no. 47)[2] a poet has used a series of related and highly functional verbal ambiguities to develop a specific poetic theme. If this suggestion is correct, then not only will our understanding of a single minor poem have been increased, but we will also have a fuller awareness of the range of dictional subtlety which we may reasonably expect in other poems of the Anglo-Saxon

[1] Marijane Osborn, "Some Uses of Ambiguity in *Beowulf*," *Thoth*, 10 (1969), 18–35; M. J. Swanton, "Ambiguity and Anticipation in 'The Dream of the Rood,'" *NM*, 70 (1969), 407–25; P. B. Taylor, "Text and Texture of 'The Dream of the Rood,'" *NM*, 75 (1974), 193–201; Fred C. Robinson, "The Significance of Names in Old English Literature," *Anglia*, 86 (1968), 14–58, and "Lexicography and Literary Criticism: A Caveat," in *Philological Essays in Honour of Herbert Dean Meritt*, ed. James L. Rosier (The Hague, 1970), pp. 99–110, esp. pp. 107–09. For an excellent general survey of the background and varieties of word-play in Old English poetry, see Roberta Frank, "Some Uses of Paronomasia in Old English Scriptural Verse," *Speculum*, 47 (1972), 207–26.

[2] *ASPR*, III, eds. George Philip Krapp and Elliott van Kirk Dobbie (New York, 1936), 205. All subsequent quotations from Old English poetry are taken from this collective edition.

period, a range which includes not merely occasional isolated punning but successions of interconnected puns organized around a central subject.[3]

The six lines of the "Book-Moth" Riddle read as follow in the *Anglo-Saxon Poetic Records:*

> Moððe word fræt.   Me þæt þuhte
> wrætlicu wyrd,   þa ic þæt wundor gefrægn,
> þæt se wyrm forswealg   wera gied sumes,
> þeof in þystro,   þrymfæstne cwide
> ond þæs strangan staþol.   Stælgiest ne wæs
> wihte þy gleawra,   þe he þam wordum swealg.

Aside from some uncertainty as to the referent of *þæs strangan staþol,* the verses offer no lexical difficulties, and R. K. Gordon's literal translation presents a fair consensus of the poem's interpreters to date:

> A moth ate words. That seemed to me a strange event, when I heard of that wonder, that the worm, a thief in the darkness, should devour the song of a man, a famed utterance and a thing founded by a strong man. The thievish visitant was no whit the wiser for swallowing the words.[4]

The only problem that commentators have found with the poem is that it seems embarrassingly unproblematic. Since it begins and ends by stating the answer to the riddle (*Moððe word fræt . . . he þam wordum swealg*), it appears to be no riddle at all. "Here," says Kemp Malone, "the riddle form was stretched to include something merely paradoxical, and even this only by identification of the ink-marks with the words they symbolize."[5] The trick question of conventional riddlers is indeed excised, and yet, if I am not mistaken, the poet has reintroduced a richly equivocal quality to the poem through a pattern of puns which achieve the "identification of the ink-marks with the words they symbolize" in a way that is both imaginative and meaningful.

Since the poet's strategy is to begin with a literal statement of his

---

[3] This paper was written during a year when a grant from the John Simon Guggenheim Foundation enabled the author to devote his full time to the study of English philology and literary interpretation.

[4] *Anglo-Saxon Poetry,* selected and translated by R. K. Gordon (London, 1954), p. 303. Gordon's translation of *gied* as "song" has no more foundation in the text than has other scholars' suggestion that the word refers to a biblical passage. *Gied* could refer to any speech, narrative, or proverb and could even mean "riddle."

[5] "The Old English Period (to 1100)" in *A Literary History of England,* ed. Albert C. Baugh, 2nd ed. (New York, 1967), p. 89.

subject and develop it to its conclusion with a progression of words used in two senses, I shall begin with the last word, *swealg* and from there work back through its other key puns. The first sense listed in Bosworth-Toller under *swelgan* is "to swallow," and this is the meaning which editors and translators have uniformly assigned to the verb in the riddle. But equally relevant in the context is the dictionary's second sense for *swelgan*—"to take into the mind, accept, imbibe (wisdom)." Among the sample quotations cited under this meaning is one which resembles the phrasing of the sentence of the riddle: *Đa þam wordum swealg / brego Caldea* [when the lord of the Chaldeans had understood those words . . .]. When *swealg* is construed in this sense, the final clause of the riddle becomes more than just an impudent rebuttal to the old maxim *Difficile est vacuo verbis imponere ventri* [It is hard to impress an empty stomach with words]; it becomes a genuine paradox: "He understood the words and yet was no wiser."[6]

Parallel with the pun on *swealg* is a pun on *staþol* in the preceding sentence. Interpreters have occasionally been troubled by this slightly odd use of *staþol* "foundation" (cf. Gordon's evasive "a thing founded"), but most agree on a literal meaning "foundation on which the words stand"—i.e. "the manuscript."[7] This no doubt is one of the senses intended. But occurrences of the word elsewhere in contexts similar to that in the riddle show that *staþol* was also used in an abstract sense to refer to intellectual foundations or to the content of a thought or an argument. In Thorpe's *Ancient Laws and Institutes of England* (London, 1840), vol. 2, p. 426, it occurs in a familiar locution which (like lines 4 and 5 of the riddle) brings together the words *cwide* and *staþol: on ðissum cwydum is se staðol ealles geleafan* [In these sayings is the foundation of all belief]. A similar shade of meaning is suggested by

---

[6] The riddler's statement that a creature was none the wiser for having understood the book may well have had special force since it denies a maxim which specifically asserts that the man who masters book-learning will always be the wiser:

> Bald bið se ðe onbyregeð   boca cræftes;
> symle bið ðe wisra   ðe hira geweald hafað.
>
> (*Solomon and Saturn* 243–44)

[He who tastes the power of books will have confidence; he who masters them will always be the wiser.]

[7] Malone, p. 89, F. G. Cassidy and W. Ringler's revision of *Bright's Old English Grammar and Reader* (New York, 1971), p. 342, and Dorothy Whitelock's revision of *Sweet's Anglo-Saxon Reader* (Oxford, 1967), p. 279, all agree on "parchment, vellum." C. L. Wrenn, on the other hand, translates *þæs strangan staþol* as "which had given strength to the strong." See *A Study of Old English Literature* (London, 1967), p. 174.

hiera geðohtes staðol[8] [the foundation of their thought] and by the fact that the derivative *staðolung* has the sense "ordinance, precept" in the Old English *Benedictine Rule*.[9] The riddle's phrase *þæs strangan staðol* finds an echo in Solomon's answer to the book-riddle which Saturn proposed to him: *Gestrangað hie* [i.e. *bec*] *and gestaðeliað staðolfæstne geðoht*[10] [they strengthen and confirm a steadfast thought]. In the Exeter riddle *þæs strangan* refers to *þrymfæstne cwide* [the mighty utterance], the entire phrase *þæs strangan staðol* [the basic argument of the mighty one] referring on one level to the intellectual content of the mighty utterance. At another level, of course, it refers to the page on which the mighty utterance stands written. The two meanings "parchment" and "intellectual content" are in equipoise, the former sense patterning with the concrete meaning of *swealg,* the latter with the abstract meaning: the insect (1) ate the parchment (2) understood the argument.

In line 4 the word *cwide* also seems to have simultaneous associations with the two levels of corporal ingestion and intellectual inquiry. The obvious meaning is "sentence, statement," but *cwide* taken in isolation could also be a form of *cwidu* "what is chewed." At first reading the grammar of the sentence directs readers' attention away from this sense of the word,[11] but the ensuing puns on *staþol* and *swealg* would very likely suggest in retrospect this other highly appropriate meaning of *cwide.*

In þystro (4) would also have yielded separate meanings in response to the simultaneous contexts of studying books and eating books. On the physical level it simply means that the moth ate the book "in the dark." On the level of studying, however, the phrase becomes paradoxical, for words cannot be read "in the dark." If *þystro* also had some of the metaphorical meaning of "ignorance" (as it often did when translating biblical *caligo* and *tenebrae*), it may pattern contrastively with *gleawra* in line 6: the benighted creature was none the wiser for having taken in so much wisdom.

---

8 See *BT s.v. staðol* II.

9 *Die angelsächsischen Prosabearbeitungen der Benediktinerregal,* ed. Arnold Schröer (Kassel, 1888), p. 112, line 24.

10 *Solomon and Saturn,* line 240.

11 As a neuter *wa*-stem *cwidu* should have *-u* or *-o* rather than *-e* in the accusative singular, and its gender would not agree with the masculine inflection of *þrymfæstne*. It should be noted, however, that elsewhere in the Exeter Book there is some wavering between *-u, -o* on the one hand and *-e* on the other; see, for example, *gewædu* for *gewæde* in *Riddle* 35, line 14; *heore-* for *heoru-* in *Phoenix* 217; *æþele* for *æþelu* in *Widsith* 5. This orthographic confusion suggests that the distinction between *-u* and *-e* was moribund by the time the Exeter Book scribe was writing, and it may already have been weakened in the Riddle-poet's day.

As the puns increasingly specify a second level of activity (a man seeking wisdom) coexisting with the literal level (an insect eating parchment), the poet's terms for the book-moth become correspondingly anthropomorphized: *moðð e, wyrm, þeof, stælgiest*. He is at first a simple moth eating words, and the prosaic Old English compound *moðfreten* [moth-eaten] suggests that *moðð e word fræt* is about as literal a statement of this act as was possible. In the next allusion to the moth he is *se wyrm*, which has the more general meaning "insect, mite," a sense which was extended to that of "poor creature" in Old English translations of the twenty-first Psalm.[12] In the last two terms the personification is complete: he is *þeof* in the fourth line and *stælgiest* in the fifth. This last term occurs nowhere else in Old English, but the second element *giest* can only mean "guest" or "stranger." The first element is always assumed to mean "thievish," presumably because of the preceding *þeof*. But it is also possible that it could mean "place," as it does, for example, in the compound *stælwyrð e* according to Bosworth-Toller. Or it could be a form of *steal(l)* and refer to the place which an abbot sets apart for the negligent members of a monastic house.[13] In the absence of other contexts for *stælgiest*, however, it is best to observe only that -*giest* indicates a complete personification of the insect and this personification enables the creature to serve as the logical subject of the punning senses of *swealg, staþol, cwide,* and *þystro* which refer to the moth as an unsuccessful scholar.

A final instance of word play on *wrætlicu wyrd* in line 2, although it does not participate directly in the dual development of the book-moth's role, nonetheless embraces the course and theme of the entire poem. Commentators have uniformly assumed that *wyrd* in this occurrence has the sole meaning "event, fate," and it is indeed the curious event to which the poet is directing our attention. But as the rest of the poem shows, it is also and particularly the words describing the event that become the real subject of his poem, for the poet's words in their double meanings both develop and resolve the paradox suggested by the event. In this context another meaning of *wyrd* comes into play, that of the etymologically unrelated homophone *(ge)wyrd* which Bosworth-Toller (s.v. *gewyrde, -wyrd*) defines as "speech, conversation, collection of words, sentence" and Bosworth-Toller *Supplement* further defines as

[12] See Psalm 21:7 in the various Old Engish Psalter translations. This verse is quoted in the *Benedictine Rule:* the Old English version (edited by Schröer, p. 29, lines 3–4) reads: *"Ic soð lice eom wyrm and no man, manna hosp and folces æwyrp"* [Truly, I am a worm and no man, the reproach of men and an outcast of the people].

[13] See Schröer, p. 68, line 11; cf. p. 12, line 19.

"copiousness of speech, verbosity." Thus *wrætlicu wyrd* means that both the event and the words reporting the event are "wondrous, curious,"[14] and the remainder of the poem demonstrates the validity of this *double entente* by using artfully equivocal words to explore the curious paradox of the event.

This second meaning of *wyrd* has passed unremarked, I suspect, first because *wyrd* "fate, event" is such a familiar and famous word in Old English and, second, because *wyrd* "speech, sentence," although it is commonly documented in derivatives and compounds,[15] occurs only here as an independent word. This latter consideration would weigh heavily against the likelihood of a pun, I believe, were it not for other factors which suggest that there was a rather close psychological association of these two words in the minds of literate Anglo-Saxons. First, both in copying of manuscripts[16] and in derivative formations from *wyrd*[17] there was a tendency to interchange *word* and *wyrd*. In the poetic context of the riddle, moreover, an association between the two words may well have been fostered by the pre-existing verse-formula *wrætlicum wordum*.[18] There is no corresponding formula linking *wrætlic* and *wyrd* "fate" (so far as the extent records show), and so the poet of the "Book-Moth" Riddle may have been playing on the expectation set up by *wrætlicum wordum*.

Aside from these points of contact, however, there was in the Anglo-Saxon period a specific philological association of *wyrd* "fate, event" and *wyrd* "speech" based on the etymology of the Latin word *fatum* "fate." *Fatum* is derived from the past participle of Latin *farī* "to speak," the original meaning of *fatum* being "the sentence (of the gods)." Isidore of

---

[14] The gender of *wyrd* "sentence" is apparently feminine (see F. Holthausen's *Altenglisches etymologisches Wörterbuch*, 2nd ed. [Heidelberg, 1963], s.v. [ge]*wyrd* 2), so that *wrætlicu* agrees equally with *wyrd* "event" and *wyrd* "speech, sentence."

[15] Most common is *gewyrd*, which is documented in phrases such as *wisra gewyrdum* [by the statements of wise men] (*Menologium* 66) and *ðæt ic mæge becuman to bræddran gewyrde* [that I may attain to more copious speech] (see BT s.v. *gewyrde, -wyrd*, where both passages are cited). But the root also occurs in compounds: *fægerwyrde* [smooth-speaking], *gearowyrde* [fluent of speech], *gewyrdelic* [verbatim], *hrædwyrde* [hasty of speech], *scandwyrde* [slanderous], *wærwyrde* [cautious of speech], etc.

[16] For substitutions of *word* for *wryd* in the copying of manuscripts, see the variant readings in *Bischof Wærferths von Worcester Übersetzung der Dialoge Gregors des Grossen*, ed. Hans Hecht (Hamburg, 1907), p. 185, line 19 and p. 223, line 20, and BTS s.v. *wærwyrde*, where *swiðe wær on his wordum* is given as one variant reading of *wærwyrde*.

[17] See for example *andwordan, -wyrdan; foreword, -wyrd; scandword, -wyrde; wærword, -wyrd.*

[18] See *Andreas* 1200 and *Christ* 509; cf. *Andreas* 92–93.

Seville explained this relationship between "fate" and "speech" in his *Etymologies,* VIII, xi, 90:

> Fatum autem dicunt esse quidquid dii fantur, quidquid Iuppiter fatur. A fando igitur fatum dicunt, id est a loquendo.

> [Now they aver that *Fate* is whatever the gods *say,* whatever Jupiter *says.* Thus from *saying,* that is from "speaking," they say *Fate.*]

This surprisingly accurate information is reflected, perhaps, in the Latin-Old English glossaries, which include such entries as these:

> Fatis . gewyrdum
> Fatum . dictum, locutio
> Fata . i. fortuna, euentus, uel dicta; locuta, gewyrda[19]

In a gloss like *fatis . gewyrdum* one cannot even be certain whether the primary sense intended in the Old English word was "fate" or "speech," and such uncertainties arise in other contexts involving *(ge)wyrd.* Bosworth-Toller *Supplement* lists the gloss "Conditio *gecwide* vel *gewyrd"* under *Gewyrd* "fate," for example, but then adds that it could equally well be taken as *gewyrd* "speech." If *gewyrd* as an individual word was as ambiguous as Toller's note implies, then it hardly seems improbable that a pun was intended in the riddle-poet's *wrætlicu wyrd.*

In one sense, the "Book-Moth" Riddle simply collapses the terms of a familiar metaphor into a paradox. The metaphor is that found, among other places, in the Old English translation of the *Liber Scintillarum:*

> . . . swa soþlice of flæsclicum mettum byþ gefedd flæsc, swa of godcundum spæcum inra mann byþ festrud and byð gefedd.[20]

> [Now just as the body is fed from corporal food, so the inner man is nurtured and fed from spiritual language.]

In his "Tinea" enigma Symphosius presented a real-life situation which reduced the simile to literal fact.[21] The Old English poet then took the

[19] The first and last glosses are quoted from Thomas Wright's *Anglo-Saxon and Old English Vocabularies* edited and collated by Richard Paul Wülcker (London, 1884), p. 235, lines 35 and 37. The second is from *The Harley Latin-Old English Glossary,* ed. Robert T. Oliphant (The Hague, 1966), p. 177, line 128. All three glosses are found in the Harley Glossary.

[20] *Defensor's Liber Scintillarum,* ed. E. W. Rhodes, *EETS,* o.s., 93 (London, 1889), p. 222.

[21] The Old English poet's source is generally presumed to have been Symphosius's sixteenth riddle:

third step of retranslating the living paradox back into the verbal realm by using a concatenation of puns to develop the subject. More than just a Mannerist experiment, his puns make the poem self-referential in a complex and sophisticated way, forcing the words themselves to display the simultaneous reality and insubstantiality of language. In doing so, he has not only achieved what Herzfeld long ago accused him of failing to do ("Neue Seiten," said Herzfeld, "hat er seinem Gegenstande allerdings nicht abzugewinnen vermocht"[22] [He was not able to give any new twists to his subject]); he has also given us grounds for suspecting that the use of a succession of related puns as an artistic device could well have been within the capacities of other poets in the Anglo-Saxon period. If a study of other Old English riddles should reveal similar uses of pun-complexes (rather than just the isolated puns which previous commentators have from time to time identified), we will then be in a better position to assess several recent and attractive suggestions that even the more serious poets of the period may have used sustained *double entente* as a means of developing complex themes.[23]

Litera me pavit, nec quid sit litera novi.
In libris vixi, nec sum studiosior inde.
Exedi Musas, nec adhuc tamen ipsa profeci.

[Writing has fed me, and I don't even know what writing is. I have lived among books, and yet I am no more learned thereby. I have devoured the Muses, and yet thus far I have not profited from it.]

See *The Enigmas of Symphosius*, ed. R. T. Ohl (Philadelphia, 1928), p. 48.

[22] Georg Herzfeld, *Die Rätsel des Exeterbuches und ihr Verfasser* (Berlin, 1890), p. 29. Consecutive punning is not the poet's only improvement on his source. Especially noteworthy is his unusual employment of alliteration on initial *w-* to knit up the poem, uniting the initial statement and closing restatement of the paradox by a phonic continuum which includes the key terms *word, wyrd,* and *wordum.* (The alliteration of accented *w* words is metrically functional in lines 2, 3, and 6; incidental in lines 1 and 5.)

[23] See the studies by Marijane Osborn, Michael Swanton, and P. B. Taylor cited above, n. 1. See further Ida L. Gordon's edition of *The Seafarer* (London, 1960), p. 30.

24

Up a Tree: To See
The Fates of Men

NEIL D. ISAACS

UNLIKE MOUNTAINS, TREES NEVER SEEM TO BE CLIMBED SIMPLY BE-
cause they are there. One climbs a tree to see, to get, or to get away
from . . . (fill in the appropriate object). It seems natural to ask, whenever there are references to tree-climbing, what the object was. Two
obscure passages in Old English have raised such questions with, I'm
afraid, ludicrous results.

The passages in question are *The Fates of Men* 21–26 and Cynewulf's *Christ* 678b–679a. The former is in a catalogue of thirteen unfortunate lots, mostly types of untimely death, distributed by God among
men: the eighth is death by falling from a tree. The latter is in a list
of important occupations in the eighth century: tree-climbing is listed
between ship-driving and sword-smithing. This list parallels a passage in
The Gifts of Men, a catalogue of fortunate lots distributed by God
among men. *The Gifts,* in turn, is similar in structure, substance, and
treatment to *The Fates.* We are, then, dealing with a common body of
material, which should help to answer the question of why climb a tree.

In 1929, Gordon Hall Gerould looked askance at the Cynewulf
passage, calling it "a little odd that so childish a pursuit as tree-climbing
should be introduced" among important occupations in the eighth cen-

tury.[1] Rejecting earlier notions of Cook, Gollancz, and Kennedy that the reference is to some athletic activity or to Christ ascending the cross, Gerould concluded that the verses refer to house-building—"one can raise the high timber aloft"[2]—which might amuse J. D. Salinger and the Family Glass.

Within two years, Edwin J. Howard responded with a different logic, though proceeding from similar premises. Bringing *Fates of Men* into the discussion he reasoned that "the methods of meeting death are those we would expect an Old English bard to list. And since all these methods except one are ordinary ways of meeting death, the inference is that it is merely lack of knowledge on our part that makes falling from trees seem an unusual way of dying."[3] Rejecting house-building and timber-erecting, then, Howard suggested the possibility of lookouts and falcon-gatherers who in the ordinary pursuit of their life might meet death.

The following year, B. J. Whiting brought forth contemporary if third-hand evidence—Ælfric reporting and enlarging upon what Bede had heard—of one falling from a tree and going to heaven. In this case, the man had been gathering leaves to feed cattle.[4] And so the matter has rested. That the tree-climbing passages refer to tree-climbing has been generally accepted, with a variety of suggestions for the reasons behind such an activity. To the gathering of leaves, of glimpses of enemies, or of eyases, one might well add the possibility of wool-gathering. But I have found no other suggestion. Even a "critical history" (with no sense of historical context and no perceptible critical principles) leaves us hanging uncomfortably in nouncerteyn.

This brief summary of a small body of scholarship on a minor issue seems to me to demonstrate the narrowness of the "special field" type of professionalism. However exhaustive and thoroughly detailed the approach, the efforts will be debilitating without broadened horizons that permit intelligible connections. Thus, in the present instance, it may help solve the puzzle of tree-climbing in Old English poetry to observe that trees are climbed in many parts of the world for a variety of ritual purposes which have nothing to do with gathering anything except special knowledge or power. But even if we broaden the horizons around Anglo-Saxon England to include initiation rituals of other peoples in other places and other times, is there any way to relate these passages to the larger context without direct evidence? I believe there is, at least inferentially if not circumstantially, by an examination of the contexts of

[1] *JEGP*, 28 (1929), 162.
[2] P. 162.
[3] *JEGP*, 30 (1931), 152.
[4] *JEGP*, 31 (1932), 256–57.

the verses themselves, an examination that will demand a challenge to the premises of Gerould, Howard, and Whiting.

The Fates of Men, The Gifts of Men, and the passage from Cynewulf's *Christ* are all made up of gnomic materials, that is, proverbial wisdom expressed in brief, general maxims. The content of this material gives every indication of being ancient or archaic, and even more strikingly, its form appears to be a rough adaptation of older structures to a far more sophisticated poetics—the conventions of Old English oral-formulaic poetry, which itself was archaic when the poetry came to be written down. In other words we have the phenomenon of a new (written) form preserving an older, traditional (oral) form, which had incorporated and preserved much older forms of preserving ancient wisdom, the lore of the ages as codified and passed down by men of knowledge. But it is one thing to argue the antiquity of the material and quite another to assert its consequent connection with ritual practices, even where those practices might relate to the gaining or earning of the very lore passed on in the material.

Here is the passage in question from *The Fates of Men:*

> Sum sceal on holte of hean beame
> fiþerleas feallan; bið on flihte seþeah,
> laceð on lyfte, oþþæt lengre ne bið
> westem wudubeames. Þonne he on wyrtruman
> sigeð sworcenferð, sawle bireafod,
> falleþ on foldan, feorð biþ on siþe.[5]

(21–26)

[One will in the wood from a high tree fall featherless—will be in flight however, turn in air, until he is no longer the forest-tree's fruit. Then dark in mind he falls onto roots, bereft of soul falls to earth, (his spirit) is (off) on the journey.]

Despite the figurative language with its metaphors of bird, fruit, and journey, no hint remains in the diction of a potential ritual origin for the matter of this fall from a tree. It is simply one example of untimely death in a catalogue of unfortunate lots. This catalogue makes up the longest section of the poem, and it is worth asking whether the frame of reference for the several items is indeed ordinary day-to-day existence. The answer is simply that it is *not,* that the majority of the items are taken from the material of heroic poetry, mythology, or folklore, sug-

---

[5] *The Exeter Book,* edited by George Philip Krapp and Elliott van Kirk Dobbie, Volume III of *ASPR* (New York, 1936), p. 154.

gesting the motifs associated with concepts of initiation and apprentice-ship, that is, preparation for special men's special duties as king, tanist, shaman, scapegoat, or representative hero.

In the list of thirteen, the first three are types of the exposed child, victims respectively of wolf, hunger, and storm. Two others are types of the maimed hero, one is an exile, one a hanged man, and another a man burnt to death. Two are the victims of overdoses of intoxicants, result-ing in murder or what is called suicide, and the other two are victims of weapons, one pierced by a spear and the other cut down in battle, pre-sumably by a sword. Every item of the catalogue, then, can be related somehow to the narrative accounts of the trials, tests, ordeals, or other special activities of men of knowledge and power, the heroes and chiefs manqué. And the poem then proceeds to account for those who achieve special skills and favored lots, that is, those who survive the labors and events which we may regard as initiatory procedures. It would be tedious to belabor the point with further detailed accounts of the individual items in the rest of the poem and in *The Gifts of Men* and the passage from *Christ* besides, but the same general frame of reference may be seen behind all three; that is, the same context or general pattern provides the ultimate source of all this gnomic material.[6]

This is not to say that Cynewulf and the other anonymous Anglo-Saxon poets or scops were consciously referring to primitive ritual prac-tices or even were aware of the allusiveness of the examples they used in compiling their loristic poems and passages. Yet the falling out of trees, which may be seen from our perspective as but one example of failing to accomplish an archetypal heroic initiation, may very well have evoked archaic ritual connotations for an Anglo-Saxon audience that have been completely lost to Anglo-Saxon philologists.

Still, a great store of material has been preserved for a late twentieth-century audience of *The Fates of Men,* a whole forest of trees to be climbed for a broader perspective. The medievalist, for example, may begin by turning to a tree in his own back yard. The best-known section of *Hávamál,* which has been called the greatest didactic poem in the *Edda,* purports to account for the origin or presence of the runes. Oðinn himself describes his experience of hanging for nine days and nine nights on the World Tree, like his own sacrificial victims. A distillation of the concept of divine martyrdom appears in the phrase "myself given to myself" (which elicits inevitable comparison with the crucifixion of

[6] See Lynn L. Remly, "The Anglo-Saxon Gnomes as Sacred Poetry," *Folklore,* 82 (1971), 147–58, for a general discussion of the value of looking at certain philological curiosities from a vantage afforded by comparative religion. Inciden-tally, two of Remly's prime examples are references to tree lore.

Jesus). Fasting, spear-stabbed, and enduring the agonies of hanging, he is able at the end of the fixed term to bend over and lift up the magical runes and thus bring secret knowledge to men. Prometheus now appears as another obvious figure of comparison.

Stefán Einarsson sees in this section of the poem reflections of "widespread initiation rites for magicians,"[7] while H. R. Ellis Davidson talks of "the visionary experience of death and resurrection endured by the Shamans of Siberia and elsewhere as part of their initiation, and as a necessary preliminary to achieving powers of prophecy."[8] To me the significant factor here is the recognition of an essential connection between *initiation* and *knowledge* in these rituals. In other words, the symbolic death and rebirth of this particular kind of initiate separates him from others *specifically* in terms of the special or magical/spiritual things he comes to know through or during the experience. While he may be marked physically at the same time (the wounds of the crucified, usually an explicit scarring or maiming of limbs), this is merely the exterior manifestation of the inner workings of his specialness—his new power, the experience which renders him magically capable.

Mircea Eliade has made numerous references throughout his works to rituals involving tree-climbing. In *Rites and Symbols of Initiation,* for example, he describes several African customs, beginning with the *Umba* ceremony of the Arunta:

> The novice has to climb a young tree that has been stripped of its branches. When he gets to the top of it, all those on the ground burst into cheers. Among the Kurnai, just before the return to camp, what is called the "opossum game" is played. . . . A similar custom is found among the Wiradjuri. Among the Karadjeri, the tree climbing constitutes a special initiatory ceremony, called *laribuga;* in the forest, the neophyte climbs a tree while the men chant a sacred song.[9]

Again, citing E. Andersson's *Contribution à l'Ethnographie des Kuta,* Eliade describes initiation into the sacred cult of Ngoye (Ndsasa) among the Kuta:

> . . . another ordeal consists in making the adept climb a tree five or six metres high, where he has to drink a medicament preserved in a *mu-*

---

[7] *A History of Icelandic Literature* (New York, 1957), p. 30.

[8] *Scandinavian Mythology* (London, 1969), p. 47.

[9] *Rites and Symbols of Initiation; the Mysteries of Birth and Rebirth* (New York, 1965), p. 17; see also *Myths, Dreams and Mysteries* (New York, 1960), p. 195.

kungu. On re-entering the village, the neophyte is welcomed by the women in tears: they weep . . . as though the neophyte were about to die.[10]

Also in *Rites and Symbols* he notes that "the initiation of the Araucanian *machi* includes the ritual climbing of a tree."[11]

The meaning of these rituals is quite clear to Eliade. Siberian Buriat shamans climb nine birches, symbolizing the nine heavens.[12] "The assimilation of the ritual tree to the Cosmic Tree is still more apparent in Central and North Asiatic shamanism. The climbing of such a tree by the Tatar shaman symbolises his ascension to heaven."[13] Most important, to Eliade the clarity of this meaning extends over a wide range of related phenomena:

> There are yet other archetypal motifs that recur in various types of initiations, notably the ritual climbing of trees or sacred poles. . . . examples of this in Australian, African, and North American initiations. . . . shamans of northern and central Asia. . . . puberty initiations (as, for example, in the north of the Gran Chaco, among the Chamacoco and Vilela tribes, among the Mandan, the Kwakiutl, the Pomo) but also in public festivals (Ge festival of the sun, various festivals among the Tupi, the Plains Indians, the Selish, the Lenape, the Maidu), or in the ceremonies and healing séances of shamans (Yaruro, Araucanian, Maidu). . . . meeting with Gods or heavenly powers, in order to obtain a blessing.[14]

Certain more pointed observations need to be made about these phenomena. The "blessing" which Eliade mentions is rather precisely a matter of specific wisdom, a special kind of knowledge associated with a special kind of being—god, king, hero, wizard, physician, magician, sage, seer, poet, etc. Initiation as separation has already taken place (or at least been well begun) when the ritual proceeds up a tree. The separation is then succeeded by a process of intensification (or development or acquisition) of the special qualities which set the initiate completely apart from and above all others. And this process is generally accompanied by a physical marking. Thus both the inner attainment of special qualities and its outward symbol involve an ordeal of suffering, a matter of pain and passion. And thus we have a description of, if not an actual

---

10 *Myths, Dreams, and Mysteries,* p. 204; see also *Rites and Symbols,* p. 74.
11 P. 94.
12 *Rites and Symbols,* p. 93.
13 *Images and Symbols* (London, 1961), p. 45.
14 *Rites and Symbols,* pp. 77–78. Mary Quella Kelly reports that at Transylvania College members of the Kappa Alpha fraternity traditionally climb a special tree when they become pinned. Members of other fraternities and of the girl's sorority heave vile objects at him (cow afterbirth is a favorite) for half an hour. He has been prepared for his ordeal by a good deal of Kentucky Bourbon.

accounting for, the assumed relationship between tree-climbing on the one hand and hanging and crucifixion on the other.

In any case, there is often a connection between the tree which is *climbed* and the man who is *bound* to it. The relationship is rendered explicit, of course, when there is a hanging upon a tree or gallows, as in the *Hávamál* and Easter myths. The tree itself may take on a mythic or cultic significance and be worthy of reverence, like ash and oak in Norse tradition or Christ's cross; or it may seem to have had such significance already, as when the tree is seen as a representative of the world-tree. Among many examples from American Indian traditions, the infamous Ghost Dance provides the most striking. The Ghost Dance was often performed around a tree, cedar being a popular choice, and the Cherokee and Yuchi contrived a myth to account for it:

> The red color of the wood comes from the blood of a wizard who was killed and decapitated by a hero, and whose head was hung in the top of several trees in succession but continued to live until, by the advice of a medicine-man, the people hung it in the topmost branches of a cedar tree, where it finally died. The blood of the severed head trickled down the trunk of the tree and thus the wood was stained.[15]

Several familiar motifs come together here in this obviously post-ritual mythography. Hero and wizard and medicine-man (the three are separate "characters" here), decapitation and hanging, the severed head and the sacred wood—the special capacities and magical knowledge of fertility and immortality, the perceptions of life and death.

Eliade has spoken of the "God who binds" as a terrible sovereign associated with the figure of king-as-magician, "the Indo-European Magician-King, master of the spells that 'bind.' "[16] But he has not, so far as I can tell, made the associations among tree-climbing initiation, ordeal by hanging, and psychological spell-*binding* toward which this essay is moving. The point is that the rituals are often so arduous as to require a special state of mind; they must be prepared for by a trance-producing process.[17] Auto-hypnosis is frequently one of the particular

[15] James Mooney, *The Ghost-Dance Religion and the Sioux Outbreak of 1890* (Chicago, 1965), p. 228. Another example is the Sun Dance ritual in which the Lakota Sioux use the Mystery Tree as the focal point. Then there is the Make a Home ritual of the Assiniboin in which the Mystery Tree becomes the central pillar of the house: Thunder is principally invoked rather than Sun, and a Thunder Nest (a bundle of sticks) is bound to the main fork in the structure, about thirty feet up the central post.

[16] *Images and Symbols*, p. 45.

[17] Two recent fictions show a contrasting understanding of this point. The movie *A Man Called Horse* manipulates a carefully researched amalgam of

skills of shamans, usually induced with the help of ritual procedures; but it is more appropriate, especially when dealing with an initiation of a first-time starter in a trancing event, to talk about physiochemical aids or artificial (that is, natural) stimulants. A good example is the peyote button or mescalito, which becomes the "ally" of a Yaqui man of knowledge, as described by Carlos Castaneda.[18]

Perhaps even more to the point is the fact that Oðinn, who acquired the secret of the runes for men, also brought them the secret of mead: the two gifts, it seems, are very closely associated, if not inseparable. The phrase "turning on" as a descriptive term for submitting to the spell of a drug or marijuana is more than an apt metaphor from a mechanically-minded age. It also elicits an association with whirling dervishes that is not at all out of place, especially when the rope-trick of the fakirs is seen as a type of mystical tree-climbing. Tree and rope, crucifixion and hanging, physical wounding and the agonies of mental/spiritual attain-

---

customs and rituals to authenticate an off-beat yet typically preposterous story. Richard Harris as the hero undergoes an elaborate initiation as a "Sioux" warrior dedicated to the sun. After twenty-four hours of standing exposed without moving, he is cleansed and led to the tent of the sun. There, before all the gathered chiefs of the nation, he speaks brave words; he is incised in the chest by ritual animal scalpel-claws; and he is hoisted into the sun and spun for an indeterminate time, by means of thongs attached to the wooden blades that had been ceremonially thrust through his chest wounds. His submission is satisfactory and his preparation adequate, it appears, because he hallucinates in the sun and comes to some mystical knowledge of the hidden ways of his adopted people. He endures. He emerges from the experience, from the faint or trance, not only with new strength but accepted as a worthy brave and a suitable mate for the chief's sister. The effect of this sequence is extraordinarily compelling both photographically and dramatically, but in ritual terms it is flawed because the impression is given that the hero's successful initiation is entirely the product of his own virtues of strength, determination, endurance, courage, and integrity. The power of the ritual itself is thus somewhat diminished; there is no indication of a trance-producing process or of administering any hallucinogenic substance. This is all very Hollywood-macho heroic, but rather more quaint than mystical in its thematic components, and therefore ultimately phony.

But see George P. Elliott's short story "Among the Dangs," first published in *Esquire*, June, 1958, then the title story in a collection published as a Compass Books Edition (New York, 1966). This may be equally off-beat and preposterous, yet the trancing process is reasonable and convincing within the fantastic (and ironic) givens of the story.

[18] *The Teachings of Don Juan: A Yaqui Way of Knowledge* (New York, 1969). In this connection, Henry B. Parks has drawn my attention to R. Gordon Wasson, *Soma: Divine Mushroom of Immortality* (New York, 1968), especially to "The Tree of Life and the Marvelous Herb," pp. 207ff., where the mycorrhizal relationship between the (sacred, ritual) birch and the mushroom called fly-agaric is discussed. If *Amanita muscaria* is indeed the Soma of the Vedic hymns, as now seems likely, then the relationship between tree-climbing initiation and prophecy under the intoxication of hallucinogens is clearly established, is perhaps itself mycorrhizal.

ment—all come together in the patterns of presentation and meaning associated with the diverse forms of such initiation rituals and demonstrations of special power.

Mythic and literary vestiges of these rituals show up in many forms. Just as the cross has been endowed with powers and meanings and then, by prosopopoeia, made the protagonist of medieval poems, so the trees themselves have been personified and enriched with dramatic roles, as in Graves's favorite Welsh myths, in the dryads of Greek tradition, and in the Ents of Tolkien's Middle Earth. Those striking images in *Macbeth* may owe something of their power to a similar tradition. Explicit association with medicine/magic is seen in the Navaho ceremony in which a patient is hypnotized by a character dressed as an evergreen. Tree rituals in the Near East very probably were associated with orgiastic practices, which would seem to account for Hebrew prohibitions against fruit from grafted trees (a suggestion of Maimonides). In the story of "Sadius and Galo," one of the most substantial of the "Courtiers' Trifles" in Walter Map's *De Nugis Curialium*,[19] an incident of "being cast into a tree" makes sense in the narrative pattern only when it is seen as having pointed reference to initiation practices that are the substance of the story as a whole and the rationale of all the relationships among the characters.

Two similar instances occur in the Arabian *Thousand Nights and a Night*.[20] On the 602nd night, the story of "The King's Son and the Ifrit's Mistress" includes the incident of the hero climbing a tree as a prerequisite to intercourse with the woman. The story revolves around the familiar plot of the father intending to put his son to death, only to have him survive, ennobled, for an ultimate triumph over the father (the foundling prince motif). But this is no especially heroic prince, as it turns out, since the Ifrit's Mistress has in her possession the gifts of over eighty other men who have climbed her tree. Thus, like many other tree-climbing rituals, this story appears to be a remnant of puberty initiations or group fertility rites. A better example is the story told on the 479th–481st nights, "The Island King and the Pious Israelite." The familiar narrative pattern involves separation by shipwreck and subsequent four-way reunion. The one detail which seems out of place is that after the future king is washed up on shore and performs his ablutions he "goes up to a tree and stays his hunger." Rather than seeing this as a careless and irrelevant indication of where the castaway might

---

[19] Translated and edited by Frederick Tupper and Marbury Bladen Ogle (London, 1924), pp. 131–55, esp. p. 143.

[20] All citations are to the ten-volume translation of Richard F. Burton (London, 1885).

have found some food, falcons, or timber, I suggest here a remnant of an initiation ritual that has lost its meagerest vestigial meaning for the story-tellers.

Within this broadened frame of reference, the passages from *Fates of Men, Gifts of Men,* and *Christ* take on new interest. Attention is now drawn to the fact that all three include the figure of the smith. Indirectly, this too adds support to the idea that Anglo-Saxon tree-climbing had, however remotely, some ritual significance, because of the ancient, well-established connection between the shaman and the smith. Clusters of gnomic wisdom regarding men of special knowledge and power (smiths and shamans) and their ritual initiations into their knowledge and power (involving fire and trees) may have been retained by habitual or traditional associations, although the rationale of the clusters' integrity may have been lost.

Fortunately, much evidence remains to demonstrate the associations. Eliade notes that "access to sacrality is manifested, among other things, by a prodigious increase in heat" and asserts an "intimate relation between the techniques and *mystiques* of fire—a relation shown by the close connections between smiths, shamans, and warriors."[21] He also observes that "traces of ancient initiatory scenarios are still discernible in the rites peculiar to masons and blacksmiths, especially in Eastern Europe."[22]

The name of Prometheus was taken in vain earlier in this essay, but he is an appropriate figure for helping to make certain connections here. Prometheus is bound *because* of the special knowledge brought to men, while Oðinn undergoes hanging *in order to* bring special knowledge to men. The common denominator is clear; but if the contradiction in cause and effect is seen as merely a confusion in mythological chronology, both stories may be seen as types of initiation of heroes whose knowledge *is* their power, and therefore related to the tree-climbing of shamans. An important kind of magical power, of course, is the knowledge and control of fire. And Eliade has devoted one of his books to a discussion of the connections among iron, magic, smith, and fertility.[23]

He finds that "the most primitive cultures look upon the specialist in the sacred—the shaman, the medicine-man, the magician—as a 'master of fire'. Primitive magic and shamanism both carry the notion of 'mastery over fire'."[24] And he also shows that human sacrifices, whether real or symbolic, performed during metallurgical operations, imitate a

[21] *Rites and Symbols,* p. 86.
[22] P. 122. One might also refer to the persistent ritual practices of Freemasonry.
[23] *The Forge and the Crucible* (London, 1962).
[24] P. 79.

mythical model and are intended to guarantee success thereby. "Smiths," he points out, "sometimes rise to the level of royalty. According to some accounts, Gengiz Khan was originally a simple smith; and the tribal legends of the Mongols link the smith's craft with the royal household."[25] He goes on to illustrate the importance of the smith-figure and the significance of the smith-lore with numerous African examples: the Mosengere and Ba Sakata of the southern Congo, among whom the master-smith is generally the founder of the village and his craft hereditary; tribes of the upper Ogome, among whom the smith is always a sorcerer and often chief; peoples of the Loango, among whom a smith-priest is charged with the care of the sacred national fire; the Ba Songués, among whom the smith ranks next after the chief in their hierarchy; and the Baholoholo, among whom the smiths rank next after chiefs and hunters, above the lieutenants and shamans.

Others who have studied these connections are Giorgio de Santillana and Hertha von Dechend, whose *Hamlet's Mill* has enlarged the scope of references to include mythology as well as culture-history and ethnology:

> It is possible to trace back the significance of the *blacksmith* in Asiatic shamanism, particularly the celestial blacksmith who is the legitimate heir to the divine "archi-tekton" of the cosmos. Several representatives of this type, whom we call Deus Faber, still have both functions, being architects and smiths at the same time, e.g., the Greek Hephaistos, who builds the starry houses for the gods and forges masterworks, and the Koshar-wa-Hasis of Ras Shamra, who builds Baal's palace and forges masterworks also.
>
> The Yakuts claim: "Smith and Shaman come from the same nest," and they add: "the Smith is the older brother of the Shaman."[26] . . . It is the primeval Smith who made the Sampo, as we know, and forged sky and luminaries in Esthonia. It is no idle fancy that the representative of the celestial smith, the King, is himself frequently titled "Smith." Jenghiz Khan had the title "Smith" and the standard of the Persian Empire was the stylized leather apron of the Smith Kavag. . . .[27] The Chinese mythological emperors Huang-ti and Yu are such unmistakable smiths that Marcel Granet drew historic-sociological conclusions all the way, forgetting the while that Huang-ti, the Yellow Emperor, is acknowledged to be Saturn. And just as the Persian Shahs held their royal jubilee festival after having reigned thirty years, which is the Saturnian revolution, so the

[25] P. 85.

[26] Citing P. W. Schmidt, *Die asiatischen Hirtenvölker* (Münster, 1954), pp. 346 f.

[27] "Leather Apron" was the name of one of those accused in the Jack the Ripper cases. The awesome power of these images re-emerges in surprising ways.

Egyptian Pharaoh also celebrated his jubilee after thirty years, true to the "inventor" of this festival, Ptah, who *is* the Egyptian Saturn and also Deus Faber.[28]

Wayland and Daedalus might well be added to this list of references, but the Finnish epic, the *Kalevala,* provides one of the best examples of all.

Many of the attributes of the hero-king, as we have been isolating them, seem to be divided up among the three sons of Kaleva—Vainamoinen, Ilmarinen, and Lemminkainen—to whom we should add the hero Kullervo, who is also called, though perhaps figuratively, son of Kaleva. Lemminkainen is the beloved one, filled with life (a type of the youngest-wisest); Vainamoinen is the master of magic song (a type of the Orphic shaman-king-god); and Ilmarinen is the primeval smith, inventor of iron, who "hammered together the roof of the sky" and "can forge more things than are found on land or sea"(a type of Deus Faber). Kullervo, a type of the hero as exile, is required, like Orestes, to make a return and carry out an act of vengeance. To become worthy of this (kingly) heroic act, he must undergo rituals of initiation, including serving at the house of Ilmarinen as a cowherd. While there, though the variants render the procedures unclear, he apparently performs a kind of initiation ritual at the divine smithy in order to acquire his weapons and armor. But in the entire poem the single most illuminating incident, for the purposes of this essay, is the episode in which Vainamoinen gets Ilmarinen to climb the magic tree. Here, dramatically, is a mythological demonstration of the shaman-smith connection, of the intimate relationship between the initiatory climbing of trees and the special knowledge— including the magic of fire and metallurgy—of men and power.[29]

To jump from these observations of cross-cultural common denominators to a reading of *The Fates of Men* as a collection of primitive initiation lore is far from the intention of this essay. The point is that when we find anthologies of accumulated wisdom, usually in gnomic passages, that suggest ancient or archaic traditions, we should not rigidly limit our apperception to a reconstruction of contemporary phenomena or contemporary modes of thought or contemporary art-forms. We must

[28] *Hamlet's Mill: An Essay on Myth and the Frame of Time* (Boston, 1969), pp. 128–29.

[29] Remote echoes of these motifs may be heard whenever stories include romantic trials by fire or dramatic rescues from the gallows. Perhaps the best example in literature comes, again, from the *Arabian Nights,* when the story of "The Goldsmith and the Cashmere Singing-Girl" is told on the 586th–587th nights. The smith is a determined man, and in order to get the girl he uses not only bribery but a rope-ladder (always suspect in Oriental material), a disguise, and a story of witchcraft.

stand back and look beyond. Trust that the preserved detail, puzzling or absurd in immediate context, has its signification somewhere; wonder at the possibilities that its meanings may be great or mysterious; and reach for the connectons that will justify its presence and our attention. Let this, then, be a dual plea: for an openness of mind, because it ill befits any humane discipline to close the book on anything, and for a quality of mind that transcends positivist strictures, because the wages of taking oneself and one's turf too seriously is the inhumane blindness of self-deception.

25

Widsith's Journey Through Germanic Tradition

ROBERT P. CREED

THE OPENING LINES OF THE POEM WE CALL *Widsith* LOOK LIKE THIS in the Exeter Book:[1]

> ÞIDSIÐ MAÐOLADe
> Þord hord onleac seþe mæst mærþa · ofer
> eorþan folca ʒeond ferde oft · he flette ʒeþah

They look like this in the standard edition by G. P. Krapp and E. van Kirk Dobbie:[2]

> Widsið maðolade,   wordhord onleac,
> se þe monna mæst   mægþa ofer eorþan,
> folca geondferde; ...

[1] I have had to consult the photographic facsimile, *The Exeter Book of Old English Poetry*, with introductory chapters by R. W. Chambers, Max Förster, and Robin Flower (London, 1933). The opening lines of *Widsith* are on folio 84b. The clearly visible raised point after *mærþa*, a mark that is used with a great degree of consistency by both *Beowulf* scribes to indicate the end of a verse (hemistich), suggests scribal confusion here.

[2] *The Exeter Book*, eds. G. P. Krapp and E. van Kirk Dobbie (New York, 1936), p. 149. Except when otherwise stated all quotations from poems other than *Widsith* are from the appropriate volume edited by Krapp and Dobbie in *ASPR*, volumes I to VI (1931–53). *The Seafarer* is in volume III (The Exeter Book), *Beowulf* in volume IV, *Genesis* in volume I (The Junius Manuscript).

In the emended and lineated text of Kemp Malone's very valuable second edition of *Widsith* (1962), the lines look like this:[3]

> WIDSIÐ MAÐOLADe, wordhord onleac,
> se þe [monna] mæst mægþa ofer eorþan,
> folca, geondferde. . . .

The two editions most used by English students of the poem follow C. W. M. Grein's (1858) lead in adding *monna* [of men] before *mæst* [most] and Kemble's (1835) lead in changing the *r* of *mærþa*, which might be translated "of famous deeds," to a *g,* thus turning the word into "of peoples."[4] By emending the recorded text in these apparently small ways, editors for more than a hundred years have gone some way toward substituting a creature of their own for the Exeter Book *Widsith*.

Malone succinctly justifies his acceptance of these emendations:

> Our next task is that of isolating the individual words and lines of verse. In passages where doing this gives bad results we have a right to suspect faulty transmission of the text. . . . there is something wrong with the second line, the on-verse of which has only three syllables. Comparison with *Judith* 181 and *Beowulf* 2645, where we find the same construction, gives us a hint of what might have happened: at some stage in the transmission of our text a copyist skipped the word *monna*. We accordingly read the on-verse *se þe [monna] mæst* and this reading gives us a perfectly normal B-type half-line. The emendation was first made by Grein. But even so, the line remains unsatisfactory because of *mærþa* [deeds of valor], which does not fit the context. It is parallel in construction to *folca* and ought to be parallel to it in meaning as well. Kemble gives us this parallelism by reading *mægþa*.[5]

In the course of this paper I will explain why I think *mærþa*, usually translated "of famous deeds," does fit the context. Malone's other point carries even less weight. I do not see why a genitive plural in this line need be parallel to one in the next. We can keep the MS reading here by linking the two genitives in a series like this:

he who traveled through (the) most *mærþa* over earth of peoples.

[3] *Widsith*, ed. Kemp Malone, revised ed. (Copenhagen, 1962), p. 23. Except for the previous quotation, all quotations of *Widsith* are made from this edition.

[4] The textual history of these lines is summarized in Krapp-Dobbie, *Exeter Book*, p. 300. There is a somewhat fuller account on p. 188 of R. W. Chamber's *Widsith: A Study in Old English Heroic Legend* (Cambridge, 1912; reprinted New York, 1965). Chambers notes that "Leo, Ettmüller(1) and Schaldemose . . . kept *mærþa*, which they rendered 'das was gerühmt wird über die Erde,' 'Mannruhm' etc. . . ." Krapp and Dobbie indicate that only W. S. Mackie (1934) among recent English editors keeps the MS reading *mærþa*.

[5] Malone, *Widsith*, p. 18.

This way we can at least dispense with Malone's mid-verse comma in 3a and indeed with both his and Krapp-Dobbie's verse-final comma at the end of 2b. But this is a small matter.

Malone refers to but does not quote *Beowulf* 2645 where *mæst* shares the line not with *mægþa* but with *mærða*, as in the Exeter Book text of *Widsith*. Nor does Malone point out that *mæst*, whether as substantive or adjective, never shares a line with *mægþa* in the surviving corpus of Anglo-Saxon poetry according to Grein-Köhler-Holthausen.[6] On the other hand, *mæst* and *mærða* appear together not only in the *Beowulf* line but also in the *Seafarer:*

> forðam he manna mæst   mærða gefremede
>
> (*Beowulf* 2645)

[for this (or: because) he most of men performed famous deeds]

> þonne hi mæst mid him   mærþa gefremedon
>
> (*Seafarer* 84)

[then they most of famous deeds among themselves performed].

Neither the lack of line-sharing of *mæst* [most] and *mægþa* [tribes] nor the two instances of such symbiosis of *mæst* and *mærða* in about thirty thousand recorded lines is statistically significant.

In attempting to run to earth all the instances of *mærðu* in the corpus, I came across this passage in *Genesis:*

> Ða þær mon mænig   be his mægwine,
> æðeling anmod,   oðerne bæd
> þæs hie him to mærðe,   ær seo mengeo eft
> geond foldan bearm   tofaran sceolde,
> leoda mægðe   on landsocne
> burh geworhte   and to beacne torr
> up arærde   to rodortunglum.
>
> (*Genesis* 1661–67)

[Then there many (a) man by his kinsman-lord,
(a) prince single-minded, bade another
that they for themselves as a-thing-to-be-proclaimed, before the many in-turn

---

[6] C. W. M. Grein, *Sprachschatz der Angelsächsischen Dichter,* revised by J. J. Köhler with the assistance of F. Holthausen (Heidelberg, 1912). This is the only presently available concordance to most of the corpus of Old English poetry.

throughout earth's bosom had to-fare-separately,
tribes of peoples in landseeking,
should-make a town and as (a) beacon (a) tower
should-raise up to heaven-stars.]

What struck me about these lines extends beyond the matter of line-sharing or collocation within a sequence of lines, although two, and in a way three, of the elements that are grouped together in the opening of *Widsith* appear in *Genesis* 1663–64: *mærðe* and *geond*(-), throughout, and a verb of traveling-about, *geondferde* in *Widsith*, *tofaran* in *Genesis*. The *Genesis* passage is about establishing a town (*burh*) as a-thing-to-be-proclaimed or known (*mærðe*) by the tribes (*mægðe* appears in the next line) before they scatter over the earth. The *Widsith* passage in the Exeter Book version seems to be about someone or something traveling about the earth *through* the *mærðu* of tribes (*folca*) or perhaps from one instance of *mærðu* to another—*geond* suggests both possibilities. Is the *mærðu* the same in the *Widsith* as in the *Genesis* passage? Or is this small group of associations merely chance? The *Genesis* passage presents a *burh*, a town, as a *mærðu*. We have no way of telling whether the composer of *Widsith* knew our recording of the Old English *Genesis*, of course. But we might consider leaving the word *mærþa* as it stands in the Exeter Book on the basis of this perhaps chance association of *mærðu* with *burh*. The *Widsith* poet might then appear to be saying something like this:

... he who traveled-between (the) most of famous-places over earth of peoples. ...

But this justification for retaining the MS reading is not only far-fetched, it is also beside my point. I prefer to keep *mærþa* in *Widsith*, line 2 whether or not the word carries with it even a faint hint of physical places. The incredibly long-lived creature designated by the first word of the poem has traveled through the *mærðu* of most of the peoples in a far more important way than touring. *Mærðu*, if it suggests a famous *place* or town at all, does so only peripherally. At the center of its meaning is the sense of *something well known, something proclaimed,* which we translate as *glory,* or *fame,* or *exploit.* Bosworth-Toller glosses the verb from which the noun appears to be derived as follows: "mæran . . . To make known, celebrate, declare, proclaim." Clark Hall glosses the verb: "to declare, proclaim, celebrate, glorify, honour." Klaeber's glosses of the noun and adjective (*mære*) send one both to the Gothic cognates and Modern German *Märchen*.

379

"Widsith"[7] has traveled through and between *mærþa . . . folca*, what-has-been-made-known / proclaimed / celebrated of peoples. He has traveled through what-is-known about all the tribes and peoples he so lengthily lists. He has, his presenter seems to be telling us, not only traveled from his home among the Myrgings to the court of Ermanaric, he has also traveled through the oral traditions of the Germanic folk.

But "Widsith," the character who speaks the body of the poem, seems to tell a somewhat different story than the one I have just suggested. "Widsith" begins, modestly enough, by stating that he has *heard* of such rulers and peoples as the Hunnish Attila and the Gothic Ermanaric —as well as the "Greek" Caesar and Alexander. *Fela ic monna gefrægn mægþum wealdan*, [I have heard-tell much of men ruling tribes], he says at line 10. Six lines later he rounds off this section with the words, *. . . ond he mæst geþah / þara þe ic ofer foldan gefrægen hæbbe* [. . . and he most prospered of those I over (the) earth have heard-tell of, 16–17].

By line 50 "Widsith" is singing a different song:

> Swa ic geondferde fela   fremdra londa
> geond ginne grund,   godes ond yfles
> þær ic cunnade,   cnosle bidæled,
> freomægum feor,   folgade wide.
> Forþon ic mæg singan   ond secgan spell,
> mænan fore mengo   in meoduhealle
> hu me cynegode   cystum dohten.
> Ic wæs mid Hunum   ond mid Hreðgotum. . . .

(50–57)

> [So I traveled through many foreign lands
> throughout (the) broad earth, good and evil
> I experienced there, separated from family,
> far from free-kinsmen, (I) followed-and-served far-and-wide.
> For-this I can sing and say tales,
> speak before many in (the) meadhall
> how those-of-good-kin were-good-to-me with-choicest-gifts.
> I was with Huns and with Hreth-Goths. . . .]

Geondferde in line 50 speaks of a real journey to foreign lands, no mere imaginary tour through tradition. "Widsith" says he *followed and served far and wide*. By line 70 "Widsith" is telling us he was in Italy with Alboin who reigned between 565–72. By line 82 he is telling us he has

---

[7] Henceforth I use double quotes around "Widsith" to refer to the supposed speaker of lines 10–134 and *Widsith* to refer to the entire poem.

been with the Israelites, the Assyrians, the Indians, and the Egyptians. He has traveled far indeed.

That is not the worst of it. At line 88 "Widsith" tells us he was a long (if this is what *ealle* [all] means here) time with Ermanaric, the Gothic king who "flourished in the third quarter of the fourth century,"[8] two hundred years before Alboin. "Widsith" begins to seem like a liar in two dimensions. What is the point of fussing over *mærþa* versus *mægþa* for a character who makes such preposterous claims for himself? Is he merely a clever but outrageous beggar as Norman Eliason makes him out to be?

Eliason sets the problem in this way:

> The fictitious *scop* depicted there [in the prologue, lines 1-9], however, is conspicuously at variance with the *scop* in the main body of the poem. The latter, by telling of travels extending over four centuries, is a man of incredible longevity. The *scop* depicted in the prologue is not.

—Or not necessarily, I would say. We may not be getting the whole story in the prologue. Eliason argues:

> In each [poem: he is comparing *Widsith* with *Deor*] there is a fictitious *scop* who speaks, and the two *scops* are alike in possessing a strange duality of character, each seeming to be a life-like human being and at the same time an utterly incredible one. Their incredibility . . . stems from the same feature, the longevity each claims for himself. . . .
> Each is intended, I think, to serve as the poet's alter ego. . . .[9]

Eliason analyzes both *Deor* and *Widsith* as begging poems in which a clever (and to us unknown and unnamed) performer represents himself as a long-lived liar to please and tip the hand of the man before whom he performs. Eliason's comparison of the two poems is almost as persuasive as he makes out the composition of the *Deor* poet to be. But *Deor* aside, if *Widsith* is a begging poem, it is not a simple or entirely unserious one. On whose (or what's) behalf is the *Widsith* poet begging? Is he really a beggar at all, or does he offer something in return for the gifts he says he has received? Does he really think he is fooling us with "Widsith's" preposterous claims? I do not think Eliason has gotten to the bottom of the matter.

Malone gives us a more serious "Widsith." ". . . the ideal scop was

[8] Malone, *Widsith*, p. 146.
[9] Norman E. Eliason, "Two Old English Scop Poems," *PMLA*, 81 (1966), 185–92. The first quotation is from p. 186, the second and third from p. 187.

more than a teller of stories. He was a historian and a sage, and his words were words of wisdom. The speech of Widsith begins and ends with well-considered reflections on royal rule. . . ."[10] Tacitus bears early witness to the importance of songs (and thus of those who sang them) to the tribes of continental Germania. He speaks of the *carmina antiqua,* [traditional songs] of the Germans of the first century A.D., *quod unum apud illos memoriae et annalium genus est,* [which is their only kind of tradition and history].[11] But these ideas about the scops and songs of Germania, though they may be closer to the truth than Eliason's beggars with their clever begging songs, are still as distant from the scene as Tacitus's Rome was from Germania or the twentieth century is from the seventh. Whatever else they were, scops were people, poets who performed before people, and without lecture notes I think. In any case one of them, the *Widsith* poet, seems to have created a character who traveled from the land of the Myrgings to the court of Ermanaric and who claimed to have traveled much farther and to have lived for centuries. I think he posed for his first audience, as well as for us, a kind of riddle.

I have noted elsewhere that two poets that I take to be traditional, Homer and the *Beowulf* poet, sing in their songs of counterpart singers on the distant scene they sing of. Homer and the *Beowulf* poet thus let us draw the conclusion that they, the present poets, derive their story from those distant poets who were with the heroes of the past. The trick is to get us to believe in the connection between the very present poet and the past one in the tale and thus to verify the tale we are listening to.[12] Now it seems to me that the *Widsith* poet might be up to something similar. There *was* a poet at the court of Ermanaric two and a half or more centuries before there was a poet singing or perhaps writing about him. If there had been no earlier poet at Ermanaric's court there would be no oral tradition about him: Ermanaric's *lof* [his praise], as well as his *leoht ond lif somod* [light and life together], would have perished from, or indeed never appeared in Germanic song, however alive his *history* was in the pages of Ammianus Marcellinus and Jordanes.[13]

---

10 Malone, *Widsith,* p. 79.

11 Cornelii Taciti, *De Origine et Situ Germanorum,* ed. J. G. C. Anderson (Oxford, 1938), *caput* 2.3. I am indebted to Anderson's notes on p. 39 for the reading "tradition and history" and to the Mattingly-Handford translation (Tacitus, *The Agricola and the Germania* [Harmondsworth, 1970], p. 102) for the phrase "traditional songs."

12 "The Singer Looks at His Sources," *CL,* 14 (1962), 44–52; reprinted in *Studies in Old English Literature in Honor of Arthur G. Brodeur,* ed. S. B. Greenfield (Eugene, 1963), pp. 44–52.

13 Malone, *Widsith,* p. 146; Chambers, *Widsith,* p. 16 f.

We think of Demodokos singing the adventures of Odysseus before Odysseus himself as Homer's fiction. But the *Odyssey* owes much to those singers who sang before Homer did, and Demodokos is Homer's graceful payment of part of his debt. We might also think of Balla Fasséké, the companion and *griot* of Sundiata, in a recently recorded telling of the adventures of that great king of medieval African Mali, as the creation of the contemporary *griot*, Djeli Mamoudou Kouyaté. Since Kouyaté sounds much like both "Widsith" and the *Widsith* poet, I will quote the opening lines of his tale of *Sundiata:*

> I am a griot. It is I, Djeli Mamoudou Kouyaté, son of Bintou Kouyaté and Djeli Kedian Kouyaté, master in the art of eloquence. Since time immemorial the Kouyatés have been in the service of the Keita princes of Mali; we are vessels of speech, we are the repositories which harbour secrets many centuries old. The art of eloquence has no secrets for us; without us the names of kings would vanish into oblivion, we are the memory of mankind; by the spoken word we bring to life the deeds and exploits of kings for younger generations.
>
> I derive my knowledge from my father, Djeli Kedian, who also got it from his father; history holds no mystery for us; we teach to the vulgar just as much as we want to teach them, for it is we who keep the keys to the twelve doors of Mali.
>
> I know the lists of all the sovereigns who succeeded to the throne of Mali. I know how the black people divided into tribes, for my father bequeathed to me all his learning; . . .
>
> I teach kings the history of their ancestors so that the lives of the ancients might serve them as an example, for the world is old, but the future springs from the past.
>
> My word is pure and free of all untruth; it is the word of my father; it is the word of my father's father. I will give you my father's words just as I received them; royal griots do not know what lying is. When a quarrel breaks out between tribes it is we who settle the difference, for we are the depositaries of oaths which the ancestors swore.[14]

Somewhat later in his tale Kouyaté says, "The generosity of kings makes griots eloquent. . . ."[15]

D. T. Niane, who took down the telling of Sundiata's adventures from Kouyaté, characterizes the *griot* in this way:

> The griot who occupies the chair of history of a village and who bears the title of "Belen-Tigui" is a very respectable gentleman and has toured Mali.

---

[14] D. T. Niane, *Sundiata: An Epic of Old Mali*, trans. G. D. Pickett (London, 1965), p.1.
[15] Niane, p. 14.

He has gone from village to village to hear the teaching of great masters; he has learnt the art of historical oratory through long years; he is, moreover, bound by an oath and does not teach anything except what his guild stipulates, for, say the griots, "All true learning should be a secret." Also the traditionist is a master in the art of circumlocution, he speaks in archaic formulas, or else he turns facts into amusing legends for the public, which legends have, however, a secret sense which the vulgar little suspect.[16]

There in the middle of the *griot* Kouyaté's tale the *griot* Balla Fasséké appears and speaks to us from the side of the thirteenth century conqueror Sundiata. In the *Widsith* poet's telling "Widsith" appears and speaks to us from the fourth century court of Ermanaric. But "Widsith" also tells us he was at the sixth century court of Alboin. How do we solve this riddle?

There was a singer at Ermanaric's court. There was also one at Alboin's court two centuries later. There was also the one whose song we have in the Exeter Book. All were indeed wide-ranging. And all were, in a way, *one,* because each was, while he lived, the living voice of Germanic oral tradition. There are no disembodied voices in an oral tradition as there are in a society that learns and lives by books. I do not believe that "Widsith's" character is a fiction in our sense of the word. The poet who sang the prologue and epilogue became himself Ermanaric's Widsith even as he sang in Anglo-Saxon England centuries after Ermanaric's death.

Donald K. Fry argues in a paper in progress that the *Widsith* poet gently mocks the character "Widsith" he allows to speak in the body of his poem. The *Widsith* poet is a Christian trying to put into Christian perspective—and thus put down—"Widsith's" exuberant affection for earthly rulers.[17] Perhaps. But I find more of a sense of the poignancy of the fate of wandering gleeman than Christian mockery, however gentle, in *Widsith*'s final lines.

Reading Fry's paper led me to think of Eric Havelock's working out of the reasons for Plato's war against the poets and particularly Homer in the *Republic*. "Plato's target was indeed an educational procedure and a whole way of life."[18] "From the standpoint of a developed self-conscious critical intelligence"—Plato's standpoint according to Havelock—"Homeric man . . . was a part of all he had seen and heard and remembered. His job was not to form individual and unique convictions

[16] Niane, p. viii.
[17] I am very grateful to Donald K. Fry of S.U.N.Y. Stony Brook for letting me refer at some length to his forthcoming paper titled "Two Voices in *Widsith*."
[18] E. A. Havelock, *Preface to Plato* (Cambridge, Massachusetts, 1963), p. 45.

but to retain tenaciously a precious hoard of exemplars. These were constantly present with him in his acoustic reflexes and also visually imagined before his mind's eye. In short, he went along with the tradition."[19]

Plato did *not* go along with the tradition. Instead, according to Havelock's elaborate and brilliant argument, Plato did what no one before him had so self-consciously done: he stood back from the tradition that claimed to be the storehouse of all knowledge and was an educational monopoly, analyzed it, and condemned it.

I am certainly not suggesting that the *Widsith* poet was an Anglo-Saxon Plato setting up and then attacking an "Homeric" "Widsith" who speaks for the "educational procedure and . . . whole way of life" offered by the tradition. But Fry's detection of a rift between "Widsith" and *Widsith* poet and Havelock's account of Plato's war on Homer may not be totally irrelevant to each other. I used to think that the *Widsith* poet went unthinkingly along with the tradition he so elaborately re-created. I am not so sure now. Instead I begin, thanks to Eliason and Fry, to sense an untraditional if small degree of self-consciousness in the epilogue:

> Swa scriþende   gesceapum hweorfað,
> gleomen gumena,   geond grunda fela,
> þearfe secgað,   þoncword sprecaþ,
> simle, suð oþþe norð,   sumne gemetað
> gydda gleawne,   geofum unhneawne,
> se þe fore duguþe wile   dom aræran,
> eorlscipe æfnan   oþþæt eal scæceð,
> leoht & lif somod.   Lof se gewyrceð,
> hafað under heofonum   heahfæstne dom.

(*Widsith* 135–43)

[So traveling they-turn as-they-must,
gleemen of men, throughout many lands,
say (their) need, speak words-of-thanks,
always, south or north, they-meet a-certain-one
skilled of songs, unstingy of gifts,
he who before his-retainers desires to-raise-up judgement,
to-perform noble-deeds until all hastens-away,
light and life together. Praise he works,
has under heaven high-and-secure judgement.]

[19] Havelock, p. 199.

The phrase *under heofonum* [under heaven] may indeed have served to remind an Anglo-Saxon audience of the better life *on heofonum* [*in* heaven] as Fry maintains. The poet of *The Seafarer,* for example, seems determined to convert men's desire for earthly *lof* [praise] into a longing for the heavenly kind.[20] But in any case the "hints and ironies" Fry finds in *Widsith* suggest a somewhat sophisticated mind at work in the epilogue. The *lof* the gleeman or scop contrives may well be secure (*heahfæst*) only *under* heaven, that is, on earth—but what a pity! Gleemen still encounter in their wide wanderings those who desire to buy the "doom," the judgement of the tradition, they can offer. But all that is decaying. I begin to hear in these lines a faint note of awareness— awareness that all that "Widsith" so exuberantly stands for may be passing away. The tradition may indeed be dying, confronted with Christianity and its claim to have all truth. It will be a long time before a mind in any way like Plato's will re-emerge in Europe, a mind insisting that each man, in Havelock's words, "form individual and unique convictions." In the meantime the *Widsith* poet sings in his epilogue a little elegy not so much for the doom of the old gods but for the doom of the heroes "Widsith" endlessly lists and occasionally briefly celebrates. What is doomed is the very way of knowing those heroes: "Widsith" is forced to sing not the *Beowulf* poet's confident and unself-conscious *We . . . gefrunon* [*we* share this knowledge], but the individual's *ic . . . gefrægn* [this is what *I* have to offer].

The tradition is dying here and there, so gleemen are forced to turn south and north and beg like the *griots* of an Africa invaded during the last century and a half by an alien individualism. But beggars or not, they sometimes (*simle* [always] in line 138 is an exaggeration probably for other reasons than mere alliteration) meet what they need more than generosity: *sumne . . . gydda gleawne* [someone skilled of songs], an understanding audience.

So I read the opening lines of *Widsith* exactly as they appear in the Exeter Book—except for lineation to guide the modern performer— even to the perhaps faltering three-syllable verse that begins line 2:

> WIDSIÐ MAÐOLADe word hord onleac
> seþe mæst mærþa ofer eorþan
> folca geondferde. . . .

That three-syllable verse lets my lyre into that line twice, the first time to sound the primary stress before the words of the line begin to be

---

[20] *The Seafarer,* lines 72–80a. See particularly I. L. Gordon's notes to these lines in her very valuable edition (New York, 1966), p. 43.

heard, the second time after *mæst* to finish the verse with a more lightly-stressed flourish. With this unusual verse pattern I am trying to call attention to something a little unusual I am saying—this:

[“Widsith” spoke-formally, unlocked (his) wordhoard,
he who traveled most through what-men-know
of peoples over earth. . . .]

I think the whole *Widsith* performance is a tantalizing, sophisticated, and profound sort of riddle. If it is a riddle, the answer to the question “Say what I am called” is not only “Widsith,” but also *mærðu, dom, lof,* ηλέος, *griot,* the singer singing within an oral tradition. In order to answer that riddle you must listen carefully to what the song really says: “I have traveled through men's traditionally-trained memories where the courts of Ermanaric and Alboin exist side-by-side—right here and now. But I know that sort of magic can exist only so long as the tradition lives.” The very awareness of the magic marks the beginning of the end.